MADAGASCAR

W

*http://geography.about.com/library/cia/blcmadagascar.htm

To Françoise Raison

Madagascar

A Short History

Solofo Randrianja and Stephen Ellis

The University of Chicago Press

Solofo Randrianja is professor of history at the University of Toamasina, Madagascar, and has written several books on the political history and ethnicity of Madagascar.

Stephen Ellis is a main researcher in the history department of the African Studies Center in Leiden. He has worked in Liberia, Sierra Leone, and South Africa in addition to Madagascar and has written widely on religion and politics in Africa.

The University of Chicago Press, Chicago 60637
HURST Publishers, London

Printed in India

18 17 16 15 14 13 12 11 10 09 1 2 3 4 5

ISBN-13: 978-0-226-70418-0 (cloth)

ISBN-13: 978-0-226-70420-3 (paper)

ISBN-10: 0-226-70418-1 (cloth)

ISBN-10: 0-226-70420-3 (paper)

Library of Congress Cataloging-in-Publication Data

Randrianja, Solofo.
Madagascar : a short history / Solofo Randrianja and Stephen Ellis.
p. cm.
Includes bibliographical references and index.
ISBN-13: 978-0-226-70418-0 (cloth : alk. paper)
ISBN-10: 0-226-70418-1 (cloth : alk. paper)
ISBN-13: 978-0-226-70420-3 (pbk. : alk. paper)
ISBN-10: 0-226-70420-3 (pbk. : alk. paper) 1. Madagascar--History. I. Ellis, Stephen, 1953- II. Title.
DT469.M285R365 2009
969.1--dc22
2008033721

∞ The paper used in this publication meets the minimum requirements of the American National Standard for Information Sciences—Permanence of Paper for Printed Library Materials, ANSI Z39.48-1992.

CONTENTS

MAPS

ILLUSTRATIONS

ACKNOWLEDGEMENTS

Together, we estimate that we have spent over fifty years researching the history of Madagascar. We have spent over ten years just writing this book.

After such a long period, we owe thanks to more librarians, archivists and colleagues than we could possibly acknowledge. So we must limit ourselves to just a few names.

Among the institutions to which we are most grateful are our own employers, the University of Tamatave and the African Studies Centre, Leiden, for facilitating our research over many years. We are grateful to the Centre d'Etudes des Mondes Africains (CEMAF), Paris, and to the University of Chicago for awarding fellowships to Solofo Randrianja. We owe an equal debt of thanks to the Institut des Etudes Avancées at Nantes for hosting Solofo Randrianja during the final phases of writing this book. A special debt of gratitude is due to Professor Ralph Austen for arranging Solofo's Chicago visits, and for extending his personal hospitality to Stephen Ellis as well, enabling us to enjoy a rare opportunity to work on this project for an extended period side-by-side. Stephen also expresses his belated thanks to Simon Ayache, who facilitated his first stay in Madagascar in 1979–80, at a time when obtaining a work permit was no easy matter.

For pictures, we would like to thank Philip Beale for the photos of the Borobodur temple and of the replica Borobodur ship at sea. Dominic Bois and Marie-Pierre Ballarin kindly gave us photos of old Antalaotra ruins. For the illustration drawn from Etienne de Flacourt, we are grateful to Editions Karthala, Paris; and for the photograph of Rainitomponiera and Razaimanana by the Rev. William Ellis, we are grateful to the British Council. For the photos of presidents Tsiranana, Ratsiraka and Ravalomanana, we are indebted to the Archives de la République Malgache in Antananarivo.

We thank Dolin Raherison for his expertise in drawing the maps.

We are most grateful to Sander Adelaar for his advice on Chapter One, and to Luke Freeman for his helpful comments on the entire manuscript, as well as to an anonymous reader commissioned by the University of Chicago Press. Françoise Raison kindly provided the photo of Jean Ralaimongo. The photo of King Tsiarasso was supplied by the Foiben–Taosarintanin' i Madagasikara.

Needless to say, we alone are responsible for the opinions contained throughout this book.

Tamatave and Amsterdam, May 2008 S. R and S. E.

INTRODUCTION

First-time visitors to Madagascar are often surprised by the island's great size—587,000 square kilometres, or two and a half times Great Britain, or a fair bit bigger than California.

Perhaps their surprise stems from the fact that Madagascar lies quite close to the coast of Africa, so that, looking at a map, we inadvertently compare the big island with the even bigger continent alongside. Without doubt another reason is that most English-speakers, other than those undertaking a specialist study, such as of the island's unique flora and fauna, simply aren't used to reading or hearing much about Madagascar, which leaves them with few ideas about the place, whether positive or negative. Even academic specialists in area studies tend to overlook Madagascar, unsure whether to regard it as part of Africa or of Asia.

Classification of this last sort is a rather modern preoccupation. The earliest written accounts of Madagascar, penned by Arab geographers around a thousand years ago, did not speculate whether Madagascar was better considered in relation to Africa or to Asia. Nor, generally, did the documents written by the first European visitors to the island: sailors and traders who visited in the sixteenth century. However, some Europeans who had travelled widely did remark on aspects of the island's people and language that reminded them of other locations or connections, such as the Dutch merchant-adventurer and the Italian missionary who, independently of one another, noticed that the main language spoken on the island bore a family resemblance to Malay. A scientific concern with classifying various population groups living in Madagascar as essentially either Asian or African became current among European writers and administrators only during the nineteenth century, in the years preceding the island's invasion by French colonial troops (a substantial number of whom were actually from West Africa or Algeria) and the subsequent proclamation that it was henceforth a colony of France. Even the finest scholars of the colonial period assumed that the population of Madagascar, although speaking dialects of what is clearly one single language, is divided into specific ethnic groups that owe their differences to an origin on one or other shore of the Indian Ocean.[1] Identifying various groups of Madagascar's people and their cultural attributes as being most closely connected either to Asia or to Africa has often been a highly ideological affair, these days taking the form of heated internet exchanges.

Too often, popular debates of this nature take little account of the painstaking work of scholars who have undertaken serious analysis of historical patterns of migration and language transmission.[2] Historians, anthropologists, archaeologists and other scholars using rigorous and sophisticated methods have not only gathered a wide variety of information about Madagascar's past, but have also reached a fair degree of consensus on its interpretation. A great deal has also been contributed to our understanding by antiquarians and history-lovers since Victorian times, both Malagasy and foreigners, including missionary-scholars like the French Jesuit François Callet, who collected written and oral histories in the nineteenth century, creating a prime source for the history of the highland region of Imerina,[3] and the Malagasy scholars who laboured long and hard on a multi-volume encyclopaedia of Madagascar that remains uncompleted.[4] The only history of Madagascar in English that is still extant was written by a British diplomat who served as his country's ambassador to the island at an early stage of a distinguished career, and who was so enamoured of the country as to learn its language and undertake serious first-hand research.[5]

Madagascar's plant and animal species evolved over a very long period in complete isolation from the rest of the world.[6] Its human population, however, is relatively recent and has never been completely isolated. On the contrary, the Mozambique Channel and the Indian Ocean have been highways of travel and migration for at least two millennia. Consequently, the unique civilization that has developed in Madagascar over the last seventeen centuries or more—from the time when the first person is known to have set foot on its shore until today—has historical connections to various of the Ocean's shores. The legend of Darafify, still told to Malagasy children, is the story of a giant who arrived on Madagascar's east coast by sea. According to the story,

Darafify made the first waves when he fell into the water after a woodcutter had mistaken one of his legs for a tree-trunk. The tale of Darafify is often regarded by scholars as an allusion to an abortive attempt by Islamized migrants arriving by sea to settle on the east coast, probably in the thirteenth century or slightly later.

The Malagasy of today attribute their wisdom and the moral values of their society or their societies to such distant periods and mythical events as these. It is their allegedly timeless values—so modern Malagasy are taught—that have enabled the island's people throughout their history to establish the codes of conduct and the civic virtues that are necessary for social life. The myth of a common ancestry is very much alive. In fact in many respects it is stronger than ever, as the modern political form of the nation-state depends on the perception that a relationship exists between members of a single national community. The preamble to the constitution of Madagascar's Third Republic,[7] for example, refers in its French version to the notion of *fihavanana*, a word designating kinship, implying that the 19 million Malagasy of today are members of one vast family. It is easy for a historian or an anthropologist to show that timeless cultures do not exist, and that the myth of common kinship is just that: a myth. A more clinical way of expressing the historical trajectory towards formation of a consciousness of an imagined community would be to say that the Big Island constitutes a bounded space within which a great diversity of peoples have lived and identifiable cultures have existed, changing over time and interacting with one another, without ever being utterly cut off from the world outside.

The threads of Madagascar's history

The fact of living on an island while also having contact with the world beyond the sea has produced a series of tensions that have translated into specific patterns of social and political behaviour traceable over time. On the one hand, throughout their recorded history Madagascar's people have shown an ideological attachment to whatever they feel pertains authentically to their island, or to a specific region within it. Practices of this sort are often called 'the customs of the ancestors'.[8] On the other hand, people, objects and technologies considered to come from overseas enjoy high prestige in certain circumstances. The dialectical logic that results from the coexistence of these two rather contradictory ideas may be considered as a thread running right through Madagascar's history. It is closely connected to another idea that may also be traced through the centuries that have elapsed since the island's first settlement, namely the notion that humans are not all of one sort, and that some are literally a breed apart. Following the anthropologist Paul Ottino,[9] most scholars today agree that the ideas of existential difference that have been typical of Madagascar throughout its recorded history show traces of the Hindu philosophy that was assimilated by populations in some of the islands of southeast Asia and conveyed through trade and migration from there to Madagascar at an early stage of its settlement.

Thus, there is evidence from Madagascar's very earliest history that certain categories of population have been perceived as being of a superior type by reason of their ancestry. Malagasy words denoting this high status are often translated into English as 'noble', a word carrying a historical baggage derived from the law and politics of Europe's Middle Ages. In Madagascar's history, 'noble' groups have sometimes been very numerous, have often been peasant farmers or cattle-herders just like their less elevated neighbours, and have not usually enjoyed special rights to fiefs or other positions of command. Nevertheless, the existence of certain families or groups who were believed to be existentially superior to others was at the heart of the formation of monarchies over centuries.[10] In Madagascar's historical kingdoms, non-noble groups were not directly comparable to the commoners of medieval Europe, as in Madagascar they have generally enjoyed specific rights and wielded considerable power within their communities in various forms that could equal the power of nobles. Some non-noble groups were bound to monarchs by ties of a type that has no equivalent in European history, but which endowed them with such substantial rights that it would be misleading to describe such groups as 'slaves' in spite of their attachment to a specific monarch or to a particular noble group. Only household slaves, apparently rather few in number in Madagascar until the early nineteenth century, did not enjoy group rights. At times, however, people of every grade and status were threatened with enslavement to feed a slave trade that flourished in the island for centuries. However, since the nineteenth century there has been a systematic and island-wide tendency for some groups of non-noble status to become assimilated to the status of proletarians, and the recent loss of status by such groups has often been projected back into the past. The effect has been that certain groups with otherwise venerable histories are nowadays said to be the descendants of slaves. This may be a useful political strategy for some people, but it is poor history.

The first identifiable wave of settlement of Madagascar, as opposed to evidence of landings by isolated parties of sailors, seems to date from the seventh or eighth century of our era. There is some evidence that these pioneer settlers were divided into distinct status-groups, as we will describe at more length.[11] In other words, systems of inequality have been a thread in the texture of Madagascar's history from the very beginning, and are still very much in existence in the contemporary republic whose legal structures are based on the French model. Researchers in recent years have published pioneering work on the contemporary position of social groups who, while enjoying modern legal rights of citizenship, suffer the stigma of having had ancestors regarded as slaves.[12] There has also been substantial research on the history of the slave trade,[13] and on the consequent formation of a Malagasy-speaking diaspora in Mauritius, Réunion, South Africa and elsewhere, that seems to have formed distinct communities outside the Big Island until at least the later nineteenth century.[14]

During colonial times especially, foreign commentators often considered Madagascar's people to be so absorbed by the customs of their own direct ancestors as to be thoroughly insular in nature. Madagascar's people have, over a very long period, spoken and developed a single language, even if some of the island's communities within historical times are known to have spoken other languages, including Bantu languages that were spoken in some remote areas until the 1930s. The Malagasy language is the main medium through which the culture of a given group has been articulated and transmitted over time. In spite of the many dialects they speak, Malagasy people can generally understand one another, and a Malagasy lingua franca exists. The fact is that, despite Madagascar's reputation for cultural insularity, its people have shown a formidable capacity to absorb foreign immigrants and foreign ideologies, including in the fields of politics and religion.

So consistent has the assimilation of migrants been, in fact, that it is more convincing to see continuity in historical patterns of settlement rather than a long series of shocks and ruptures. In every age, newcomers have rarely been numerous enough to impose themselves over a large area, or over a long period, other than by the force of their cultural attributes. Cultural action has been more important than military force in allowing immigrants to survive through assimilation or through assertion, with the result that processes of cultural change have produced new patterns without wiping out older ones. Not having vast reserves of strategic resources such as slaves or gold, Madagascar was rather marginal both in the expansion of Muslim-dominated trade in East Africa in the ninth to eleventh centuries that was associated with the rise of Swahili civilization and in the formation of European commercial empires in the seventeenth and eighteenth centuries. During the latter period, in the age of mercantilism, Madagascar did not feel the influence of Europe so intensively as to change the history of its civilization fundamentally. Despite the rival ambitions of Portuguese, Dutch, French, British and others, it never underwent the same fate as the second-largest island of the Caribbean, for example, divided into French-speaking Haiti and the Spanish-speaking Dominican Republic. Not even colonization by France made a fundamental difference in this respect. The initial patterns of Madagascar's cultures have been robust enough to become a fugue, a musical form in which distinct lines combine to form a harmonious whole.[15]

The history of Madagascar is the story of how this civilization was formed. But in relating this, we have to take great care not to commit perhaps the most subtle of all the errors to which historians are liable, that of teleology. In this case, we must avoid the assumption that it was inevitable that various population groups would form a people having the characteristics of a nation, and that the country would acquire the political form and legal status of a sovereign state. The political aspects of the island's history have shown definite centrifugal tendencies as well as patterns of interaction.[16] The diversity of Madagascar's people and of their readings of their own past still provides material for politicians to work with today, and centrifugal impulses will surely continue to exist in future. But there is also no doubt that there exist specific ways of managing such differences, and that these techniques are at the heart of Madagascar's civilization. These mechanisms for the management of difference have evolved from a gradual awareness, formed over centuries, that every group of people living in Madagascar shares the island with a variety of human societies. Even in the seventeenth century, the French official Etienne de Flacourt, who wrote the first full-length book on Madagascar after seven years' residence at its southern tip, described how societies in the southern part of the island were divided into two social orders, the so-called 'blacks' *(mainty)* and 'whites' *(fotsy)*, both of which were further sub-divided into grades, and he mentioned the existence of numerous population clusters that we might today call ethnic groups. The relations between these various sections of the population were complex. It is hard to believe that, even at that time, well-established cultural mechanisms were not at work in different conflicts and, more often than not, prevented people from pursuing their quarrels to the point of death.

A similar principle broadly holds true of governance in general: while the sheer size of Madagascar has caused people to gather together for sustenance and self-protection, its wide open spaces have also facilitated escape. The older forms of government always made allowance for both these elements, rather as in the Malagasy board-game of strategy and skill, *fanorona*. Victory in a game of *fanorona* is obtained not by occupying the opponent's position, nor in removing his pieces from the board entirely, as in draughts, but rather by restricting an opponent's freedom of movement by steady approach, through turning the enemy into an ally. Only a poor *fanorona* player attempts to eliminate the adversary entirely. In a country where, two centuries ago, there were probably barely two million people, the spirit of *fanorona* corresponds to a need to conserve human resources. This fundamental logic was to change only in the nineteenth and twentieth centuries. The last eighty years or so have seen an astonishing growth in population that shows no sign of slowing down, as is also the case in mainland Africa. A leading historian, John Iliffe, maintains that Africa's population growth has been on a scale and at a speed unique in the known history of the entire world.[17] In this respect at least, Madagascar may be considered part of Africa.

Instant communication, the growth of population and economy, and the increasing dependence on the rest of the world that was a feature of the late twentieth century, are not unambiguous gains for a massive island that remained for so long on the margins of the main currents of globalization and trade. Madagascar has one of the world's lowest rates of infection by AIDS, while nearby southern Africa has one of the highest. The recent discovery of oil, in a world thirsty for this precious mineral, will no doubt sharpen appetites for power both outside and inside Madagascar. All of these challenges will test the capacity of the civilization of the ancestors to adapt without losing its soul.

Reading the present into the past

If a streak of nationalist ideology is unmistakeable in many twentieth-century works on Madagascar's history, this is not only because Madagascar gained sovereign status in the second half of that period, but also because of a particular conception of history of European origin that has been assimilated by Malagasy intellectuals. History in its modern sense is hard to separate from the view held by generations of Europeans and North Americans that time itself has a meaning, and that history proceeds through a series of ever-higher stages. Many professional historians these days are not so confident as they once were in the notion that history is the medium for the advance of humankind, but the fundamental idea of history-as-progress has proved long-lasting among the general public in Europe and North America. The exact conception of what the end-goal of the passage of time might be has changed throughout the decades.

It was in the eighteenth century that historians began to label the most basic chronological phases as ancient, medieval and modern periods. Victorian authors inherited this division of time into blocks and added to it an assumption that the European system of states was the political expression of progress. When the European colonial empires were dismantled in the twentieth century, it turned out that elites in Africa and Asia had generally adopted a similar view, making them susceptible to reading the history of their societies in earlier times as a prelude to the achievement of national sovereignty.

It is largely for this reason that historians of Africa have conventionally organized material into precolonial, colonial and postcolonial periods. But this practice is increasingly open to question, not least because it implies that formal colonial rule—a period of no more than three generations in much of Africa and in Madagascar—is the pivot around which the whole history of a continent revolves. Nothing seems more debatable. But if we abandon the convention of regarding the colonial period as a unique historical watershed, then we are left with the problem of identifying other criteria to take its place. Dividing the past into specific periods seems unavoidable, if only for the practical reason that historians conventionally divide their books into chapters. They have to decide what the main theme of each chapter should be, and where to break off and start a new section. Writing one continuous text with no chapters would hardly solve the problem, as the story would still take a narrative form, and each individual string of data would still need a beginning and an end.

In the case of Madagascar, the story of humankind begins around the middle of the first millennium, when the first people are known to have settled in the island. A major problem for the historian is how to consider the seventeen centuries or so between then and now. A few of the themes that run like threads through Madagascar's history could potentially be used as criteria for making sense of the past. Some of them could reasonably be interpreted as signs of progress, not necessarily in moral terms, but certainly in the sense of an expansion of scale. Most obviously, the island's population has increased over time from a few hardy pioneers to the 19 million people who live there now. The more people have lived in Madagascar, the more they have altered the natural environment. In particular, they have cut down trees to use for firewood or for building or just to clear the ground for planting. Victorian historians were quite likely to regard this sort of activity as progress towards a rational mastery of nature. Today's readers, for many of whom Madagascar is a prime example of environmental destruction, may be more inclined to believe the opposite. But whether deliberate alteration of the land represents progress or not, it is an example of a thread that can be traced throughout the island's history.

Dividing the past into specific periods rarely corresponds to distinct ruptures in people's lived experience. It mostly involves identifying symbolic events that suggest a larger and more complex truth about how the world has changed. The sack of Rome, the storming of the Bastille, the fall of the Berlin Wall, are taken to be events of deep resonance. Regarding Madagascar's history, it is not self-evident which events might be identified as epoch-marking. Certainly the appearance of the first European navigators—the handful of Portuguese who landed on the island at the start of the sixteenth century—cannot be regarded as a historical tipping-point, as Madagascar was already well-established on the fringes of the main shipping-lanes of the Indian Ocean, and the arrival of Europeans in itself changed little.[18]

A better argument could be made for taking the rise and fall of major political units as markers of Madagascar's history. Many writers have taken such an approach. As far as anyone knows, the first large political organizations that could be described as kingdoms appeared in Madagascar in the seventeenth century. But it is impossible to affirm this chronology with full confidence, as much remains to discover concerning Madagascar's history, in spite of the advances that have been made. For example, there is clear evidence, requiring further investigation, that substantial home-grown polities existed on Madagascar's northwest coast before the seventeenth century.[19] Archaeology, still relatively undeveloped in Malagasy studies, surely has more to reveal concerning the island's earliest inhabitants. In this book, we have devoted considerable attention to the Sakalava kingdoms founded in the seventeenth century because they are the first large-scale political structures in Madagascar that are the subject of extensive eye-witness accounts, but also because they were particularly influential, being directly related to the formation of the Betsimisaraka kingdom and having a major effect on Imerina in the central highlands.

The rise and fall of those kingdoms that are known to have existed in the seventeenth century are too important to be assigned to a minor place in history, not least because they imply an increase in political scale and a growing concentration of power that are significant elements in the story of the great red island. On the other hand, none of these kingdoms succeeded in extending its rule to the whole country, not even the monarchy based in Antananarivo—today's capital—that was recognized by major powers in the nineteenth century as the Kingdom of Madagascar. The control of people was more important than territorial sovereignty in all the island's historical kingdoms.

There were significant connections between all of the kingdoms known to have existed in Madagascar's past, including in terms of political and religious ideologies, which makes it misleading to treat them as separate entities entirely. Perhaps they should be judged by the same standard as the different forms of vernacular speech in Madagascar, which can indeed be considered independently of one another, but which also have to be assessed in terms of their degree of mutual comprehensibility. Whether in regard to political units or speech patterns, centuries of interaction, warlike and pacific alike, have amounted to systems of exchange.

There is another factor, too, that weighs against organizing a historical narrative around the story of the main kingdoms, namely the Sakalava monarchies of the seventeenth and eighteenth centuries and the self-styled Kingdom of Madagascar of the nineteenth century (the latter being to a considerable extent the vehicle for an oligarchy of largely Merina families). For whereas Jan Vansina has shown[20] that monarchical constructions have had a definite tendency to store texts concerning their ruling groups in oral form even where they lack documentary skills, concentrating too much on such texts may imply that the substantial areas of Madagascar that were never incorporated into a major kingdom or made subject to a central power until colonial times were therefore politically backward. Moreover, included in Madagascar's known kingdoms were groups of people that have been largely invisible to historians, either because they were held under subjugation or simply because they lived far away from the centre of power. Their stories remain substantially unwritten. Included in this category are not only slaves, but also former ruling elites that were defeated or overthrown. Just as the pharaohs of Egypt erased inscriptions relating to earlier rulers, so too did ruling groups in Madagascar, usually by way of manipulating oral traditions.

One aspect of Madagascar's history that could provide a less arbitrary division into periods concerns historical sources. There are very few known documents describing Madagascar or its people before European traders, sailors and missionaries began to frequent the island. There is therefore a case for saying that the late sixteenth or early seventeenth century marked a definite change of phase simply in terms of the quality of the information available to modern readers. By the same token, the early nineteenth century saw the first attempt by any Malagasy group or institution to create administrative documents and maintain archives in the sense familiar to anyone who has lived under a bureaucratic system of government. This, too, marks a change of phase. Successive innovations in forms of storing information coincided with significant shifts in techniques of governing, corresponding roughly to the rise of kingdoms in the seventeenth century in the first case, and the emergence of a state that aspired to conquer the whole island in the second. Each of these periods has left traces that can provide material for historians. We must, however, recognize that the writings or other productions of Asian traders and navigators have not been comprehensively investigated, and nor have the texts of early European geographers.

All things considered, we believe it is useful to make a broad distinction between, first, the age of Madagascar's settlement; second, the age of kingdoms; and, third, the island's entry into intercontinental systems of commerce and exchange so pervasive that they caused a permanent change in the quality of life of most Malagasy, connecting Madagascar to the exterior in a more profound sense than ever before. In our view, an entry into international relations of this intensity occurred in the early nineteenth century, although there were signs of such developments for decades previously. Its most obvious symbolic expression was the signature of a treaty between King Radama I of Imerina and a representative of the British governor of Mauritius, Sir Robert Farquhar, in 1817.

In regard to the colonial period, the French conquest of Madagascar in 1895–6 marked a clear change in the island's relations with other countries. So too did its international recognition as a sovereign republic in 1960, although we will argue that this did not either cause or signify any profound change in the nature of Madagascar's relations with France. The most important historical developments actually occurred in between these dates, notably with the beginning of a major population growth that shows no signs of levelling out, and with the establishment of a state that makes a rhetorical and actual commitment to improving the condition of its people through bureaucratic action. Madagascar's First Republic was often regarded as a neocolonial regime, and this was an accurate perception insofar as the island's formal independence did not in itself signify a radical break with France. Such a break occurred more than a decade later, somewhere between the revolution of 1972, with its anti-imperialist rhetoric, and the agreement with the World Bank in 1980 that was central in Madagascar's renegotiation of its place in an international order based on neoliberalism rather than on the colonial link with France. For these reasons, we may say that a new phase of Madagascar's history began in the 1930s or 1940s and that there was another change in the late 1970s or early 1980s. In the narrative of development, international recognition of Madagascar's national sovereignty in 1960 constitutes an event rather than a point of rupture.

The texture of change

Not only is it possible, then, to discern distinct phases in Madagascar's history, but it could also be said that this history has not proceeded at a uniform speed. For example, the Prophet Mohammed died in Arabia in the year 632 (measured by the European calendar). It took at least four centuries before his teachings made a clear impact in Madagascar, beginning with some coastal areas, and gradually penetrating populations further inland. As time went by, international developments came to Madagascar at greater speed. The Spanish conquest of South America in the sixteenth century produced great quantities of silver that were to have a marked effect on Madagascar within 150 years, when trade in silver coin, mostly of American origin, was to become an important element in the formation of major kingdoms in Madagascar; in turn, these kingdoms exported slaves, sometimes as far as the Americas. (Madagascar was already implicated in the seaborne slave trade before this date, to East Africa and southern Arabia especially, but the European connection introduced significant new elements). By the twentieth century, developments half way around the world were making themselves felt in Madagascar far more rapidly. Large numbers of Malagasy soldiers fought in France in the First World War. Reports of the founding of the United Nations inspired an anticolonial rising in Madagascar in 1947. Africa's wave of democratization, itself influenced by the fall of the Berlin Wall and by the release of Nelson Mandela in South Africa, reached Madagascar when crowds brought down the socialist government of Didier Ratsiraka in 1991.

While international communication has speeded up enormously over the centuries, so too has the number of Malagasy increased. Estimates are always rough, but it is likely that the number of people living in the island has grown from several hundred thousand around the start of the second millennium, to some two and a half million in 1900, six million in 1960, and some 19 million in the early twenty-first century. It would be a fine point to debate whether more people necessarily make more history. But, considering demographic growth together with the speed of change and the improvement in the quality of historical sources, it is almost inevitable that in this history we are obliged to examine events in more detail as time goes by. Thus, chapter one covers some seven centuries of history, chapter two, three centuries, and chapter seven, only thirty years.

In the last resort, the history of Madagascar narrated in the present volume is the story of the people who have lived in the island, interacting with one another through war and through commerce as well as through strategies of marriage and other forms of peaceful contact. We believe this to be a more accurate vision of the country's past than a narrative of separate groups that have developed largely in isolation from one another.

Any general history is bound to leave out more than it includes, and will always be a partial view of the past. If this book seems to portray Madagascar as more disposed to intercourse with foreign parts and foreign people than some readers can easily recognize, it is perhaps inevitable in a volume that tries to compress so many centuries of history into just a few pages. In any case, it is at least a corrective to the many books that have represented Madagascar as a world unto itself.

A note on place-names

Nearly all Malagasy place-names have been spelt differently over time, often depending on writers' nationality. Thus, the leading seventeenth-century port known to navigators from East Africa and Arabia by the Arabic word *manzalajy* ('harbour'), was called by Portuguese sailors Mazalagem Nova, transformed into Matthewlodge by the English and Maselage by the French, and so on, in each case with many variant spellings. Place-names became standardized during the nineteenth century, and particularly after the imposition of colonial government. In the 1970s, the government of Didier Ratsiraka decreed the use of Malagasy versions of the names of the country's main towns, but to this day many Malagasy still use names of European origin, referring, for example, to Diego Suarez, rather than using the official name of Antsiranana. In this book, for the sake of clarity we refer to towns by the names that are generally best-known. Thus, we refer to Madagascar's capital city throughout as Antananarivo, which is both the usual Malagasy spelling as well as the one widely used by English-language writers in the nineteenth century. The colonial spelling—Tananarive—now looks rather dated in an English text, although it is regarded as standard in French. We nevertheless continue to refer to other leading towns by names that were officially changed in the 1970s, such as Diego Suarez, Fort Dauphin, Majunga and Tamatave, simply because they are most often called by these names, even inside Madagascar. We use the official form when referring to the modern provinces, such as Antsiranana (Diego Suarez) and Toamasina (Tamatave).[21] This is perhaps not ideologically consistent, but we hope it aids understanding.

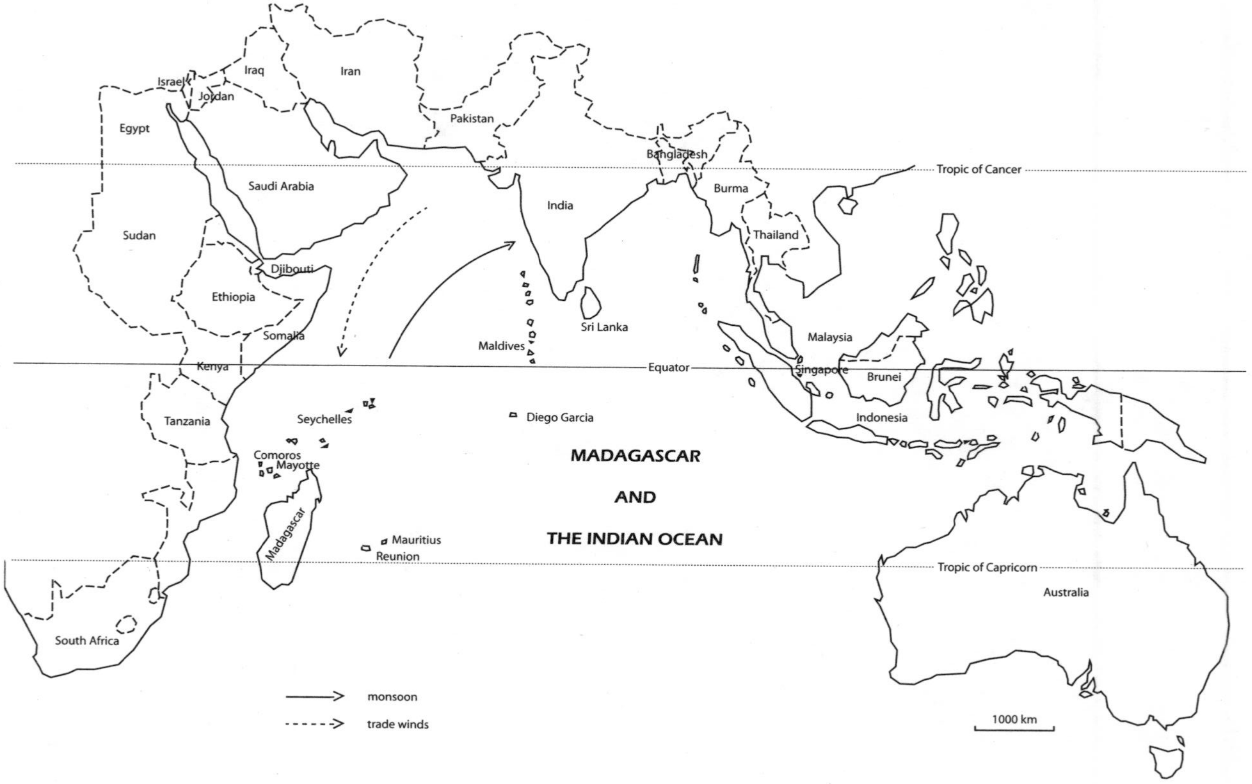
MADAGASCAR
AND
THE INDIAN OCEAN
Tropic of Cancer
Equator
Tropic of Capricorn
Egypt
Israel
Jordan
Iraq
Iran
Pakistan
Saudi Arabia
Sudan
Djibouti
Ethiopia
Somalia
Kenya
Tanzania
South Africa
India
Bangladesh
Burma
Thailand
Sri Lanka
Maldives
Malaysia
Singapore
Brunei
Indonesia
Seychelles
Comoros
Mayotte
Madagascar
Diego Garcia
Mauritius
Reunion
Australia
monsoon
trade winds
1000 km

1

SETTLEMENT 400–1099

Of all the world's oceans, the Indian Ocean is the friendliest to sailors. Its two halves, separated by the Indian sub-continent, are like two massive lungs. The air that gives them life comes from the monsoons, the prevailing winds that change direction with some regularity and create seasons in the tropics. Well over two thousand years ago, seafarers living on various points of the Ocean's rim had learned to use the winds' predictability to advantage.

In much of the Ocean's western half, the winds blow for part of the year from the northeast, making possible a journey from India to East Africa. In the best month for undertaking this journey, December, a good sailing-ship can reach Africa in 20–25 days. By April the prevailing winds turn to blow from the southwest, making a return journey possible. A similar system of winds in the eastern half of the Ocean encourages seasonal voyages between India and the string of islands that stretches from the southeast Asian land-mass to Australia. Real sailors, of course, know that no weather system is ever dependable. In some years there are freak winds. Some parts of the Ocean are liable to severe cyclones, while even the most favourable wind has to be used in combination with local variations and currents.[1]

On the fringes of the Indian Ocean, some of the world's first cities developed, in Mesopotamia and northwest India. Both of these were home to large populations with sophisticated governments more than two millennia ago, sucking in merchandise from a wide area.[2] Later, Greeks and Romans, travelling from ports on Egypt's Red Sea coast, also sailed into the waters known to the Romans as the Erytrean Sea and developed a working knowledge of the system of monsoon winds. Greek and Roman merchants and skippers and their commercial agents were active throughout the western 'lung' of the Indian Ocean, sailing down the East African coast as far as the modern Mozambique and eastwards to India. Greek sailors are known to have travelled to Sri Lanka, where Roman coins of the fourth and fifth centuries have been found. Europeans traded there with merchants from Austronesia.

Austronesia has never been a single political unit, not even after Dutch colonizers in later times had imposed a single authority over thousands of islands to form the modern Indonesia.[3] Islands strung over thousands of miles contain a wide variety of populations, including dark-skinned Melanesians and lighter-skinned peoples, living from widely differing systems of agriculture, fishing and trade. The island of Borneo[4] to this day contains inland populations living in forested mountain areas difficult to reach, speaking languages whose use is restricted to small zones, even though its coasts have been visited for at least two millennia by sailors and traders who, over time, have spread the use of trade languages, goods and cultural knowledge, including political and religious ideas.

Two thousand years ago, sailors from Austronesia were already heading westwards in their distinctive boats, usually equipped with outriggers, as the Roman geographer Pliny recorded.[5] There were regular maritime relations between Austronesia and India, and merchants and sailors from Sumatra and Java carried goods between India and China. Austronesian trade-goods, and perhaps even Austronesian sailors, were thus reaching Africa even before the Christian era, as has been suggested by the discovery of bones from a chicken—an animal of East Asian origin—found by archaeologists in a cave on Zanzibar and carbon-dated as being over two thousand years old.[6] Many commodities and plant-varieties of Austronesian origin no doubt reached Africa indirectly, traded first to India before being taken further westward by stages. What is clear, however, is that the Indian Ocean was already an old system by the time Portuguese navigators rounded the Cape of Good Hope and sailed to India. Probably before the start of the first millennium, Chinese travellers had discovered the existence of this vast ocean. They sailed in these waters to reach India, perhaps from as early as the second century, although it is possible that Chinese traders preferred to travel in Indian, Persian or Arab ships. If the Chinese were held back, it was not by a lack of technical skill or knowledge, but by an awareness that African and Indian peoples were already subject to rulers of their own. For the Chinese, political considerations were more important than the pursuit of maritime or economic progress. China's ruling classes generally considered long-distance sea journeys to be expensive, unpredictable and unnecessary. They found it better to rely on the use of middlemen and to limit their own exposure to risk. They became more actively interested in Indian Ocean trade only at the time that Arab arrivals on their own coasts declined, in the thirteenth and fourteenth centuries.[7]

At some point in ancient times, at the far southwestern point of the wind-powered navigational systems they habitually used, sailors found an island without any human population. They had discovered the island of sub-continental size that is today called Madagascar.

Discovering Madagascar

The sophistication of ancient systems of navigation and trade in the Indian Ocean suggests it is quite likely that a ship's crew, perhaps caught by a cyclone or in search of water, would have touched Madagascar in the course of an ocean voyage at an early date, and that humans may have set foot on the big island long before it was permanently settled. Some scholars believe that settlers from East Asia may have arrived in Madagascar as early as the fifth century BCE.[8] While this cannot be ruled out, it should be said that there is no hard evidence of such an early human presence on the island. Iron implements had replaced stone in large parts of both Africa and Asia by the second century BCE, and yet no archaeologist has ever found a site in Madagascar containing traces of the systematic use of stone tools.[9] The absence of any finds, though, is not conclusive evidence, since Madagascar has received only a relatively small amount of attention from archaeologists. No doubt future discoveries will continue to produce surprises, and may cause historians to revise their theories on the timing and exact manner of Madagascar's settlement.

Among the oldest worked objects found by archaeologists in Madagascar are animal bones that show traces of having been marked by tools, notably some bones from an extinct species, the dwarf hippopotamus, that were found in the southwest of the island by the nineteenth-century scholar-explorer Alfred Grandidier and taken by him to Paris.

These have been carbon-dated to the early years of the first millennium of the current era.[10] Samples taken from old sediment cores in lakes show traces of pollen from imported plant-sorts,[11] also suggesting human influence from a period that has not left any more substantial remains and lending weight to the argument that stronger evidence of early human settlement may be lying in the ground awaiting discovery. The safest statement is probably to the effect that if mariners did indeed land on Madagascar before the first centuries of the current era, no traces of them have yet been found.

At present, the clearest direct archaeological evidence of people living in Madagascar that can be dated with some degree of accuracy comes from caves in the hills around what would later be called the bay of Diego Suarez—nowadays officially known as Antsiranana—near the island's far northern tip. One site has revealed animal bones and remains of locally made pottery that have given carbon dates from roughly 685 to 745 CE, and these cover a lower level dating from perhaps 405 CE. This latter date, then, given the current state of knowledge, is the earliest at which it can be said with some confidence that there were people on Madagascar. These traces are from rock-shelters most probably used as temporary accommodation by sailors who had sailed into Madagascar's best natural harbour.[12] As a specialist on the archaeology of Madagascar has put it, physical remains of this sort provide no more than 'very limited evidence of transient human occupation' for the earliest identifiable stage of the island's history, perhaps in the fifth century CE.[13] It seems quite likely that these remains were left by mariners who stayed in Madagascar for only short periods. The first humans to set foot in Madagascar are unlikely to have intended to establish a permanent settlement.

Whoever those sailors were, eating their meals and sleeping in shallow caves or under overhanging rocks close to the sea shore, they probably spent no more than a few weeks there at a time, with hundreds of kilometres of uninhabited wilderness to the south of them. For them, the northern point of Madagascar possibly became a source of timber for building and repairing ships. Madagascar has a native variety of tree that produces a timber highly resistant to rot. Perhaps the island gained a reputation as a useful source of raw materials more generally, or perhaps it became known as a landfall for crews blown off course around the Comoro Islands in the Mozambique channel. It was also a place for taking on fresh water and food. Certainly, the sailors of the Indian Ocean were good enough navigators to be able to reach Madagascar whenever they wanted, once they had discovered its existence. As time went by, some ships' crews must have decided to spend the whole of a monsoon off-season on the island, knowing that it would be weeks before the winds turned and allowed them to sail back to their port of origin. It could be that a few took to staying from one sailing-season to the next to cut wood for export. It is quite probable that they did not immediately realize they were perching on the edge of an island, believing that it was the shore of an already known continent.

The island these early travellers discovered is huge, about 1,600 kilometres long and up to 570 kilometres wide. It lies some 400 kilometres from the African coast and 6,000 kilometres from Austronesia. Also to its east, about 800 kilometres away, are the two islands of Mauritius and Réunion, which appear to have been uninhabited until the seventeenth century but which were to play an important role in Madagascar's history thereafter, when they became European colonies that needed their giant western neighbour to supply them with basic necessities. Almost a thousand kilometres from Madagascar's northernmost point is Mahé, the central island of the Seychelles.

Of all these islands, Madagascar is the only one not formed by volcanic activity. Its central spine consists of a long series of mountains, some up to 3,000 metres high. The mountains rise abruptly from a narrow eastern plain, forming a barrier to easy movement from east to west. The western side of the island is less rugged, consisting of wide, rather flat, plains. Madagascar's great size and its considerable variety of terrain are combined with sharply differing patterns of rainfall. The south of the island is dry and in places is virtual desert, its main vegetation being cactuses. The east coast, by contrast, is hot and humid, receiving some 335 centimetres of annual rainfall in the wettest areas, where the trade winds blowing from the southeast hit the escarpment that rises up from the narrow coastal strip, bringing heavy rain in the southern summer months. The heaviest rainfall on the eastern coast compares with just one-tenth that amount in the dry south. The hinterland consists of a series of high plateaux and broad valleys with a mild climate and plentiful rainfall. The island has several large rivers, but most of them have rapids or other obstacles that make them unsuitable for navigation along their whole length.

At the time of the island's first settlement, the eastern, northern and central areas of the island were generally heavily wooded, providing a natural cover whose modern-day remnant is the thin and rapidly shrinking strip of rain forest close to the east coast, once a band of dense and lush forest hundreds of kilometres long. Recent studies of natural prehistory suggest that at the time of its first settlement Madagascar was much drier than it is today. Thus, the great expanses of open grassland typical of the centre-west of the island may not be the result of settlers cutting down trees, but a feature of the island since before it was populated. Fire existed before human settlement, and wildfires that started as a result of a lightning strike, for example, may have burned for long periods. Even the steep, eroded gullies so characteristic of the highlands that their name in the Malagasy language—*lavaka*—has become a technical term in geography, may have been primed by natural conditions rather than being entirely the product of agriculture. The ecology of the island was already 'dynamically changing' before the arrival of the first people.[14]

Having originally formed part of a vast landmass known as Gondwana and become separated from other continents some 150–500 million years ago as a result of a tectonic shift, Madagascar hosts unique flora and fauna, like that other island-continent of the Indian Ocean, Australia. Today, some 80% of Madagascar's plants are reckoned to be indigenous, as are many of its animals. Among extinct species native to Madagascar were a dwarf hippopotamus and an enormous flightless bird, the aepyornis, a larger version of the ostrich that is known to have lived into historical times. Sometimes, people still find fragments of its eggs, which were eaten by early settlers on the island. The most famous of Madagascar's unique animal species to survive today is the lemur family of forest-dwelling animals that look like a cross between a cat and a monkey and have long, furry tails. When the first people arrived, there were no poisonous snakes or dangerous carnivores other than the crocodiles that infested the island's rivers.

We can do no more than speculate on the exact circumstances in which the first humans set foot on Madagascar, and the course of events that led some to stay there for extended periods and, at some unknown date, for the first baby to be born on the island. Some inhabitants must have been locally born from an early stage, living and dying without ever leaving the island. It is difficult to know what name to give to the earliest native-born inhabitants of the island. It would be misleading to call them 'Malagasy', as this would imply that the very first generations assumed a political and cultural identity that was in fact formed centuries later. Much of the academic literature refers to 'proto-Malagasy', but perhaps it would be more accurate to call the earliest inhabitants 'pre-Malagasy'. Whenever it was that the first person waded ashore on Madagascar, and whenever the first baby was born there, it was not very long ago by the standards of human history. In any case, it seems that there was no settlement that could remotely be described as a town in Madagascar for a considerable period, perhaps even for centuries, after sailors had first set foot there. Madagascar's settlement was a process more than an event, unfolding long after other parts of the Indian Ocean's shores had become home to substantial populations with a knowledge of trade, navigation and ship-building, some of them living in towns.

There is evidence that people were setting fires, possibly to clear land for planting, before the sixth century, as may be deduced from sites in which fossilized pollen is mixed with charcoal deposits in layers of sediment that can be dated.[15] At some point, early visitors began to spend the length of an agricultural cycle on Madagascar, making it possible to plant crops and stay long enough to harvest them. In time, groups of people who spent a succession of agricultural seasons in one place became permanent settlers. One of the two most important of the known early settlements is Irodo, a site on the northeast coast of Madagascar that shows traces of continuous occupation from the ninth to the sixteenth centuries,[16] or possibly even from slightly earlier. Archaeological excavations at Irodo provide the most unambiguous evidence of permanent human habitation in Madagascar at an early date, although, once more, this observation does not exclude the possibility that evidence of fixed settlements of older date may still be discovered.

Irodo may well have been established by people arriving from the Comoro Islands. But wherever its founders came from, they no doubt remained in regular communication with their home ports overseas. It is not surprising to find that most of Madagascar's oldest identified sites are located on its coasts or in estuaries, suggesting that the earliest human occupants remained in communication by sea with other centres of population, in the Comoros, in other parts of Madagascar itself, or further afield. The earliest coastal sites do, though, show signs of having had distinctive livelihoods, suggesting that they were sufficiently isolated from one another to acquire a degree of self-sufficiency.[17] Having been established by long-distance traders and navigators, they were cosmopolitan from the start. Irodo, for example, contains shards of pottery of Mesopotamian origin dating from the eighth to ninth centuries.[18]

Places of origin

The archaeologist Pierre Vérin has written that Madagascar was 'undoubtedly discovered from the Comoro Islands',[19] but this observation alone does not tell us much about what sort of people the discoverers were, since the Comoros, like their giant neighbour, were settled rather late in human history and for a long time remained a stopover for the argonauts of the Indian Ocean rather than the home of a long-established population. Even if the Comoro Islands were a regular stepping-stone for the first generations who reached Madagascar, they are unlikely to have been the only sea-lane in use. The first visitors may have included people travelling directly from Africa or even from Austronesia, with others travelling via the Comoros or some other point of the Indian Ocean. For east-west travellers the most likely stopover is the Maldive Islands, and if ships called there en route from Austronesia to Africa and Madagascar, it might explain how cowrie-shells, which exist in large quantities in the Maldives, became such a widespread currency in Africa from an early period.[20] It is quite possible that the first visits to Madagascar were by Austronesians who had already established colonies in East Africa, intermarrying with Africans. However, this theory must take account of the fact that any such Austronesian colonies have left no discernible trace in East Africa itself beyond some archaeological data, such as the 2,000-year old chicken bones found in Zanzibar,[21] and this is far from conclusive evidence because the chicken, a bird of Asian origin, could have been traded by stages to Africa rather than having been brought directly by settlers.

On the whole, probably the most accurate way to imagine the earliest period of Madagascar's history is to think of small groups arriving in Madagascar, sometimes staying for only short periods, but in other cases settling in the island, and this over a period of centuries. Nevertheless, there are compelling reasons for believing that one particular early wave of settlement eclipsed all others. This deduction is based on the analysis of language. All Malagasy nowadays speak tongues considered by linguists to be close enough in grammar as to be classed as dialects of a common language. The classical Malagasy of today is a standard form produced by modern government, education and mass media, originally on the basis of the language spoken in the central highlands, but the many regional dialects are not so diverse that people are completely unable to understand one another. The various dialects spoken in Madagascar are closer to each other than are, say, French, Italian and Spanish. On the other hand, even today the differences are such that two people conversing in a deep dialect can be hard to follow for a third person who comes from a different part of the island. Differences between dialects were certainly greater in the past, before mass education and mass media had produced a homogenizing effect. In the view of linguists, there is no doubt that all Malagasy dialects form part of the Austronesian language group, which consists of some 1,200 distinct tongues—20% of the world's current total—spoken today by some 300 million people in Indonesia, Polynesia and parts of southeast Asia.[22] 'All Austronesian languages are currently considered to derive from a single parent language, probably spoken on Taiwan over 5,000 years ago', according to recent scholarship,[23] in the same way as languages of the Indo-European family, spoken in most of western Europe, are thought to have a common origin somewhere in northern India. From Taiwan, the supposed Austronesian ancestral language is assumed to have spread to southeast Asia and to the archipelago lying between Malaysia and Australia. Malagasy is the most westerly member of the Austronesian language-family.

These linguistic observations, although of enormous value as information about Madagascar's past, have to be considered cautiously if they are to be used as historical evidence. Linguists are able to identify similarities and relationships in language-patterns that are not always obvious to native speakers, implying a degree of unity and commonality that may be more apparent in intellectual analysis than in lived experience.

That the Malagasy language has close connections with some languages of southeast Asia has been clear to scholars for a long time. The first people to engage in written speculation on the Malagasy language included a seventeenth-century Italian Jesuit priest and a Dutch trader who, independently of one another, recognized the similarity of the dialects spoken in Madagascar to the Malay language. The Dutch trader Frederick de Houtman, who had visited Madagascar in 1595 and again in 1597 and learned some of the language, was later imprisoned by a ruler in Sumatra for over two years. He used his enforced idleness to compare words with fellow-prisoners, compiling a vocabulary of Dutch, Malay and Malagasy words. On his return to the Netherlands he had the list published in Amsterdam, compiling in effect the first Malagasy dictionary.[24] However, while the grammatical structure of modern Malagasy clearly shows its resemblance to other members of the Austronesian language-family, there is also a consensus among experts that the Malagasy language must have undergone a substantial degree of African influence at an early date. The mixing of Austronesian and African elements could have occurred in Madagascar itself, but may also have taken place in the Comoros or in East African ports prior to migration to the great island. Accounts of western Madagascar written in the seventeenth century record the presence of substantial communities of people speaking African languages, chiefly Swahili, but also others.[25] The fact that Madagascar's people have a documented history over a long period of absorbing other languages may provide clues as to older patterns whereby an established population, speaking an Austronesian language, assimilated groups of immigrants speaking mother-tongues from Africa or other parts of the Indian Ocean, including some that appear to have been related to languages of Mozambique and Zimbabwe.[26]

Thus, although the settlement of Madagascar took place over a long period, and may have included people coming via a variety of sea-routes, the preponderance of early settlement in Madagascar was of people speaking a language or languages of the Austronesian family, probably arriving via the Comoro Islands in the first instance. But this does not necessarily mean that all the very first inhabitants of Madagascar came from the eastern shore of the Indian Ocean, nor does it even necessarily mean that the majority did. After all, the dominant language of the USA today is English, despite the fact that people from England were not the first inhabitants of North America and that people of predominantly English ancestry do not form a majority of modern Americans. Until about 1800, the majority of overseas immigrants to the USA actually came from Africa. To take another modern example, the people of the Caribbean islands of Martinique and Guadeloupe are overwhelmingly of African origin, and yet they speak French. These cases demonstrate the point that the language that becomes dominant is not necessarily the mother-tongue of the majority of settlers. There are various reasons why entire populations may end up speaking a language that was introduced by only a small percentage of their ancestors. Moreover, languages can spread by means other than the mass migration of those who speak them. Therefore, native-speakers of Austronesian languages may or may not have been a majority among the people who came to Madagascar during its first few centuries of settlement. They were, however, preponderant.

If speakers of Austronesian languages were not a majority among early immigrants, then there must have been circumstances that caused their way of speaking to become the most widely-accepted language in the island. Immigrants from Austronesia might, for example, have exercised domination over another population. Nineteenth-century writers on Madagascar, attached to theories of racial evolution and the survival of superior species, were generally drawn to this idea. They often supposed that invaders from Austronesia or India established themselves in Madagascar by conquering a mysterious race of darker-skinned aboriginals and imposing their own culture. Consciously or not, they were making an implicit analogy with Europe's colonization of many parts of the world inhabited by dark-skinned people, supposing that this reflected a law of nature.[27] Although Madagascar abounds in legends featuring mysterious dwarfs and nature-spirits, there is no strong evidence that any such racial clash ever occurred in Madagascar, and no scholar today supports a theory along these lines. Arguments about the relative importance of the Austronesian element, the Bantu element, or some other influence in the composition of the early ancestors of the Malagasy[28] has become highly ideological, tending to follow quite closely the political needs of the moment, according to whether proponents would prefer to regard Madagascar today as a country related primarily to Asia or to Africa.

Any convincing explanation of Madagascar's settlement has to reconcile the undoubted prominence of Austronesian ancestor-languages with the admixture of other elements in the Malagasy language, notably reflecting influence from Africa. It has to state how early migrants from across the Indian Ocean came to adopt the Bantu words and particularities of speech that exist in modern Malagasy, sometimes deeply embedded. It also has to take account of the great variety of Austronesian civilizations. All of this adds up to a giant puzzle. One prominent historian liked to refer to the early history of Madagascar's human settlement as 'the world's most pleasing enigma'.[29]

Detailed comparison of modern Malagasy dialects with other members of the Austronesian language-family produces finer-grained explanations. Specialists in the comparative study of languages have reached a consensus that, of all the sub-branches of the Austronesian language-family, the one most closely resembling Malagasy is the group of southeast Barito languages nowadays spoken by quite a small number of people on the Indonesian island of Borneo.[30] There is also broad agreement that modern Malagasy contains traces of early borrowing from the Malay language, including from parts of the Austronesian archipelago other than Borneo. Malay is a traditional language in Sumatra, the Malay peninsular and west Borneo, and it was imported at an early stage to Java too. A Javanese influence in Malagasy is also detectable.[31] Linguistic analysis of modern Malagasy suggests that early migrants to Madagascar were already speaking a mixture of various Asian languages even before they sailed across the Ocean, and in particular had absorbed the influence of Malay. Careful linguistic comparison can suggest dates for early migrations. Most western Austronesian languages today contain a substantial number of words of Sanskrit origin as a result of the Hindu influence that spread from southern India through Sumatra and Java from about the third century CE.[32] Malagasy, however, contains rather few words derived from Sanskrit, and those that it does contain almost all occur in Java and Sumatra as well. This suggests that the Malagasy language became separated from others in the Austronesian group at a relatively early period in the spread of Hindu influence. Similar historical deductions can be made from old Arabic-based words in Malagasy. Some of these are associated with rituals derived from Islam and must therefore have been transmitted after the spread of Islam, probably reflecting not a direct immigration to Madagascar by Arabic-speakers, but the absorption of Arabic words into southeast Asian languages and their subsequent spread from there to Madagascar. We may recall that the Prophet Mohammed died in the seventh century as measured by the Christian calendar.

On the whole, linguistic evidence suggests that migration from parts of the modern Indonesia and from elsewhere in the Austronesian world to Madagascar can hardly have reached significant proportions before perhaps the seventh century CE at the earliest, the date at which a Hinduized Malay civilization was developing in Sumatra. It is also increasingly clear that immigration to Madagascar occurred in a wider context of trade and travel connecting the east and west shores of the Indian Ocean. These provisional conclusions based on linguistic analysis are borne out by modern studies of genetic evidence, including recent research finding that roughly half of the genetic lineages of today's inhabitants of Madagascar suggest an origin in Borneo, and half indicate a connection to East Africa.[33]

The close kinship between the Malagasy language and its Barito cousins suggests that settlers whose ultimate origins were in Borneo had such overwhelming influence among the earliest settlers, whatever form that may have taken, and established themselves so firmly in Madagascar, as to absorb successive generations of newcomers who, arriving in Madagascar at later periods, eventually adapted themselves to the language they found already widely spoken there.

The cosmopolitanism of many ports around the Indian Ocean's rim at an early period, and continuing immigration to Madagascar from all directions throughout the centuries, mean that it is usually fruitless to try to identify the precise place of origin of any single Malagasy community of modern times. However, it does seem likely that there was a connection between early emigration from the islands of southeast Asia and events associated with the existence of Srivijaya, a Malay kingdom in Sumatra that arose in the seventh century and flourished for the next six hundred years, its rulers strongly influenced by Hindu ideologies. Srivijaya was a sea-power controlling maritime trade between India and China as it passed through the straits of Malacca.[34] The kingdom owed its prosperity largely to its ability to oblige ships passing through these narrow straits to pay customs-dues. An inscription concerning Srivijaya written in Singhalese on rocks at Anuradhapura in Sri Lanka, as well as traces of old Malay settlements in Sri Lanka more generally, testifies to the extent of Srivijaya's influence.[35] The rise to power of Srivijaya appears to have been accomplished through war.[36] Like a succession of old Malay states, Srivijaya was chronically short of manpower, causing its princes, soldiers and merchants to search for slaves from overseas. 'The Malay states', notes one author, making an illuminating comparison, 'resemble nothing so much as the Viking system of trading, raiding, and slaving'.[37] Just as seafarers from Scandinavia, at roughly the same date, were impelled by domestic circumstances to sail astonishing distances in search of trade, plunder and land, making a ferocious reputation for themselves in the process, so too did the Malays. Like other Malay states, the rulers of Srivijaya saw themselves as upholders of cosmic order over peripheries that they considered geographically remote and culturally inferior. This style of statecraft led to major population movements, typically in the form of flight from the central node of the state to the outlying areas by people escaping from the government, at the same time as the central power sought slaves. Srivijaya was a polity 'riddled with centrifugal tendencies'.[38] Quite a few states in history have been like this, simultaneously projecting their power from the heartland outwards while also causing people from the core area to migrate, producing patterns of settlement in which political allegiances between the centre and periphery are complex mixtures of affiliation and rejection.

Some old texts by Arab geographers hint at the possibility of emigrations caused by war in the Austronesian islands.[39] There is interesting written evidence that at least one party of emigrants from Borneo passed through an area of Sumatra under the influence of the maharajahs of Srivijaya, and that these people had some relationship to Madagascar. A stone inscription found in 1892 at Kota Kapur in Sumatra, dating from 686 CE, is written in two languages, one being Old Malay, the other disputed but bearing some resemblance to modern Malagasy. It contains an imprecation against people rebelling against the authority of Srivijaya.[40] The Malay text includes the word *tapik*, meaning a military expedition. This word has disappeared from Malay[41] but appears to be related to the modern Malagasy *tafika,* meaning 'army'. There are therefore grounds for considering that part of the Kota Kapur inscription may be written in a proto-version of modern Malagasy, with Malagasy retaining a word that has become obsolete elsewhere. Early Austronesian emigrants to Madagascar may have included people escaping from Srivijaya, or at least the immediate descendants of such fugitives. Thereafter there were further waves of emigration from Borneo westward, via Sumatra and on towards the western shore of the Indian Ocean.[42]

It is also worthy of note that the names of the points of the compass in Malagasy indicate a change in orientation from those in some other Austronesian languages. The names for the different points of the compass in Malay have 'slipped' by ninety degrees in the Malagasy language, so that *timur* ('east' in Malay) corresponds to the Malagasy *atsimo* ('south'), and so on. Since the basic axis of orientation in Austronesian societies is traditionally between the inland and the sea, identification of the cardinal points can vary according to location. Detailed investigation suggests that the vocabulary for the points of the compass that is used in Malagasy is partly borrowed from Malay, and that the system itself must originally have been acquired from Malays in south Sumatra, which is where Srivijaya was probably situated.[43] The most likely hypothesis is that Malays were the main actors in the voyages across the Indian Ocean, with other Austronesians (and, later, perhaps Africans) being subordinated to them in some way or form.[44]

By the time the rulers of Srivijaya were asserting their authority, Madagascar had already hosted a human population, at least occasionally, for a couple of centuries or more. However, the numbers of permanent residents in the island (if any) would have been tiny. The influx of a relatively large wave of refugees from Borneo, possibly via Sumatra, would go some way to explaining why this later group had such a formative influence on the language spoken on Madagascar, replacing or assimilating whatever tongue or tongues were spoken there up to that time.

Although many authors have considered that emigrants would have made their way around the rim of the Indian Ocean, possibly over quite long periods, a direct sea crossing was also possible. That this is feasible even in small craft was demonstrated by accident in 1930, when fishermen from the Laccadive Islands in the Bay of Bengal were blown off course and landed in Madagascar.[45] A direct crossing from east to west of the Ocean by sail is possible in only 30–40 days according to Ibn Majid, the famous Arab navigator often credited with having guided Vasco da Gama to India,[46] while some other commentators maintain that a journey from the Sunda Straits, between Java and Sumatra, to the Chagos islands, about half way to Madagascar, could be made in just ten days or less in the right season.[47] Some scholars[48] believe that migration may have taken place directly from east to west across the Ocean. Well over a thousand years ago, the maritime communities of southeast Asia were able to build and sail ocean-going ships of very substantial size, at least as big as the Portuguese caravelles that were later to make their appearance in the eastern seas. Such large, ocean-going craft are depicted in carved reliefs at the eighth- to ninth-century temple at Candi Borobudur in Java.[49]

A plausible theory of Madagascar's settlement also has to account for the fact that all Malagasy dialects contain features and words of Bantu origin, embedded in such a way as to suggest a considerable degree of mixing between Austronesian language-speakers and East Africans at an early period. Some leading scholars account for this by maintaining that small numbers of Bantu from Africa may have been living in Madagascar before the large-scale immigration of Austronesians,[50] and that the two populations subsequently mixed. Otto Christian Dahl, the Norwegian missionary and scholar who first proved that Malagasy's closest linguistic relatives were in Borneo, considered that some Bantu words unlikely to be loans (such as the names of native animal species) and also certain grammatical features and typical forms of pronunciation (such as aspirated consonants, common in East Africa) amount to evidence of what he termed a 'Bantu substratum', indicating a formative Bantu influence on the Malagasy language.[51] The first Bantu migrants from the African interior, ancestors of the later Swahili, probably arrived on the East African coast from central Africa between 200 and 400 CE. At that stage they had little maritime technology,[52] although there were old trading contacts between the Middle East and East Africa predating the rise of Islam, with which the Swahili associated themselves at an early stage. The predominance of Bantu vocabulary in Malagasy words associated with women and typically female household tasks, such as cooking, suggested to Dahl that there may have been intermarriage at an early period between African women and groups of Austronesians who were mostly men,[53] although in this regard Dahl's hypothesis is based on selective evidence and is judged by some other experts to be unconvincing.[54] Also suggestive of an early African influence are Madagascar's zébu cattle, with their long horns and humped back, which are of African origin, as are the word used to designate them *(omby)* and many of the techniques used for breeding them.[55] Zébu cattle, introduced from Africa by early settlers, soon became wild and were captured for use in sacrifice or for other ritual purposes.[56] In fact, it is notable that almost all the words used for domestic animals in Malagasy are of African origin. However, notwithstanding the existence of early Bantu influence on Madagascar, there is a growing consensus among historical linguists in favour of the overwhelmingly Austronesian nature of the early Malagasy language, which has essentially retained most of the original Austronesian morphology and syntax that the first major influx of Austronesian settlers brought with them. It does not have the characteristics of a true pidgin language, and even the older Bantu words it has assimilated may have been acquired over a long period.[57]

Besides the hypothesis of Bantu and Austronesian migrants meeting in Madagascar, it is also possible that a mixing of Bantu and Austronesian languages occurred before emigrants from Borneo and Sumatra had actually settled in Madagascar. If this were so, it would explain how African influences were incorporated into the Malagasy language from a very early stage, even while its various dialects remained predominantly Austronesian. There is strong evidence from the fields of archaeology, botany and material culture of Austronesian influence in Africa as early as 200 BCE.[58] Asian plants that were brought to Africa at an early period include bananas, plantains, taro and yams, and domestic animals following the same route include chickens, all of which soon became African staples.[59] But this does not necessarily mean that Austronesians crossed the ocean, since their goods could have moved from east to west indirectly, being traded by stages. The transfer of these plant-sorts and animal species to Africa, direct or indirect, seems to have happened before the settlement of Madagascar, as is shown by the mention of plants of southeast Asian origin in the manuscript known as the *Periplus of the Erytrean Sea*, probably written by a Greek merchant in Alexandria in the first or second century CE.[60] There may also have been a lasting Austronesian influence on Africa in the form of boat-building technology and musical styles, the latter once the subject of a bitter academic dispute among musicologists.[61] Conversely, African musical styles may have influenced Austronesia, and there is an argument to be made for the xylophone being an African export to Austronesia.

Analysing cultural patterns as though they were archaeological strata, to be scrutinized layer by layer in a search for historical evidence, is fraught with difficulty and risk of error. While technologies certainly do spread from one place to another, similarities cannot automatically be taken as evidence of mass migration. People in two separate places may develop a certain technique or cultural practice independently from each other, or one group may adopt imported styles and practices for reasons unconnected with large-scale migration, simply by learning them from individual travellers. But when cultural similarities are supported by evidence from other sources, they can provide useful evidence of connections between geographically separate areas. For example, in Madagascar, the use by blacksmiths of bellows made of bamboo tubes, and the extensive use made of bamboo more generally, as well as conventions of house construction, are very similar to techniques found in parts of Indonesia and southeast Asia.[62] This could in principle be a simple coincidence, but since there is overwhelming linguistic evidence of migration between Austronesia and Madagascar, it is reasonable to suppose that the use of bamboo bellows was a technique brought by the early migrants. Regarding early African influences on Madagascar that left traces at later periods, these include a snake cult, still strong in western Madagascar as well as the southern highlands, and the use of poison ordeals to detect witchcraft.

Taking all these factors into account, many historians and anthropologists think it possible that there were Austronesian colonies established on the coast of East Africa from the first centuries of the first millennium or even slightly earlier.[63] In addition, Austronesians and Africans may have lived alongside each other and intermarried on the Comoro Islands, and settlers may have headed from these places to Madagascar having already absorbed a significant degree of African influence.

Voyages between Africa and Madagascar, particularly those going via the Comoros, may have been connected with an international trade in slaves. It is known that slaves were one of the cargoes carried eastwards from Africa at an early period, and it is possible that the Comoros were used as a convenient depot for holding slaves pending their transport to points further north and east.[64] 'The entire African region from Ethiopia to Madagascar had become a major source of slaves for markets from Europe to China' by the fourth century CE, according to two experts.[65] Baghdad was the biggest city in the world at this time, with a population of one and a half to two million people, and it was a major importer of slaves. A major slave rebellion in Iraq in the ninth century seems to have included large numbers of slaves of East African origin.[66] An inscription of 860 CE indicates that Javanese traders were among those who shipped slaves from East Africa, known to Arab travellers at that time as Zanj, the name generally used for the whole African coast south of Mogadishu, including Madagascar.[67] (Zanj is the origin of the modern word Zanzibar). Chinese sources record the

Chinese government receiving slaves of apparently East African origin from its provinces among the islands of Austronesia in 724 and 814 CE.[68] It seems, therefore, that not only were boatloads of people leaving Austronesia in search of peace or prosperity elsewhere, but that there were also traders, including Austronesians but perhaps also Arabs or Persians, regularly employed in taking slaves from East Africa to the Persian Gulf and even to Austronesia. Madagascar, as yet barely populated, can hardly have been an important source of slaves, but its settlement is best understood within the context of these commercial networks, which constituted an integrated system.[69]

A Persian source describes how in 945 CE an Arab sailor met a fleet of ships, probably in the Mozambique channel, which he describes as being from Waqwaq.[70] This fleet, almost certainly Austronesian, had raided the coast of East Africa.[71] The name Waqwaq—encountered in more than twenty medieval texts of Arab provenance[72]—has been the subject of much discussion, and there are various theories as to the actual place designated by this name. Arab geographers of the time probably believed the Indian Ocean to be a vast lake, ringed by land, and Waqwaq was the name they applied rather vaguely to its southern and eastern shores and to Austronesian cultures more generally. Some scholars have noted the similarity of Waqwaq to *vahoaka*, the modern Malagasy word meaning 'the people'. In the opinion of both Gabriel Ferrand and Otto Christian Dahl,[73] two leading scholars of early migrations, an antique word resembling the modern *vahoaka* may have been the Austronesian name for Madagascar, becoming deformed into Waqwaq in the mouths of people speaking Arabic.[74] This raises the question of what name a modern historian is to use in describing the modern island of Madagascar when referring to older times. The island has been called by a variety of names, as we shall see, but it is difficult to avoid using the modern word for ease of comprehension, even in regard to early centuries.

Research as to where the ancestors of the pre-Malagasy came from and how exactly they planted themselves in their new home has shown definite progress. Gradually, historical linguists, archaeologists and human geneticists have reached a consensus on the connection of early settlers in Madagascar with Borneo. Given the present state of knowledge, it is plausible to suppose that Madagascar, a previously uninhabited island, was occasionally visited by crews of sailors from other parts of the Indian Ocean in the early centuries of the first millennium. These early visitors may have included both East Africans and Austronesians. Although the Indian Ocean contained some thriving trade routes, Madagascar contained so few people that it rarely figured as a destination, perhaps serving as an occasional port of call for people in search of raw materials. According to the present state of our knowledge, it is difficult to give a precise date to the transition from seasonal or semi-permanent human occupation to permanent settlement. The site of Andavakoera, for example, seems to have been occupied intermittently over a long period from the end of the fourth century, although we have insufficient data to say whether it was a site of permanent occupation from the outset, or an occasional shelter that evolved into a permanent settlement, or whether settlements of both types coexisted. Austronesians dominated ocean-going commerce in this period, trading with destinations as far away as East Africa. Fierce commercial competition for control of the strategic Malacca straits, the channel for trade between India and China, and the emergence of the powerful thalassocracy of Srivijaya in Sumatra, led to a stream of emigrants making their way across the Indian Ocean to East Africa, possibly calling en route at Sri Lanka and other places. Some of these migrants may have spent time in East Africa and the Comoros, intermarrying with local people and assimilating local customs and patterns of speech before settling in Madagascar. Many of the emigrants were people originally from southeast Borneo, who had spent some time on Sumatra and may have been enslaved or otherwise made subject to the ruling Malay dynasty of Srivijaya. These were people who had left a society with strong social and political distinctions, making use of originally Hindu ideas of purity.

Settler politics and society

Over centuries, the slave trade, and commerce more generally, both within Madagascar and with the various sea-powers that influenced communities living there, stimulated contacts between the various groups of pre-Malagasy. Trade, wars, alliances, patterns of inclusion and exclusion, all served to impose a common destiny on the island's inhabitants. This was no doubt reinforced by their sense of living on an island, even such a big one. It is reasonable to suppose that at a certain point, probably well before the year 1000, Madagascar's first inhabitants became aware that they were surrounded by sea, and not living on an outcrop of a known continent. By that time, the early settlements, a handful of which have been extensively excavated by archaeologists, must have contained substantial numbers of people born in Madagascar. We do not know what the people living in these settlements called themselves. They almost certainly did not have any consciousness of belonging to a single community in the sense of aspiring to a single political authority.

Broadly speaking, there are two theories as to how the early settlers in Madagascar came to form communities with distinctive and durable social and political characteristics. Some have suggested that groups of pioneers, perhaps having already achieved a high degree of synthesis of African and Austronesian traits and language in Africa or the Comoros, landed on the northeastern coast of Madagascar and spread from there.[75] If this was so, then the main stream of migrants via the Comoros must have dried up relatively early, as Comorans seem to have been speaking a language of the Sabaki sub-group, related to Swahili, for the last thousand years;[76] if the islands had continued to host streams of migrants from Austronesia, one would expect this to have had a major influence on their speech. A second, less plausible, theory is that small communities settled at different points on Madagascar's coast at an early date, and that their speech and cultural patterns gradually converged as they learned to co-exist in Madagascar over the centuries.[77] If this is so, then speakers of a southeast Barito language must have been preponderant among them.

It is indeed very likely that the great majority of the first settlers in Madagascar arrived on the northwest and northeast coasts of the country, the areas most easily accessible from the African mainland and the Comoros and the ones with some of the oldest archaeological sites. A survey of Malagasy dialects using the controversial technique known as glottochronology suggests that the northern dialects of Malagasy are the oldest, again supporting the suggestion that this is the original area of settlement.[78] Certainly, the earliest settlers in Madagascar were seafarers *par excellence*. Building their houses next to estuaries where they could fish, perhaps trading with other estuary-settlements scattered around Madagascar's coast, they may have made seasonal trips to East Africa or further afield for trade. Excavations of early hamlets suggest that people in both Madagascar and the Comoros followed a similar way of life, living in the same types of houses and using simple pottery and ceramics that also resemble remains of houses and household objects from the same period found in East Africa. Some of this pottery was imported from more distant parts of the Indian Ocean via entrepots at Lamu and Zanzibar. Early settlements on Madagascar's northern coasts maintained a strong connection to the Comoros for centuries, with Swahili or other African languages being spoken in northern coastal areas of the big island. Later immigrants from the east, speaking Austronesian languages, perhaps did not pass via the Comoros, as we will see.[79]

The earliest settlers remained very close to the sea by which they had arrived and which connected them to colonies on other parts of the coast or overseas. Once the internal settlement of the island had begun in earnest, when substantial groups of people began moving deep inland and founding durable communities there, before the end of the first millennium, some of the island's inhabitants must have ceased direct contact with communities overseas and abandoned any notion that they formed part of a diaspora. Some settlers became specialists in herding; others turned their backs on the sea and developed an attachment to the land. The early settlers knew how to work iron, and they made objects from the soft stone found in Madagascar. They lived in small communities, a mode of organization that was to be dominant for many centuries and continues to be the norm in many parts of the island even in the twenty-first century. Most people lived dispersed in hamlets or villages even in those areas where climate, soil and manpower combined to make intensive rice cultivation possible. From the outset, these small communities made adjustments to the habits and cultural understandings that they had brought with them from their places of origin in the light of their experiences in the big island.[80] They grew rice, millet and other crops using slash-and-burn techniques largely introduced from Austronesia, and they seem to have given Austronesian names to plants and animals which they found in Madagascar whenever they thought that these exotic new species had similar properties to certain Austronesian varieties, as well as keeping the original names for imported species such as sugar cane and mountain rice.[81] They also gathered wild fruits and hunted game from a wide variety of ecosystems.

People living in small settlements became deeply attached to specific locations, considering property to be held collectively. Their social organization was formed largely by the need to work in groups, particularly for rice-cultivation, an activity that benefits from intensive labour. The life-style of early pastoralist groups is less well known,[82] but cattle-herders were relatively mobile by nature, constantly searching for new pastures. In some parts of what remained until the twentieth century a generally thinly-populated island, numbers of people in the early centuries probably lived semi-nomadic lives, especially in the least-frequented areas such as the middle west and the centre-north, grassfields where wild cattle roamed, later to become classic zones of settlement for runaway slaves or fugitives from oppressive political regimes. In some of the more remote areas, groups of hunter-gatherers were living even until the early twentieth century. Inland from the east coast and even in parts of the highlands there was a tradition of rather impermanent settlement necessitated by the demands of the slash-and-burn method of farming that required cultivators to move frequently in search of virgin land.

There is interesting linguistic evidence that some of the first groups of migrants to settle in Madagascar included slaves, or at least people in a position of subjection to others. It has already been mentioned that the Malagasy language contains relatively few words of Sanskrit origin, and that these came via Malay and Javanese rather than being a result of direct Indian influence on Madagascar.[83] It is instructive to consider the vocabulary that the Malagasy language borrowed at an early date from Malay and Javanese since it includes, for example, nautical terms and words for certain parts of the body.[84] This and other clues suggest that the first major wave of migrants from Austronesia to Madagascar may have come from quite a sharply differentiated society, possibly one in which a Malay-speaking elite commanded ships' crews composed of common sailors or slaves who were predominantly from southeast Borneo and spoke a different language.[85] The Malay origin of the names of parts of the body may be explained by the prevalence of taboos associated with a superior class, causing loan words to double for certain body-parts.[86] Thus, the most substantial waves of early settlers in Madagascar may have arrived in groups that maintained sharp distinctions of status. The consciousness of hierarchy was maintained in the first continuous communities in Madagascar, perhaps in the form of bondsmen and bondswomen attached to particular households.

If this was a society that followed the custom widespread in Austronesia of regarding certain words as taboo, and used a special vocabulary in regard to the bodies of those regarded as ritually superior to the common people, it would explain the presence in the speech of pre-Malagasy communities of a Malay vocabulary containing words from Sanskrit, markers of elite status in a Barito language spoken by the mass of the population.[87] This is not as unusual as it may sound. It recalls, for example, the linguistic pattern of medieval England, marked by the presence of a Norman-French elite amid a much more numerous English population that at the outset spoke a different language. Certainly, it is on balance more likely[88] that the pre-Malagasy lived in a stratified society than to suppose that early settlers arrived in groups with little social or political structure, and that hierarchies developed only through interaction between local communities and later visitors or settlers. The matter is complicated by the fact that settlement took place over an extended period. Forms of social organization brought by new immigrants were sometimes superimposed on existing structures.

The establishment of settlements on Madagascar in which a high status was accorded to a minority of the population, reflected in the language they spoke, would also explain how these populations were able over centuries to absorb migrants from other areas into their population, through marriage or otherwise, while still retaining the essence of their Austronesian speech. Madagascar's societies have demonstrated over many centuries an impressive ability to assimilate new immigrants, each incoming group losing its original language within a few generations and adopting a Malagasy dialect instead. This is also reflected in wider matters of culture, as immigrant groups adopt habits and patterns of activity that they have learned from the existing population, in respect of farming techniques, house-building, and so on. By the same token, immigrants have introduced new technology, ideas and words that have been absorbed by established communities. Most immigrants have also come to make use of genealogies that make no mention of their foreign origin, reciting lists of their ancestors to imply they have been living in Madagascar for many generations and that they therefore enjoy rights of residence. An important exception to this last observation concerns some elite groups that, on the contrary, emphasize their exceptional status by claiming that they have a collective memory of their ancestors coming from abroad, typically from some highly prestigious place such as Mecca. The subtle interaction between an insular pride in whatever is felt to be authentically Malagasy and the opposite principle—that whatever is exotic and foreign is most prestigious—has long been at the heart of the way in which Madagascar's people think about their history and their very identity. A rigid division of society into categories considered to be of fundamentally different types, requiring careful selection of marriage partners to maintain the purity of the upper strata, is an old feature of the Austronesian societies of Java and Sumatra, reflecting their assimilation of Hindu thought.[89]

Part of the ideology that the settlers brought with them concerned river estuaries, where the mixing of waters indicated a fusion of elements of the world above and the world below. Sumatra in particular was also noted for the importance of its estuary-towns: rulers or other high-status groups lived on the banks of river-mouths, placing their vassals up-river. In Madagascar, to this day some of the most prestigious groups bury their dead on estuary shores, as they were probably accustomed to doing in the Malay city-states that had such influence on the origins of the settlers.[90] Places of burial seem to have been of importance from an early stage, as successive generations of immigrants, when they encountered previous inhabitants who by this time had acquired the status of first-comers, reached accommodations expressed through practices such as recognizing the rights of the oldest communities by appointing them as guardians of cemeteries.[91]

The pre-Malagasy seem to have had a notion of a cosmos that was regular in design. The normal functioning of fertility and harmony within this system was constantly threatened by inversions that could be operated by ill-intentioned magicians and sorcerers. From an early stage of Madagascar's history, one of the most reliable means of detecting sorcery was thought to be an ordeal in which poison was administered to an animal, taken to represent a person suspected of this antisocial crime. If the animal died, it was taken as a sign that the accused person was indeed guilty. In some communities at least, part of the population was regarded as having a close association with the sky and the heavens, another part with the earth. This was more of a ritual division than a political one in any modern sense, not least because the first settlers were hardly numerous enough to form complex states, but it contained within it the potential for the political inequalities that were later to emerge in the form of kingdoms. People considered themselves to belong to kinship groups based on common descent, probably no more than a few hundred strong, and headed by an elder whose authority was based on supposed religious powers.

Small communities were often composed of several distinct groups organized around the notion of kinship *(fihavanana),* ascribing their social connections to the natural order. It is possible to detect in such groups the forerunners of what would later become ethnic groups, although it would be risky to assume that the development of 'ethnic' characteristics was either steady or inevitable. If one such group reached a certain size, it was likely to subdivide, perhaps accompanied with a greater or lesser degree of violence, and one faction would depart to found a new community elsewhere. There is every reason to suppose that in the earliest period lineage heads had little or no wider authority. Widespread rituals probably included animal sacrifices. There were earth cults that incorporated the existence of 'masters of the earth' *(tompon-tany)*, families or groups regarded as being descended from the first occupants of an area and having a special relationship with the spirits of the earth. Some of these earth cults were probably brought from Africa, one of the many striking resemblances between political and religious ideas current in Madagascar over many centuries and African models. One researcher speaks of the 'astonishing similarities' between old beliefs and rituals among the people of the south-central highlands of Madagascar and those of kingdoms in Africa including among the Shona, the Janjero of modern Ethiopia, and in the Great Lakes region.[92] The oldest cosmological system used in Madagascar is one of eight cardinal points, overlaid at a later date by a twelve-house system of Arabic origin.[93] Among the ideas of ritual purity brought from Austronesia were, most probably, taboos on eating certain foods and on the use of certain sorts of language, both of which have remained central to Malagasy religious ideas.

Similarities like these are quite likely to result from migrations a thousand years or more ago, but it is unsafe to conclude on such grounds that particular groups of today's Malagasy are therefore of essentially African origin while others are of Asian origin. Ideas introduced in one part of the island have been assimilated by other groups, and Malagasy over time have produced inventions of their own. For example, a key political and religious idea that is most probably of Austronesian origin is the notion that excellence is at the centre, not the periphery, and yet this has spread to all parts of Madagascar, including the west coast that faces Africa and has most often received immigrants from the continent nearby. A map of Madagascar's human settlement remains to this day influenced by the history of migrations. The relatively densely populated areas of the northwest, northeast and southeast were early zones of habitation. The far south was more thinly populated. In the earliest centuries, so too were the highlands, the last area to welcome large-scale immigrant groups, mixed with other groups moving inland from the coast. Taken together, all these migrations were at the origin of surprising combinations of human diversity and a relative coherence of culture that were to be strengthened in later centuries.

Central to political and religious thought was the notion of a force known in Malagasy as *hasina*.[94] This key Malagasy concept, which was probably present among the earliest settlers, has changed its meaning over time.[95] *Hasina* is a spiritual quality that was the essence of social and political organization against the forces of disorder and wilderness. In time, it was to be incorporated into complex ideologies of kingship in which the sovereign was regarded as an essential channel for the spiritual virtue necessary for human society to endure. According to Pierre Boiteau, a professional botanist as well as an historian, among the plants introduced by the first settlers was dracaena, perceived by the settlers as having magical powers and therefore planted as a sign of claiming the wild bush. It is called in Malagasy *hasingola* or *kosingola*, related to the word *hasina*.[96]

By the beginning of the ninth century all the basic elements of a distinctive civilization were in place, articulated by small communities. At first these pioneers clung to the coasts, and only hesitantly began to explore the island's interior, remaining in communication with one another and with other settlements overseas.

SITES OF EXCAVATIONS AND DATATION BY THE CENTRE D'ART ET D'ARCHEOLOGIE, ANTANANARIVO

First human occupation of the sites

- ● before the VIIth century CE
- □ between the VIIIth and the IXth centuries CE
- ▲ between the Xth and the XIIth centuries CE
- △ between the XIIIth and the XVth centuries CE

1. Sculpture of an Austronesian ship. Borobudur temple, Java, 8th–9th C

2. Reproduction of an Austronesian vessel, of the type probably used by early settlers in Madagascar

3. 'White' and 'black' families as recorded by Flacourt, mid-17th century

4. Ruins of Antalaotra settlement, northwest coast

5. Rafaralahy, governor of Foulpointe under King Radama I

6. King Radama I

7. A senior army officer and his wife, 1860s. Rainitomponiera and Razaimanana

8. King Tsiarasso of Nossi-be, 1899

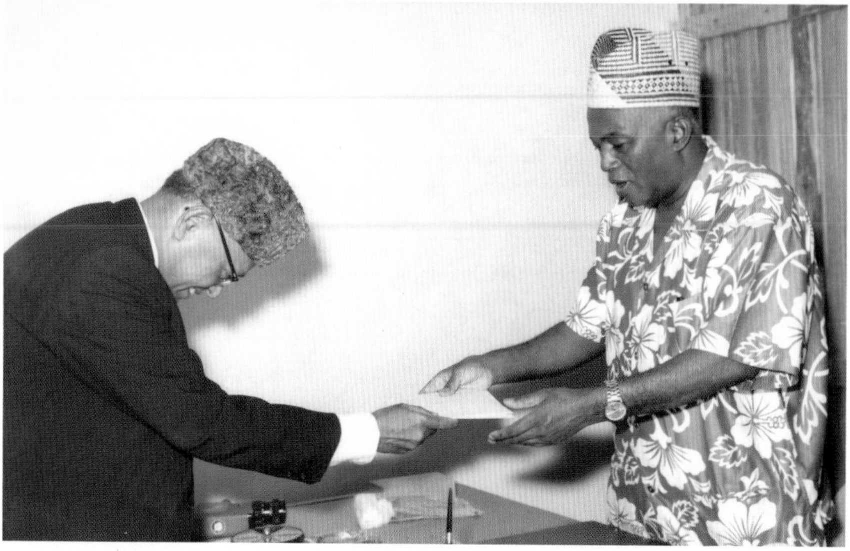

9. Philibert Tsiranana

10. Jean Ralaimongo (above, far left) with Malagasy comrades from the First World War

11. Didier Ratsiraka

12. Marc Ravalomanana

2

TRANSFORMING THE ISLAND 1100–1599

Modern travellers to Madagascar are often struck by the changes wrought on the land by its people. The airborne visitor looks down to see rivers red with the soil washed from hills that are treeless and bare. The dense rainforest of the east coast has shrunk even in the last couple of decades in the face of inroads by people in search of land to cultivate or of timber for fuel or building. International environmental organizations have set up offices and field projects in an effort to stop the loss of ecosystems and plant and animal species in an island world famous for its unique flora and fauna.

Ecological change in Madagascar is not new: only its current momentum is. Humans, although few in number, were already transforming Madagascar's environment at a very early period. A thousand years ago, the island's population was growing mostly as a result of immigration, probably by this time including newcomers from the Persian Gulf or other parts of the Indian Ocean's northern rim as well as ongoing arrivals from Africa and Austronesia. While most of the earliest settlers seem to have clung to locations near the coast and on the shores of estuaries, there were also hardy pioneers who moved deep inland. Evidence from pollen and from the increasing presence of charcoal in deposits analysed by archaeologists suggests that herders and hunters were active in Madagascar's highlands from the eighth century, although the first identified sites of permanent settlement there are from somewhat later, implying that the highland regions may have remained a frontier-zone for quite a long time.

Even if population density remained very low, the small number of people living in Madagascar was enough to cause the extinction of animals that had never known any predator in the millions of years of evolution since the island had separated from the prehistoric land-mass known to palaeo-historians as Gondwana. By the thirteenth century, the dwarf hippopotamus, various species of lemur, and, perhaps most famously, the giant, flightless, aepyornis bird, had all become extinct, most probably as a result of hunting and other human activity.[1] An array of skeletons and other remains of extinct species is to be found today on public display in the basement of the Académie Malgache, the learned society situated in Antananarivo's Botanical Gardens.

If the early centuries of settlement was the period in which humans transformed Madagascar's ecology, with some help from climate change, they were also the years that witnessed the development of cultural patterns that can be identified as distinctively Malagasy. But a paucity of information makes the first centuries of Madagascar's history, until the arrival of Portuguese navigators at the start of the sixteenth century, its most obscure period. Contemporary documents from those times are limited to a few accounts by sailors and geographers writing in Arabic, often mixing navigational details with myths and fables. Linguistic analysis is less helpful than for the first period of settlement, since the basis of the Malagasy language was already established. Archaeology remains a vital technique for investigating the history of the island. Even with the very limited sources available, however, it is clear that, over a long period roughly contemporary with Europe's Middle Ages, Madagascar, like other parts of the Indian Ocean rim, was influenced by the spread of Islam via the sea-lanes and trade networks in which the island had a marginal position. Contemplating the impact of Islam on Madagascar, identifiable roughly from the eleventh or twelfth century onwards, not only helps to explain how the island's people came to acquire cultural traits different from those of the generations that we have labelled 'pre-Malagasy', but also puts into perspective the later arrival of the Portuguese and other Europeans, by no means the first seaborne traders to leave their mark on the island.

Early towns

Mahilaka is the name of a small town—possibly the island's first settlement worthy of that name—that existed over a thousand years ago on Madagascar's northwest coast. Its remains have been investigated, and the record of this excavation[2] gives us an idea of how people lived in at least one part of Madagascar in the early years of the second millennium, when Mahilaka flourished, roughly from the ninth to the fifteenth centuries. The people of Mahilaka lived in wooden houses equipped with a range of household implements and tools made within their community. Among them were traders who imported ceramics from overseas. There were blacksmiths who forged iron using bellows fitted with pistons, a technology common in the islands of southeast Asia. The smiths' bellows were made of bamboo, a plant introduced from Asia that the early inhabitants of Madagascar used for a great variety of purposes. People in Mahilaka used the distinctive soft stone found in the island to carve vessels and other useful objects for themselves, and this stone they also exported, together with timber and copal resin. Another export product, which probably also left Mahilaka at least occasionally, was rice. This was shipped as far as Aden, where fifteenth-century records reveal that rice was imported from the great island via Kilwa, one of the leading wholesale marts of the western Indian Ocean.[3]

Further nuclear settlements have also been discovered on Madagascar's northeast coast, where the most important site, Irodo, shows the oldest traces from about 870 CE. Excavations elsewhere on the same stretch of coast, at Sandrakatsy, have shown traces of people living in 'a small, central village composed of several distinct quarters, with outlying hamlets',[4] in clusters slightly less concentrated than at Mahilaka. Here, too, people were making their own pottery—much cruder than the Chinese and Middle Eastern wares that figured among Madagascar's imports—forging iron, and carving soft stone to make water-jars, cooking-ware and ovens. By the tenth century, people had already moved slightly inland from the northeast coast itself and were building houses on the hillsides and in the bottoms of the area's fertile valleys.[5]

Although the evidence suggests that Madagascar's northern coasts, easily accessible from the Comoros, were the initial places of settlement, it remains possible that there were early landings on the southern coasts too. Certainly, there were people living in permanent settlements quite far inland in the southern part of the island at an early date. One site in the centre-south that has been excavated, Andranosoa, dates from about 940–1060 CE.[6] Andranosoa's inhabitants practised mixed agriculture, ate beef, made their own pottery, and used iron tools, although it is not clear whether these were self-made or imported, as there was certainly trade with the coast. An interesting observation is that the ecological conditions in this region, which is today very dry, were clearly better a thousand years ago than now.[7]

By 1100 CE, there was no single region of Madagascar, including the hinterland, whose most favourable points were not occupied, even if the total population of the island remained very small.[8] Just how many inhabitants there were at that date cannot be known, but it was presumably a few hundred thousand at the very most. To judge from the scanty archaeological evidence, and considering what is known of later patterns of settlement, it seems likely that the main clusters of population were in the estuaries and valleys of the east coast, easily accessible to the open sea but also providing avenues into the hinterland and offering good land for farming. The highlands, later to become one of the most densely-populated parts of the island, probably did not host many communities in the very first centuries of settlement. Archaeological research on vegetable sediments suggests that there was a period of marked environmental change around 1000 CE in the northwest and slightly later in the highlands, probably corresponding to the arrival in those regions of pastoralists.[9] Early highland settlements contain evidence of the import of ceramics, including some from China and the Middle East, meaning that early settlers in the highlands were in touch with the coast.[10]

During these obscure centuries of Madagascar's history, the most sophisticated trading settlements were those on the northwest coast, like Mahilaka, connected by sea to East Africa, the Middle East and further afield, and by land or water to the centre of the island.[11] Rivers and the sea provided possibilities for fishing, the land for agriculture. There were no horses, donkeys, camels or draught-oxen for transport, and people covered formidable distances on foot. Those who ventured inland would have discovered that along Madagascar's mountainous central spine, running from north to south, there are two wide passes that permit easy passage between the island's west and east coasts, one at Ihosy in the south-central highlands, and the other at Androna in the north. Both were to become corridors for commerce and migration over the centuries. Nevertheless, it is hard to imagine that people from the north coast of the island, which probably housed the majority of early settlers, would have journeyed well over a thousand kilometres overland to create new settlements like Andranosoa in the far south, travelling through the temperate, and largely malaria-free, valleys of the central highlands on the way but declining to settle there. It is more likely that sailors, hugging the coast, spread from the northern settlements to establish new colonies in estuaries further south, perhaps joined by newcomers from other parts of the Indian Ocean who settled directly on the southern coasts without any lengthy sojourn in the Comoros or in the north of Madagascar, and that settlers moved inland from these coastal nodes. It appears that, even in such a thinly-populated country, there were violent conflicts for control of key strategic sites. When the first substantial accounts were written of what various groups of people in Madagascar had to say about their own history — transcribed by European visitors in the sixteenth and seventeenth centuries — they included oral histories of bloody clashes between groups occupying the main estuaries and newcomers trying to wrest control from them. The losers in these struggles headed for other points along the coast or moved inland.

Even though new migrants often came from the same places of origin as the earliest pre- or proto-Malagasy, it is not certain that immigrants arriving in Madagascar by the twelfth century would always have recognized their connections to those inhabitants whose ancestors had arrived three or four centuries earlier. The earliest settlers had adapted to their new home to the extent that latecomers would have found the cultures of Madagascar familiar, but also showing differences that they may have found significant. Attachment to a specific territory seems to have become an important trait among societies in Madagascar at an early date, even among semi-nomadic groups, and it is one that survives to the present. Migration and other forms of contact within the island encouraged the diffusion of new techniques including in social conventions, agriculture, and herding, generating strong similarities in the various regional patterns of culture, most obviously in regard to language, as new migrants were obliged to adapt to their environment. The emerging Malagasy language was itself an instrument for the transmission of a distinctive cosmology and, consequently, of ideas about society and the place of humankind in the cosmos.

Throughout these centuries, it is unclear what name, if any, the people living on Madagascar used to designate their island. We have said[12] that Waqwaq was an Arabic name that could have reflected an Austronesian word designating Madagascar, but this is highly speculative. One of the first Europeans to write a detailed account of Madagascar, the Italian Jesuit Luis Mariano, recorded in the seventeenth century that the people did not have a name for the country as a whole.[13] One oral tradition, written down only in the early twentieth century, maintains that the oldest indigenous name for the island was Nosin' omby ('Cattle Island').[14] Arab navigators and geographers of the time had a variety of names for Madagascar including Al-Qomr, which is also the origin of the name Comoro Islands.[15] An old Swahili word designating Madagascar and its people is Buki, which some authors have thought might echo the name of the Bugi of Sulawesi[16] in today's republic of Indonesia. Europeans knew the island from an early period as Madagascar, a name derived from a simple mistake by the great traveller Marco Polo, who confused hearsay accounts of various places in the western Indian Ocean that he had not visited personally.[17] It was also known by the name Saint Lawrence, given to it by early Portuguese visitors.

Different communities within the island surely had collective names for themselves and used specific names to designate other groups living on the island. In some settlements, people in early times may still have called themselves by their places of ultimate origin, in the same way that, at a later period and on another continent, it took several generations before early English settlers in North America ceased to label themselves primarily by reference to England. As we have seen, most of Madagascar's people probably already spoke dialects that were forerunners of the Malagasy of today, with its basically Austronesian grammar and admixture from Swahili and other languages. Since the emergence of a distinct Swahili language, Madagascar's northwest coast has always been home to some Swahili-speakers, sometimes constituting sizeable communities, including recent arrivals who have not yet fully assimilated the Malagasy language. In the case of Swahili merchant communities, their speech has been constantly renewed by intercourse with the African coast. In the past, there were almost certainly communities especially on the northern coasts that spoke dialects of the Sabaki group, similar to the language spoken in the Comoros for the past thousand years. To judge from later patterns, the island's early settlements may also have included pockets of people speaking other

Bantu languages that have disappeared over time as they have acquired the dominant language of the island.

Scanty as it is, the evidence points to these small settlements as being self-governing in the early centuries of their existence. Authority lay with heads of lineages and individuals regarded as having exceptional religious powers. These may well have included priests considered able to mediate with the spirits of the land, and therefore essential for agriculture, but there may also have been other cults associated with the sky, whose ritual specialists came from families considered of high status. The anthropologist Louis Molet caused a minor uproar in 1956 when he published a book claiming that some groups living in Madagascar in the distant past had a ritual practice of eating the dead as a means of incorporating their spirits.[18] This suggestion was subsequently supported by another eminent anthropologist, Maurice Bloch.[19] If this was so, then it was a custom that disappeared with the later rise of kingdoms.

To judge by later developments, it seems unlikely that authority in communities of the early second millennium was transmitted from one generation to the next through any single system of inheritance, such as from father to son or from father to sister's son, and that various rules of inheritance were in operation in different parts of the island, reflecting the influence of different ultimate places of origin. When large kingdoms later arose, one of the main problems they faced was in establishing orderly rules of succession after the death of a particular king, suggesting that there was no universally recognized rule of inheritance in ancient times also. It is possible that the highly localized powers of ritual experts were associated with a repertoire of recognized symbols, such as the large masts or poles that are erected in some parts of Madagascar nowadays to 'humanize' a territory, to mark it as the property of a particular group, demarcated from the surrounding wilderness, or the standing-stones or obelisks used to commemorate events or to enhance fertility, a custom perhaps brought from Africa. Cattle, introduced from Africa at a very early period, were not only a major form of wealth but also served a religious purpose, being sacrificed on important occasions. The great diversity of political groups was noted by an Arab geographer who in 1224 wrote, concerning the island he called Al-Qomr, that it lies 'in the middle of the Sea of Zandj which contains no island larger than it. It comprises a great number of towns and kingdoms. Each king makes war on the other.'[20]

The large-scale settlement of Madagascar's central plateaux and valleys appears to have begun in the twelfth century or thirteenth century. This was probably the consequence of a conjunction of several population movements. New arrivals on the coasts caused armed conflicts, pushing the losers deeper into the hinterland. Those who headed inland may have included both new immigrants who had failed to establish themselves in the estuaries and the descendants of earlier settlers, obliged to cede their homes to newcomers; the coexistence of groups of Asian and African origin led at an early period to the emergence of distinctive styles of living that would subsequently be labelled 'black' *(mainty)* and 'white' *(fotsy)*.[21] It is possible that population movements on the East African coast may have led to the departure of Austronesian communities previously established there, leading them to seek refuge in Madagascar. Further groups of newcomers from Austronesia arrived via Madagascar's east coast in the decades thereafter,[22] turning these inland plateaux and valleys into one of the most densely populated parts of the island, rivalled only by the estuaries of the southeast coast.[23] By the seventeenth century, one region alone of the central highlands was able, according to one contemporary source, to assemble 100,000 people.[24] Although there are no eye-witness descriptions of the central highlands earlier than the eighteenth century, archaeological evidence suggests that settlements there were for centuries built on hill-tops, often surrounded by ditches for defence, local equivalents of the fortified hill-towns common in southern Europe. The large, sparsely-populated tracts of land that surrounded the highlands formed a clear geographical frontier to the central district known from the seventeenth century as Imerina. But these marches, though extensive and functioning as frontier-zones, never formed a serious obstacle to movements of people. In times of trouble, inhabitants migrated to find new opportunities or safer environments, while in times of calm some of them travelled to trade.[25] In the flatter and drier regions of Madagascar's far south, less densely populated than the highlands even centuries ago, people often lived in enclosures formed by impenetrable hedges of thorn-trees. Nomadic fishing communities preferred temporary shelters that were easily transportable. Migration, interaction, integration into commercial circuits, and the slave trade established at an early period, were all causes of conflicts between, or sometimes among, small communities. Petty wars were themselves a form of intercourse, redistributing wealth and creating contacts between autonomous communities, not least by means of the negotiations that bring conflicts to an end.

The maintenance of dialects that were mutually intelligible and of a range of customs held in common, one of the key achievements of the pre-dynastic period, suggests the existence of fairly regular contacts between individual settlements. There must have been individuals or small groups who travelled extensively on trading or hunting expeditions, taking them many miles from their communities of origin. The cattle that were imported from Africa by early settlers soon went wild, providing a source of meat in the absence of other large game-animals. Archaeological excavations reveal the existence over widely separated areas of similar designs used in handicrafts, suggesting that fashions and techniques were transmitted from one area to another.[26] To judge from later patterns it is likely that, as so often in continental Africa,[27] sacred sites became places of pilgrimage that attracted people from far afield. The exchange of cattle between families or communities, including for religious sacrifice, lubricated relationships that connected otherwise disparate communities.

The growth of Islamic networks

All around the Indian Ocean's rim, communities gradually absorbed influences emanating from the rise of Islam in the centuries following the death of the Prophet. This was a slow process. The Prophet's death was in 632 CE; less than two centuries later, the first mosques were appearing in towns connected to maritime trade routes on the Swahili coast.[28] It is not clear whether the first mosques were built for the convenience of visiting traders or for local communities, but from the late eleventh century mosques in East Africa were serving a local public as increasing numbers of people embraced Islam,[29] perhaps suggesting a gradual conversion to Islam over generations. Madagascar was similarly touched by the spread of Islam, coming both from Africa and from others of the Ocean's coasts.

One of the key trades of the towns along the East African coast was in gold from Zimbabwe, far in the continent's interior. It is generally accepted that gold mining in Zimbabwe was at its height from the twelfth to the fifteenth centuries,[30] stimulated by demand on the coast. The gold was carried from the mines to the port of Sofala, near the mouth of the Zambezi, in today's Mozambique. Sofala lay at the southern tip of the system of monsoon winds, too far for merchants from the Middle East or India to make a round-trip in one season. New ports therefore emerged, at Mafia Island and Kilwa, where cargoes from Zimbabwe could be stored and where traders from further north could wait out the season of adverse winds until conditions were right for them to set sail back to their home-ports with their African gold.[31] Ivory and slaves were other major African exports to the Middle East and India, while beads, cloth, ceramics and luxury objects were carried from Asia to Africa. The Indian Ocean as a whole constituted the world's most advanced integrated trading system of the time, in which Madagascar's small ports and trading establishments occupied only a peripheral place. The discovery of a gold coin dated AH 515 (1121–2 CE) in northeast Madagascar, in the grave of what appears to have been a Muslim Arab or Swahili, indicates that at least one individual Muslim had visited the island at that date, and in course of time flourishing Muslim communities were to emerge in Madagascar consisting of traders connected to Africa's Swahili coast and to southern Arabia; knowledge of Islam was also spread by migrants from Austronesia, who introduced Arabic script. It is notable, however, that just as Madagascar has shown over centuries a formidable ability to absorb immigrants speaking other languages, turning them into Malagasy-speakers in the course of a few generations, so it has done in matters of religion too, at least until recent times. Thus, while there is abundant evidence of immigration by Muslims of diverse origin, novelty in religion has been absorbed over time in the same manner as novelty in language, leaving traces in more diffuse patterns of Malagasy cultures. Until very recently,[32] Madagascar had little tradition of indigenous Muslim communities in spite of the immigration over many centuries by Muslims—the mosques in recent times have been frequented mostly by people of Indo-Pakistani or Comoran origin. Language and religion, considered over the *longue durée*, have in fact been vectors of integration more than they have acted as markers of separate identities.

One of the most durable trades of the Indian Ocean was in slaves. At an earlier period, the Indian Ocean slave trade included an important route from the Horn of Africa to Mesopotamia. This branch of the commerce in human beings declined from the ninth century, although there was a continuing movement of human cargoes from East Africa to India and the Middle East for use as soldiers especially.[33] Javanese shippers were carrying slaves from Africa in the eighth and ninth centuries.[34] One twelfth-century Arabic text speaks of raids being carried out on the East African coast by Buqqiyin—people from Madagascar—via the Comoro Islands, suggesting that Madagascar's coastal settlements in places like Mahilaka were powerful enough to organize raids overseas.[35] The Buqqiyin referred to in this text, however, may not have been natives of Madagascar, but might have been sailors from elsewhere using the island as a staging-post, allied to the local inhabitants by commercial and cultural links maintained over generations. Perhaps they were Malays, redoubtable sea-raiders, who had come across the ocean from Sumatra and were using a temporary base among their distant cousins in Madagascar for the duration of a slaving-expedition. According to one modern source there are traces from an early date of slaves from Madagascar being sold in Persia, Yemen and Arabia.[36] The Arab chronicler Ibn al Mudawir in 1228 stated that slaves from the Comoros and the coasts of Madagascar were shipped to Yemen and Jeddah.[37] These suggestions that slaves were occasionally exported from Madagascar could be taken to imply that the island already contained a population large enough to constitute a minor source of slaves, although it seems likely that the bulk of slaves traded overseas were re-exports of slaves originally taken from the African coast.[38]

According to another Arab chronicler, the people living in Madagascar did not have boats suitable for sea crossings, and the island's ocean trade was served by ships from Oman and elsewhere that travelled as far as Java. He went on to note that 'People from Djavaga [Java] come in large ships and export products from Madagascar because they speak the same language'.[39] Malay-speaking sailors from the powerful and warlike kingdom of Srivijaya are known to have visited East Africa in the twelfth century, including Sofala, the terminus for trade with Zimbabwe and its gold-mines. Some scholars believe that there may have been Srivijayan settlements at Sofala and Zanzibar.[40] Even during the centuries when Arab sailors and traders were acquiring commercial supremacy in the western half of the Indian Ocean, Madagascar continued to maintain relations with the Austronesian islands with which it had such historic connections. Some of the first Portuguese navigators in the Indian Ocean met Austronesians who could recall earlier voyages to Madagascar, a fact suggesting that regular, direct contacts between Austronesia and Madagascar may have lasted until the late fourteenth century.[41] Oral traditions collected in the sixteenth century imply that some Javanese even at that late date recognized the Malagasy as related to themselves.[42] Javanese ship-building was certainly adequate for such long ocean voyages. Austronesian vessels are known to have reached not only Africa and Madagascar but also Taiwan, New Zealand and Easter Island.[43]

In much of the Indian Ocean, the profession of Islamic faith functioned as an international brotherhood attractive to long-distance traders, winning adherents from East Africa to Java and making it difficult to distinguish clearly between religion and commerce in the spread of Islam. As Islamic networks came to dominate the Ocean, sea-captains and geographers produced guide books and navigational aids written in the Arabic *lingua franca* that reveal a sophisticated knowledge of navigational skills and foreign ports. Arabic-speaking sea-captains used navigational instruments of Chinese origin such as the compass and the astrolabe. Nevertheless, probably the main reason for Arab commercial success after the eleventh and twelfth centuries was not so much navigational skill—which Malay sailors especially also had in abundance—as the stability of their currency, the dinar. The dinar's strength was based on the prestige of a powerful state ruled by elites that had realized the usefulness of minted coins as an instrument of commerce. Coins from Egypt have been found in Madagascar from the time of the Fatimid dynasty,[44] which overran North Africa in the tenth century and flourished for two centuries. Increasingly, Islamized traders, Arab or Swahili, began to build mosques in the ports on Madagascar's northern coasts, and in time these were to be constructed in stone. The northern coasts of the island could boast a handful of modest port-towns replete with stone-built houses and mosques, but none of these was home to more than 10,000 people at most. Inasmuch as activity in these towns was associated primarily with commerce or small-scale manufacturing rather than with agriculture, they were probably centres of new forms of sociability. The handful of towns, being centres of cosmopolitanism and commerce, may have provoked curiosity and envy. It remains an open question whether there may not be sites of early towns destroyed in local warfare that are still awaiting discovery.

Indian Ocean sea-routes gained in importance after the signature in 1345 of a treaty between the Mameluk ruler of Egypt and the republic of Venice, superseding Middle Eastern land routes that were controlled by Mongol rulers. The Arab domination of sea-trade facilitated new population movements from one part of the Indian Ocean rim to another, to the extent that there was a small Arab community in the major Chinese port of Canton, while no less than a quarter of the population of Mangalore in India is said to have been Arab by the sixteenth century.[45] In the opposite direction, movement along the sea-lanes from east to west resulted in the establishment of a detectable Indian influence in East Africa.

Because Islam was itself a medium of communication over large distances, the spread of Islamic influence to Madagascar cannot automatically be taken as sure evidence of migration by people from Arabia. Rather, just as earlier Indian influence on Madagascar was spread indirectly, through the transmission of Hindu religious ideas to Java and Sumatra, and thence to Madagascar, the propagation of Islam was similarly indirect. Madagascar's west coast was regularly visited by Islamized traders from the African coast, many of them travelling so often on dhows to and from southern Arabia as to have adopted an Afro-Arab identity, wearing turbans or skull caps and long robes, and sometimes speaking Arabic. Often called by Europeans 'Arabs' or 'Moors', they were known in Madagascar as Antalaotra ('People of the Sea'), and it is by that name that we will refer to them here.[46] It was Antalaotra traders who founded the settlements of Langany and Kingany, both situated on islands in the inlets that are characteristic of Madagascar's north-west coast.[47] These entrepots attracted dhows from the continental towns of Malindi and Mombasa, bringing the products of Africa and Arabia in exchange for slaves and rice. When one of Madagascar's port-towns was sacked by a Portuguese fleet in 1506, the Portuguese found that it contained enough rice to fill twenty ships.[48]

Settlement on small islands, easily reachable by sea and also easily defended from attack from the mainland, was characteristic of Swahili towns in Africa and of Antalaotra settlements in Madagascar. When, after the fifteenth century, the Portuguese became the first Europeans since antiquity to enter Indian Ocean waters regularly, they adopted the same pattern. Madagascar's existence seems to have been known to European cartographers already, since it was mentioned by Fra Mauro in 1459[49] and the name is marked on the first globe made in Europe, by Martin Behaim in 1492.[50] The Portuguese originally acquired much of their knowledge of the area from local navigators. When Vasco de Gama made his famous first trip to India, he was guided by a Gujerati pilot he had met in Malindi, on the Swahili coast.[51]

New immigrants, new ideologies

In the first centuries of its diffusion outside its Arabian heartland, adherence to Islam linked influential groups across countries and continents. In many places where it took root, it was a religion of traders and ritual experts rather than farmers. Islamic knowledge was prestigious, being connected with new technologies regarded as efficacious. Among these were systems of measurement known to Arab science, including the calculation of time reckoned by lunar calendars and associated with divination. The introduction of new ways of thinking about the world was, over a long period, to change the ideas of Madagascar's inhabitants on many matters. Yet few of the new immigrants who transplanted Islamic ideas to Madagascar from perhaps the twelfth century came directly from the Middle East, even though their descendants sometimes cited genealogies claiming that their forebears were from the holy city of Mecca. The great majority of Islamized immigrants came from Africa and Austronesia, bringing with them the ideology and the practise of Islam as it was lived in those places. By the same token, we should add, there were immigrants from parts of Africa that had not been Islamized, who brought with them ideologies related, for example, to the systems developed in the gold-rich lands of Zimbabwe, and most probably there were immigrants from southern Ethiopia as well. The combined result, over a period of centuries, was to introduce to Madagascar ideologies that emphasized hierarchy and esoteric knowledge, which were soon absorbed into the existing cultural knowledge of the islanders.

The earliest Islamized immigrants had only a superficial knowledge of Islam, or perhaps adhered to minority traditions within Islam. Their decision to migrate from their countries of origin, in Africa, Austronesia, probably Persia, and elsewhere, does not seem to have been connected with any desire to proselytize. In time, different patterns emerged among immigrants from Africa and those from the eastern shores of the Ocean. Swahili-speaking, Islamized settlers from East Africa and south Arabia—the Antalaotra—characteristically remained in close contact with Swahili communities in East Africa. When they settled in Madagascar, generally in the northwest, these Antalaotra created Swahili-speaking communities, sometimes becoming rulers of their own city-states on the coast. High-status new immigrants on the east coast, on the other hand, of Austronesian origin, perhaps found it more difficult to maintain regular contact with their more distant places of origin. Unable to find Muslim marriage-partners in Madagascar, the overwhelmingly male newcomers tended to take wives from local elite families, which encouraged their integration. They acquired a status as ritual experts, having exclusive rights to slaughter cattle, for example, but losing much of their claim to Muslim orthodoxy over time. There are traditions that early Islamized immigrants brought slaves with them.[52]

Among the innovative ideas brought to Madagascar by people who had assimilated Islamic ideas was a particular concept of exchange. Islamized groups, particularly the Antalaotra with their connections to the trade of the Swahili coast, were especially inclined to use coin, the most efficient means of storing wealth that could be transported and actuated at a moment convenient to the holder. The implications of the use of coin were far-reaching. It revalued existing forms of exchange between people, since various social obligations could now be regulated by money and thus capitalized or imagined as debt. The Antalaotra and other Islamized groups had their own calendar, based on a seven-day week and lunar months, and their own system of weights and measures, and their technical knowledge enabled them to create new spheres of commerce inseparable from their religious and astrological expertise. Cattle, which had had a ritual and political function in Madagascar from the earliest times, acquired new significance by these means. Some Islamized groups gained control of cattle-sacrifices by virtue of their high prestige, performing the rituals of slaughter in the Muslim fashion. In the southeast of Madagascar, this tendency became so ubiquitous that descendants of an Islamized group gained monopoly control of all cattle slaughter, asserting this privilege among groups of people with no previous experience of Islam. This explains how Islamized immigrant groups were able to acquire ownership of cattle and to generate small amounts of coin by the purchase and sale of livestock, creating the beginnings of commerce in something like its modern sense. Cattle-dealing directly concerned only small numbers of people, who thereby gained elite status, in a population that lived largely from agriculture or herding and had little use for coin. The employment of silver coin for certain branches of trade did not lead to the general use of money.

Some Islamized immigrants at a relatively early date brought with them knowledge of writing in Arabic script, regarded as a potent religious technology. This was adapted to the Malagasy language, and from perhaps the fifteenth century a tiny number of scribes were producing manuscripts in Malagasy written in Arabic characters, known as *sorabe* ('big writing').[53] The oldest surviving manuscript written in this esoteric script dates from the seventeenth century and is today conserved in a library in Paris. Some seven thousand pages of *sorabe* written in Malagasy dialects transcribed in Arabic script still survive, some of them of quite recent creation.[54] Expert studies of *sorabe* suggest that knowledge of the script came most probably from Java, transmitted by immigrants who had already absorbed Islamic learning before their departure from the east.[55] The Malagasy word *soratra* ('to write') comes from the Arabic *sura*, a chapter of the Qur'an, testifying to the mystique that writing acquired in Madagascar. Knowledge of *sorabe* writing in Madagascar was confided to only a handful of people per generation.[56] To this day, some groups of Antemoro religious specialists claiming to be descended from high-status immigrants have a secret language that is passed on among initiates from one generation to another. Analysis reveals it to be largely of Arabic origin, with a substantial element of Swahili and Persian.[57] However, Antalaotra merchants and rulers in the northwest were also writing business letters in Arabic or Swahili by the seventeenth century, using the Arabic script for secular purposes.

The esoteric knowledge brought to Madagascar by Islamized groups has had a permanent influence on the history of the island in many respects. The itinerant holy men known as *ombiasy*, who probably existed previously, were increasingly expected to have knowledge of Islamic divination and of writing. Older techniques of divination, notably that known in Malagasy as *sikidy*, became mixed with new ones. Descendants of Islamized groups regarded their specialist knowledge as secret, the possession of particular families. However, certain new practices became very widespread, including circumcision, which spread to most parts of Madagascar. The very houses that people lived in became repositories of the new knowledge, a measure of just how important Islamic ideas were in the formation of what later generations were to regard as characteristically Malagasy cultural practices. Thus, increasingly as Islamic influence spread, right up to the twentieth century, most Malagasy built their houses according to a standard orientation whereby, in all but a few regions of the island, the northeast corner was regarded as the most auspicious part, reflecting the importance of this sector in systems of divination based on Arab and Islamic learning. It was in the northeast corner of the house that people performed rituals in honour of their ancestors or kept revered objects. Other than the Antalaotra with their mosques, the Malagasy had no dedicated temples until they began building churches in the nineteenth century, even if certain natural sites, often mountain-tops or springs, were places of pilgrimage. Each family had its own shrine, normally in its own house. Everywhere people extrapolated from calendars and astrological charts to calculate auspicious and inauspicious periods. Not only were some days taboo, but in some places children born on those days were put to death out of fear of the destiny governing their birth.[58]

The Islamized settlers

There is more information available on the Islamized immigrants than on earlier settlers thanks largely to the writings of early European visitors to the island, particularly the Italian Jesuit Luis Mariano and the French official Etienne de Flacourt, administrator of the local establishment of an early chartered company. Mariano visited Madagascar in 1613–14 and again in 1616–17,[59] while Flacourt lived there for seven years from 1648, later writing a book based on his experiences.[60] Both left enough descriptions gleaned from their discussions with Malagasy informants that, supported by other sources, their writings allow us to trace the outlines of a history of immigration by Islamized groups on Madagascar's east coast. The first of the new high-status immigrant groups to arrive in Madagascar, perhaps in the twelfth century, or even slightly earlier, was the Zafibrahim ('Descendants of Abraham'). They claimed to be descended from the prophet Abraham but otherwise seem to have borne few traces of Islamic practices, leading some authors to speculate whether this may have been a group of migrants from somewhere in the Middle East who had left their first home before the establishment of Islam. Some Zafibrahim families remained in coastal settlements in northern Madagascar, their first place of settlement, while others gradually migrated southwards down the east coast over generations.

The next arrival was the Zafiraminia, who were to have a major influence on the organization of communal life in Madagascar in matters of both politics and religion. In this regard, it should be said that until parts of the island underwent more intensive European influence in the nineteenth century, the Malagasy language did not have separate words for 'politics' and 'religion', both notions being integrated in a concept of power whose spiritual and material aspects were considered to be inseparable. One Zafiraminia king, Bruto Chambanga, recalled the mythical origin of his family in conversation with Luis Mariano in 1613. The king's title, *bruto,* is an honorific term indicating royal status and is probably of Austronesian origin.[61] Mariano's description was as follows:

> [The king] said that he had no Portuguese blood and that his origins lay in Mangalore and Mecca, at which places his ancestors originated, who, losing their way in one or more ships heading from the coast of India, came to land on the north point of the island and, little by little, increasing in number, they had arrived in the south. This movement had taken place over many years. By one line he counted seventeen generations and by the other fourteen, and it is thus that all along the east coast there are people who were part of this expansion.[62]

The Jesuit Father Mariano had no hesitation in classifying the Zafiraminia he met in southern Madagascar as Muslims. They knew of the Qur'an and of the annual fast of Ramadan, they did not eat pork, and they practised circumcision. A distinctive feature of the Zafiraminia was their recognition of a ruling elite whom they called Roandriana, a word probably derived from a similar title used in Java and among the Bugi of Sulawesi. A Roandriana had to be of noble ancestry on both maternal and paternal sides, a requirement that caused the highest-status families sometimes to practise incest.[63]

Bruto Chambanga's statement that his ancestors came from Mangalore in India and Mecca in Arabia is a myth, a claim to high prestige rather than a memory of a historical point of departure. The Zafiraminia are generally thought to have had their origins in the northernmost part of Sumatra, a centre of Islamic influence from the thirteenth century.[64] This region was known to Arab geographers as ar-Ræmyn. Thus, the name Raminia designates a Sumatran,[65] and the meaning of the name Zafiraminia is 'Children of the Sumatrans.' There are still extant today *sorabe* manuscripts recording the alleged landfall of the Zafiraminia on Madagascar's northeast coast and their movement southwards,[66] and Madagascar's east coast contains several villages whose names suggest the historical passage of Zafiraminia or other Islamized groups from Sumatra and Java. The date historians usually give for the arrival of the Zafiraminia in Madagascar is the thirteenth century, deduced by simply counting the number of generations given by the informants of Mariano and Flacourt. In fact, Ramini and other ancestors whose names figure in the genealogies may be a personification of waves of immigrants arriving from Sumatra between the twelfth and fourteenth centuries.[67] It is quite likely that there was no one single group of Zafiraminia that arrived in Madagascar and stayed together during their subsequent peregrinations inside the island, but that this name was given to a series of high-status immigrant groups from Sumatra and Java who landed on the east coast. A pattern emerged whereby incoming groups tended to lose many specific features of an Islamic identity as they adopted the existing cultural patterns of Madagascar. However, their Islamic knowledge was occasionally renewed by the arrival of more recent immigrants from such centres of Islamic culture as Persia, Sumatra or East Africa, in search of marriage partners from suitably high-status groups after arriving in their new island home.

The exceptional ritual knowledge and high prestige of the Zafiraminia constituted a form of capital as surely as did the commercial expertise of these and other Islamized immigrants in matters of currency and trade. Attached to elaborate genealogies and joined to older knowledge already existing in the island, these cultural attributes were eventually to form a basis for the foundation of monarchies. Although there were certainly other influences bearing on the gradual formation of ideologies of royal sovereignty, the Zafiraminia were probably the most influential single purveyors of such ideas. In the highlands, for example, later to produce the most powerful of all the monarchies in the island, although some later oral traditions suggest that new political-religious ideologies associated with royalty came from a separate identifiable wave of immigration,[68] there are also traditions implying that the new nobility that was to emerge in the centre of Madagascar originated in a junior branch of the Zafiraminia moving inland from their coastal settlements.[69] There is not necessarily a contradiction between the two accounts, if we think of the Zafiraminia not as one single group of immigrants, but as the name given to waves of Islamized immigrants coming particularly from Sumatra, but perhaps also from Java and other Austronesian islands over several generations. For the same reason, it is possible that it was not the ancestors of the Zafiraminia as a group who introduced the knowledge of writing to Madagascar, but that it was a skill they learned only after its introduction to Madagascar by another immigrant group, and which the Zafiraminia later claimed as their own. The suggestion that the Zafiraminia were not one single group, but arrived in successive waves of migration, not always by the same routes, is strengthened by the observation that they appear to have acquired some traces of Swahili language on their travels.[70]

Many of the migrants arriving from Austronesia in the thirteenth and fourteenth centuries were leaving homelands that were themselves undergoing political and religious tranformations, and indeed it is possible that some immigrants came to Madagascar as refugees from these upheavals, as others had arrived centuries earlier as refugees from Srivijaya. The notion that there were powerful centrifugal forces operating in Austronesia is reinforced by the observation that emigration to Madagascar was still taking place at the same time that Austronesian sailors were settling in New Zealand.[71] Java witnessed the rise of Mojopahit. Established in the late thirteenth century, this was a state formed in a distinctive tradition, a mountain kingdom in which a divine monarch ruled over a rigidly hierarchical society based on intensive rice cultivation. Monarchies of a comparable sort arose in other parts of southeast Asia, including Angkor. Although the ideas underpinning Mojopahit and other kingdoms bore some resemblance to Hindu originals, these were homegrown monarchies that developed over centuries. Austronesian clerics and princes assimilated 'classical' ideas from India not as a result of conquest or domination, but out of admiration, rather in the way that Europeans took ancient Greece and Rome as their model.[72] The mountain kingdoms of Austronesia held strongly to the notion that excellence was situated at the centre of a concentric universe. This was not only a prescription for the construction of a state that was politically centralized, but a reflection of a spiritual philosophy, a science of the self mastered only by an elite.[73] The king was a visible god who presided over a microcosm of the cosmos, at the centre of rituals designed to uphold harmony.[74] His status was reflected in the construction of his palace, itself an *imago mundi*.[75]

Scholars who have studied both the highland monarchies of Java and those that were to arise in highland Madagascar are so struck by the resemblance between the two that they tend to believe that this could be no coincidence, given the linguistic evidence of connections between Austronesia and Madagascar.[76] One scholar comments in regard to similar kingdoms in central Madagascar: 'It seems to me today that the resemblance with Mojopahit is more than similarity, but the reconstruction in Imerina of ideas brought by immigrants who themselves had absorbed the influence of concepts deployed by the sovereigns of Mojopahit.'[77] In the central highlands of Madagascar, the concept of the universal sovereign, living in a high place at the centre of a kingdom considered as extending to eight points of the compass from the king's residence, was to combine with the emergence of territorially-based groups called in Madagascar *foko*. It is notable that these double-descended kinship groups closely resemble social formations known in East Timor with the almost identical name of *fukun*.[78] Among other technologies probably introduced by new immigrants from Austronesia were the art of fortifying hilltop settlements including by digging moats that also emphasized the concentric nature of the power wielded by local rulers, and perhaps also significant new techniques of irrigation that were to have a major influence on rice-growing.[79] Ideologies of religion and politics, new techniques of production, and novel forms of social organization, influenced one another.

Prestigious immigrant groups whose names were recorded by early European travellers or transcribed from oral histories by later chroniclers included the Zafirambo, originally from East Africa, who are believed to have passed through the Comoros and settled in northern Madagascar in the late fifteenth century,[80] and the Zafikazimambo, another group of African origin, perhaps from the Zambezi valley.[81] Just like the Austronesians, they brought with them ideas and techniques that were prevalent in the places from which they emigrated. Successive groups of newcomers to Madagascar's fertile east coast competed with the already established Zafiraminia for power, probably clashing over privileges relating to cattle. The privileged right of slaughter was key to the control of trade in cattle, and therefore had an importance that was religious, political and commercial in equal measure, each aspect being inextricable from the others. The losers in these sometimes very violent struggles were forced gradually down Madagascar's east coast.

These wars between Islamized groups could be considered as commercial conflicts, but were perhaps justified by reference to the Islamic notion of *jihad*.[82]

The coexistence of new claims to authority alongside older ones was to lead to political solutions that have marked Madagascar's history and social habits to this day. The institution of strict endogamy among high-prestige groups at this point of Madagascar's history may have been the genesis of true ethnic groups, substantial populations having an ideology of common descent that often corresponded to a high degree of inter-marriage, as opposed to groups of people having simple collective names derived from the place where they lived. The institution of a new type of rule also contained the germ of a more extensive and aggressive power, as was noted by the thirteenth-century chronicler Ibn Sa'id who wrote concerning Qomr, one of the names sometimes used to designate Madagascar in Arabic manuscripts:

> Included among these settlements is Leyrané ... It is ruled by Muslims, but its inhabitants are a mixture of people from various countries ... The sheikhs who wield authority there try to remain on good terms with the prince of the town of Malây which is to the east ... This king sometimes manages to conquer the greater part of the island but does not retain much advantage from his victories, because the distances are great and the people divided.[83]

Many of the Islamized immigrant groups were quite small in size, and although the new ideas and practices they brought with them were to have an important and lasting effect on Madagascar, there were also regions that remained little touched by these new influences, unsurprisingly in a country so large. Even close to Madagascar's east coast, a favourite venue of traders and new immigrants, by the late seventeenth century there were still communities with little tradition of monarchical rule, although they had absorbed practices associated with Islam such as circumcision and, sometimes, the Muslim rite attached to the slaughter of animals. In these small-scale settlements with no tradition of monarchy, according to the administrator of the French fort established in the far south of Madagascar in the mid-seventeenth century, Etienne de Flacourt:[84]

> ... slaves are not regarded as such, but their masters consider them more like children. The masters freely give them their daughters in marriage, if they consider them to have earned it through their good services. Each village forms a separate government, whose chiefs are called Philoubei,[85] among whom they choose an elder to be an arbiter among the other Philoubei, each one of which

dispenses justice in his own village. They come to each other's assistance when they make war against others who are not of their community; but if some Philoubei make war with each other, the remainder will intervene only to try and reconcile them, and otherwise will leave them to fight each other.

The perennial encounter between newcomers and existing communities encouraged the emergence of a distinctive set of ideas concerning the simultaneous existence of dual sources of political legitimacy, although it may also be noted that similar distinctions were current on the Swahili coast that was so influential in Madagascar's history.[86] These notions of duality became grafted on to still older ideas about the separation of earth and sky. Groups of people claiming descent from the original occupants of a territory became referred to as *tompontany*, 'masters of the land' (or in some coastal areas *tompon-drano*, 'masters of the waters'), while other groups who derived prestige from their esoteric ritual knowledge made a virtue of their external origin, vaunting their descent from an immigrant ancestor like Raminia or from the sky. High-status groups of this latter sort are referred to by a variety of names in Malagasy, often translated by European writers as 'nobles'. Such groups are distinguished by their rigid ideas of hierarchy and purity, requiring inter-marriage within elite groups. The fact that ideas concerning the existential inequality of different types of population, defined by their degree of ritual purity, may have been present in Madagascar from its first settlement, affected the way in which new Islamic ideas were received and assimilated. Similar ideas concerning radical differences of human types are to be found in many Austronesian cultures, often connected with specific colours, such as in Java, where there is a distinction between white, considered the colour of Islam, and red, the colour associated with the earth, or in Sulawesi.[87]

In time, the existence of multiple standards for measuring legitimacy and a strongly dualist conception of the cosmos generally was to lead to a division of the population in many parts of Madagascar into two parallel social orders known as *fotsy* and *mainty* ('whites' and 'blacks' respectively). Each hierarchy had specific ritual functions, creating a system of political and religious checks and balances. These were not originally representations of political power in the modern sense so much as distinctions of rank: people of high status might in some circumstances command fewer resources and have no more coercive power than those of lower status. The tendency of Europeans to translate certain conceptions of rank current in Madagascar over the centuries as 'noble' can therefore be misleading. 'White' *(fotsy)* groups were indeed considered noble in the sense of belonging by birth to a higher and purer breed of person. However, they have always been more numerous in Madagascar than in western Europe, where the nobility has never constituted more than a small percentage of the total population. People of noble birth in Madagascar have never, as a group, enjoyed rights to extensive estates or high government office in the same way as in European history.

It is notable that the regions of Madagascar that adopted the notion that social groups belong to one of two hierarchies labelled 'black' and 'white' were the same areas that later developed powerful monarchies, a coincidence suggesting a connection between religiously-based ideas of inequality and purity and the development of complex political structures. In Madagascar's history over the last five or six hundred years, nobility has emerged as a concept applied to people supposed to have a blood relationship with a sovereign either living or dead. After the death of a king or the demise of a dynasty, all of those descended from the king were likely to claim continuing noble status for as long as the memory of their revered ancestor remained current, a fact that gave considerable political importance to royal genealogies. It contrasted interestingly with a possibly older tradition, still maintained by some groups in later times, whereby the name of a ruler became taboo after his death, and was replaced by a posthumous name.

Some authors have seen in the categories 'white' and 'black' a description of physical characteristics,[88] and Europeans in colonial times were inclined to see them as racial markers. The original purveyors of new ideas of nobility, such as the Zafiraminia, were indeed rather light-skinned—yet, some dark-skinned groups of African origin, like the Zafikazimambo, also became regarded as 'whites'. An indicator of *fotsy* status at least as important as skin colour was long, straight hair.[89] The two categories of 'blacks' and 'whites', then, reflected physical appearance, but were above all attempts to classify the type of power wielded by different social groups and to reach a balance between them.

The creation of high-status categories as a result of the arrival of new immigrants possessing new ideologies and technologies created a vocabulary of prestige that could be applied to a wide variety of elements and not only physical appearance. *Fotsy* status, typically maintained by strict endogamy, could be marked by the right to slaughter cattle, the wearing of the colour red, and special forms of personal address. Food was also classified in this way, with the old staple taro becoming regarded as a quintessentially 'black' food, and the new style of riziculture making rice an archetypal 'white' food.[90] Thus, the adoption of new ideas concerning existential purity was associated not only with new religious and political practices, but also with innovations in material technology. In this way, new techniques of agricultural production and of commerce or in other fields were to become inseparable from the development of kingdoms, new modes of organization that were associated with a strict hierarchy of social groups. New systems of monarchy were associated with a great number of other technical innovations, too, including the construction of citadels, the placing of tombs inside settlements rather than in the wild lands outside, and a relationship between elevation and power.[91] High places were for people of elevated standing. In the highlands, royalty became associated with the clearing of forest land for rice-planting, one reason for the deforestation that is thought to have occurred in the highlands in the fifteenth and sixteenth centuries, and eventually with intensive rice-cultivation.[92] However, forests were also destroyed by pastoralists in search of grazing for their cattle.

Settling the highlands

The earliest inhabitants of Madagascar's mountainous interior, as we have seen, were probably small groups of cattle-herders and hunters, later followed by slash-and-burn farmers. It is likely that fugitives or people displaced from coastal settlements deliberately formed communities in remote areas, or attached themselves to existing communities in those places, not unlike the maroons or runaway slaves who were later to emerge on European-ruled plantation islands like Mauritius and Réunion. We do not know what the very first inhabitants of the highlands called themselves, but they were later known as *lava-sofina* ('long ears') because of their practice of lengthening their ear-lobes with heavy ear-rings.[93] An early name for the central highland region was Ankova. There are various accounts of how it got this name, or how the people there came to be called Hova,[94] but *hova* seems to be an old word originally used to describe free peasant communities living without masters.

The first identifiable settlements in the highlands—as opposed to evidence of the passage of small groups of semi-nomads or other transients—date from shortly before the turn of the first millennium. Early highland settlements were integrated into networks of exchange connecting them with other regions and indirectly with overseas, as may be deduced from traces of ceramics of Chinese and western Asian origin.[95] Thereafter, the rather rapid development of a dense population in the central highlands seems to have been the consequence of a major wave of immigration by relative newcomers to Madagascar or of a series of waves over a short period. Highlanders throughout recorded times have spoken a dialect of Malagasy that shows traces of a late departure from Austronesia, suggesting the arrival of groups of immigrants originating in a fairly limited geographical area in Sumatra, and perhaps later from Java, and in sufficient numbers as to have absorbed the small numbers of people who had lived in the highlands previously. The new immigrants developed intensive rice-cultivation, and the highland population grew rapidly,[96] to the extent that the highlands had become the main source of slaves for export from Madagascar's northwest coast by the seventeenth century. At that time, highlanders were recorded as sometimes travelling to the coast to trade, [97] receiving in exchange for their slaves and cattle small quantities of silver and imported consumer goods, such as pottery.

The oral traditions of the central highlands claim that immigrants, probably from Austronesia, arriving seemingly via the east coast, encountered an earlier population whom they killed, expelled or assimilated. The new settlers referred to these mythical predecessors as Vazimba, represented as primitive dwarfs. Later oral traditions suggest that virtually every useful technology or social virtue or accepted cultural practice in the highlands was introduced by the immigrants and by the royal dynasties that were later to emerge among them. European scholars in the nineteenth century often took the oral traditions at face value, assuming that the Vazimba were a technologically primitive aboriginal population, racially distinct from the light-skinned, straight-haired immigrants from Sumatra and Java. This is now considered to be a wrong assumption. It is far more likely that the scant population encountered by the first major waves of Austronesian newcomers to the highlands was descended from earlier immigrants, who also included people with ancestors from Asia. Archaeological investigations in a reputed *vaz-*

imba village in the highlands, at Fanangoavana,[98] have revealed traces of metal-working from the thirteenth century, earlier than suggested by oral traditions that maintain metallurgy to have been the gift of a prestigious dynasty of a later period. This finding suggests that the earliest occupants of the highlands were not as primitive as they have been portrayed by oral traditions. Furthermore, groups in the highlands today who are reputed to have *vazimba* ancestors are no different in physical appearance than their neighbours, again suggesting that there never was any mysterious race of aboriginals.

Thus, the name *vazimba,* which has acquired such a mythical character, is best understood as referring not to a defunct ethnic group, but to the way of life in an imagined state of nature, considered as predating the discipline of social organization. The word is associated with notions of ancestors whose precise identity has been forgotten and who are connected to earth spirits, not only in the highlands but also in the forest of southeast Madagascar.[99] *Vazimba* spirits are thought to linger in wild, non-human places, outside the bounds of civilization as represented by societies organized according to the principle of royalty. To this day, it is said in the highlands that the original *vazimba* lived in water or in the forest, were semi-feral, ate only raw food, and so on. Some scholars have noted that words similar to *vazimba* are used in East Africa in suggestively similar situations.[100] Regarding populations that have disappeared as having entered the spirit world is widespread in Africa, and the word *wazimba* (singular: *mzimu*) has been reported to have been widely used in east and central Africa to designate 'spirits' or 'ancestral ghosts'.[101] Among the numerous explanations that have been advanced to explain the origins of the word *vazimba*, therefore, is the suggestion that it was 'a term imported from Africa, possibly by Islamic people, to refer to the populations living a primitive way of life in the interior'.[102] It is a generic term designating people who operated a pre-dynastic political system, shorn of any prestige in the monarchical age. In time, most of the kingdoms that arose in Madagascar were to represent themselves as having replaced a generation of primitives known by generic names such as *vazimba.*[103]

The hypothesis that the word *vazimba* is of African origin is strengthened by the observation that comparable changes of meaning have occurred with some other words and concepts imported from Africa, such as Masikoro. It is reported that, in Tanzania, a similar word may be used to designate persons coming from the interior.[104] In Madagascar, Masikoro is today the name of an ethnic group. Thus, in the case of Masikoro, as with the name *vazimba,* a word originally applied vaguely to people with a distinctive style of living, has also become the name of a specific group. In fact, a group of people calling themselves Vazimba still existed in the west of Madagascar in recent times. Robert Drury, a cabin-boy on an English ship who was shipwrecked on the coast of Madagascar, and who lived on the island for some fifteen years and learned fluent Malagasy before returning to London to tell his tale, left a brief description of some people calling themselves by this name whom he met in the early eighteenth century. He recorded that they were bilingual in Malagasy and another language.[105] One of the most complete descriptions of a Vazimba group in the twentieth century was by a Norwegian missionary, Emil Birkeli, who visited the centre-west of Madagascar in 1914. Birkeli recorded that the people he interviewed there did not regard themselves as 'pure' Vazimba, but as having intermarried with others. He believed that they had assimilated immigrants from overseas and from elsewhere in Madagascar. Like Robert Drury two centuries earlier, Birkeli found that the Vazimba of west Madagascar spoke a different language from other Malagasy, which the Norwegian thought to be related to languages from the upper Zambezi valley. A neighbouring group, the Beosi, said to be purer descendants of the original Vazimba, used many archaic Malagasy words and a distinctive grammar.[106] To add to the piquancy of this puzzle, it may be noted that a group known as Zimba existed in East Africa in the sixteenth century.[107]

The 'real' Vazimba, in the sense of a group of people using that name as a self-chosen label, and whose historical existence is documented, do not represent the scattered remnants of an aboriginal population. Rather, they are a social group that has kept alive cultural or social practices that have become obsolete elsewhere. Foremost among these cultural attributes is a certain form of political organization. It may include the practice of declaring the names of the deceased to be taboo (as some west coast peoples do to this day), a trait that was replaced in other parts of Madagascar by the memorizing of complex genealogies in which kings' names were remembered as they had been used in life.[108] The term *vazimba*, therefore, has two meanings. First, it is the name of an ethnic group in western Madagascar that has existed for at least the last three centuries. Second, it is the name of mystical beings symbolizing an obsolete way of life.

Culture as a historical stratum

Analysing the meanings of *vazimba* is an example of how difficult it is to glean historical information from people's cultural attributes. Fortunately, though, the quantity of evidence from other sources, including documents and archaeology, is good enough to make it a worthwhile exercise in the case of Madagascar.

From an early period, there were techniques in widespread use in Madagascar—for example, for forging iron and building canoes—that were almost identical to methods used in Asia, and were surely introduced by very early settlers. By the same token, other practices used from the earliest period closely resemble African models, such as techniques of animal husbandry.[109] When more sophisticated forms of political community arose in Madagascar, centuries later, these too were associated with techniques that bore a close resemblance to foreign models, such as the rice-growing monarchies ruled by a god-king that were to emerge in the highlands of Madagascar, so astonishingly similar to the highland monarchies of Java and elsewhere in Austronesia. Equally evident, but less rigorously investigated,[110] is the striking number of political-religious techniques used in later statecraft and ritual that have obvious parallels in Africa, such as the special rights of the maternal uncle in systems of inheritance, the custom of burying the body of a venerated leader in a riverbed after death, the notion of snake ancestors, the use of liquid poison in trials by ordeal, freemen assemblies that modify the powers of chiefs in government, the social importance of cattle and the habit of marking their ears with complex patterns, all of which have been noted among groups in south-central and western Madagascar especially.[111] Lists of this sort are rich in implications about the flow of ideas to Madagascar from all parts of the Indian Ocean rim.

Before we can reach any provisional historical findings on the basis of such data, however, it is important to consider how much weight can be attached to cultural practices and their attendant beliefs as a source of historical knowledge. There are three main difficulties in any attempt to equate culture with evidence of origin. First, it is clear that there was a great deal of mixing in Austronesia, probably on the east coast of Africa and, probably too in the Comoros, among early groups that were in the process of migration to Madagascar. Thus, as we have seen, the introduction of Islamic knowledge and Arabic writing almost certainly reflects the arrival in Madagascar not of people from the Arabian peninsular, but of Islamized groups from Sumatra, Java and East Africa. Second, groups resident in Madagascar for a long period assimilated new customs introduced by new settlers, and, vice versa, newcomers adopted the language and customs of the island's older generations of residents. Third, knowledge of processes may be spread by word of mouth unaccompanied by actual migration. The essential aid to interpretation is the information provided by other sources, mainly documentary or archaeological. Only when taken together do these make it possible to interpret culture in historical terms.

In advancing these interpretations, it is necessary to take into account the role played by culture and ritual in an essentially oral society. In the general absence of written record-keeping (although *sorabe* were used to a very limited extent as administrative instruments) ritual and custom became key mechanisms of social life and politics, a means by which the status of groups and individuals may be asserted or maintained and rights and duties recalled. Cultural practices become a matter of great importance in an essentially oral society. In the type of monarchy that was to arise in Madagascar after the immigration of the Islamized groups, cultural practices became connected to a clear geographical element. In a concentric monarchy, power was channelled through the king, the centre of excellence and the upholder of the cosmic order. The king lived in a perpetual present, even when he was introducing innovations. Time was not autonomous, but emanated from the person of a king. In Malay political thought, those living on the periphery of a system were not just out of reach of the government, but 'exemplars of all that is uncivilized, barbaric, and crude'.[112] There was a constant flow of people from the centre to the periphery. Typically, these were fugitives, such as escaped slaves or people fleeing from taxes or forced labour, or the losers in factional disputes. Conversely, there were people from the outside who came to the centre. The relation between the centre and periphery was comparable to that of plantation and maroons in a slave economy.[113] Customs could be acquired or lost over time, and this invariably implied a change in political relationships. So it is that western Madagascar is home to several groups that are notable for not practising circumcision and includes pockets of population that have not adopted various customs widely observed elsewhere on the island.[114] The concept of centre-periphery so deeply embedded in many Austronesian societies, including in Madagascar, tends to result in the people living on the fringes of monarchies being those with the most archaic cultural features, like the Vazimba.

Movements of people and the cross-fertilization of ideas in Madagascar over centuries, and their interaction with dynamic networks of overseas commerce, eventually caused identifiable clusters of interests to coalesce around certain strategic activities. Among the most important of these were the right to slaughter cattle, which was connected with a series of commercial and political privileges, and access to overseas trade. Of all the branches of long-distance trade, it was the slave trade that became the most important, especially after European traders had begun to visit Madagascar, following the first Portuguese landfalls at the beginning of the sixteenth century. In the following 150 years, Europeans of various nationalities established semi-permanent trade establishments called 'factories' in the English vocabulary of the time, and regular ports of call. European traders generally felt most comfortable dealing with kings, a political form that they easily recognized and that they found most suitable for their type of business. But the Europeans did not invent kingdoms in Madagascar, and nor did they invent the slave trade. Structures of this sort existed before the arrival of the first Portuguese, as traditions collected in Madagascar testify.

During the seventeenth and eighteenth centuries monarchies with quite extensive control were to emerge in several areas of the island, particularly in places where kings were able to combine a higher ideology of monarchy with an enhanced commercial role that was partly the result of the growth in trade with Europeans. The rise of powerful kingdoms makes the seventeenth century a turning-point in Madagascar's history.

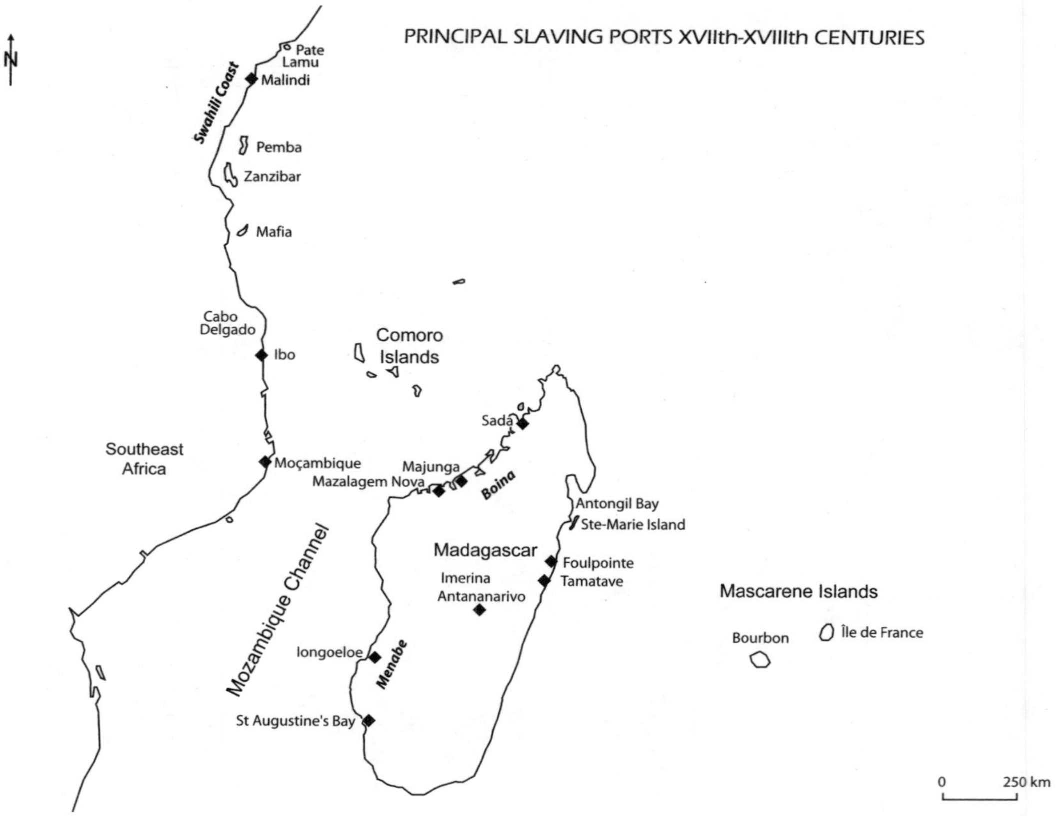
PRINCIPAL SLAVING PORTS XVIIth-XVIIIth CENTURIES
N
Pate
Lamu
Malindi
Swahili Coast
Pemba
Zanzibar
Mafia
Cabo Delgado
Ibo
Comoro Islands
Sada
Southeast Africa
Moçambique
Majunga
Mazalagem Nova
Boina
Antongil Bay
Ste-Marie Island
Madagascar
Foulpointe
Tamatave
Imerina
Antananarivo
Mozambique Channel
Mascarene Islands
Bourbon
Île de France
Iongoeloe
Menabe
St Augustine's Bay
0
250 km

3

ROYALTY AND THE RISE OF KINGDOMS 1600–1699

Etienne de Flacourt, a native of Orléans in central France, arrived in southern Madagascar in December 1648 at a place the French called Fort Dauphin. An official of the Compagnie Française de l'Orient, recently established by Cardinal Richelieu to trade with Asia, in imitation of the Netherlands' brilliantly successful United East India Company (the Verenigde Oostindische Compagnie, VOC), Flacourt had orders to found a permanent settlement. Travelling with him were a company of soldiers, some civilian officials, and a handful of Catholic missionaries who were to make the first systematic efforts to produce Christian literature in the Malagasy language. Flacourt acquired a considerable knowledge of south and southeast Madagascar and eventually wrote the first full-length book on the island. Fort Dauphin was situated in a kingdom that the Frenchman called Madécase or Madécasse, probably because he had encountered a group of this name, and he subsequently applied the term to the whole territory. Thus, thanks to the influence of Flacourt's book, at least three names for the island were current among Europeans by the late seventeenth century: Saint Lawrence, Madagascar, and Madécase. The latter word was in course of time to be turned into the word 'Malagasy' as a name to designate the island's people.

Flacourt wrote an acute description of a distinctive form of dual authority whereby the population of the area surrounding Fort Dauphin was divided into two hierarchies, one classified as 'white' (*fotsy*), the other 'black' (*mainty*). The king of Madécase told him, much as his father had told Father Mariano some thirty-five years earlier, that the royal family, at the top of the 'white' hierarchy, was descended from a group of immigrants known as Zafiraminia who had reached Madagascar some seventeen generations previously and migrated gradually down the east coast before arriving in the far southeast. The system of double authority reflected an accommodation between the Zafiraminia immigrants and the local peoples. Immigrants and indigenes had learned to live with each other by creating parallel structures that, over time, had developed complex rights and obligations towards each other. There was no doubt that the 'whites' had the higher status of the two. Flacourt compared the *fotsy* to the aristocracy of his native France, referring to the most prestigious among them as *'les Grands'*.[1] It was apparent to him, as it had been to Mariano, that the Zafiraminia displayed a marked degree of Islamic influence, although they did not respect the five basic duties considered essential in orthodox Islam.

After their arrival in Madagascar, the Zafiraminia, according to their own oral histories, had been challenged by another Islamized group, the Zafikazimambo, immigrants who probably arrived around 1500. They had made war on the Zafiraminia and seized control of their privileges,[2] driving the Zafiraminia further south. Although the Zafikazimambo had come from Africa, possibly with origins in Zimbabwe, they were also generally recognized as 'white' or *fotsy*. Nevertheless, Flacourt considered that the terms *mainty* and *fotsy* represented physical types in addition to constituting a social hierarchy. He wrote :

> The whites are divided into three categories, called Raondrian, Anacandrian and Ondzatsi. The blacks are divided into four types, which are Voadziri, Lohavohits, Ontsoa and Ondeves. The Raondrians are those who are, as it were, the princes of the race of whites. The Anacandrian are the degenerate descendants of nobility....The Ondzatsi have reddish-brown skin and long hair, as do the Raondrians and Anacandrian, but they are more lowly ... The Voadziri are the richest and most powerful of the blacks ... They are of the race of masters of the earth, before the arrival [of the whites] ... The Lohavohits are also considered as an aristocracy among the blacks ... The Ontsoa are superior to the Lohavohits and their relatives. The Ondeves are slaves ...[3]

It seems difficult to avoid the conclusion that early inhabitants of Madagascar, certainly by the seventeenth century but perhaps even from very early times, identified the existence of human categories in which skin colour and quality of hair were key criteria in the classification of people into the hierarchies known as *fotsy* and *mainty*. It is less clear to what extent such physical attributes were regarded as decisive in social and political arrangements. In the kingdom described by Flacourt, *fotsy* lineages provided kings, with the chiefs of *mainty* lineages playing a constitutional role.

The same terms, associated with similar principles, have continued in use ever since in several parts of Madagascar, with a signification that has changed over time, but with an enduring association with distinct physical types. *Fotsy* and *mainty* categories, in fact, can be considered to form a thread throughout Madagascar's history. Even in those parts of the island that may not have explicitly used these two words, similar grades of status have existed. Since whatever period the physical characteristics associated with these twin markers of status came to play a role in the management of communal matters—well before the seventeenth century—social groups have tried to preserve their genetic characteristics by in-marrying. This was to become one of the key elements in the constitution of royal dynasties.

The customs of the ancestors

An undoubted revolution associated with the arrival of European visitors was in the production of documentary information concerning Madagascar.[4] From this time on, we have a steady supply of first-hand accounts of Madagascar that enable us to analyse social and political developments with increasing sophistication, and even to catch glimpses of everyday life. Madagascar's people in recent centuries (and no doubt for much longer than that) have liked to justify contemporary behaviour by reference to what their forebears allegedly did. The evocation of the customs of the ancestors, when compared with contemporaneous documentation, has enabled modern anthropologists to investigate the substance of tradition in some historical depth.[5]

Flacourt in particular has left us with precious eye-witness descriptions of people in the seventeenth century and these, taken with information from other sources, provide us with precious information on some of the aspects of daily life as it was lived in the south of the island in his time. Virtually all Madagascar's inhabitants, other than in the handful of towns, lived in small communities, social units that enabled people to find protection and to survive. The cohesion of these groups was assured by rules and styles of living that were transmitted by word and deed from one generation to the next by reference to past practice, described as 'the customs of the ancestors' (*fomban-drazana)*. A Victorian missionary was later to capture this attitude quite nicely when he wrote that 'The commands of a father or an ancestor are held as most sacredly binding upon his descendants'.[6] Old accounts leave no doubt that the system of thought associated with the ancestors was strongest before the introduction of widespread literacy and of colonial government. Conformity to tradition served to regulate social conduct and, in effect, as a filter for new ideas and practices. The societies of old Madagascar certainly experienced innovation—sometimes very rapid—but always via the ideological prism of tradition, as measured by the customs of the ancestors. Among the major innovations over the centuries were the introduction of a lunar calendar and the seven-day week and the new military technology connected with firearms. Several European visitors noted the speed with which people in contact with foreign traders learned the use of firearms and even became adept in their use.[7]

Madagascar's people lived, Flacourt thought, 'very like our ancient patriarchs'.[8] He made this comparison with the patriarchs of the Old Testament in an effort to convey the sense of extended families living close to the land, with their herds, under the authority of family-heads, acutely conscious of a cosmos that had a rigorous design. A pervasive habit was to regard anyone in authority as *ray amandreny,* 'father and mother'.[9] As described by Flacourt in regard to the south of the island, the family was built around the couple of man and woman and their children, but also included various other dependents, whose number and functions varied according to wealth and social standing. Polygyny existed in many parts of the island but was not general. Individual strategies of social promotion developed via alliances of inclusion and exclusion. Domestic slavery was a basic institution, and no doubt some form of internal commerce in slaves had long existed, connected to the Indian Ocean slave trade that was already of great antiquity in Flacourt's time. Kings and other rulers lived no differently from commoners in many respects, generally dwelling in similar houses, made from such perishable materials such as reeds, bark and wood until a shortage of timber caused highlanders in the eighteenth century to begin building with baked mud. Only in the Swahili-influenced towns of the northwest coast were there buildings of stone. There was nevertheless an acute sense of social differentiation. One French missionary noted that the upper classes (*'les Grands'*, he called them, using the same term as Flacourt) treated slaves like dogs; another claimed that they gave slaves bones to eat by throwing them on the ground.[10] A Dutch trader in

1715 thought that household slaves were half-starved, watching 'with amazement how greedily and enjoyable [sic] these miserable creatures ate our rotten and discarded food remains'.[11]

The use of the English word 'slave' is somewhat misleading since it covers various types of dependency that in the Malagasy language were designated by a more nuanced vocabulary. The type of slave with the fewest rights was the *andevo* or household slave, but there were distinctions to be made between people born in this condition and those taken as prisoners of war. Kings who acquired great numbers of dependents might give them a special status, in some respects conferring greater privileges on their own 'slaves' or personal retainers than on persons of free rank. In many respects slaves and freemen seem to have led a fairly similar material existence. Before the nineteenth century Madagascar had no system of plantation agriculture, and the main tasks of slaves were cattle-herding or other routine agricultural work or domestic tasks.

The division into *fotsy* and *mainty* hierarchies extended even to ways of eating. According to Flacourt, most people in the region where he lived, in the south of the island, ate two meals a day, in the morning and the afternoon, but Zafiraminia aristocrats ate sometimes as often as five or six times per day.[12] In the south and east, people ate only with other members of their own group; this was possibly a distant reflection of Indian ideas of caste that had circulated via Austronesia.[13] People made no use of ovens, but ate cooked food either boiled or grilled.[14] In some parts of the island, they did not use cutlery or tableware, eating with their fingers from banana-leaves, but archaeological finds suggest that some families from an early period used spoons and plates fitted with a short pedestal, making them a convenient height for a diner seated on the floor. Diners shared the same dish. [15] Flacourt, a gentleman from a country undergoing a rapid refinement of etiquette and sensibilities, thought that the Malagasy prepared their food very well but that they had poor manners.[16] Staple diets in various parts of the island included rice, beans and pulses, yams and manioc. In the south, but probably also throughout the island, the basic diet was sometimes supplemented by fish, game or the meat of domestic animals. People ate meat only occasionally, especially at festivals with a social and religious connotation, such as funerals, weddings, circumcision ceremonies, and so on. Meat came from cattle, sheep, goats, chickens, guinea fowl, and ducks. There were river-fish and salt-water fish. In the south, pork was taboo, as it was also among some higher-rank status groups in the highlands, perhaps a reflection of Muslim influence. Fruits included bananas, coconuts, sugar cane and many others. Alcohol was widely consumed in the form of beverages made from honey or sugarcane, and heavy drinking was widespread, although in the highlands alcohol does not seem to have been generally used until the nineteenth century. Some of the kings who obtained distilled liquor from European traders held stupendous drinking-sessions that could end in unconsciousness or even death. They were 'great lovers' of alcoholic drink, thought Robert Drury, 'and some of the ordinary fellows as great sots as any in England'[17]—this, at a time when English society was notorious for its attachment to strong drink. Then as now, in those parts of the island where alcohol was consumed, circumcisions, burials and other family feasts in Madagascar were occasions for heavy drinking by men, women and children.

There were considerable differences in people's personal appearance not only between social groups in one community, but also between one region of the island and another. One aspect was skin colour, varying from light to dark, but there were also clear regional distinctions in personal adornment and clothing. The few descriptions of highlanders before the nineteenth century, for example, suggest that it was common for the men to lengthen their ears, as some people in Africa do to this day, by inserting heavy plugs that caused their ear-lobes to stretch, although this custom was also known elsewhere. When Robert Drury met two highlanders travelling on the coast he asked them about this, and they told him that a hole was made in the ear-lobes of young children, 'and a piece of lead put in it at first; after the wound is healed they have a small spring-ring put into it, which dilates it by degrees,' until the hole was big enough to take a silver plate.[18] Flacourt wrote that over time the holes in their ears became big enough to pass an egg through.[19] This led to one of several nicknames given by people living on the coasts to the highlanders that they saw only rarely—*lava-sofina* ('long ears').[20]

Highlanders, no doubt because of their colder climate, had a characteristic way of wearing the *lamba*, a large cloth wrapped around the upper body like a Roman toga. People living in the tropical heat of the coasts wore less. The southern men described by Drury, Flacourt and others wore a cloth around the waist, leaving their upper body bare other than perhaps for a string of beads worn as decoration, while women wore a similar cloth without underwear, covering their torso with a simple shift. People of both sexes and all social classes went barefoot. Only in the west-coast ports, visited by Swahili traders, was Muslim dress common, in the form of long robes and turbans. Local cloth was often made from the soft inner bark of a tree, beaten to provide a surprisingly soft textile, but one that could not be washed. 'The outer bark they take away,' Drury observed, 'and the inner, which is white, they peel off entire, and beat with a stick till it is soft and pliable, and then it is fit to wear.'[21] Rich people wore imported calicos and other foreign-made cloth. In the highlands, silk was produced and was particularly used for weaving funeral shrouds. Both men and women wore armbands and beads of copper or silver, while kings often sported ornaments of gold, regarded as a royal metal. The use of jewels seems to have been introduced by Muslims and to have spread from the northeast of the island.[22] People paid extraordinary regard to hair-styles. The long, straight hair of the *fotsy* groups was particularly esteemed, but all classes went to great trouble in braiding, plaiting or otherwise dressing their hair. Hair texture and coiffure were a marker of social class and even of political relationships.

One of the most striking differences between life in Madagascar and that in Europe was in regard to gender roles and sexual freedom. In general, there was a division of labour between women and men, although exactly what form this took varied from one region to another. Women played a key role in agriculture on the east coast, for example.[23] Sexual relations in general began at a young age and, according to Flacourt, were not in principle associated with any notion of sin, pollution, or transgression. Interestingly, despite the importance of the division of Madécasse society into the status-categories of *mainty* and *fotsy*, sexual relations (though not marriage) between men and women of different condition were frequent. This is one reason why it is unsatisfactory to refer to the different divisions of Madagascar's society as 'castes',[24] since ideas of existential purity, although they persist in Madagascar to this day, do not appear ever to have been applied as rigorously as would be suggested by referring to various status-groups in this way. In Flacourt's time, the fact that a relatively high degree of sexual liberty was combined with a notion that high-status groups should retain their purity through in-marriage within their group resulted in a large number of unwanted children being aborted or killed after birth. Young children were considered still to belong largely to the wild domain of the untamed and the non-human, and to become fully human only as they reached the age of seven or eight.[25] *Fotsy* women who became pregnant by a *mainty* routinely aborted their babies or killed them after birth. Both men and women were free to have sexual affairs more or less as they pleased until marriage, and premarital sexual relations were even encouraged. 'If the men are sensual', wrote Flacourt, 'the women are no less so, and miss no chance to amuse themselves, having always, besides their husband, one or more men friends to dally with.'[26] After marriage, adultery in theory became an offence, although it often occurred. Flacourt, again, noted of the women that 'if their husbands annoy them, they leave them and spend their time with whomever they please'.[27]

According to Flacourt,[28] there was no homosexuality in Madagascar, but he was certainly mistaken in this judgement. A Dutch trader was present when a powerful Sakalava king sat to judge the case of a man who had slept with one of the king's nephews.[29] It is quite possible that homosexuality was most frequent among the royal families of the Sakalava, as the high importance attached to endogamy (which also provided an incentive to royal incest) made them more disposed to same-sex love affairs that carried no risk of children. Flacourt did notice, though, the existence of a category of transvestites,[30] apparently an old feature of Malagasy life. 'They are', Flacourt wrote, 'effeminate and impotent men who look for boys, and act as if in love with them, pretending to be girls and dressing as such, giving them presents to induce the boys to sleep with them, even giving themselves girls' names'.[31] Flacourt was assured that these transvestites remained sexually chaste, but it seems debatable whether this was usually the case. They were half-way between entertainers and diviners, regarded as having particular insight into religious matters and being protected by rulers throughout the island.[32]

Almost all Malagasy before the nineteenth century engaged in fishing, cultivation, herding or other agrarian activities, sometimes combined with blacksmithing, weaving, or other craft work. In some of the more remote areas there were groups of hunter-gatherers. Inland from the east coast and even in parts of the highlands there was a tradition of rather impermanent settlement necessitated by the demands of the slash-and-burn method of farming that required cultivators to move frequently in search of virgin land. Communities varied in form from the scattered villages of the arid south, fenced by cactuses, to the hill-top villages of the district known from the seventeenth century as Imerina, surrounded by defensive ditches and earth ramparts, many of which are still to be seen today. Central Madagascar was already deforested by the late eighteenth century.[33] In times of trouble, people migrated to find new opportunities or safer environments, while in times of calm, certain of them travelled to trade. There are signs that, even among an agrarian population that had no form of transport other than their own feet, having neither horses nor donkeys nor ox-carts, nonetheless there were people who travelled widely, from the earliest times. Flacourt noted the existence of itinerant clowns, dancers and singers, who did no farming work but lived entirely from the hospitality of patrons, moving from the compound of one ruler to another.[34]

'*Mamy ny aina*', Malagasy people sometimes say, meaning 'life is sweet'. Although Etienne de Flacourt described aspects of a life that was often marked by hunger and material hardship, and although he considered his Madécasse neighbours to be warlike and treacherous, he also recognized the more pleasant aspects of their way of life, judging that they lived more pleasantly *('doucement')*[35] than the people of his homeland.

War, commerce, fate

Madagascar was exporting slaves and commodities, at least occasionally, for centuries even before the coming of the Europeans. But there appear to have been few full-time traders other than the Antalaotra merchants based on the west coast. Nevertheless, the Jesuit missionary Mariano noted the role played by the Hova people of the highlands in bringing slaves and cattle hundreds of kilometres to the northwest port of Mazalagem Nova[36] (the first historical reference to the Hova), as other seventeenth-century visitors also recorded.[37] When two travellers from the highlands met the shipwrecked sailor Robert Drury, they told him that their countrymen also traded with the southeast coast and the far south of the island,[38] implying the existence of island-wide commercial networks. The highland traders exported slaves, cattle, iron, cloth and some other manufactures. From the coast they imported silver coin, cattle, firearms, and foreign-manufactured cloth and other wares. Regular markets did not exist until a relatively late period, perhaps not until the seventeenth century. They eventually emerged not only as a place for the purchase of imported goods,[39] but possibly also because of the need to negotiate ransom-payments for family-members captured in local wars.[40]

This was the age of mercantilism, a concept deployed by Europeans to designate the idea of trade as a finite sum, to be wrested from rivals by means fair or foul. It was also the age of the slave trade, not coincidentally, for commerce and war were bedfellows. In Madagascar also, these two were associated in various ways, including in the almost ritualized activity of cattle-raiding. Warfare is in itself a form of intercourse between social groups, often associated with trade and the transmission of ideas. People who fight each other are not socially isolated, especially when wars are small in scale and short in duration.

The earliest detailed accounts of Madagascar often refer to constant minor wars. Father Mariano, sent from the Asian headquarters of the Portuguese government in Goa to conduct a survey of Madagascar as a possible mission field, noted that the island's rival rulers were engaged in 'many and continual wars'.[41] Flacourt too found the people of the island to be very warlike. In the highlands, he reported, there were 'perpetual wars of one against the other, the overall aim being to steal and carry away cattle, under pretext of long-standing quarrels.'[42] Rival princes had every reason to compete by means of ownership of cattle—a form of currency as well as a source of sustenance—as well as for control of people. It is a moot point, however, to determine the extent to which the petty wars noted by early European observers may have been caused at least partly by the Europeans themselves. In the south of the island, the French colonists who for thirty years struggled to found a permanent base at Fort Dauphin launched constant raids on their neighbours,[43] while the west and east coasts were increasingly frequented during the seventeenth century by European traders and pirates selling guns and encouraging their local interlocutors to enslave their countrymen for sale. 'The epidemical evil of this island is their frequent quarrels with one another, and the very cause so many of them are sold to the Europeans for slaves', wrote Drury.[44]

Warriors were generally not specialists, but simply farmers whose life was dictated by the rhythms of the agricultural year. Wars seem to have taken place especially in the hungry period before the harvest, between December and March. One of the aims was to steal the enemy's grain reserves, which had the effect of causing deaths from hunger far more often than from wounds during times of war. To judge from contemporary accounts, cattle-raids of the sort witnessed by Flacourt and experienced by the London ship's-boy-turned-slave Robert Drury were mid-way between war, economic exchange, and a violent sport. Both Drury and Flacourt describe raids in which a physical attack was preceded by a formal exchange of insults, the singing of war-songs, and the preparation of magical charms intended to incapacitate the enemy. Sometimes action went no further than these aggressive rituals, battles being contests by rival magicians unleashing invisible forces against each other. But there were also far more deadly conflicts, such as in the south, where it was customary to refuse quarter in battle to men of the Zafiraminia aristocracy, with only women and children being spared, while a king's ordinary subjects were taken as prisoners.[45] The Zafiraminia were to become more or less extinct by the late eighteenth century, a fate also befalling ruling elites in other parts of the island when their prominence made them particular targets. Some visitors recorded occasions when enemies were literally cut into pieces to defile their bodies after death.[46] However, it was less the physical elimination of the Zafiraminia aristocracy that caused its disappearance, but rather a political evolution that led to the dispersal of its various branches.

For people of all ranks, death and life were closely associated with notions of destiny, a force that could be channelled via ritual but that was more powerful than humankind. People considered hidden destiny, *lahatra*, to be an integral part of a cosmos that had a regular and fixed order. They aimed to maintain a balance of cosmic forces that would enable them to survive and even prosper. This was done largely by respecting numerous taboos. An illness, for example, was routinely ascribed to having transgressed a taboo or otherwise having disturbed the harmony of the cosmos. Illnesses could be treated by plants, and there were families with specialized knowledge of pharmacology.[47]

In every part of the island people believed that cosmic forces could be discerned by means of divination, dreams and esoteric knowledge such as that possessed by the *ombiasy* clerics from the southeast of the island, a group whose qualifications included their redoubtable knowledge of *sorabe* writing. According to some modern scholars, it is possible to identify separate chronological layers in this corpus of mystical knowledge. The pre-Malagasy, Philippe Beaujard considers, brought with them a concept of the universe divided into the sky, the earth and the lower world, that was later overlaid with philosophies attached to the knowledge of cardinal points and, later still, complex notions of astronomy.[48] Many think that the system of divination known as *sikidy* is probably one of the oldest components of Malagasy culture. There seems little doubt that an older knowledge of divination was complemented by Islamic learning at a later date, just as Islamic techniques of astrology were grafted onto the cosmological patterns attached to the existing practice of building square houses considered as microcosms of a vaster universe.[49] The standard orientation of houses meant that anyone, even sitting indoors, could identify at a glance the points of the compass, essential knowledge in societies where daily life was governed by observance of the cardinal points in everything from the way to face while praying to the ancestors to the way to lie at night. The house even constituted a sort of instant sundial, as before the advent of clocks, people could tell the time by reference to the rays of the setting sun shining through the door, always facing to the west, slowly reaching inside as far as the central pillar of the house to throw a shaft of sunlight onto a flattened earth floor.

All over the island, too, family heads performed religious duties on behalf of their families. 'Every man here', wrote Robert Drury, 'a poor man as well as a lord, is a priest for himself and family, and expects an answer by the demons in his dreams.'[50] The cosmological order imposed a discipline in the form of a felt need to observe a wide range of taboos that generally included avoidance of certain foods, regarding some days as taboo, and the attribution of significance to particular colours. The colour red, for example, was reserved for kings or their close relatives. Every person constantly applied this highly-developed and detailed cosmology to notions of time and space. As in other essentially oral cultures, ritual practices assumed a wide range of functions that helped communities to cohere and provided the sinews of political relationships. This was the case with the custom of male circumcision probably introduced by the high-status groups that transmitted Islamic knowledge, although to this day there are groups, perhaps including the descendants of people who had migrated to the island before the arrival of Islam, who do not practise circumcision. Another widespread ritual replete with cosmological and political significance was purification through bathing at the start of a new year. Like circumcision, the bathing ritual became associated with royalty through the work of the *ombiasy* ritual masters who played such an important role in creating and articulating ideologies of power.

Deeply shocking to European visitors was the widespread practice of killing babies born on inauspicious days. The fact that this occurred in a country that was thinly populated in most regions, and where power and wealth consisted largely in the control of people, is testimony to the importance attached to the arts of divination and astrology. A child born on an inauspicious day was considered to have an unfavourable or an evil destiny, as determined by a diviner, and was generally taken to a remote place and simply abandoned to the elements.[51] Flacourt identified several dates and times considered inauspicious in this way. Such ideas were current in all parts of Madagascar and could be as binding on sovereigns as on their subjects. A Dutch slave-trader who met a powerful west-coast king in 1715 noted that he had killed those of his own children who were born on a Sunday or a Tuesday, considered inauspicious by his diviners.[52]

Guns and silver

An English trader who did business in Madagascar in the late seventeenth century gave a list of the main imports and exports:[53]

> The comodityes that at present strangers carry thither and the natives esteem most are good powder and armes, flints, beads, sissors, knives, looking glasses, needles, glass beads, corall, agate and cornelian beads, silver, brass and tin monitoes [?], Iron, lead and brass, painted & striped clouts, rings and several other toyes, and cases of spirits. These are commonly exchanged for slaves, beeves, rice, yams, hony, wax, tamarins, dragon blood and several other things that the country affords.

Although Madagascar had imported and exported goods throughout its history, the entry of European traders into Indian Ocean waters was gradually changing the nature of an ancient trading system. The Europeans enjoyed military superiority by virtue of their ship-mounted cannon and had a commercial edge over rivals for the control of the Indian Ocean carrying-trade because of their easier access to silver bullion and coin from American mines. In just a century and a half from about 1500, the Mexican silver *real* became the unit of account throughout the Indian Ocean, later replaced by the Maria Theresa *thaler*.[54] In fact, most of the silver mined in the Americas after the Spanish had begun their colonization of the continent eventually found its way to China and Asia, where it was exchanged for local products.[55] American silver joined the old Indian Ocean trade system to the Atlantic, a foundational element in the making of the modern world.

Portuguese merchants often financed their voyages with silver borrowed from Antwerp bankers, who after 1550 began to lose ground to competitors from the Netherlands, at that time under the Spanish crown.[56] The outbreak of a rebellion in the Netherlands in 1568 caused leading financiers to relocate from Antwerp to Amsterdam, aiding the emergence of the new Dutch republic as a major sea-power. In 1602, consortia from six leading Dutch trading-cities joined together to form the VOC, the world's first modern multinational company. It was run by a committee known as the Heren XVII ('the Seventeen Gentlemen') sitting in Amsterdam, home to an advanced ship-building industry and a banking community that developed a range of new financial instruments including notably the world's first stock exchange, making Amsterdam a pioneer of capitalism.[57] The success of Dutch commercial institutions inspired imitators in France, Denmark and elsewhere to create their own government-licensed companies for trading with the Indies; England had founded its own East India Company in 1600. Each of these aimed to create a monopoly of trade with the Orient, leading them to compete fiercely with each other and with regional traders.

Several European governments sponsored early schemes to create a settlement in Madagascar, like Flacourt's at Fort Dauphin, but all such attempts at creating a permanent, substantial and self-governing base in the island were to fail until the nineteenth century. Madagascar was only on the fringes of the Indian Ocean's trading system and produced little, other than slaves, that the Europeans valued enough to carry over long distances. The islands today known as Réunion and Mauritius came to fulfil many of the needs of the Dutch, British and French in the region. Although they sometimes called at points in the northeast and southeast, early European traders favoured doing business on the west coast of Madagascar, relatively accessible from the Dutch settlement at Cape Town, established in 1652, or from Mozambique. They generally found that the best place for buying slaves was the northwest coast, where they could benefit from the commercial networks pioneered by Antalaotra traders.

All the main ports in Madagascar's northwest had a strong connection to Africa. The main port of earlier times, Mahilaka, was abandoned before 1500,[58] probably in the face of competition from rivals. Dynamic new ports arose, like Sada, which was sacked by a Portuguese fleet in 1506. It was incorporated into the kingdom of Tingemaro or Guingemaro, whose ruler was considered by an English visitor in 1640 to be the 'greatest king of all the country'.[59] One scholar[60] has recently assembled evidence to suggest that power in Guingemaro was held by former slaves who had escaped the control of Mahilaka and created a kingdom of their own, whose ruler attracted subjects with a promise not to enslave his own people. Mariano described him as an African *('cafre')*.[61] By 1640, the king of Guingemaro had no fewer than 400 wives and concubines and was regarded 'as a God'. 'King's children cannot inheritt, but it must be the King's eldest sister's son that hath right to the Crowne', an English traveller noted.[62] Like the Portuguese and the Dutch, the rulers of Sada and other port-cities had frequent recourse to war in their struggle for control of Madagascar's overseas trade.

In the late sixteenth century, a new entrepot was founded by Antalaotra traders on the island today called Antsoheribory, in Boina Bay. This soon grew into a town known to the Portuguese as Mazalagem Nova[63] (so called from an Arabic word for a harbour), a name deformed by English sailors into Matthewlodge and generally known to the French and Dutch as Masselage. Mazalagem was a fierce competitor of Sada, and grew to prominence so quickly that the Dutch governor-general of the VOC settlement in distant Java already in 1615 knew the reputation of both towns, considering them the best places in Madagascar to buy slaves.[64] By about 1650, Mazalagem Nova had displaced rivals to become the most flourishing port in the whole of Madagascar.

Essentially an Antalaotra town, Mazalagem Nova was very cosmopolitan. It boasted houses, mosques and tombs made of stone. It had some 6–7,000 inhabitants, virtually all Muslims, and attracted seaborne trade from all over Madagascar.[65] The people wore Arab-style robes and turbans. The most widely-spoken language here was Swahili, followed by Malagasy and various African languages.[66] A fair number of people spoke a smattering of Portuguese or other European tongues; a few who had been to Europe or to one of the European entrepots in Asia were fluent. Mariano, for example, met in 1614 a man from northern Madagascar who had been enslaved some twenty-five years earlier, sold to an Antalaotra trader and taken by his master to the Comoros, Arabia and Mozambique. He had then been captured by an English ship, visiting France and the Netherlands before returning to Madagascar.[67] Probably most of the island's slave exports were shipped from Mazalagem Nova. Traders from Pate, Malindi, Lamu, Surat and other ports came with each monsoon to buy wood, tortoise-shell and slave boys whom, observed a Portuguese writer, 'they send to Arabia to serve their nefarious purposes',[68] hinting at sexual services. More probably, their main use in Arabia and the Persian Gulf was as agricultural and domestic workers and eunuchs. A Dutch visitor described the ruler of Mazalagem Nova, Sultan Hamet Boebachar, in 1676.[69] The sultan was dressed 'in the Arab manner', he noted, wearing a turban. About thirty-six years old, he spoke passable Portuguese and was married to a Swahili or Arab woman, although he also had various Malagasy concubines. He was said to govern some 300 households and to be able to raise 3,000–9,000 soldiers for war, plus their slaves.[70] Sultan Hamet was in regular contact with the ruler of Anjouan in the Comoros, to whom he asked his Dutch visitor to carry a letter for him,[71] and with potentates in Arabia and Muscat.

The Antalaotra merchant-princes in Mazalagem Nova were uninterested in extending their formal political rule deep into Madagascar's hinterland, aiming to control import-export trade and relations with their overseas partners rather than to acquire authority over large numbers of people. The slaves they needed, whether for personal use or for export, they bought from inland traders, generally in return for cloth, beads and other wares.[72] To their overseas partners they re-sold these slaves in return preferably for piastres and silver chains. The existence of a demand for slaves, cattle and other export goods led to the development of a regular trade-route from the highlands, hundreds of kilometres away. Every year, Mariano noted in 1614, 'large caravans brought from the interior large numbers of cattle and slaves'[73] to the northwestern ports, a trade that seems to have continued throughout the seventeenth century.

The description of Mazalagem Nova under Sultan Hamet is redolent of a way of life that had evolved over the centuries with the incorporation of northwest Madagascar into the Arab-dominated trade of the western Indian Ocean. It was a period now ending under joint threat from European traders and the rise of powerful new kings with roots in Madagascar's interior. These new-style kings waged wars with the aim of capturing slaves whom they could sell directly to Europeans, or they sponsored expeditions to sell cattle or imported cloth for slaves obtained from the interior of the island.

Priests and war-kings

It was among the population known as Antemoro, nowadays regarded as an ethnic group, clustered around the main estuaries of southeast Madagascar, that there evolved the first system of durable, institutionalized authority in the island that fully merits the name 'royalty'.[74] The ruling elite in this area were the Zafiraminia, some of whose kings recounted the oral histories of their line to Mariano and Flacourt.[75] Claiming family origins in Mecca, they were the most prestigious ritual experts in all of Madagascar, their reputation being based on their mastery of the esoteric arts of writing, divination and astrology.

The high reputation of Zafiraminia elites was also related to their privilege in regard to the slaughter of cattle. According to orthodox Islamic dietary laws, meat may only be consumed if it is from a beast that has been slaughtered in the correct ritual fashion. The act of slaughtering cattle is called in Malagasy *sombily*, a word derived from the Malay *semblih*, itself a corruption of the Arabic *bismillah*, 'in the name of God', the word uttered at the moment of cutting a beast's throat. In Madagascar's southeast, the Zafiraminia, using the ritual knowledge they had brought with them from Austronesia, successfully asserted the privilege of being the only people allowed to butcher cattle. Flacourt witnessed at first hand how keenly kings aimed to acquire cattle, a symbol of royalty and a necessity for religious rituals, that royal dynasties were to turn into a tradeable commodity. Chronic cattle theft was one of the most common causes of war between rival kingdoms. Some Zafiraminia kings extended their role as controllers of a vital resource to rice as well as cattle. This they did by building stocks of grain at harvest-time and exchanging or redistributing it later in the year.[76] It is possible that they also exchanged some of their dependents or subjects with other kings or traders, as the main Antemoro estuary of Matitanana was also one of the earliest ports of call for European slavers. The right to slaughter cattle became the central element in a many-sided dominance of society.

It is well established[77] that the Zafiraminia and other elite groups from Madagascar's southeast were instrumental in spreading advanced ideas about royalty to other regions of the island, where these ideas were grafted onto existing ideologies. At the time Flacourt was living in Madagascar, a new royal dynasty was arising on the west coast that was later to become the most powerful in the island's history until that point. Its supporters, for reasons that remain unclear, acquired the name Sakalava. The original Sakalava ruling dynasty, the Maroseraña, were cattle-herders living in south-central Madagascar who moved to the southwest, where they gained recognition as kings. They brought with them elements of an ideology of royalty that they had acquired from Islamized ritual experts.

Like other royal families in Madagascar, the Maroseraña furnished themselves with a genealogy that attributed their origin to a founding ancestor superior to the ordinary race of men and women, suggesting that they were a breed apart. Although this claim could be taken as evidence of a foreign origin,[78] it also reflects a convention regarding the uniqueness of kings. Included in their genealogies were the names of royal ancestors whose names appear allegorical. One Maroseraña ancestor was Andriamandazoala, 'the Prince who Destroys the Forest', quite possibly a reflection of the tendency of the Sakalava kings to cut down trees in order to establish grazing lands for cattle. Archaeological investigation of a site in the area of south-central Madagascar where the Maroseraña originated suggests that the occupants were connected to international trade even before the rise of the Sakalava monarchies, to judge from Chinese and Middle Eastern ceramics found there.[79]

All over the island there were nature-cults connected to notions of fertility, sometimes used by sovereigns to articulate the power of a dynasty, sometimes existing as popular practices outside royal control.[80] Broadly speaking, the oldest such cults dated from predynastic times, but were later assimilated by royal families as part of their apparatus of legitimation. Popular ancestral cults were co-opted by royal dynasties in such a way that the royal ancestors became objects of veneration, providing legitimacy to the political system. By a dialectical process, the tombs and memories of past kings re-entered the popular religious repertoire. Rituals based on the memory of royal ancestors provided an effective connection between rulers and ruled that could at times constitute a formidable instrument of control in societies that otherwise lacked much in the way of bureaucracy or an apparatus of government. In the kingdoms that arose in Imerina, for example, the sovereign's formal annual bath was the signal for every family to cleanse itself, removing the pollution of the dead year and bringing blessings for the season ahead. Sakalava kings publicly washed the relics of their dead ancestors in a similar act of renewal, ensuring the coherence of society.

Everywhere in the island, particular importance was attached to ancestors, and very often to the funeral ceremonies by which a living person made the transition to the world of the dead. The details of funeral ceremonies varied widely. There are many examples of rites used in various parts of Madagascar showing strong similarities to comparable ceremonials in Africa and Asia, suggesting an important field of research on early patterns of migration to Madagascar. Thus, kings on the west coast in the early seventeenth century were described by Mariano as having a particular funeral ritual whereby the body of a deceased sovereign was placed on a wooden platform where it was allowed to rot, and the liquid of the putrefying cadaver was gathered in a receptacle. Only after the corpse had been drained was it buried.[81] Similar practices of waiting for royal bodies to rot and to emit vital fluids have been recorded in other parts of the island. A practice of waiting for a maggot to leave the corpse of a deceased king shows clear similarities with royal funerary practices in Zimbabwe, Ethiopia and the Great Lakes region.[82] One of the political usages of such a ritual was to provide a time-limit to the interregnum and attendant political and social confusion that followed a king's death.

In view of the obvious importance that Madagascar's people attached to the supposed existence of an invisible world, home to the spirits of the ancestors, it is striking how consistently early European authors wrote that the island's inhabitants had no religion. This was not because these European travellers were unobservant, but rather because they were applying particular ideas about religion that reflected the European societies they came from. What struck them in Madagascar was the lack of religious buildings or sacred texts or an organized hierarchy of clerics, and it was this that caused them to conclude that there was no religion. It was clear that Madagascar's people believed that the spirits of ancestors continued to be a source of power and that it was possible to communicate with these and other invisible forces that were deemed to exist. It was for this reason that people wore protective amulets, sometimes mounted with gold or silver and beads, made offerings and used sacrificial blood to protect their houses.[83] In this way they could attract *hasina*, blessing or spiritual power.

The pervasive sense of a rigorous cosmological order that includes complex taboos has, over centuries, created in Madagascar a strong sense of a culture in which silence is at least as important as what is said.[84] Perceptible to this day, this was noted by Flacourt in the seventeenth century. Commenting on the sexual liberty he found in southern Madagascar, the Frenchman remarked that the men were not disturbed if their daughters or female relatives had discreet affairs, but were concerned only that this should be kept secret and not exhibited publicly.[85] Yet this was also a culture of words, in which people entertained each other with stories, knowledge was conveyed in ancestral proverbs and oral histories, and oratory was considered a fine art. 'They love to gossip and make fun of one another and make a thousand jests', observed Flacourt, 'and adore listening to stories and fables of olden days. They pass their evenings listening'.[86] It is small wonder that Madagascar's literature, whether written in the Malagasy language or transcribed in European langauges, includes many collections of folk-tales and oral histories. The most famous is the *Tantaran' ny Andriana*, oral histories of highland kings collected in the mid-nineteenth century and published in four fat volumes, or the *hainteny*, oral literature and poetry.[87]

It was the ubiquity of the discipline provided by rigorous and precise cosmological knowledge that provided a sense of political order in an island in which modern concepts of politics, government and religion were in many respects non-existent before the nineteenth century, when Europeans transcribed the Malagasy language into Latin script and circulated printed texts. The ultimate roots of the mythology that made political order possible were of Indian and Islamic provenance, both mediated via Austronesia, and also of African origin. The precise weight to be attached to the various influences is a matter of debate among scholars. Whatever the arguments in favour of Asian or African or other early influences in regard to any particular custom or rite, it is clear that a distinctively Malagasy culture was formed at a date early enough for this corpus to assimilate new ideas from orthodox Sunni sources brought by waves of migrants.[88] The ubiquitous Malagasy myth of Ibonia, a hero rather in the manner of the Greek Heracles or Odysseus, is a portrait of the divine nature of sovereignty. It is a version of God's delegation of authority rather different from that contained in the classical Christian and Muslim ideologies, since it represents power as being divided between God in heaven and the visible god on earth that is a king.[89] '*Iboniamasiboniamanoro* is the myth of Man, of his authentically human and religious meaning, as it is perceived by more or less all humanity outside the modern, non-Christian, West.'[90]

The assimilation of ideas from various sources into ideologies of power sometimes created practical difficulties that were to have a considerable bearing on the course of Madagascar's history. Perhaps the prime example was the lack of a clear rule of succession to positions of authority. At least three different systems of succession have been in regular operation within recorded times. One system provides for succession to pass from senior to junior males within one generation, or in other words from an older to a younger brother. Another tradition is that of matrilineal inheritance from a king to his sister's sons, which is known to have existed in western Madagascar in the seventeenth century. Simple male primogeniture, in contrast—the same system as was usual in Europe until recently—was probably introduced to Madagascar by orthodox Sunni Muslims. The coexistence of all three systems reflected the exceptionally broad range of influences that migrants had brought to Madagascar from the Indian Ocean's shores. More prosaically, in any specific political dispute, succession was often decided by force of arms, subsequently justified by appeal to alleged custom.

4

THE SLAVE-TRADER KINGS 1700–1816

The rise of a dynasty with origins in south-central Madagascar[1] to form a political identity known as Sakalava is arguably the single most important political revolution in the history of Madagascar. The founders of the Sakalava kingdoms[2] attributed to themselves a ritual role closely connected to their control of cattle. By marrying their religious powers to their commercial acumen and military might, the Sakalava kings permanently altered the form of the island's social organization, changing fundamentally the moral values of the small communities into which people had been divided for the previous thousand years throughout Madagascar.

The Sakalava kingdoms were to become the first of successive monarchies that benefited from major population movements, with far-reaching consequences. As a Dutch official, Hendrik Frappé, noted after visiting the northern Sakalava king Toakafo in 1715, 'because all his undertakings were crowned with success ... this region flourished and increased enormously in population, with people taking shelter from other regions'.[3] The same phenomenon existed in other areas, where whole communities placed themselves under one or other warrior-king to secure protection from enslavement.[4] Frappé further noted that Toakafo was 'honoured and feared like a god' by his subjects,[5] like other kings who were regarded, in Flacourt's words, as 'great Magician[s]' by virtue of the cult objects in their possession.[6] Systems of royal rule spread to all parts of the island along the main corridors used by migrants, travellers and herders. Sakalava kings, and others after them, turned to advantage occasional visits by European traders and acquired guns, although the unwieldy matchlocks on offer were prestige objects. While guns certainly made their owners powerful, they did not in themselves revolutionize ways of waging war.[7]

The Sakalava kings

According to their own genealogies, the Maroseraña, the ruling dynasty of the Sakalava, originated in a village called Bengy, probably in the sixteenth century. They moved westwards towards the southwest coast, and from there, in successive generations, junior branches moved northwards to new locations, thus extending the dynasty over a wide area and creating a series of Sakalava kingdoms, all of them organized around the sacred person of the monarch. The Sakalava kingdoms were characterized by large-scale cattle-herding and organized slave-trading.

One of the first kings[8] in the line of the reigning Maroseraña dynasty, according to royal genealogies, was Andriandahifotsy or Lahifotsy[9] (c.1614–1683), and he is the first who can positively be identified as a historical rather than a semi-mythical figure, since his name was recorded in contemporary European documents. He is even quoted verbatim in Dutch records.[10] Taking control of ports on the southwestern coast, Lahifotsy—known to English traders as King Lightfoot—became a key partner of the European sailors and traders who were coming to Madagascar in increasing numbers, originally often to buy supplies for their ships' crews, but, increasingly from the 1660s, in search of slaves too. The people Lahifotsy sold were transported as far afield as the Americas and the eastern headquarters of the Dutch East India Company at Batavia.

According to some oral traditions,[11] Lahifotsy came to power by killing his own uncle. He then tried to establish a rule of succession through the eldest son of his first wife, herself a princess, attributing to her descendants the epithet *volamena* ('red silver', i.e. gold). Many of these princes developed a practice of incest, marrying their own sisters in order to keep the kingship within the dynasty.[12] When Lahifotsy died, a son of his senior wife duly took control of a kingdom based on Madagascar's central west coast and, fearing trouble from other members of the family, expelled his junior brothers, who set off to find their fortunes elsewhere. The most successful of the fugitives was Tsimenata (c.1668–c.1709). Acquiring firearms from English traders via a local ally, he set off northwards and conquered a large swath of territory including the vital port of Mazalagem Nova, killing its Antalaotra sultan in the process. Tsimenata made himself into the island's leading slave-exporter and most powerful king. His kingdom of Boina was to remain probably the most powerful monarchy in Madagascar for about a century afterwards.

There are several eye-witness descriptions of King Tsimenata in his prime. He was described by a Dutch official in 1695 as 'clever, strong and robust', but also a 'brute and tyrant', with, like his late father, a formidable appetite for strong drink.[13] Thirteen years later, another visitor described him as being aged about forty, by now grown 'rather fat', but still 'tall and handsome'. He was described by the same visitor as being 'almost black'. He received visitors on a throne carved of ebony with inlaid ivory, wearing a golden crown, sporting diamond rings on his fingers. On one of his upper arms he wore a small silver box, probably containing the relics of one of the royal ancestors. He had eighteen wives.[14]

A striking aspect of the early history of the Sakalava kingdoms is the succession problem that split Lahifotsy's descendants into rival branches. The lack of an agreed rule of succession created a permanent factionalism among Sakalava ruling elites, consisting of the king's extended family plus the leaders of various subject groups that became Sakalava while also retaining their original identity. Kings took junior wives or concubines from these subordinate groups or gave their female dependents in marriage to important vassals, binding their subjects to the ruling house by these arrangements.[15] The kings required headmen from their various subject groups to attend them, the more easily to supervise them. But no precaution was enough to prevent permanent dynastic in-fighting, including assassinations, palace intrigues and constant revolts from uncles, brothers and other close family members. A British slave-trader who was present in the Sakalava kingdom of Menabe during one round of feuding was told by a chief that 'it was a sett of Freemen of this country who had entered into a conspiracy against [King] Rangeeta and had put him to flight'.[16] An added layer of complexity consisted in the fact that, from the beginning of the dynastic history of the Sakalava, the *mainty* section of the population played an important role in the nomination of a sovereign.[17]

Rather than ruling the key port of Mazalagem Nova directly, Tsimenata, the first Sakalava king of Boina, installed a client-government nominally under the control of a group of Antalaotra merchants headed by his own infant granddaughter, whom he gave in marriage to an Arab from Surat.[18] Thanks to these commercial links the Sakalava kings had far greater access to firearms than other rulers. This permitted them to organize powerful armed forces, which in turn enabled them to accumulate wealth, to regulate commerce in their own interest, and to raid for slaves. They regularly bartered slaves in return for guns, gunpowder and ammunition. Even in the mid-seventeenth century one west-coast ruler was described as sending his captains 'to travel through the country with one or two hundred soldiers and to exchange either cattle or Portuguese textiles for slaves, to such effect that he was able to acquire all the slaves in the north of the island', for later sale to European merchants.[19] For the most part, Sakalava kings' wealth 'consists ... in the great number of their slaves and all their wars have no other object than to acquire prisoners in order to enslave them'.[20] Firearms were to play an increasingly important role in these wars. A Dutch trader who visited the mid-west coast in 1719 noted that local men could handle muskets as expertly as any European, whereas 'not even a century ago, they were so afraid that a single man armed with a musket could put to flight' a much larger number of warriors.[21] Tsimenata made effective use of European pirates as military advisors and mercenaries.

European merchants used Madagascar as a revictualling point on the route to the Indies but occasionally too as one of their sources of manpower for colonies as far away as Java and even North America and the Caribbean. However, this was nowhere near the scale of the Atlantic slave trade at that time.[22] Sakalava kings and their European partners developed a fairly standard pattern for doing business. They opened negotiations for the purchase of slaves by sharing the alcohol the Europeans brought as a preliminary gift. This was usually a spirit, arrack, but could also be red wine from the newly-planted vineyards at the Cape. This period of socialization often involved very heavy drinking, ending with one or both parties needing a couple of days to recover from their hangovers. King Lahifotsy in fact died as a result of such an orgy of heavy drinking.[23] His subjects, convinced that he had been poisoned by the crew of the brigantine that had supplied him with liquor, [24] took their revenge by killing their European visitors. A later visitor from the Dutch East India Company, after negotiating with the king of Boina, a great-great-grandson of King Lahifotsy, wrote in 1741 that 'the arrack bottle is indispensable in commerce with these people ... when you give them a calabash full of arrack, they keep going until they have drunk it to the last drop.'[25]

After the king's diviner had identified the most auspicious day to begin proceedings in earnest, trade negotiations opened between the king and whatever European traders he was dealing with, mostly Dutch, French, Portuguese, English and English-American, or Danes. Generally, the west-coast kings aimed to monopolize the trade of slaves for arms. Only when the king had finished his business was it customary for him to allow his subjects to deal with the Europeans, sometimes for the provision of a few more slaves, but mostly for the sale of ships' victuals or other supplies. European trade became closely linked to extensive networks of commerce and war much further inland, especially through the slaves-for-arms nexus.

According to the Dutchman Hendrik Frappé, who in 1715 visited King Toakafo's court, this grandson of Lahifotsy owned 300,000 head of cattle, and some of his courtiers had 70–80,000.[26] While these look like exaggerated estimates, they serve to emphasize the stature of the new style of kings as traders and plutocrats. Obligatory gifts of cattle to a chief were to turn into the first form of taxation operated by the new kings. Rulers in other parts of the island were to become associated with other forms of economic enterprise, such as the highland monarchs who encouraged intensive rice-cultivation. This was a reflection both of their ability to organize collective labour for communal work on dykes and irrigation systems and also of their perceived ability to channel a mystical quality of fertility. Acquiring, breeding, and herding cattle—or its economic equivalent in the highlands, securing and protecting valuable farmland—became one of the material bases of royal power, requiring a concentration of armed force that was to lead to the development of royal armies. Increasingly, rulers with a reputation as channels of power and fertility could also secure the allegiance of people in need of protection, whom they could then require to provide them with gifts of cattle and military or labour service, thus creating a logic of power and reciprocity. King Toakafo was described as carrying a loaded musket at all times,[27] demonstrating his role as a military commander.

The main west-coast ports received visits from European ships that increasingly were in search of slaves, including even vessels from New York and Barbados. This trade linked Madagascar's main ports into global systems of exchange. Largely through the sponsorship of Tsimenata and his son Toakafo, the slave trade to the Americas flourished to the point that no less than 1,400 slaves from Madagascar were imported to the colony of Virginia between 1719 and 1721,[28] many of them probably bought at Mazalagem Nova. Like the Antalaotra slave-traders before them, the Europeans made no effort to capture slaves themselves, but only to buy them. For this purpose the advantage of maintaining correct relations was clear to both European traders and Sakalava kings after the rupture in relations with the king of Menabe that had followed Lahifotsy's death in 1683 and the violent reaction of his subjects. In 1738, Charles Barrington, a British slave merchant travelling aboard a Danish ship, gave three reasons why Mazalagem Nova was the best place in Madagascar to buy slaves:[29]

1. that as it is a place where the annual Johanna[30] ship comes, I should think it as considerable as any place on the island, if not more so, and the people there by a constant traffick, under a better and more regular polity and government, than the wilderness frequented [sic] parts of the island.

2. the government at Massaleage [Mazalagem Nova] by anything I could learn is not at all disturbed, as it is here [Iongoeloe, in Menabe] by rival kings, parties and factions.

3. I find that the terms and prices of trade are scarce to be settled, but where there is a king, who has a settled authority to back and maintain what is concluded on with him, that a great part of the slaves are to be had from the king, which may be the case at Masseleage.

The rise in demand for slaves gave potentates in Madagascar every incentive to wage aggressive wars in order to capture slaves for export. Furthermore, it caused them to consider in a new light the use that could be made of their own dependents; it was not unknown for kings to sell members of their own family, and even their own wives, into slavery.[31] This sort of opportunism was politically risky, however, as it could provoke subjects into placing themselves under the protection of a rival sovereign, either by making use of local factional intrigues or simply by migrating.

Like Muslim traders in earlier times, Europeans brought new ideas about political power and its representations that had a clear effect on local potentates. The foreigners tended to regard all rulers as sovereign without inquiring too closely into the exact nature of their power. As

Barrington again wrote, some minor rulers who were in fact beholden to greater lords elsewhere 'have passed as kings, with us Europeans, who generally dubb all as such whom we find the Head Men of a people, not declaring themselves subject to others'.[32] The Sakalava kings studiously adopted symbols of royalty that would impress their visitors. King Toakafo, for example, received his Dutch visitors in 1715 wearing 'a massive gold, star-shaped crown' studded with agates, sporting gold and silver chains around his neck and with golden armbands and rings.[33] Moreover, some kings went considerably further in making practical use of technical assistance from foreigners, taking Europeans directly into their service as administrators or, especially, as mercenaries and military advisers. Tsimenata engaged the services of twenty sailors from two ships owned by Frederick Philipse of New York to help him in his original conquest of Mazalagem Nova and an adjacent stretch of coast.[34] There was a growing number of Europeans ready to perform services of this sort. By the 1690s, northern Madagascar was home to between 400 and 830 European pirates, according to various contemporary estimates. These had been expelled from their previous haunts in the Caribbean and were attracted particularly by the prospect of attacking seaborne pilgrims from India and the east on their way to Mecca. The pirates' military skills and access to high-quality firearms made them formidable, and they were to constitute a major element in the balance of power on Madagascar's northern coasts until they were driven out by Britain's Royal Navy in the 1720s. One or two pirates actually claimed to rule small areas of Madagascar themselves. The children they had with local women often received particular recognition from local rulers as a guarantor of privileged relations with foreign traders in exactly the same way as the Sakalava kings treated leading Antalaotra merchants. Some pirates married into royal families and were assimilated into local dynasties.

One such case is exemplary. An English pirate, Tom by name,[35] married the daughter of a local chief near Foulpointe on the northeast coast. She bore him a son, probably in 1694 or 1695, whom the English pirates also called Tom. His local name was Similaho, and he was often known by both names, as Tom or Tam Similaho. In later generations his Malagasy name gained the honorific prefix 'Ra' to become Ratsimilaho. The young Ratsimilaho is reported to have visited England with his father, and perhaps also India. He used his advanced knowledge of European military techniques and access to firearms to become a potentate in Madagascar. At first he worked as the chief minister of King Toakafo,[36] the second Sakalava king of Boina, but soon branched off to set up a new kingdom of his own in eastern Madagascar. His subjects took the name Betsimisaraka ('The Many Undivided'), and this was the origin of one of Madagascar's recognized ethnic groups today.[37] His main military innovation was the use of extended campaigns, European-style, whereas previously there had been a tendency for groups at war to admit defeat after just a single engagement.[38]

James Armstrong has suggested that between 40,000 and 150,000 slaves were exported during the seventeenth century from Mazalagem Nova,[39] Madagascar's most active slave port. Other authors, making use of Portuguese archives, estimate that 2–3,000 slaves were exported from Madagascar annually during this period by Swahili merchants working out of Lamu and Pate particularly, excluding those who were shipped via the Comoros.[40] Many of these were ultimately intended for markets in Arabia and Oman. Total slave exports from Madagascar during the seventeenth century may have been as high as 3–5,000 per year, excluding those exported by Europeans.[41] While the slave trade seems to have grown even larger at a later stage, even at this relatively early date it had important implications for Madagascar's internal politics. The Sakalava kings obliged rulers in many other parts of the island to pay tribute to them, including in the central highlands, probably the main reservoir of slaves by reason of its dense population. Minor kings in the central highlands raided each other's territories for slaves whom they then assembled into caravans that were marched to the northwest coast for sale, together with cattle.[42] Later oral traditions collected in the highlands recalled how Sakalava kings and warriors stimulated domestic quarrels which provided captives that they could then sell as slaves.[43] European traders, despite their long-term interest in dealing with strong kings, also sometimes encouraged factional wars as a way of generating slaves.

The Antalaotra traders who were established on the northwest coast as vassals of the Sakalava king of Boina were able by the late eighteenth century 'to do business just about all through the island', a French slave trader reckoned.[44] By that time Mazalagem Nova had gone into decline, eclipsed by Majunga, today one of Madagascar's provincial capitals. The same French trader described Majunga in 1792 as being home to 'more than 6,000 Arabs and Indians with their families' and as containing mosques and schools. The leading traders were in regular communication with Surat,[45] the main banking centre for Indian merchants. Majunga's traders are reckoned to have drawn an annual income of about 20 or 30,000 silver piastres from Madagascar, acquiring a monopoly of exports of handicrafts for sale to the Banyans of Surat and Bombay.[46]

By the time that Mazalagem Nova lost its commercial vocation, eventually to become the ruin that it is today, the Sakalava kings and their Antalaotra vassals were suffering the effects of a shift in the location of demand for their main export commodities, slaves and cattle. Europeans were losing their former interest in the west coast of Madagascar. Dutch officials in Cape Town had long been dissatisfied with Madagascar's reliability as a source of slaves, and, more importantly, there was a rapid increase in demand for plantation workers on the French possessions of the Ile de France and the Ile Bourbon (today called Mauritius and Réunion). The small number of French settlers at Bourbon had been buying slaves from Mazalagem Nova and from the southeastern port of Matitanana from the 1720s, but demand expanded fast as the cultivation of coffee and, later, sugar, developed on the two islands from the mid-eighteenth century. Plantation-owners looked to buy slaves from Madagascar's east coast, the closest to the two islands. The first political-military entrepreneur to profit from the shift in direction of the slave trade was the pirate's son Ratsimilaho (c.1695–1750). After his death French slave-traders on the east coast cynically played off rival factions, encouraging them to make war on one another so as to keep the slave-markets supplied, and his Betsimisaraka kingdom did not last. Moreover, as in the island's other kingdoms, the rules of succession were unclear, giving rise to family quarrels.

Ideologies and groups

Starting with the reign of Lahifotsy from the 1650s to 1683, the Sakalava monarchies were broadly able to satisfy contemporary European requirements in matters of trade, and they therefore received commensurate commercial and diplomatic attention from Europeans. Comparable political formations were soon to emerge elsewhere in the island, including on the east coast and in the central highlands, all of them successfully articulating global currents as well as domestic pressures or opportunities. Furthermore, relatively durable leagues were to emerge that had a distinctive identity, but without a strong central monarchy of the sort developed by the Sakalava. By the eighteenth century, some such groups had acquired names that are still in use today to designate what are now called ethnic groups. In some cases they gained their name from the geographical zones where they lived, like the Tanala ('Forest People') or the Bezanozano ('Many Reeds'). Other ethnic identities, however, were a reflection of political arrangements, like the Betsimisaraka ('Many Undivided'), created from a number of distinct descent-groups by Ratsimilaho around 1720 after he had learned his business as prime minister to the Sakalava king of Boina. A similar political genesis may have been at the origin of the collective identity of the Betsileo, for although there is some dispute as to the origin of this name,[47] it may have been derived from that of a seventeenth-century ruler. The mass of the people in the central highlands seems to have been known by the word *hova* from an early period, while being divided into numerous minor polities.

All of these large conglomerates were porous in nature. They were disparate in many aspects of culture and organization, being themselves composed of large numbers of smaller, named units. Aristocratic lineages could pass from one group to another. The English expressions 'caste', 'social class' and 'ethnic group' are all imperfect descriptions: the names for such entities in Malagasy suggest aspects of all three. Prestigious lineages like the Zafiraminia, as we have seen, jealously guarded the high status that made them a quasi-caste.

In view of the nature of the social units that had formed in Madagascar over time, it seems misleading to refer to the Sakalava construction as the island's 'first empire', as some historians have done.[48] This term implies the assertion of centralized political control over groups having a significantly different political and cultural tradition and with a developed consciousness of their autonomy, accompanied by the assignation of superior status to the population of the core area of the state. While the Sakalava kings indeed exerted their authority over many distinct groups and over a territory hundreds of kilometers in extent, it is doubtful that the political and cultural identities of specific groups had previously hardened to the extent that it is accurate to think of the Sakalava kingdoms as states exerting control over essentially foreign populations. Moreover, while Sakalava kings asserted their own elevated status, they did not privilege the population group at the core of their kingdom. For all the power associated with the sovereign's person, Sakalava kingdoms were characterized by constant centrifugal movements. The relation of ideas of monarchy to migration is also worthy of note: models of political organization were carried along the routes most often used by people on the move, in search of new homes or for seasonal trade, like cattle-herders. The Matitanana valley in the southeast, the Ihosy plateau in the centre-south, Imerina in the highlands, the long coastal plain of the west and the Androna gap in north-central Madagascar were all highways for the transmission of ideas as well as people and goods.

Key to the articulation of royal power in all parts of the island was the notion of *hasina*.[49] This designates the invisible essence of power and fertility that can be channelled to human beings, particularly through ancestors. Some of the most fundamental Malagasy ideas concerning political hierarchy arose from the prestige associated with a person or family considered to be a channel of exceptional virtue by reason of their ancestry.[50] The transmission of *hasina* required respect for the ritual obligations and taboos that bound members of a family or a community to each other, to nature, and to the land. The foremost principle of political authorities throughout the island was that they should embody this life-force and bestow it on their subjects. Conversely, a subject was considered to grant *hasina* by an act of allegiance, making the relationship between sovereign and subject a reciprocal one. Various customs and institutions deemed to be of ancestral origin were associated with the transmission of such power. Nevertheless, while *hasina* is among the oldest[51] ideas of political authority in Madagascar, it has been constantly enriched with new inventions and imports.[52]

The rulers of all the many polities in Madagascar transmitted this metaphysical essence by invoking the invisible forces of the cosmos through word and ritual gesture, by securing the services of diviners, and by arranging their affairs, in details ranging from the shape of their houses to the naming and treatment of their children, in conformity with what they believed to be the pattern of the cosmos. The fundamental task of a sovereign was to reign: to dispense blessing, notably through the practice of appropriate rituals, and to ensure fertility, to prevent the subversion of the natural order, and to channel the *hasina* of royal ancestors to royal subjects. The increase in the command of material resources through trade and war reflected in the history of the Sakalava kingdoms and, later, the Betsimisaraka and other kingdoms, did not detract from the fact that the core of political legitimacy lay in the ability to channel the spiritual quality of *hasina*. It is for this reason that European travellers from the early seventeenth century often claimed that kings in Madagascar were regarded by their subjects as gods.

The combination of ritual supremacy and commercial and military power assured by the Sakalava style of kingship is clearly conveyed in a fascinating account written by Otto Hemmy, a German employee of the Dutch VOC who visited the royal palace of the kings of Boina at Marovoay in 1741.[53] Hemmy noted that the king's dwelling consisted of several enclosures and was, he thought, bigger than the mansion of the Dutch governor of Cape Town. Altogether there were four or five concentric rings of wooden palisades surrounding the king's residence. The king's grandfather, Toakafo, had, in his time, received visitors in a complex of 18 or 19 buildings standing on a fortified hilltop, surrounded by a wooden palisade, with four entrances, presumably at the four cardinal points.[54] This concentric layout was apparently adopted not only for defence, but also to impress on people the king's place at the centre of the cosmos. A similar arrangement may still be seen at the royal citadel of Ambohimanga, near Antananarivo, one of Madagascar's leading tourist sites.

It is apparent from this and other descriptions that the Sakalava kings, like the Zafiraminia in the east and south, regarded themselves as being at the centre of the cosmos, no matter how limited their actual domains. One of the Zafiraminia myths was that the whole of Madagascar had once been under the control of a single king,[55] articulating a vision of primeval perfection. One southern king, Dian Ramach (unusual for having been educated by the Portuguese at Goa), was described by Flacourt as calling himself 'king of the whole island of Madagascar'[56] despite the fact that he was clearly just one of many rulers even within his own region of the island. His title reflected an ideology rather than a statement of fact.

Various features of the display seen by Hemmy concern elements of kingship that had obviously been imported, emphasizing cosmopolitan connections. The king showed his visitors storerooms containing dozens of boxes of goods, gifts and luxury items. He proudly pointed out his lacquered throne, an object of Chinese manufacture that had been given to him by French traders. They saw a Japanese vase filled with punch. The next day, he received his guests wearing a long, white, Arab-style gown, a silver-pommelled scimitar hanging from his belt. On another occasion he wore Persian clothes. He asked his Dutch visitors whether they could provide the services of a tailor to repair the European clothes that he also owned. In short, he had sets of costumes that reflected a wide range of influences. Visitors noticed that, like his forefathers, the king was an enthusiast for strong drink, yet he also invoked the Prophet Mohammed, indicating a religious eclecticism as great as his sartorial variety. The search for cosmopolitanism seems to have made Sakalava kings particular lovers of all things exotic, like King Toakafo, who asked Dutch visitors in 1715 to bring him on their next visit breeding-pairs of horses, peacocks, ostriches and hunting-dogs.[57] In conformity with their universalizing vision, Sakalava kings of Boina considered their European visitors as their own potential subjects.

Hemmy was also privileged to view the relics of the king's ancestors, kept both as a proof of royal descent and as a perceived source of power. In the Sakalava monarchy, these relics were at the centre of an elaborate royal ritual combining religious ideas from a wide variety of sources in which the bones of dead kings were periodically washed in a river in a public ceremony. These and other physical remnants were kept in an ossuary that itself became a powerful ritual object. Thus, a pretender to the kingdom of Menabe, when seeking support among minor kings, summoned them 'to pray at his ancestors' tombs'.[58] The cult of ancestral relics was probably adopted by the Sakalava kings from the pre-dynastic rulers of the west coast, as, even before the rise of the Sakalava, Mariano had noted the importance of a cult of the ancestors, observing how people wore around their waist a belt that had sewn into it relics of the dead, including 'hairs from the beard, fingernails and the cloth worn by their fathers.' High-status families placed such objects in a small box that they attached to their belts and carried into battle.[59]

Although the circulation of ideas from one part of Madagascar to another generally took place rather slowly, it is possible to follow some quite specific examples over relatively short periods of time, such as the diffusion of styles of dress from one place to another. There is evidence, for example, that princes and potentates in the highlands in the early nineteenth century imitated styles of dress that were current at the courts of their Sakalava overlords, as may be seen from some contemporary pictures and texts.[60] Less than a generation later, the same strata of highland society were to adopt European dress on a large scale, encouraged by European and American traders eager to spread the products of industrial manufacture. The adoption of new forms of clothing and personal adornment was accompanied by changes in social organization and in many other spheres as well.

The last of the major kingdoms to emerge in Madagascar was in the central highland district of Imerina, traditionally part of the larger area known as Ankova. The kingdom of Imerina is the one that has been most often described by historians. One reason for this is that Imerina's capital city, Antananarivo, has been the seat of governments that have aspired to rule over the whole island of Madagascar from the early nineteenth century until today, but a further reason for the relative abundance of books on Imerina is because of the number of oral histories recorded by scholars working in Imerina at an early period,[61] not to mention the volumes of other documentation. However, the attention that has been given to Imerina should not divert attention from the fact that it, like other highland kingdoms, was influenced by developments elsewhere in the island.[62]

The earliest known use of the name Imerina, in the seventeenth century, designated a geographical area only, which became a single political unit briefly in about 1700, only to split into rival kingdoms. In the 1780s and 1790s, the whole area was again made subject to one king, who then changed his name to Andrianampoinimerina ('The King at the Heart of Imerina'). Thus, the Merina kingdom was not the political creation of an ethnic group that had maintained a homogeneous cultural or political identity from the time of its arrival in Madagascar centuries before. Rather, the word 'Merina' originally designated the subjects of a given ruler and his dynasty,[63] just as was the case with the Sakalava and the Betsimisaraka. All three names were originally political labels. In each case subject groups continued to retain their existing identities alongside their new, political one.

Imerina

By the eighteenth century, the central highlands of Madagascar, including the areas today known as Imerina and Betsileo, had for some time already been one of the most densely populated parts of the island, ever since its large-scale settlement by neo-Austronesian immigrants in the thirteenth to fifteenth centuries. Highland kings were in regular contact with rulers and *ombiasy* in other parts of the island. Antemoro clerics are known to have supplied them with protective amulets,[64] and Antalaotra traders from the west supplied them with silver coin via the slave trade. After the rise of the Sakalava kingdoms in the seventeenth century, many highland rulers were obliged to pay tribute to Sakalava kings.

Situated in the mountainous interior of Madagascar, highland rulers were ideally placed to use the topography of the land as a demonstration of political ideology. A highland king sat god-like at the centre of a hierarchical social order reflected in the geographical form that royal government assumed, with power being closely associated with the spatial dimensions of height (the king lived on a hilltop) and breadth (power emanated from the centre). The king was the embodiment of excellence, the lord at the centre of the universe. The peripheries were anti-social and represented also archaic forms of organization.[65] In material terms, the domination by a centrally-located ruler of subjects living in valleys beneath corresponded also to a need to organize labour for intensive riziculture, as was done in the highlands from around the sixteenth century. Perhaps the lack of direct access to seaborne trade was also a stimulus to the intensive use in the highlands of labour for agriculture.

The development of exalted notions of royalty led families in the highlands related to a king to claim a particularly high status, and they became referred to as *andriana*, a royal title. There were so many petty kings that, in the nineteenth century, 'a fourth part of the whole free population of Imerina', or slightly less according to other sources, was considered to be descended from royalty and therefore classed as *andriana*.[66] Even today there are graphic reminders of the division of the highlands into dozens of autonomous political units at an early period in the form of the literally thousands of fortified hilltops that are best seen from the air,[67] dominating valleys and plains where rice was grown by villagers living under the domination of the lords above. Each individual king offered protection to the peasants under his rule in return for allegiance and payment in rice or other goods, and individual rulers frequently raided each other's lands. These petty wars helped keep the west coast supplied with slaves for export, first, to the Middle East, later to Cape Town and the Americas, and, later still, to the plantations of the Ile de France (Mauritius) and the Ile Bourbon (Réunion). The bulk of the population remained classed as *hova*, or commoners, and highland traditions describe *hova* communities as self-governing before the imposition of rule by *andriana*. As in the southeast of the island there were parallel hierarchies of *fotsy* and *mainty* families. Early European writers generally considered the population of the central highlands to form a single territorial group that they called Hova, using the name of the most numerous social class.

Several of the numerous highland kingdoms were temporarily united under one king, Andriamasinavalona, in the early eighteenth century, at a time when some highlanders benefited from the commerce that was thriving in the northwest of Madagascar, where Hova traders are known to have been active. Andriamasinavalona's kingdom collapsed into civil war after his death, which occurred some time before 1740, although he appears to have divided his kingdom among his four sons and abdicated well before that date. This conflict was 'the first instance we heard', according to a later chronicler, 'of a war and bloodshed caused by Hova people against one another'.[68] For several decades until the 1790s, the central highlands were devastated by slave raiding and 'terrific civil wars', that 'ravaged Imerina, and caused the deaths and slavery of thousands and thousands of Her miserable people'.[69] War destroyed many of the fortified hilltop villages and displaced large numbers of people.[70] Peasants expelled from their villages founded new groups, which sometimes themselves became militarily powerful. Some displaced people formed themselves into robber-bands or into political leagues, providing a political opportunity for any king or other leader powerful enough to give them protection.

The first extant eye-witness description of political conditions in the highlands was written by a French slave-trader, Nicolas Mayeur, in 1777. Mayeur's memoirs[71] of his travels concord in many ways—and differ interestingly in others—when they are compared with the oral narratives collected two or three generations later. He recorded a densely populated region and an industrious population living from rice cultivation. Intensive cattle-grazing at an earlier period in central Madagascar had contributed to the deforestation of the area, so noticeable today, even by the late eighteenth century.[72] Imerina was also known for its manufactures of pottery, cloth and iron goods especially, which were quite extensively traded for cattle and imported goods with neighbouring areas. 'The Europeans who have frequented the island of

Madagascar', Mayeur wrote, 'and who read these memoirs, will have difficulty believing that one may find in the interior of this huge island more enlightenment, more industry, a more active government policy than on the coasts, whose inhabitants are in constant relation with foreigners'.[73] This seems a rather rosy picture of a region scarred by civil war and enslavement.

While the civil wars of the eighteenth century plunged many highlanders into misery, they allowed others to amass fortunes of unprecedented size. The most ruthless power-holders, including the rulers of some of the micro-kingdoms in the central highlands, did not hesitate to enslave and sell their own subjects. It had previously been common for highland families engaged in petty feuds to capture members of rival groups and hold them to ransom,[74] a tactic that encouraged circulation of the very limited supplies of silver coin, a practice reminiscent of cattle-raiding among the island's pastoralist populations. Captives now became more likely than previously to be sold for export. Enterprising individuals like these slave-merchants were situated between descent-groups, with their strong levelling ethos, and their king, the personification of hierarchy and inequality. The resulting tension was fertile ground for jealousy, suspicion and rivalry.[75] The growth of individual fortunes led to accusations of witchcraft, which the most unscrupulous rulers exploited as a means of convicting people who could then be sold as slaves. People accused of witchcraft were a significant source of slaves for export not only in Imerina but in some other parts of the island too.[76]

Just as the founders of the Sakalava kingdom in the west and the short-lived Betsimisaraka kingdom in the east had made use of the opportunities created by overseas commerce, so too in Imerina did a minor prince exploit the existence of the slave trade to extend his power and subdue rival kings. This was Andrianampoinimerina (c.1750–1809), the most famous king in Madagascar's history, who began his conquests by deposing the king of the hill-settlement of Ambohimanga, capital of a micro-kingdom, in 1778.[77] The king he deposed had made himself unpopular by enslaving his own subjects and manipulating accusations of witchcraft. The leading slave-traders and long-distance merchants were among Andrianampoinimerina's earliest and most loyal supporters, and he rewarded these families with privileges that were to accumulate throughout later reigns. Unlike his Sakalava and Betsimisaraka counterparts, however, the victorious King Andrianampoinimerina represented himself as the transmitter of an existing political heritage rather than the creator of a new polity. Once installed as king of Ambohimanga, he went on to overcome by conquest or diplomacy all the other kings of the central highlands, becoming the undisputed master of Imerina. He made skilful use of political relations countrywide, securing an alliance with the Sakalava ruler of Boina, still the most powerful sovereign in Madagascar at the start of his reign. He summoned from the southeast of the island one of the most famous Antemoro clerics, Andriamahazonoro (died 1828).[78]

Andrianampoinimerina transferred his capital to the centre of one of the kingdoms he had conquered. This was Antananarivo, whose name means literally 'the Town of a Thousand', which emerged as a major centre of population. War-weariness gave him the opportunity to offer protection to all who accepted his authority. In effect, he offered to subject groups a pact: physical protection and recognition of their right to territory in return for recognition of his authority, with only certain noble lineages having the right to move their place of residence. The practice in Imerina of building massive family tombs, that many Malagasy today believe to be a custom dating from time immemorial, is probably an innovation of the period of Andrianampoinimerina,[79] as newly-settled groups cemented their links to the land by investing in tombs. He exploited an existing system of group protectors, ritual objects made by *ombiasy*, often from the southeast, that were considered to protect the groups that owned them. Each time Andrianampoinimerina conquered an area, he either co-opted or destroyed its religious objects, according to political criteria, making copies of group talismans where appropriate. Developing many of the techniques of statecraft used by his predecessors, 'he plucked from obscurity local or tribal amulets to turn them into the official protectors of all the Merina', noted a later scholar, codifying their accompanying rituals and making them obligatory. He often entrusted these powerful objects to his leading generals, 'creating, so to speak, a state religion' based on a national pantheon.[80] Like some of the princes he defeated, Andrianampoinimerina exploited the fear of witchcraft, using the poison ordeal to dispose of his enemies.[81] Kings in Madagascar routinely believed themselves to be surrounded by political opponents in secret possession of powerful charms. It was logical that an expansion of royal power would take the form of searching for possible dissidents with dangerous, unlicensed amulets that represented unofficial, and therefore potentially subversive, channels of the cosmic force *hasina*.

Closely allied to leading slave-traders, yet promising his subjects that he would not sell them into slavery, Andrianampoinimerina turned to advantage the demand for slaves from French plantations in the Mascarene islands. He used his strength to raid areas outside his kingdom for slaves and to establish himself as the intermediary for any slave trader who wished to export from Madagascar's east coast. Cornering control of the main areas of the highlands from which slaves could be obtained, he used his new power to drive up prices and assemble a substantial war-chest and a powerful arsenal. So successfully did he monopolize the supply of slaves that the Betsimisaraka kings of the east coast, the successors of Ratsimilaho, took to raiding in canoes as far as the Comoro Islands and the East African coast in search of new sources of slaves for sale to French planters,[82] their expeditions sometimes gathering hundreds of canoes at a time, each with dozens of paddlers. Between 1767 and 1810, the Ile de France and the Ile Bourbon imported some 110,000 slaves, of which perhaps 45 per cent were from Madagascar.[83] The proportion of slaves originating in the central highlands is a matter of controversy,[84] but it is clear that highland kings until the late eighteenth century were heavily involved in the export both of war-captives and of their own subjects, the number of slaves remaining in Imerina in domestic service being small.

Having established a strong government at his capital of Antananarivo, Andrianampoinimerina in effect ratified many aspects of custom, representing himself as the centre of the natural order, the pillar between earth and heaven.[85] He reinforced the old ideal of the monarch as the father and mother of his people, constantly emphasized in royal speeches, in which the king would repeat that 'it is not I who has sought to reign, but you who have invited me'.[86] He has remained famous in popular memory among the Merina—the name applied increasingly after the early nineteenth century to the whole population of the central highlands in the kingdom founded by Andrianampoinimerina—largely because he succeeded in convincing subjects who remained loyal that they were safe from enslavement under his rule. In regard to those outside his kingdom, on the other hand, he was a major conqueror and slave-trader. In formal speeches, he addressed free communities that accepted his rule as Ambaniandro ('Under the Sun'). The increase in the number and security of his subjects led to a rapid development of intensive riziculture, enabling the king to fix the peasantry on precise territories, which in turn allowed him to impose various taxes or other obligations. The customary offerings made by subjects to a monarch became in Andrianampoinimerina's hands a systematic obligation on freemen to perform public works. In parts of Imerina, politically-directed communal work led to the construction of an impressive system of dykes and hydraulic works that facilitated agriculture, making Imerina into the most productive rice-growing region. The rapid development of agriculture under Andrianampoinimerina was the apogee of a process that had developed over a long period, probably from the sixteenth century.

Andrianampoinimerina's rule in Imerina marked an important break with the reign of the earlier 'brigand-chiefs',[87] the minor kings that had dominated Imerina for centuries. It constituted a more intensive and sophisticated form of government than had previously been seen. Although some earlier highland kings had followed a similar logic of political consolidation and of the encouragement of agrarian economies, in every case sustained development had been snuffed out by political conflict. Less than a century earlier, King Andriamasinavalona had succeeded in uniting Imerina but his sons had quarrelled over their inheritance, in just the same way as rival factions in Sakalava royal families had always done.

In 1809[88] King Andrianampoinimerina died in Antananarivo, the commanding hilltop settlement which he had made into his capital. By the time of his death it was already the largest town in Madagascar, reckoned to have 25,000 inhabitants,[89] surrounded by a large plain whose 'infinite number of canals and rivers' and massive system of dikes and sluices watered 'an immense area of ricefields divided into squares of a greater or lesser intensity of green, depending on their stage of maturity', as a visitor described it at a slightly later date.[90] With his combination of diplomacy, commercial acumen and military skill, Andrianampoinimerina had turned himself into the most powerful king in Madagascar, whose dominion covered the whole of the central highland region. His only serious rivals were those princes who could also command a significant share of foreign trade, like the dynasties descended from English pirates who controlled the east coast harbours at Tamatave and Foulpointe, home to most of the island's French traders, or like the ruler of the west-coast kingdom of Boina who enjoyed excellent relations with Antalaotra and Arab slave-dealers, but whose trade was suffering from the shift in the direction of trade to the east coast, where European rivals held sway. Andrianampoinimerina was respectful enough of the power of various west-coast rulers that he sealed marriage alliances with them and even received military help from them for his wars.[91] His people, according to a Malagasy writing a half century later, 'had great fear of the Sakalava people, who are famous for their bravery and great skill in the use of fire-arms'.[92]

Like the first historic Sakalava king, Lahifotsy, Andrianampoinimerina came to power by killing his own uncle—apparently a classic route. Seeking to avoid the disputes that had plagued the Sakalava kingdoms, Andrianampoinimerina arranged his own heritage by killing those of his own family who could have impeded succession by his favourite son Radama, no more than fifteen or sixteen years old when he became king of Imerina on his father's death.[93] In his first years in power the young Radama was surrounded by the advisers, diviners, and comrades-in-arms who had served his father and who had grown wealthy from the slave trade.

Madagascar and the Indian Ocean

Perhaps even more than his father, Radama was preoccupied by war throughout his reign. Within a couple of years of his accession, he was faced by risings in some areas that his father had conquered only recently, notably in the south and east of the highlands. In central Imerina the resulting campaigns were remembered as having taken men away from their farms for long periods during which they suffered terribly from fever and hunger, with the result that there was much veiled criticism of the new king.[94] These campaigns produced slaves whom the king and his counsellors could export in exchange for silver piastres or for weapons and ammunition, exactly as Andrianampoinimerina had done previously. But the interdiction on enslaving the king's own subjects meant that royal armies in search of new populations to enslave now had to go ever-greater distances towards the coasts, involving a degree of logistical organization beyond the scope of the army of unpaid farmers that highland kings had previously used. It was for this reason that one Franco-Mauritian with long experience as a slave-trader, received by King Radama in Antananarivo in July 1816, wrote that 'this trade is not far from disappearing of its own accord'.[95]

It had been Andrianampoinimerina's policy to oblige French slave-traders living on Madagascar's east coast, and apparently also Antalaotra merchants on the west coast, to travel hundreds of miles to Antananarivo to buy slaves at source, rather than sending his own caravans to the coast. This policy enabled the king to impose higher prices and to ensure that it was the foreigners who bore the risk of losing cargo on the return journey. Managing caravans of slaves from Imerina to the coast was a frankly dangerous business. For several years before the old king's death, groups of people living in the Ankay plain between the highlands and the coast, including refugees displaced by Andrianampoinimerina's wars, regularly attacked slave-caravans heading towards the sea. So serious did this become that Franco-Mauritian traders urged Andrianampoinimerina to take personal control of Ankay so as to assure freedom of passage.[96] The chronicler Raombana, writing later about events which were still in living memory, confirmed that King Radama, like his late father, was led to conquer the east of the country by a need to restore security to the trade routes as well as by the desire to seize new slaves for export.[97] As Radama pushed on with his conquests the numbers of slaves exported from Imerina increased, perhaps to as many as 4,000 per year exported to the east coast where they arrived 'formed into gangs of from 50 to 200, with iron handcuffs on their wrists'.[98] Most of these unfortunates were probably war captives, but some were re-exports, for there continued to be a brisk trade in slaves imported from Mozambique to Madagascar's west coast, and taken from there to Antananarivo by Antalaotra merchants,[99] while some Merina traders were buying slaves from elsewhere in Madagascar.[100]

In seeking to control Madagascar's east coast hinterland, Radama also had in mind a new strategic relationship.[101] This was with the British governor of Mauritius, Sir Robert Farquhar. Just a year after Andrianampoinimerina's death, British forces took control of the Ile de France, which had been used by their French enemy in the Napoleonic wars to harry British ships sailing to and from India. The island, now renamed Mauritius, was reliant on slave imports to work its plantations. The international slave trade, however, had been declared illegal by the British parliament. This placed Governor Farquhar in a difficult position. As early as 1811 he appears to have considered taking some measure to regulate the slave trade from Madagascar,[102] and he ordered one of his aides to compile extensive documentation on Madagascar which would give him the information he needed to plan his diplomatic moves.[103]

For some time the British pinned their main hopes for identifying a reliable ally in Madagascar on a prominent east-coast ruler, Jean-René. Born in 1773 in Mauritius of a French father employed by the Compagnie des Indes and a mother from Fort Dauphin in the far south of Madagascar, Jean-René had worked for the French agent at Tamatave before lending his services to the British as an interpreter, and when the British took control of Mauritius, they helped Jean-René to impose himself as the ruler of Tamatave. Only after Jean-René, himself a leading slave-shipper, had refused Farquhar's terms for a ban on slave exports[104] did Farquhar turn to Radama to offer similar terms. Contacts were established between envoys of the British governor and the king of Imerina, and they reached a series of agreements. Radama sent two of his younger brothers to be educated at Mauritius, while a sergeant of the British army, the Jamaican James Brady, was seconded to work with the king as a military advisor. These arrangements were formalized by a treaty signed in 1817 and subsequently renewed twice.

The alliance between Britain, a world power on a scale without precedent after its victory over France, and Radama, the young and ambitious demi-god in Madagascar's highlands, was to change Madagascar's history.

5

THE KINGDOM OF MADAGASCAR 1817–1895

In the middle of 1817, King Radama's army marched to Tamatave in a campaign to assert control over the main trade route from his highland domain to the coast, an arduous journey through steep terrain and thick forest. The ruler of Tamatave, Jean-René, was obliged to sign a treaty recognizing his visitor from inland as his brother, and Sir Robert Farquhar, the British governor of Mauritius, in contact with both men, agreed to mediate in the event of any further dispute.[1] Radama received a permanent political agent acting for the British government, an army sergeant named James Hastie. Later in the year, acting on behalf of his home government, Hastie signed with the king a peace treaty by which Radama agreed to forbid all slave exports from Madagascar and the government of Mauritius undertook to send him a range of military supplies in compensation.

Radama's alliance provided the king with the diplomatic and military support of the world's pre-eminent power, Great Britain, enabling him to increase his military strength beyond anything previously seen in Madagascar. In some of his future campaigns, Radama was even assisted by British warships. Furthermore, British influence was enhanced by the arrival in Imerina of missionaries from the London Missionary Society (LMS) in 1820. Radama regarded their educational work as a complement to his aim of building an effective army and bureaucracy, while LMS craftsmen also set to work making useful manufactures and teaching such skills as weaving and printing. The king personally supervised the missionaries' transcription of the Malagasy language in the Latin alphabet. With the exception of a period between the mid-1830s and 1861, British Protestant missionaries were to be close to the royal government in Antananarivo for the next seventy-five years, rejoicing in the conversion of a later queen and prime minister, in 1869, and, subsequently, of thousands of their subjects. Madagascar came to enjoy a modest reputation in Victorian Britain as a successful example of Protestant missionary endeavour.

The 1817 treaty with Great Britain was a historical turning-point. Earlier potentates had sometimes been pleased to be styled as kings of Madagascar,[2] but this was the first time that any ruler in the island had tried to conform to the new norms governing world affairs, those concerning the relations of states one with another, each constituting a stable apparatus controlling a territory and a population. Henceforth, international recognition was a major factor in Madagascar's politics. 'The relationship with the West was in the nineteenth century the major problem of power and elites', Françoise Raison has observed. 'There was a permanent transfer of institutions, technologies and representations of power in society and in the cosmos.'[3]

Sovereigns, generals, subjects

Strengthened by his British alliance, Radama I set out to submit the whole of Madagascar to his rule. He was able to put some 40,000 troops into the field.[4] They were composed, a British officer noted, 'of the ordinary peasantry of the country, led by their local chieftains, under the supreme command of the king or his officers'.[5] But, for all the manpower and the imported weapons at his disposal, Radama found that his more distant campaigns, notably in the far west of Madagascar against the Sakalava kingdom of Menabe, were beyond his logistical capacity. With British technical assistance, the king therefore designed a series of measures intended to create a standing army. It consisted of an elite permanent force trained by an army commander seconded by the British government, the Jamaican James Brady, and a rank and file conscripted on the basis of a rudimentary census of the population. Those of his subjects classified as civilians, meanwhile, were liable to forced labour on public works or any other service the king pleased to require from them.

Despite the scale of this reorganization, the king's new model army continued to suffer massively in the absence of a proper supply-train. The royal army lost as much as fifty percent of its soldiers during some of Radama's campaigns of the 1820s,[6] overwhelmingly as a result of disease and hunger. The worst losses were when they served outside the highlands. An elder described by a British missionary as 'an aged person of rank', asked 'whether this country was not more depopulated when the slave trade was carried on or now when their children are dying in the war every year', replied: 'It is quite as bad if not worse'.[7] Women took over some of the agricultural tasks traditionally performed by men,[8] their labour augmented by that of slaves captured on campaign. No longer liable to be sold for export, war-captives were instead taken back to Imerina. Radama's armies killed the whole adult male population in some areas, sparing only women and children for use as slaves. The king remained superbly unconcerned by the human cost of his campaigns and, using such methods, by about 1825, he had succeeded in conquering most of the economically useful areas of Madagascar and, crucially, in installing garrisons in the main ports.

An enthusiast for technical innovations, Radama affected a European style in personal appearance as well as in regard to military arrangements. He spoke and wrote Creole French as well as being able to write the central highland dialect of Malagasy in both Latin and Arabic scripts. He personally supervised the LMS missionaries in formalizing the transcription of the language in the Latin alphabet.[9] An Irish traveller, Henry Keating, who met the king in 1825, found him wearing a French uniform of blue with gold embroidery. At dinner, he ate in the European manner, using a knife and fork.[10] Keating described the king as five foot six or five foot seven inches tall (less than 1.68 metres), 'his face very boyish looking, so much as not to have the appearance of more than 21 or 22 years of age, although he is 33 in reality. His colour a light copper with black glossy hair cut in the English fashion and evidently a good deal of pains bestowed on it.'[11]

Alongside a standing army, Radama aimed to create a centralized bureaucracy, and to this end the LMS schools in and around Antananarivo were soon producing graduates literate in the Malagasy language whom the king employed without pay. 'Many of you are nobles', he said in an address to one of the first classes to be enrolled at an LMS school, 'and have received the honour from some noble acts done by your fathers and forefathers and not by you yourselves, but I shall consider those individuals, nobles, who would be able to read and write and do business for me as secretaries, and those alone shall receive certain marks of honour from me'.[12] He intended this new, literate, elite of service to include people from all parts of Madagascar and from various social categories.[13]

Radama followed the precedent set by earlier sovereigns in Madagascar, like the Sakalava kings of Boina, in his eclectic choice of counsellors and functionaries. His main representatives in negotiations with the British prior to the signature of the 1817 treaty, for example, were two brothers from southeast Madagascar who were literate in the *sorabe* script.[14] Included in the upper reaches of power were the French mulatto ruler of Tamatave, Jean-René, and, later, Jean-René's nephew, Aristide Coroller. Radama chose some key officials and advisers from ruling families from outside the central districts of Imerina that constituted the core of his kingdom. He often took junior wives from these families and gave his own female relatives in marriage to cement relationships with royal dynasties from various parts of the highlands outside his father's home province of Avaradrano. Both King Radama I and the sovereigns who succeeded him after his death in 1828 appointed British and French nationals to positions in their service as technical experts. The most famous of these was Jean Laborde (1805–78), who became a fixture at the royal court in Antananarivo in the middle years of the century. A blacksmith's son from France's southwest, Laborde arrived in Madagascar in 1831. His remarkable talents as a craftsman led to his being employed by the government to build an arms and munition factory and to supervise other attempts at manufacturing local copies of imported goods. In the 1840s Laborde had no fewer than 20,000 forced labourers working in his factories at Mantasoa.[15]

By the time Laborde appeared at court, power was no longer in the hands of the sovereign, but lay rather with the leading officers of the army. After Radama I's death in 1828, the succession was rigged by a coterie of generals from the Avaradrano district in favour of one of the late king's wives, who took the title of Queen Ranavalona I (1828–61). In effect, her accession was the result of a military coup, and from that date until the eventual collapse of the state in 1895–6, the leading military officers and traders, endlessly manoeuvring for factional advantage, were the real power behind successive monarchs. The only exception was during the brief reign of Radama II, king from 1861 to 1863. He tried to reassert royal independence and was murdered by a group of officers and senior officials, confirming the grip of the oligarchy.

The attempt to create institutions of government that were a hybrid of indigenous and imported models was a major theme of Madagascar's nineteenth century. European contemporaries, believing that their own models of government represented progress, applauded innovations that they saw as positive, and were alarmed by the ostentatious revival of traditional religion that was a feature of the reign of Queen Ranavalona I. From the late 1860s, this state was ruled by a constitutional monarch and her consort, Prime Minister Rainilaiarivony, grandson of one of Andrianampoinimerina's generals. In 1877, the government passed legislation to free imported slaves, a measure greeted by most missionaries as progress, and to establish European-style institutions. To many British missionaries of the time, this looked like real evidence of the advance of civilization. The government in Antananarivo was considered in international law and diplomacy as the capital of the sovereign state of Madagascar, a fledgling member of the international family of states.

None of this was what it seemed to Europeans at first sight, however. Imported institutions functioned in a local context; foreign ideas and practices were understood in indigenous terms. The apparent lurch from Radama I's thirst for innovation, through his successor's attempt to revive indigenous forms of government, to an outwardly Victorian style of Protestant respectability among the upper classes, overlay a discernible continuity in dynastic power and patronage. As a colonial official later wrote, 'this whole administrative facade, although of recent creation, was, at the time we assumed control, a ruin in Imerina, and a utopia in other parts'.[16]

Oligarchy

The main architect and chief beneficiary of successive attempts to fuse the type of state recommended by British missionaries and foreign diplomats with local economic and social realities was an oligarchy that was able to operate in repertoires both indigenous and foreign. The most powerful oligarchs were from families from the Avaradrano district of Imerina, the micro-kingdom where King Andrianampoinimerina had come to power in 1778. These oligarchs created durable relations with provincial elites far distant from the centre of the island, giving a degree of stability to the political system created by Radama I and modified in subsequent reigns. The disconnection between a Victorian ideal of progress, on the one hand, and the reality of a government that was massively wasteful in human life and cared little about economic efficiency, on the other hand, became increasingly apparent over time.

A key element of the oligarchic system of government was labour. Throughout the nineteenth century, many population groups that were subject to the effective control of the government in Antananarivo were required to work without pay, either as slaves or as forced labourers.[17] Command of unpaid labour was a mainstay of political rule. The mass recruitment of workers, for example to haul huge tree trunks dozens of kilometres to build a royal palace, often had little economic rationale, serving rather as a display of political control. The lack of wages depressed markets for consumer goods, concentrating wealth in a small circle. In the first half of the century, before royal armies had lost the ability to conduct sustained campaigns, senior officers grew rich through slave-raiding and plunder. 'The booty obtained in War is nearly all divided among the Officers and of course the higher the rank the larger the share', noted an LMS missionary in 1833, 'so that a mere fragment falls to the last of the great mass.'[18] The same officers also enjoyed a near-monopoly on import-export trade with Mauritius and Réunion since they could control all of Madagascar's harbours and fix prices through their networks of clients and retainers. The only exceptions were a few west-coast ports that, at least until the advent of steamships, were too far away to be able to participate in the most important overseas trade, which was with the two Mascarene Islands. The leading plutocrats owned vast herds of cattle, tended by their slaves, in the grazing-lands adjacent to Imerina. They used these herds to supply beasts for export to Mauritius and Réunion islands. From 1845 to 1854 the government in Antananarivo imposed a ban on trade to the two islands as a result of a diplomatic incident, but this was a two-edged weapon, since these sanctions hurt the magnates as well as their customers. Later in the century, when free trade had reduced the profitability of the key export trades, senior officials in Antananarivo could use official postings in the provinces as sources of income. A government minister could sell an official title as a prebend, and the purchaser would then use the position to make money. By the 1890s an important governorship could cost as much as 30,000 piastres.[19]

The relative distribution of wealth between the sovereign and the leading families of the oligarchy changed during the century. In Radama I's time, the annual royal revenue from all sources — mostly customs dues and taxes on captures of slaves — varied between 22,000 and 50,000 silver piastres,[20] Madagascar's most widely accepted form of coin. Thirty years later Queen Ranavalona had a treasury containing some 500–600,000 piastres. This sum was less than the fortune of some individual courtiers; by comparison, the French trader Napoléon de Lastelle, who ran various industrial and shipping projects in partnership with government officials, is reckoned at the height of his career before 1845 to have been worth some 2.3 million piastres. He owned thirteen ships in partnership with Julien-Gaultier de Rontaunay.[21] In 1855, the crown prince, the future Radama II, signed a contract with a syndicate of French entrepreneurs led by one Joseph Lambert, granting these businessmen a vast land concession, a monopoly on mining and extractive industries, and numerous other provisions, in exchange for a promise of political support. The crown prince signed this document in a bid to undermine the power of the leading oligarchs by using a foreign alliance as leverage. On learning of Lambert's charter, the government carried out a series of arrests, and there was a sharp rise in anti-European feeling. When the young prince succeeded to the throne as Radama II in 1861, he continued his pro-European line by implementing a free trade policy. 'The King authorised every man to become his own salesman, to dispose of his goods on his own terms; and, in order to imitate free trade in its widest possible exent, he abolished all export and import duties', the Reverend William Ellis, a leading British missionary, noted with satisfaction.[22] The king wrote to the governors of Mauritius and Réunion with an invitation to traders and settlers to establish themselves in Madagascar. He allowed missionaries to return and proceeded to sell them land in spite of a traditional interdiction on alienating land to foreigners[23]— a provision that exists, in theory at least, to the present day. He signed foreign treaties in September and December 1862.

It was not only powerful courtiers who were offended by Radama II's reforms, but also large numbers of his subjects, profoundly disturbed by the rupture of the rituals of royal service that were required to ensure ancestral blessing. Some became possessed by ancestral spirits, articulating a form of protest.[24] Just two years after his accession, the king was murdered by conspirators from an elite faction. These events led to a serious haemorrhage of coin from Madagascar, as the government was obliged to pay France an indemnity of 240,000 silver piastres for cancellation of the disastrous Lambert charter. Of this sum, 140,000 piastres came from the royal treasury, and the rest from loans to the government from the prime minister and his family.[25] Some twenty years later, in 1886, after France had won a brief war that it had fought only half-heartedly, the government in Antananarivo was obliged to accept a loan of 15 million francs, at six per cent interest, from a French bank, in order to pay a further indemnity. Interest on this loan was paid regularly up to 1895.[26] By then, the royal treasury contained only about 400,000 gold francs (roughly equivalent to 80,000 piastres), earmarked for arms purchases and the expenses of the court.[27] By that time the leading oligarch, Prime Minister Rainilaiarivony, grandson of one of Andrianampoinimerina's generals, had a personal fortune, including in property, cattle and slaves, reckoned at 140,000 piastres.[28]

For almost three-quarters of a century after the coup of 1828, power in the kingdom of Madagascar was exercised through several intertwined elements. One was the existence of a network of officials who were formally regarded as administrators carrying out the wishes of the monarch, but who in fact were placemen in the service of one or other of the rival ministers and generals who were the arbiters of power. Senior generals enjoyed the personal allegiance of hundreds of junior officers known as *deka* (a word derived from *aides-de-camp*). They also had many other retainers and dependents whom they placed in strategic positions. Junior officials of the government could try to improve their standing by manoeuvring between the patronage networks of rival grandees. Top officers, noted a son of Rainilaiarivony, the prime minister and royal consort who dominated the government from the 1860s to 1895, 'not knowing what to do with [their] aides de camp, sent them to the coasts to trade on their behalf'.[29] Since no official received a salary, state functionaries maintained themselves at the direct expense of the populations they were formally required to administer. A second element of the system of government was the vital role of the monarch in sustaining the cosmic order. The most important duty of sovereigns was to transmit blessing—*hasina*—from the royal ancestors to the people. This they did through rhetoric and ritual, emphasizing the real and deep bond between themselves and their subjects. The monarch's religious role was in fact probably the main factor keeping the kingdom of Madagascar in existence. Its ritual form was to change on several occasions during the nineteenth century, but most notably after Queen Ranavalona II and her prime minister, Rainilaiarivony, converted to Christianity in 1869. A third pillar of government depended on the circulation of wealth, especially in the form of silver coin, cattle and slaves. Members of the ruling oligarchy used their command of unpaid labour to keep control of these assets and undercut the commercial activities of foreigners. During the second half of the nineteenth-century European governments and the USA became increasingly insistent that the commercial interests and legal rights of their own citizens be respected, and this resulted in increasingly frequent diplomatic wrangles.

In reality, neither King Radama I nor his successors ever achieved effective authority over the whole of Madagascar. After Radama's initial success in installing military garrisons at strategic points along the island's coasts in the 1820s, areas of western and southern Madagascar hundreds of kilometres long and broad escaped all real control by the government in Antananarivo. For, despite the formal adoption of European conventions of statehood, the exercise of royal power remained concerned primarily with the management of people, in time-honoured fashion, rather than with the systematic control of territory as a mark of sovereignty, in the European manner. Army deserters and fugitives from forced labour, escaping from the grasp of officialdom in the central districts of the kingdom where the government had the strongest grip, formed bandit-groups or 'maroon' communities that could, over time, acquire a distinct social identity. Some of these agglomerations of fugitives put themselves under the protection of independent Sakalava kings in the west, or of Bara kings in the south of the country. Some groups, particularly in the sparsely-populated areas to the west, north and south of the highlands, existed on the margins of two royal authorities and professed loyalty to each or to both, depending on the circumstances. Hence, it would be misleading to think of Madagascar in the nineteenth century as being divided into independent states with clear boundaries, for not only were the frontiers between different polities unclear, but so were degrees of allegiance imprecise. Many groups composed of fugitives from Imerina maintained contact with kin and other networks in the highlands, while at the same time declaring themselves to be Sakalava or Marofotsy, the latter being a group formed by slaves who had escaped from the regions of Imerina and Antsihanaka.

The ready adoption of political labels by minor lineages or leagues of families that nevertheless retained their original name illustrates the profusion of identities, their adaptability, and their often conjunctural nature. The nineteenth-century kingdom based in Antananarivo retained the fluid political identities that are one of the red threads of Madagascar's history. However, it is also possible to detect in the activities of royal officials and the writings of Protestant-schooled scholars the faint beginnings of a colonial-style ethnography.

Bandits and raiders of all sorts became steadily more aggressive as the royal army became ineffective outside its core area, due to poor organization, the low morale of unpaid conscript soldiers, and the primacy accorded by officers to commerce and politics rather than to military affairs. A list of military expeditions compiled by a senior government official indicates that by the 1850s the government was hardly capable of fielding more than 2,000 men on an expedition outside its own borders.[30] Thirty years later, the government had so little influence over large tracts of southern and western Madagascar that kings from rival dynasties implanted in these areas, Sakalava in the west and Bara in the centre-south, were able to organize raids for cattle and slaves deep into the highlands. It is notable that even this degree of military weakness hardly threatened the existence of the kingdom based in Antananarivo, as the Sakalava and Bara kings who benefited from slave-raids and the mass theft of cattle showed no inclination to assert any system of regular territorial control over the highlands.

As the government in Antananarivo weakened during the course of the nineteenth century, Sakalava kings especially, being in effective control of much of the west coast, were able to secure commercial alliances with European, American, Antalaotra, Arab and Indian traders in a revival of the system of commerce and power that had existed on the west coast a century and more earlier. They benefited from the boom in demand for cloves and ivory that was fuelling a demand for slaves to work in Zanzibar. The East African island was a possession of the sultans of Oman, rulers of a thalassocracy that spread from the ports of western India to Muscat and East Africa. The brokers and bankers of this commercial empire were Indian merchants. Its slaves came from Africa and, sometimes, Madagascar. Arab, Indian and Swahili networks cultivated the traditional East African and south Arabian connection with parts of west Madagasacar that were effectively independent of

Antananarivo. An Anglican bishop who visited the northwest coast in 1876 found the port of Anorontsanga to be 'quite as important as Tamatave, but with this difference, that here you have no Europeans. The Arabs and Kutch men are the traders. There are also many Swahili from Zanzibar. There is also a large number of Mozambiques [i.e. African slaves], and there can be no doubt that it is a great centre of the slave trade.' Anorontsanga, the same visitor noted, had two mosques and six imams.[31] This, we may note, was the probable site of the port of Sada that had flourished two-and-a-half centuries earlier.

In places like Anorontsanga, local elites enjoyed extensive autonomy. Governors and other officials appointed by Antananarivo became steadily more inclined to make common cause with local notables and to immerse themselves in local politics and commerce rather than to follow the orders of the central government or to act in its interest. The changing relationship of trade and investment in central Madagascar had the significant (and, by Europeans, unforeseen) consequence of causing an increase in the slave trade, as slaves were increasingly imported to Imerina from Africa not for their capacity as labourers, but simply, wrote one missionary, because 'slaves are often bought as cattle are bought as a good money investment'.[32] Another British missionary writing in the 1870s noted that 'not seldom were pure African slaves, knowing but little of the Malagasy tongue, met with in the Capital and other parts of Imerina. The people in general know them as "Mojambikas".' These were people imported from East Africa to satisfy a continuing demand for slaves in Imerina. The same writer found slaves imported from East Africa 'still more numerous ... in the seven garrison towns in the north west.'[33] Sakalava kings were well placed to benefit from the trade both in Merina captives taken in raids into the central highlands, whom they sold on to Arab traders, and, vice versa, from the commerce in African captives imported and sold on to Imerina.[34]

A good description from the later nineteenth century of the military forts intended to guard the borders of the kingdom and to oversee trade came from the pen of the Reverend James Sibree of the London Missionary Society after his visit to the southeast of Madagascar in 1876. He described a typical garrison, a wooden fort with guards posted at its gates. 'Like most of the Hova [i.e. Merina] colonies and military posts all over Madagascar', Sibree wrote, 'the four forts in this south-eastern part of the island ... were built at the close of the first Radama's reign or in the early part of the first Ranavalona's', [35] or in other words around 1825–35. At another government post Sibree found a garrison that contained twenty-seven soldiers, a church with ten members, twenty people able to read and write, and a school. The governor, in harness for twenty years, owned a wine-store stocked with claret. On formal occasions he wore an old-fashioned European uniform from the Duke of Wellington's day, complete with cocked hat. He owned 500 cattle and 200 slaves, which, Sibree observed, made him 'very rich'.[36] Not the least striking feature of Merina garrisons in coastal areas like this was the strong memory of what Sibree called 'the cruelties practiced by Radama's and Ranavalona's generals.' As a result of the slaving expeditions of the 1820s and 1830s, he noted, 'a large proportion of the slave population of Imerina are descended from the Taimoro, Taisaka, and other tribes on this south-east coast'.[37] Sibree had recruited his porters in Imerina, and some of them, while they were travelling with the missionary in the southeast, met relatives from whom they had been separated since being seized as war-captives in their childhood. 'The most remarkable circumstance was that our cook discovered that one of the governor's wives at Ankarana was his mother's sister'.[38] This observation concerning the origin of so many of Imerina's servile class tells us much not only about popular memories of the wars of the early nineteenth century, but also about the nature of ethnicity at the same period, as it meant that a high proportion of the highland population had a recent origin in other parts of the island. Even many free lineages that lived in Imerina had recent histories of migration. 'Merina' itself was a political identity, without great genealogical depth, while some Sakalava and other groups consisted largely of fugitives or emigrants from the central highlands.

The state internationally recognized as the Kingdom of Madagascar, then, did not exercise a homogeneous or consistent power over a precisely-defined territory. Nor did it seriously aspire to safeguard the welfare of its subjects, not even in its heartland of Imerina—the Merina peasantry was to be one of the most evident victims of the oligarchic system of government that was established in the 1820s and that lasted until the last years of the century. A French Jesuit who visited Antananarivo in 1855, Marc Finaz, and who received information from Jean Laborde, concluded that the class of free peasants that constituted the backbone of Merina society was being destroyed by forced labour and military service.[39] In general, forced labour was used steadily less for agricultural or industrial production or for works of real public usefulness, and functioned as the public performance of a political relationship of inequality. One paradoxical result noted by Finaz was that 'many slaves refuse manumission if it is offered to them'.[40] If they were mistreated, slaves were liable to run away and join the maroon communities which existed in various parts of Madagascar, to the extent that many of the servile communities established by the leading officials and plutocrats to keep their vast herds soon ceased to do much more than make a token gift of cattle to their masters and were otherwise left largely to their own devices. Freemen, by contrast, were tied to their ancestral land by social and religious obligation and could not move so easily. In the course of time the lot of a slave became easier than that of a freeman in Imerina in more ways than one. It became increasingly common for slaves to insist on remaining nominally attached to their masters even when they had virtual freedom.[41] In truth, the entity internationally known as the Kingdom of Madagascar was based not so much on slavery as on the forced labour of subjects who were only nominally free.

There exists no account of the middle years of the century more revealing than the chronicles written by the Queen's private secretary, Raombana. Born into one of the royal families of Imerina that had been eclipsed by the line of King Andrianampoinimerina, he was sent for education in Manchester at the height of Radama I's alliance with Britain and joined the royal service on his return. He wrote in English as a precaution against his often scathing comments being read by others.[42] Raombana described how generals and oligarchs became enormously wealthy, owning hundreds of slaves and thousands of cattle. He confirmed that 'these [military] expeditions has costed [sic] Her Majesty the deaths of thousands of her soldiers, which almost depopulated Imerina'.[43] Thousands more royal subjects died in purges of people accused of various forms of religious subversion, the accusations often being manipulated or initiated by royal officials for reasons of self-interest, either to confiscate the goods and lands of a convicted person or to attack supporters of rival political factions.[44] In 1839 and 1840, for example, the queen's chief minister eliminated the leading independent traders of the east coast by having them accused of witchcraft.[45]

Of all the exactions visited on the population, forced labour was the most unpopular. It was an old-established principle—recorded, for example, in southeast Madagascar in the seventeenth century—that subjects should do team-work for their sovereign as a public performance of a political bond.[46] Labour-dues were already being used for productive purposes in the highlands in the time of the slave export trade, when some highland kings put their subjects to work on intensive rice cultivation. During the nineteenth century, forced labour became simply a general obligation to be performed at the royal whim or, in practice, at the behest of officials. After 1869, following the same logic, Christian monarchs presented an obligation to attend school as a form of compulsory royal service.

With the passage of time, this burden of unpaid labour fell on a decreasing share of the population. Although population figures are very imprecise, [47] a fair estimate may be that Madagascar had at the very most three million inhabitants in the mid-nineteenth century, of whom up to one third lived in Imerina. The first systematic census of the whole island, in 1905, was to give a figure of 2,650,000 natives.[48] These figures, apart from being unreliable, do not reveal the major changes in the composition of the population during the nineteenth century. This occurred especially in Imerina, where there was a reduction in the numbers of free families in the sense of those belonging to the categories of *hova* and *andriana*, the only ones regarded as full subjects of the queen. This decline was because of the loss in their numbers due to military service and forced labour, enslavement for debt or other offences, and simple penury. After the relaxation of controls on internal migration in the 1860s, there was a marked emigration of Merina freemen as settlers to Betsileo and the east coast. Probably half or two-thirds of male freemen in the central province were classed as soldiers, although the army had become incapable of effective military action by this date.[49] By the late nineteenth century as many as 40–50% of the population of Imerina belonged to the category of household slaves,[50] perhaps 300,000 of them in central Imerina alone.[51] Around Antananarivo, as many as two out of every three people were slaves.[52] As we have seen, many of these slaves had family origins in other parts of the island or in East Africa; they may be regarded as Merina only insofar as they lived in the province of Imerina. This fact obliges us to regard with the greatest caution notions of colonial origin concerning the racial homogeneity of specific ethnic groups, and regarding the stability of these units over time. Some of these ideas concerning ethnic purity have been used in more recent times by ethnographers and anthropologists in an effort to define the essential characteristics of each group, as well as by politicians of an ethno-nationalist persuasion.

Such changes in the composition of the population had an adverse effect on agricultural production. It was again Raombana who remarked that 'By thus continually getting new recruits for to supply the place of those who dies in the wars and in the military stations, Imerina is in a fair way of getting depopulated and as the country is not so well cultivated as formerly on account of this, and the numerous feudal services, provisions are getting very dear...'.[53] There was a decline in the infrastructure of dikes and irrigation canals that had so impressed visitors a hundred years earlier by its efficiency and orderliness, a source of popular pride. By the late nineteenth century the army was incapable even of defending its heartland against raids from independent areas of the island in the west and south, which by the late 1880s were very heavy.

What sort of regime was this? Despite the domination of the government after 1828 by a handful of families from the area immediately north of Antananarivo, it is, on balance, misleading to describe the state as a 'Merina empire' as one historian has argued.[54] 'Empire' remains an elusive term, used to designate a great variety of political and economic regimes, but is usually thought to designate rule over different ethnic communities.[55] The kings and queens who reigned in Antananarivo were known by the same title—*mpanjaka*—as sovereigns in other parts of the island, suggesting that people did not perceive them to belong to a different category of power-holder that would require a different name. To call it 'the kingdom of Imerina'[56] risks implying that this government purported to rule over a specific regionally-based group in something approaching the modern sense of the word 'ethnic', which was not the case, as successive sovereigns of Antananarivo aimed to incorporate all the island's people under a single sovereignty. None of the island's polities was ever based on a vision of continuous territorial control. Before the twentieth century, Madagascar was not divided into distinct, non-porous ethnic groups in the sense conveyed by the latter term today. While there were notable regional variations in language, dress and other cultural markers, there was also a long history of migration between different parts of the island, including by ritual experts, traders, slaves and others circulating from one region to another. As earlier chapters have described, the circulation of ideas and people had resulted in a certain continuity in matters of royal organization, ideology and personnel between kingdoms in various parts of the island. The tendency for ethnographers to consider the Merina as a distinct population of a type different from other Malagasy was largely the consequence of the conscious import of techniques and ideas by the Antananarivo government during the course of the nineteenth century.[57]

In the last resort, in this book we have chosen to call this entity by its formal name, the Kingdom of Madagascar, while being aware of the oligarchic nature of the state and of its failure to control large areas of the island. The sovereigns in Antananarivo were not the first potentates to claim to be the paramount rulers in Madagascar,[58] without being able to give the title the substance of homogeneous territorial control. However, in securing formal recognition from Great Britain, Radama I set the island on a distinctive path, often marked by extreme violence. He had an ambition to exert his sovereignty over the whole of Madagascar, and his strategy of enlisting foreigners to this end was to mark its history indelibly.

Visions of society

Formal recognition by the major powers of the day, starting with Great Britain, later joined by France, the USA and others, was a key element in the establishment and survival of the Kingdom of Madagascar as well as an indicator of just how strong the new global currents of diplomacy and commerce were. States operating on a global scale required reliable partners and interlocutors in all parts of the world, and European diplomats and traders were no longer satisfied to do business with individual potentates or entrepreneurs in the same way as they had a century earlier. Thus, even when Sakalava and Bara kings became able to launch heavy raids into the highlands, in the last quarter of the nineteenth century, European and American diplomats maintained formal recognition of the Kingdom of Madagascar as a sovereign state, in conformity with the policy of their home governments. French strategists were often tempted by the idea of forming a Franco-Sakalava alliance to counter what they saw as a British-Merina axis, but their arguments never altered the French government policy of maintaining formal recognition of the Kingdom of Madagascar until the moment of colonization. As for business operators, while some American traders, in particular, were active on the west coast,[59] most European merchants continued to cluster on the east coast or in Antananarivo, despite the general lack of economic dynamism of these areas in the later nineteenth century. There is no clearer demonstration of the primacy of the government in Antananarivo, for all its many weaknesses, than the fact that later, after France had occupied the island and declared the Kingdom of Madagascar to be abolished, French colonial officials soon found themselves adapting much of its legacy and human resources for their own purposes.

From today's vantage point, we may wonder why the Kingdom of Madagascar lasted as long as it did. Its longevity was due largely to the emerging European demand for formal, legally binding agreements concerning consular and commercial matters that the government in Antananarivo was able to satisfy better than any of the island's independent kings. The leading global powers increasingly sought to do business with authorities having an institutional existence solid enough to sign binding treaties and agreements covering trade rules, land purchase, title-deeds, and a growing range of emerging global issues, and able to implement these same measures. Lobbies were developing in the leading industrial and military powers of the world that took an interest in the internal affairs of distant places like Madagascar on humanitarian or religious grounds, such as the Anti-Slavery Society and the various missionary societies, or that pressed for market access for their manufactured goods, and they were able to put pressure on their home governments to enforce measures intended to further these aims. European governments and their US counterpart increasingly took formal responsibility for the welfare of their citizens worldwide, and were prepared to hold others to account in terms of an emerging body of rules and conventions that constituted the growing field of international relations and international law. A leading British political economist, writing in 1867, referred to the quality necessary for correct commercial and financial dealings as 'national good faith'. This could, he thought, be reduced to three elements: 'a continuous polity; a fixed political morality; and a constant possession of money'.[60] This was a succinct description of the requirements of the world's leading financial and diplomatic powers. It was in early pursuit of a continuous polity of the sort required by global powers that British advisers in the 1820s had fed Radama I's ambition to create a uniform national language and a standing army, calculated to enable him to dominate the island of Madagascar and thus to become a partner valuable to Britain. In indigenous terms, Radama's aspirations emerged from a historical notion of the universal sovereign that was deeply embedded in local political culture.

It would have been logical if one of the Sakalava kings were to have profited from the military weakness of Antananarivo in order to turn his own superiority into a formal status of sovereignty with the recognition of France or some other powerful state, taking over the role of leading interlocutor with external powers. That this did not happen was because systems of government operated by kings independent of Antananarivo were unsuitable for the purpose of global player, depending as they did on slave-raiding and plunder, the same qualities that had made them suitable trade partners for European traders in an age of mercantilism two centuries earlier. In European or American terms, the Sakalava and Bara kingdoms were archaic in the sense of not conforming to contemporary Western ideas of order or utility. For these reasons, it is not accurate to suppose that there was a renaissance of Sakalava monarchies in the 1870s or 1880s, even though the power of Sakalava kings increased relative to that of their Merina counterparts, and even though west-coast traders profited from the prevailing conditions.

The relationship between Malagasy sovereign and global power was thus an ambiguous one, from which both parties strove to draw advantage. This relationship, moreover, developed during a long period of rivalry between France and Britain for regional influence in the Indian Ocean, which sharpened after a resumption of Franco-British-Malagasy commercial relations in the 1850s, following a diplomatically-induced suspension in 1845, and in the face of factional rivalries within the royal court in Antananarivo that were reflected in competing patronage systems that spread countrywide. Pressures to create new types of trade agreement came not only from without, but also from within. Although Queen Ranavalona I was under the influence of army officers who profited from wars of plunder and the capture of slaves, she also had to take account of the existence of a class of merchants with wider commercial interests, allied to the generals who controlled the seaports. The leading military and commercial faction was known as Andafiavaratra.

The problem of legitimacy

The Andafiavaratra faction was the real arbiter of power after the coups of 1828 and 1863, but the families that constituted this group could not make any serious claim to authority in their own right based on custom or precedent. Like earlier kingdoms in Madagascar, the royal government in Antananarivo was held to be properly ruled only by an *andriambahoaka*, the universal sovereign at the centre of the earth. It was therefore essential for these ambitious oligarchs to control the monarch, the centre of legitimate authority. The Andafiavaratra faction was originally formed around a *hova* family that commanded military expeditions on behalf of King Andrianampoinimerina when he set out to conquer all of the highlands in the 1780s. A hundred years later, the leader of the faction was Rainilaiarivony, the grandson of one of these generals. Appointed prime minister in 1864, he married three queens in succession and remained the real leader of the government until the French invasion of 1895. He built a massive palace on the top of the rugged crest that dominates Antananarivo, alongside the royal palace, symbolizing the nature of a power that had become bicephalous. The prime minister's palace still stands today, next to the carcass of the royal palace gutted by an arson attack in 1995, now being rebuilt.

It is instructive to consider the means that were used by elite factions to stay in power over several generations. Andrianampoinimerina rewarded his leading friends and supporters from his home province of Avaradrano with high office and other trappings of power, including guardianship of the *sampy* or religious talismans that he had confiscated from conquered groups and that he built into a national pantheon. After the death of their original benefactor in 1809, the Andafiavaratra and other leading families strove to maintain their position in a kingdom that was both greatly enlarged and radically transformed in nature. The most powerful officials of the Kingdom of Madagascar were drawn from families that had established themselves in positions of privilege and power at nodes of internal and external networks at key moments, notably during the wars of conquest by Andrianampoinimerina and the military coup of 1828. Over three or four generations, these oligarchs showed little sign of any ideological aspiration to govern beyond the interests of their own family or faction; this was not a government that maintained any general commitment to improving the welfare of its subjects, other than in occasional rhetorical declarations.

Broadly speaking, from the coup of 1828 until Radama II's brief reign in 1861–3, leading oligarchs aimed to stay in power by associating themselves with popular reverence for the monarch, deemed to join heaven and earth and to be the dispenser of *hasina*, the power to live and to fertilize the land. There was intense popular attachment to rituals connected with the monarchy, such as the circumcision and new-year ceremonies, and to the religious talismans that were held to embody local power. These became part of an expanded system of government.

The networks most closely associated with traditional cosmology and its attendant rituals generally consisted of local notables at the village level. These were connected to competing factions at the royal court. Religious authorities at local level included diviners and clerics, village heads, and others, sometimes collectively dubbed by Europeans 'the old *hova* party'. An astute French diplomat late in the century described this social stratum as consisting of 'small landowners, people receiving rents, all those who don't work and are afraid of contact with foreigners and the rapid increase in prices'.[61] Associated with these networks was a redoubtable arm of factional competition — the power to launch or adjudicate accusations of spiritual subversion or witchcraft. According to custom, the surest way of testing this was to impose a poison ordeal on the person suspected. With power effectively unregulated other than by factional intrigue, but expressed in terms of traditional ritual and performance, use of the poison ordeal became very widespread. A series of purges from the 1830s to the 1850s killed tens of thousands of people and ran out of control. Local officials sought quotas of victims to demonstrate their loyalty to the government, while rival courtiers accused provincial officials in order to install their own placemen and extend their client-systems.[62]

The need to claim legitimacy for a regime which, although decked in outwardly traditional forms, in reality articulated some radical new forces, led to a massive inflation of representations of power. During Ranavalona I's reign, lauding the queen as a living embodiment of the high god, her courtiers organized elaborate ceremonies and formal balls where they wore sumptuous, exotic costumes based on Arab and Sakalava as well as European originals. Visitors recorded being received by the queen 'seated on crossed legs and atop a sofa, shaded by a red silk parasol bordered with fringes and gold embroidery' in the oriental manner previously used by Sakalava kings.[63] The Reverend William Ellis, received at court in 1856, saw dances in the Sakalava style performed before courtiers rigged out in Arab costumes that included enormous turbans. This was followed by European-style dances. Invited to join in, the puritanical Ellis confessed that he did not know how to dance. 'It was a scene which it was perhaps well to witness once in a lifetime', he thought. 'It appeared something like the reality of what the gorgeous and imposing pageants of our theatres are reported to represent'.[64] (He appears never to have seen the inside of a theatre personally.) For one court occasion, a headdress was ordered from the costumier of the Paris Opera, via one of the small group of French traders who had an entrée at the court.[65]

Grafted on to networks that were constituted by quasi-traditional forms were those produced by such innovations as the standing army and the schools, both first established in the 1820s. The first cohorts of graduates, though relatively few in number, assumed key bureaucratic positions in the royal government. It was reckoned that by the time the LMS missionaries were expelled from Antananarivo in 1836, 'there were four thousand officers employed, who transacted the business of their respective departments by writing'.[66] Many of the elite who occupied senior bureaucratic and military positions being graduates of the LMS mission-schools, they were privately quite well disposed to Christianity even during the 1840s and 1850s, when there was ferocious persecution of dissidents or perceived opponents of every type, including the martyrdom of dozens of Christian converts. Although there were only a few hundred baptized Christians, obliged after 1835 to hide their allegiance on pain of death, some rich families retained mission-trained tutors at home to teach reading and writing to their children. In the worst period of persecutions and purges, a form of opposition coalesced around the person of the crown prince, the very signatory of the disastrous Lambert charter, negotiated in a bid to secure foreign support. Passionately interested in Christianity and European thought, he was considered by many to be a messiah who would soon come to rescue his people from their troubles.[67] By the time he ascended the throne as Radama II in 1861, the number of Christians was, at the very most, no more than about 4–5,000 people in Antananarivo and 2,000 in the rest of Imerina.[68] Religion was inseparable from political allegiance, and thus the emergence of a Christian community was also taken as a contestation of the traditional religious forms that constituted the institutions of government in the mid-nineteenth century. For those who held to older religious ideas, adherence to Christianity was tantamount to an act of allegiance to a foreign king and his ancestors, for was not Christ described by the missionaries as a king?

Religious practice also shaped individual behaviour. Both Radama I and Radama II, conscious of the existential superiority bestowed on them by their royal status, articulated ideas of ethics, duty and taboo strikingly different from those of their subjects.[69] Radama I once told a French painter who was busy with his portrait, André Coppalle, that he didn't believe in religion or divination at all. 'He even laughs about this sometimes, and he ... told me that it was a political affair', Coppalle wrote. 'He questioned me one day on my own religious opinions, and having in my turn put a few questions to him on this subject, he replied to me among other things that religions were merely *political institutions, good for guiding children of all ages*.'[70] The Reverend William Ellis, who visited the country three times in the 1850s, thought that many courtiers 'belong to a numerous class here, neither Christian nor heathen, but simply shrewd worldly men'.[71] These foreign visitors may have misinterpreted political cynicism, wrongly identifying it as religious agnosticism.[72]

A succession of European missionaries, diplomats and travellers urged Malagasy ministers and officials to implement radical measures intended to promote what the Victorians were inclined to call 'civilization', the direct ancestor of the twentieth-century notion of development. Such measures generally included abandoning certain aspects of traditional religion deemed to be offensive, maintaining the ban on slave exports, encouraging the spread of literacy, and stimulating foreign trade. Christian missionaries also urged religious conversion, both in its outward forms and in regard to processes of personal self-fashioning. There were senior government officials who showed real interest in European ideas of economic and political progress, as Radama I and Radama II both did. The royal archives contain circulars from 1839–40 addressed to garrison commanders ordering them to report on the possibilities of developing their areas, and at a later date, the official gazette encouraged governors to extend agriculture in empty regions.[73] Among those who learned to read and who were exposed to European and Christian thought, there were some who developed an intense curiosity towards new ideas about the nature of the world and of society.

The establishment by European missionary societies in the 1860s of Christian congregations with freedom to worship opened a space of discussion on the nature of society, small though it was, that was the precursor of an enduring connection between Christianity, education and erudition, and politics. Christianity contained within it the germ of a genuine civil society. When Prime Minister Rainilaiarivony converted to Christianity in 1869, it was largely as a means of taking strategic control of the growingly influential Christian faction. The political and intellectual space formed by practitioners of imported religion grew in importance each time the governing power tried to incorporate it.

Whether under the guise of technical innovation, or of the restoration of religious tradition that was official government policy from the early 1830s to 1861, or of Christianity, oligarchic rule played havoc with the constitution of Imerina as it was represented in oral traditions and historical precedent. It is clear from a careful reading of the many oral traditions written down in the mid-nineteenth century, as well as from the events after the eventual colonization of the island by France, that there was a general perception throughout central Madagascar that Imerina had a classical constitutional form dating from the period before the establishment of the Kingdom of Madagascar.[74] Briefly, monarchs were traditionally represented as ruling through a compact made between themselves or their predecessors and the descent-groups often labelled by European contemporaries 'clans' or 'tribes', which the Merina call *firenena*. These compacts were recalled during national rituals such as circumcision ceremonies or the annual feast of the royal bath. Group rights were confirmed by popular acclaim at mass meetings. The *sampy* — the group talismans that Andrianampoinimerina had gathered from different parts of his kingdom and assembled into a national pantheon — were key components of the unwritten constitution. Thus the official burning of the *sampy* in 1869 was a consequence of the royal conversion to Christianity that also marked a repudiation of older constitutional guarantees. Tens of thousands of royal subjects formally adopted the new religion out of loyalty. Adherence to Christianity, particularly in the Protestant form favoured by the LMS, was seen as a test of political reliability. Most conversions were in the highlands, where the sovereignty of Antananarivo had its deepest roots. In more distant parts of the island, few people adhered to Christianity other than royal officials or families that had emigrated from the central districts.

Religious legitimacy and political loyalty to the queen of Madagascar being now expressed in the register of Protestant Christianity, outward display at court was no longer of Oriental finery, but of a northern European sobriety of gesture and dress. The new Christian elite, often frock-coated and sometimes top-hatted, had a taste for European imports of everything from pianos and tea-cups to books and boots. The new court fashion of dressing in European clothes caused many 'to incur expenses beyond their means',[75] and the injection of a significant amount of new cash into the economy pushed up prices. 'The relative value of money and labour has been considerably altered since the death of Ranavalona I', wrote one missionary in regard to changes since 1861. 'The large amounts spent in the capital in the building of the memorial churches, the residences, school-houses, and other buildings belonging both to the Protestant and Roman Catholic missions, have raised wages and the price of many articles of food.'[76]

The decline of divine monarchy

Since the sovereign was expected to channel blessing and fertility by performing appropriate rituals and by following the advice of diviners or other experts, ignoring these conventions carried a high social and political cost. While the adoption of Christianity brought certain benefits to the government, it was not a religious ideology able to penetrate to the heart of daily life in agrarian communities in the way the older cults did. The adoption of Christianity weakened the mystical relationship between subject and monarch and transformed the concept of *hasina* radically and permanently. Many people remained discreetly attached to cults of the *vazimba* and to practices of divination that were now deemed backward and even disloyal, and in some places people still consulted in secret the *sampy*, the talismans that were the guardians of local tradition and local privilege.[77] Traditional religious experts—*ombiasy*—lost power to missionaries and officials of the state church. Some royal subjects thought that banning various forms of divination meant that communication with the invisible world had become more difficult, with the result that 'everyone keeps their thoughts to themselves'.[78] Henceforth, opposition to the regime tended to be associated with the underground cults of the *sampy* that were now officially banned.

Not only did forms of religious practice change radically in central Madagascar during the nineteenth century, but so did some of the most basic social formations. The creation of a standing army in the 1820s split a substantial part of the male population from the kin-groups that were the core of society. The vast influx of slaves created a substantial section of the population that did not share fully in the intimate dialogue between monarch and subjects. The free population, divided into both 'white' *(fotsy)* and 'black' *(mainty)* groups, saw its rights trampled by a succession of oligarchic measures that included the use of the army as an instrument of power, the extension of forced labour, and, later, growing exposure to a market economy. Groups living in central Imerina, unless they had the direct protection of a prominent courtier, were particularly vulnerable to these processes. More distant communities were sometimes able to fare better, since they were far enough from the centre of power to negotiate accords with the government from a position of relative strength.[79] Living far away from Antananarivo, even groups theoretically considered as personal slaves of the monarch developed relations with other protectors, such as with the many Sakalava kings in the west.

New practices of governance over two or three generations had a major effect on the way people lived in various parts of the island. Antananarivo grew into a real city, sometimes described as having 100,000 inhabitants by the 1890s,[80] of whom as many as 60,000 were slaves, although these figures seem to include many surrounding villages on the densely-settled plain below the royal city on its imposing crest. A completely new town arose, modelled on the capital, at Fianarantsoa in the southern highlands. Christianity redefined relations between the Kingdom of Madagascar and those areas of the island where its writ did not run, no longer officially represented as a relationship between a monarch situated at the centre of the universe and her subjects at all the cardinal points, but as one between a Christian centre and a heathen periphery. Substantial communities of people of Malagasy origin were established overseas, largely as a consequence of the slave trade, especially in Mauritius and Réunion and at Cape Town. The Malagasy language continued in use at these places for a couple of generations but seems to have died out in the later nineteenth century.[81] On the other hand, Malagasy has been spoken in some parts of the Comoros since before the nineteenth century, while the largest Comoran community in France, in Marseille, is also largely Malagasy-speaking. Emigrants from the Comoros have contributed substantially to the existence in Zanzibar of spirit cults originating in Madagascar.[82]

Throughout the last decades of the nineteenth century, the government was under constant pressure from European partners. Not only were traders and missionaries from Europe and the USA[83] settling in Madagascar, but so too were increasing numbers of penniless creoles from the sugar-colonies of Mauritius and Réunion, in search of land. All of these foreigners benefited from the diplomatic protection that Britain, France and other powers were intent on enforcing. The Christians, although not numerous, had emerged as a significant political faction with great influence in the army. Rainilaiarivony's premiership began in 1864 amid great difficulties, as not only did France demand compensation for the cancellation of the Lambert charter, but the murder of Radama II had led to a popular insurrection in the western highlands that was ruthlessly suppressed. Nevertheless, the prime minister succeeded in imposing his authority throughout a period of reforms that inspired great enthusiasm among Protestant missionaries, at least until his government ran out of steam in the 1880s.

In many ways, the establishment of a Christian government in 1869 was the centrepiece of Rainilaiarivony's tenure. In the years following, with help from British and Norwegian Protestant missionaries, the government of Madagascar established an administrative system in which churches and schools played a key role. French Jesuits established a rival Catholic network of churches and schools that the government viewed with less sympathy. The authorities in Antananarivo promulgated a series of written law codes, including items concerning the sale of land.[84] Other measures establishing administrative institutions of a European type followed in quick succession: universal school education for children over the age of eight; universal male military service for five years, with exemptions for Christian pastors, the sick, and others designated by the queen; regular taxes to be paid on slaves and cattle; the outlawing of polygamy.[85] A law was promulgated in 1877 formally emancipating imported slaves, known as Mozambiques. In 1881 the government established eight ministries, to function in the manner of European government departments. There was a growth in education, with hundreds of schools being built by Protestant missionary societies, and a smaller number by the Catholic church, and by 1882 there were some 150,000 school students registered. There was a rapid development of literacy. The first newspapers and periodicals were published, and there emerged a small number of what we might term intellectuals. These new-generation administrative measures were instruments in the hands of an oligarchy that remained devoted to factional self-interest. At the coronation in November 1883 of the last ruler claiming to be the monarch of all Madagascar, Queen Ranavalona III, the queen was flanked by a bodyguard of '400 of the elder scholars from the chief city schools in uniform carrying Remington rifles with fixed bayonets and officered by their teachers', most of them from mission schools.[86] As we have seen, Christianity took over some of the ritual function previously ensured by indigenous cults and it articulated the monarch's legitimacy.

It was after 1883 that Rainilaiarivony's premiership entered its second period, one of stark decline. The British missionaries who played such a prominent role in the formation of the Kingdom of Madagascar continued, at least in public, to regard it as a successful example of political development, but in private they became less sanguine. 'I have known the Malagasy Government now for many years', the Reverend Richard Baron wrote in 1894, 'and my deliberate opinion of them now is this: they are corrupt to the core; their one idea being to get wealth, they are the veriest oppressors and bloodsuckers'.[87] French officials, less inclined to expressions of sympathy with what they considered an anglophile government, nevertheless tended to make the same mistake as those British officials and missionaries who over-estimated the significance of the modern-looking institutions created by the government of Madagascar. French diplomats often believed that indignities inflicted on French citizens were the result of political hostility, and failed to recognize the government's weakness and administrative incapacity.

Madagascar and the great powers

One way of considering Madagascar's nineteenth century is to see it as the beginning of a gradual convergence between external and internal elements. On the one hand was a European vision of political modernity, projected into the western Indian Ocean with increasing force. On the other hand were Madagascar's historic political cultures. King Radama I and his successors realized that there was a certain concordance between their own traditional position as *andriambahoaka*, universal sovereigns, and the European convention requiring a state to be equipped with a formal structure and a recognizable figurehead, representing a defined body of the population. Thus, the sovereign who was to his subjects *andriamanitra hita maso*, 'the visible god', was likely to be viewed by Europeans in terms proper to their own tradition. Radama I, for example, was often seen by Europeans in the 1820s as an enlightened despot, and his later nineteenth-century successors, queens dominated by their ministers and generals, could easily be seen as ceremonial heads of state not unlike Queen Victoria. William Ellis, writing in 1838, made a spirited effort to classify the Malagasy government according to the categories prescribed by Montesquieu. He concluded that there were too many public assemblies of the people and too much customary law for the government in its classical form to be considered despotic. He noted that 'for some years past, however, the increasing power of the military officers, and the extent to which the troops have been employed by the sovereign, have rendered the government almost a pure military despotism'.[88]

At the same time, there were other ideas and conventions current in Madagascar that hardly rhymed with fundamental European notions at all, such as the social division of the population into *fotsy* and *mainty*, or institutions that Europeans regarded as obsolete, such as slavery. Noteworthy in this respect was the Malagasy tradition of regarding political space as discontinuous and time as being of uneven texture. Successive monarchs and their ministers actually made little attempt to impose a consistent form of political authority of the type recommended by European advisers, generally preferring a patchwork of relationships that left some regions with a considerable degree of autonomy and others exposed to the full range of labour-dues and taxes. After Christianity had been adopted as the official state religion in 1869, some villages very close to Antananarivo emerged as hostile to the new religion and to the royal officials with which it was associated. In areas like these, there was much suspicion of schoolteachers and pastors, seen as agents of a government that had forfeited its legitimacy. At the same time, however, some distant provinces were relatively immune from the attentions of grasping officials and enjoyed effective self-government. It is notable that some distant provinces like these, populated mostly by non-Merina, were to express their support for the Kingdom of Madagascar during the anti-French risings of 1895–8. This sometimes puzzled French administrators who, applying a European logic of statecraft and ethnicity, expected to be greeted as liberators in any province that was not peopled by Merina.[89] Patterns of loyalty or disloyalty in regard to the sovereigns in Antananarivo who styled themselves as kings and queens of Madagascar can not be convincingly explained by reference to ethnicity in its twentieth-century form.

Despite the advantages it derived from international recognition, the government of Madagascar was ultimately unable to satisfy its international partners in vital respects. The British imperium that acquired a hegemonic position in the Indian Ocean at the start of the nineteenth century was of a type different from the influence wielded by the Austronesian voyagers of the early centuries or even the Portuguese or Dutch seaborne empires of early modern times. British influence, like that of its French rival, which was to revive during the later nineteenth century, was centrally coordinated and was based on a strategic conception of national interest in the world. Both Britain and France projected their naval power from Mauritius and Réunion, and this grew more formidable over the century with the development of steamships and improvements in artillery. Britain especially was able to mobilize capital and produce goods on a scale so enormous that they penetrated not only the ports of the Indian Ocean, home to merchants for many centuries, but also societies deep inland, including the highland region of Imerina. American merchants too were very successful in Madagascar, but unlike their British and French counterparts they were not backed by a government having much strategic interest in the Indian Ocean. Nor were these the only global business interests with a foothold in Madagascar, as German companies, for example, also became active.

France (on one occasion joined by Great Britain) launched at least four military expeditions against Madagascar in the nineteenth century, in 1829, 1845, 1883–5 and, finally, 1894–5, the latter culminating in the island's formal annexation as a French colony in 1896. It became steadily more difficult for the island's rulers to defend themselves militarily against such intrusions, or to resist the economic incursions of British and French citizens. After the treaty ending the 1883–85 war, France acquired a theoretical protectorate over Madagascar, although it was almost entirely ineffective. In the face of a growing European imperial rivalry as well as a social crisis induced by its extreme economic problems, the government in Antananarivo was weaker than ever. Unable to defend its own sovereignty, it granted some 25–30 land concessions to Europeans between 1886 and 1894, some of them of considerable size,[90] generally on the basis of a joint venture with the prime minister.[91]

The adoption of a more aggressive policy towards Madagascar by the French government in the last two decades of the nineteenth century proceeded by degrees.[92] After the bout of hostilities in 1883–5, the government in Antananarivo was obliged to accept the presence of a French Resident whose main task was to oversee the application of a peace treaty that had created a formal French protectorate over Madagascar. The most significant aspect of the 1885 treaty was an obligation placed on Madagascar to pay an indemnity of ten million francs to the French government. Unable to find the required sum, the government borrowed the money from a French bank, the Comptoir National d'Escompte, after the French government had pressured it not to borrow in the City of London. The Parisian bank took control of the customs receipts of Madagascar's main ports as security for its loan. The island's customs revenue was not enough to cover the Comptoir National d'Escompte's loan, and so Prime Minister Rainilaiarivony instituted a special form of forced labour that consisted in panning for gold in the country's rivers, which was unpopular in the extreme. These financial and economic arrangements had political repercussions that weakened the royal government still further. Labourers deserted en masse. Among the political elite, there were a few who thought that a French takeover of the government in some form was a solution to Madagascar's problems. A small and influential group of politicians from the French island of Réunion saw the colonization of Madagascar as a solution to their demographic problems, and pushed for an aggressive policy by the French government.

Nevertheless, it was only after France and Britain had agreed on their spheres of influence in the western Indian Ocean in August 1890 that France enjoyed a free hand in Madagascar. By then France was actively encouraging the development of a pro-French party in Antananarivo in preparation for the eventual departure of the prime minister, Rainilaiarivony.[93] It was a kingdom utterly drained of power and in a state of effective collapse[94] that confronted the final assault—a full-scale military expedition—that was to transform Madagascar into, first, a full protectorate and, shortly after, a colony of France.

MADAGASCAR, MAIN ROADS, HYDROGRAPHY, POPULATION DENSITY

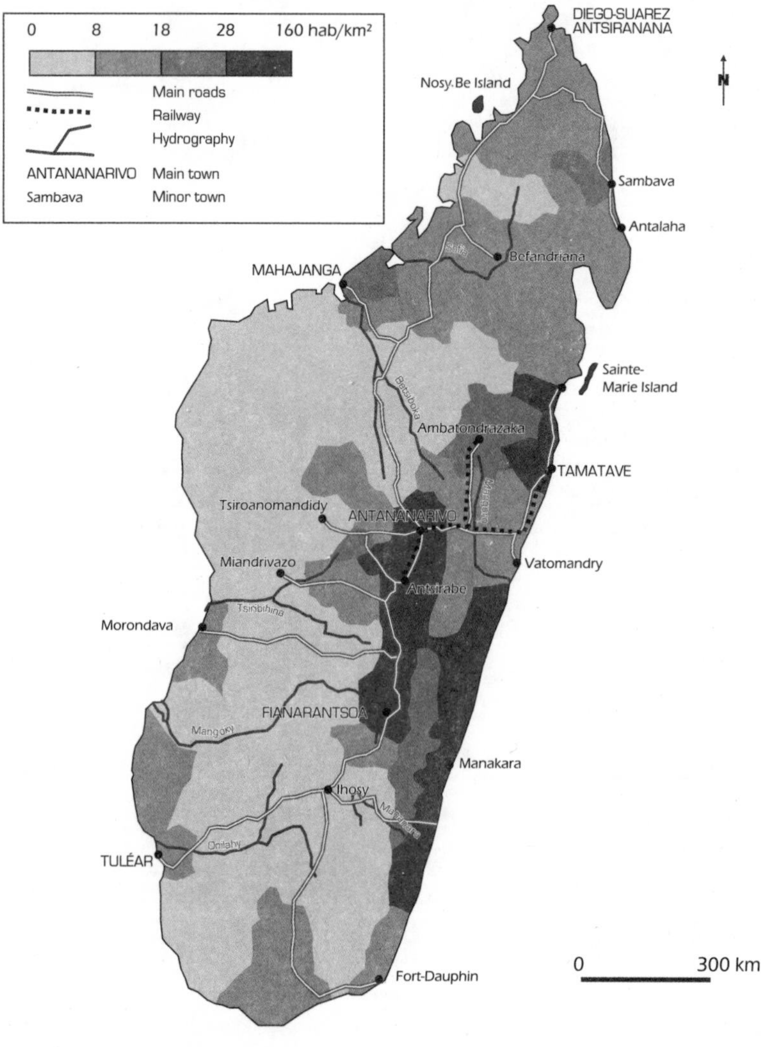

6

THE FRENCH PERIOD 1896–1972

By 1894, Madagascar was a matter of considerable frustration to the French government. Suspecting the authorities in Antananarivo of bad faith in failing to implement fully the 1885 protectorate and to respect the rights of French citizens, the foreign minister asked the Chamber of Deputies for money to fit out an expeditionary force. The deputies assented by 377 votes to 143. An expeditionary force duly landed at Tamatave on 12 December 1894, followed three days later by a second landing at Majunga, on the west coast. The Malagasy royal army, superior in numbers but demoralized and weakened by corruption, put up almost no resistance. On 30 September 1895, French soldiers entered Antananarivo after a campaign that saw half of the 15,000 colonial troops—including perhaps 1,500 West Africans or Algerians—perish from disease. The rickety bureaucratic apparatus of the Kingdom of Madagascar effectively collapsed.

For more or less the next three generations, Madagascar was remodelled in pursuit of a French dream of shaping the island and its people in conformity with French ideas and values. First came the period of conquest. Later, between the two world wars of the twentieth century, the process took the form of making Madagascar part of '*la plus grande France*', symbolized by the successful 1931 Colonial Exhibition. The Second World War and its diplomatic consequences brought a change in the form rather than the substance of this ambition. Throughout these decades, many of the policies implemented by the government in Madagascar were similar to those employed in other French colonies, in pursuit of the centralizing vision of French policy-makers.

Demands by local elites to share power, added to the general unpopularity of the colonial system, led to a major rising in 1947 that reflected changes taking place worldwide. In every continent there was a growing feeling that political independence, inspired by ideologies of difference, was the best way to secure the emancipation of colonized peoples. Madagascar duly acquired sovereign status by degrees, through a series of legal measures, with 26 June 1960 being generally accepted as the date of independence. Yet for all Madagascar's legal independence after 1960, from then until 1972 the essential components of state sovereignty were subject to the continuing ambition of building a Greater France in which the big island would be just one element. To cite one example among many, Madagascar's First Republic included several French ministers.

Only in the 1970s did it become clear that there was a deep current of dissatisfaction among many Malagasy that translated itself into a wish to distance the island from France. This political project took the ideological forms of nationalism and socialism.

The colonial state

During the first months after French troops had occupied Antananarivo in September and October 1895, large areas of Madagascar remained out of reach of a central authority that was itself in chaos. French military and civilian officials squabbled with each other, echoing the quarrels between rival ministries 10,000 kilometres away in Paris. France's second attempt at a protectorate in ten years had no chance of success under these circumstances. In the east, Vorimo insurgents launched a series of attacks between November 1895 and February 1896,[1] looting goods in transit on the vital route linking the east-coast ports to the interior. There was serious unrest in the central districts of the island. The French parliament accordingly resolved to take direct control of the situation, approving a formal act of annexation on 6 August 1896, with 312 deputies in favour and 73 against. The government in Paris decided to replace Hippolyte Laroche, the first French resident-general after the conquest, vilified by the press and often disdained by the military, with a man of action. The person chosen was Colonel Joseph-Simon Gallieni, who had long experience of military campaigns in West Africa and Tonkin. Promoted to the rank of general, Gallieni landed in Madagascar on 28 September 1896 to become the island's first military governor. Unlike Laroche, he concentrated power over both military and civilian bureaucracies in one pair of hands.

In the last days of his own tenure, before his handover to Gallieni, Laroche in a fit of pique had decreed the abolition of slavery, declaring with a simple signature that some half a million slaves were now free, 60 per cent of them in Imerina, out of a total population of perhaps two and a half million people.[2] This made the situation still more chaotic. Insurgent movements generally referred to by French soldiers as *fahavalo* ('enemies') were operating over large swathes of territory, and the extent of these movements was closely related to the abolition of slavery in circumstances of acute economic crisis and amid the collapse of the old royal government. In the west, some minor kings fought to free themselves both from the leading Sakalava kings of the west coast and from the sovereigns in Antananarivo or from the French.[3] Within the heartlands of the defunct Kingdom of Madagascar, some middle-ranking officials of the old regime saw in the political vacuum that followed France's military expedition of 1894–5 an opportunity to rebuild the old state according to what they saw as its proper constitution.

Arriving in Antananarivo in October 1896, in an effort to produce quick results Gallieni had some leading officials shot by firing-squad after show-trials. The victims included the queen's uncle, Ratsimamanga, and Rainanandriamampandry, former commander of the royal garrison at Tamatave and a leading Protestant intellectual.[4] Gallieni decreed the abolition of the monarchy and in February 1897 sent Queen Ranavalona III and her leading courtiers into exile. Nevertheless, the rebellion in the centre of the island by those later referred to as *menalamba* ('red togas') was to last for some three years.[5] In 1904, one Kotavy, who had himself served the French as a militiaman, led a serious rising in the southeast of the island, initiating a new cycle of violence. The series of uprisings caused by the collapse of the old royal government and the imposition of a colonial administration was to last until 1915–17.[6]

The *menalamba* bands that roamed the highlands in 1896–8 were generally composed of peasants, brigands, escaped or freed slaves, and often former soldiers and minor officials of the former regime. Some groups were more inclined to banditry than others. In some cases the insurgents' political notions amounted to an ideology of self-rule that could be described as a form of nationalism. Several armed groups were led by people who could be described as on the fringes of Madagascar's former political elite. Various factions tried to turn the prevailing situation to their advantage. In areas where neither the old royal government nor the French wielded any authority at all, large bands of raiders operated with complete impunity. One of the future leaders of the Malagasy anticolonial movement of the 1930s spent part of his childhood as the captive of one such bandit-group after his family had been killed in a raid.[7]

Gallieni organized a campaign of military pacification that crushed all the insurgent and bandit movements one by one. His troops confronted their greatest difficulties when they were faced with relatively well-organized groups that had some political vision, like those *menalamba* groups that were organized by former officers of the royal army, or like King Toera of the Sakalava kingdom of Menabe, with his 7,000 soldiers. Ultimately, Gallieni imposed peace by methods quite similar to those used by King Radama I less than a century before, by building a network of forts in strategic locations, with secondary positions one or two days' march away that were to develop into administrative centres as armed resistance ceased.

Peace was the precondition for the establishment of a colonial administration and a series of measures aimed at placing Madagascar squarely in French hands. Gallieni was convinced that far-sighted measures could secure support for colonial rule by showing its advantages to these new subjects of France, but his big ambitions were not matched by the size of the budget at his disposal. In 1900, the parliament in Paris passed a law requiring the governments of French colonies to finance themselves from their own resources. Gallieni reacted by soliciting the establishment of chartered companies. Areas the size of a French *département* were given to French concerns, but many of these used their concessions simply to inflate their paper value and their share-price on the Paris stock exchange without investing a single centime in Madagascar. Of the 900,000 hectares given to settlers at this period, 550,000 ended up in the hands of just six companies, the rest being distributed among some 2,000 individuals.[8] Would-be migrants were discouraged by Madagascar's poor reputation in France and by its sheer distance, and the settlers most willing to move to Madagascar were penniless adventurers from Réunion. Madagascar's infrastructure was hardly sufficient to attract French capital,[9] and the island's population was too small to be an attractive market. The few new economic

ventures by French interests in Madagascar bus
with the pillage of natural resources, leading t
several species.

The only effective way of implementing Fre
Madagascar was by government action. It is in t
ry of colonization becomes inseparable from th
Madagascar.[10] The state was not only the sole organ capable of ensuring security, but it was also the only one able to build new infrastructure, without which there could be no increase in production. Gallieni invented the term 'moralizing taxes' *('l'impôt moralisateur')*[11] to designate fiscal measures intended not just to raise revenue for infrastructure projects but to instil a new type of social and personal discipline. These obligations were imposed on a population that was overwhelmingly rural and included in the monetary economy only superficially.[12] Financial requirements made it essential to reinforce the government's administrative control, and some Malagasy were therefore hired as junior officials to implement state policies. These were overwhelmingly people from the central highlands, the area with the highest rate of school-enrolment under the old regime, where there were some 200,000 registered pupils in school at the beginning of the colonial period.

Hemmed in by lack of resources, Gallieni resorted to setting up a string of mini-protectorates in order to incorporate local kings into a system of indirect rule, an expedient possible only in parts of the island with kingdoms solid enough to facilitate some degree of central control, mostly in the west and centre-south. These measures were part of what Gallieni called a *politique des races*, a policy used in several French colonies where he had served earlier in his career. This form of ethnic administration was to have a lasting effect throughout the colonial period and even beyond, helping to entrench a political tribalism that set people with family roots in the central highlands against populations closer to the coast. Use of the two categories 'highlanders' and '*côtiers*' ('coasters', 'coastal populations') was to become normal during the colonial period and was enshrined in studies by ethnographers, many of whom were actually state officials, like Raymond Decary and Hubert Deschamps. This crude bifurcation was more ideological than scientific—some groups considered as *côtiers* actually lived in the interior districts of the island, like the Bara, while the populations of the highlands were far from homogeneous.

[illegible]y enough, it was a French general who realized King Radama [illegible]mbition of placing the whole island under a single political author-[illegible]y. Nevertheless, for all the undoubted continuities in the form and function of the state from royal to colonial rule, there were also differences so major that it becomes impossible to doubt that colonial rule marked a rupture in key domains. These included the imposition of the conventional French colonial vision of a civilizing mission that was in fact notable for its ambiguity, stuck between an aspiration to form active citizens and a need to organize compliant subjects. This, together with a fragile, state-dominated economy[13] single-mindedly reoriented to serve French interests, and an exhausted population, was the legacy Gallieni bequeathed to his successors when he left Madagascar for the last time in 1905.

Civil administration and the population

After Gallieni, successive colonial ministers in Paris preferred to appoint civilian governors-general. Every one of them faced fundamental problems stemming from the relative scarcity of Madagascar's population, allied to its formidable size, in a context where the metropolitan government continued to enforce a general principle of self-financing for the colonies. This was later described by a French member of the Antananarivo chamber of commerce as follows: [14]

> Madagascar has been no more privileged than any other overseas territory. The few hundred million francs in loans that made possible modest growth in 1904–5 and the development of the years 1930–1938 were entirely the work of the local administration. These loans were productive but insufficient … Other than in the short period of establishment up to 1906, Madagascar has cost France nothing—it has had to pay for its own development. Madagascar's own economic activity has been at the heart of a budget that has increased steadily to finance the equipment that the country needs. It is thanks to self-financing that our businesses have reached their current state of development. External capital has been of little importance.

The broad vision of colonial development announced by colonial minister Albert Sarraut in the 1920s, and a loan in 1927 for infrastructure projects, were early signs of a rethinking of the rigid financial self-sufficiency that was characteristic of the early colonial period. In the next decade, the metropolitan government loaned to the colonial administration in Antananarivo 730 million francs, repayable with interest. Nevertheless, for most of the colonial period, governors-general owed their careers largely to their success as tax-collectors, and tax recovery rates were as high as 90–95 per cent,[15] a figure that testifies to the oppressiveness of the colonial system as well as to the efficiency of its tax collection apparatus. Key administrative and legal structures, such as the law code applied to native subjects, the *code de l'indigénat*, were in practice oriented towards bringing in the tax-revenue the government needed. In 1936, for example, out of 240 people imprisoned in the small town of Vatomandry for infringements of any one of the five articles of the *indigénat*, 94 percent were locked up for failing to pay their taxes on time.[16] Since many people hardly used money at all, the colonial administration had recourse to taking taxes in kind, in effect continuing the old royal practice of forced labour. Every able-bodied man between sixteen and sixty was obliged to work for the state for a specified period that varied according to the whim of individual governors, but that could be as much as three months per year. On 3 June 1926 these labour requirements were consolidated into a programme known as the Service de la Main d'Oeuvre pour les Travaux d'Intérêt Général, similar to a system of military conscription. SMOTIG was to last until 1946, despite being condemned by the International Labour Organization in 1930.[17]

A vicious circle developed. The government's main source of income was direct taxes. Imposing such taxes, however, reduced the already meagre purchasing-power of the peasantry, leading to a reduction in the consumption of imported goods. A fall in consumption in turn led to lower income from indirect taxes, and thus a reduction of state revenue, leading to an intensification of fiscal pressure. This was a basic structural problem of the colonial system. Added to it were periodic crises, notably after the Wall Street crash of 1929 and during the early years of the Second World War, after Madagascar's colonial authorities had declared themselves in favour of the Vichy government. Britain and its allies reacted by imposing an economic blockade on Madagascar, depressing economic activity and leading the government to raise direct taxes by half. The combination of reduced economic opportunities and heavier taxes in the early 1940s resulted in arguably the most extreme misery of the entire colonial period.

With hindsight, it is apparent that many foundational aspects of modern Madagascar's place in the world came into existence in the years between the two world wars. The regular repayment of official debt with interest inaugurated the pattern of financial dependency that has held Madagascar in thrall ever since. In time, the system of state loans was to encourage the colonial administration to develop a social policy that was initially oriented towards urban populations. Subsequently, in 1947, the establishment of the Fonds d'Investissment pour le Développement Economique et Social (FIDES), an investment fund financed largely by the metropolitan government, was intended to inaugurate an ambitious policy of both infrastructure improvement and the development of agricultural production. But the main consumer of tax revenues was the state apparatus itself, with some 60% of tax receipts in the 1940s being earmarked for civil service salaries. By 1955, 4,000 French and 12,000 Malagasy functionaries were absorbing 80% of the state budget.[18] In this sense the colonization of Madagascar was a process more administrative and political than economic in nature.

A paradox of the colonial period was that by impeding the development of a modern private sector—such as occurred at the same period in India, for example—the state's role in financing infrastructure projects encouraged a rate of population growth that the economy could not match. In effect, state action was producing a new generation that looked to the state for development. A perceptible increase in population began in the 1910–20 decade. Slow at first, population growth was interrupted by occasional blips corresponding to economic crises, the Second World War, and epidemics such as the 1919–20 Spanish influenza brought to Madagascar by soldiers returning from the battlefields of Europe and the 1925 outbreak of bubonic plague.[19] The effect of these epidemics was compounded by government policy, as workers recruited for forced labour were obliged to leave crops standing in the fields, leading to food shortages that contributed to the high mortality of those years. Meanwhile, diseases such as malaria, venereal disease and tuberculosis were endemic. At the same time, a high birthrate among the rural population and a fall in mortality resulting from colonial public health policies stimulated population growth. The budget of the medical service, known as the Assistance Médicale Indigène, increased from two million francs in 1919 to 20 million ten years later.[20] The number of Malagasy doubled in the space of just half a century. From an estimated 2.1 million in 1900, the population increased to 3.7 million in 1930 and four million ten years later. After a fall in the war years caused by blockades and other disruption, the overall population figure increased relentlessly to 5.2 million in 1960 and 6.9 million by 1971.[21]

During the colonial period as a whole, the rate of population growth caused a corresponding drop in the average age. By 1935, over a third of the population was under the age of 15, a proportion that was to rise steadily. The colonial administration thus left to successor governments a demographic time-bomb, the economy being dominated by a state that lacked the means to implement a sophisticated social policy, and economic growth being out of phase with the increase in the number of people.

At the same time there was an obvious and rapid change in the way people lived, particularly evident in the major towns. In 1900, only about 2.4 percent of Madagascar's people lived in towns. Antananarivo, with 43,000 people,[22] was the biggest city by far, followed by Tamatave with 7,000 people. Thirty years later, the urban population had risen to 3.9 percent, or 216,000 people, after which it really took off, with Antananarivo alone counting more than 200,000 people by 1960 and 600,000 a mere ten years later. The increase in the urban population was a reflection not only of demographic growth in general, but also of a profound reorientation whereby towns became attractive to rural migrants. The population of Isotry, for example, a popular quarter of Antananarivo, increased from 9,000 to 20,000 between 1939 and 1948.[23] Towns were the political and economic nerve-centres of the colonial system. In 1927, Governor-General Marcel Olivier divided the island into six new administrative regions and designated the six main urban centres as provincial capitals.[24] Communication between towns improved dramatically. When Queen Ranavalona III and her entourage headed into exile in 1897, it had taken them almost two weeks to get from Antananarivo to Tamatave. But when in 1938 the body of the late monarch was repatriated from her place of exile in Algiers, it took just 17 hours for a cortege to travel from the east coast to Antananarivo by train, and the official ceremonies to mark her return were efficiently organized thanks to the telegraph and the telephone. Yet these two events were separated by little more than one generation. Apart from the railway, the colonial administration also oversaw the construction of thousands of kilometers of roads, some of them usable all year round, even if fewer investments were made in infrastructure in Madagascar than in any other French colony.[25] The island was endowed with an airline service in the 1930s, by which time several ships per month linked Madagascar to Europe in a journey-time of just three weeks.

Hence, town-dwellers became generally more mobile. Government officials, traders and labour migrants were all increasingly inclined to travel, and political activity increased correspondingly. The first modern nationalist group, Vy, Vato, Sakelika,[26] developed in the second decade of the twentieth century in towns on the main road and railway networks. In 1936, *Le Prolétariat malgache*, the Communist party newspaper, was being distributed in the main towns as well as in more remote areas of Madagascar. Copies found their way even as far as Cambodia. It was through his reading of the foreign press that, as early as 1900, the Protestant pastor Ravelojaona, one of the first nationalist intellectuals, grasped the global nature of colonization and understood that it was likely to last for a long time. The colonial authorities paid close attention to the ideas propagated by the numerous newspapers. In 1936, thanks to the development of air transport, the Communist leader Paul Dussac was able to send words of encouragement to his friend and comrade Jean Ralaimongo, recently arrested: 'Ever since you have been so shamefully imprisoned', he wrote, 'I have been in weekly airmail communication with our comrades in Paris. They are informed of everything that has happened here, and of your unhappy experience.'[27] After 1945, Malagasy deputies sitting in the French Constituent Assembly and the National Assembly were able to travel by air and also to work their Malagasy constituencies by car, abandoning the use of palanquins, the chairs carried by teams of porters that were favoured by colonial administrators of the inter-war period.

Towns were open to the world. It was here, especially, that the presence of foreign communities brought an air of cosmopolitanism to Madagascar, encouraging the island's elites to develop the idea of Malagasy nationalism. In 1933, in addition to French citizens, the island was home to 2,500 other Europeans, including 1,604 British, plus 2,500 Chinese and 7,000 Indians. However, the total number of foreigners never exceeded 50,000 people until the very eve of independence; the great majority of these were French, mostly Réunionnais. In this respect, too, it is apparent that colonial government cut across the grain of earlier history. For centuries, Madagascar had been a site of immigration, with newcomers of high status contriving to establish themselves as ruling groups in various parts of the island. But ever since the introduction of colonial government, immigrants were no longer able to assert themselves in this way—the basic logic of political rule had changed. Older networks tended to lose their influence in the face of a globalization that was integral to France's colonial empire, whose heart of course lay in the colonial metropole itself.[28] Those Malagasy who had the wherewithal made their way to France, and witnessed at first hand the original version of the civilization that administrators regularly invoked to justify the colonial project. Thus, resigning his position as a schoolteacher and getting a job as a domestic servant with a French administrator bound for home, the future anti-colonialist leader Jean Ralaimongo left Tamatave on 4 August 1910, arrived at Marseille on 26 August, and was in Paris the next day.[29]

Ralaimongo, who had spent most of his childhood as a slave, had begun his school education at a late age at the hands of Malagasy Protestant missionaries. Assimilating French ideas of citizenship, particularly while serving in France as a soldier during World War One, he went on to work in favour of equal civic rights for all Madagascar's people. He is just one example of how an individual could acquire a range of new ideas tending towards a consciousness of an individual's ability to shape their own destiny in the world.[30] This was just one of the new varieties of experience made possible in towns. It was there that the colonial system demonstrated most convincingly that social status was not only inherited, but could be acquired by hard work and respect for the new rules. The towns were filling up above all with immigrants from the countryside. Before the Second World War, of 37,750 townspeople surveyed, 27,000 had migrated from rural areas.[31] These newcomers, like urbanites born and bred, were absorbed by the idea that the towns were islands of a new civilization, as most towns were multiethnic from the outset. In provincial towns, the grid street-pattern and the existence of an administrative quarter, plus distinctive patterns of suburbs and native townships, formed the classic colonial town layout. With the exception of Antananarivo, town centres were reserved for administrative buildings and organized for the convenience of Europeans and those few natives who had attained the status of *assimilés*, while plots were allotted around this nucleus for the numerous Malagasy families arriving from all parts of the island. At the same time, immigrants often followed their own particular ways in town, limiting the degree of ethnic mixing and the growth of individualism, and the colonial government encouraged the formation of ethnic neighbourhoods as a technique of control. Chinese residents, for example, were from 1896 obliged to be members of an official organization chaired by a person appointed by the colonial authorities, a system originally developed in Indochina to simplify the government of the many Chinese communities that had grown up there.[32] Comoran and Karana (Indo-Pakistani) immigrants were organized along similar lines. The government encouraged the creation of this kind of ethnic association even in Antananarivo,[33] the least planned of all Malagasy towns.

The urban style of individualism coexisted with new forms of solidarity such as trade unions, mutual organizations and home-town associations. A modern citizenship showed timid signs of emergence by way of elections to consultative positions, membership of economic delegations and town councils. This political tissue was to develop quite fast. In 1939, the Reverend Ravelojaona was elected to represent Madagascar on the Conseil Supérieur des Colonies. At the end of the Second World War, deputies elected in Madagascar sat, first, in the French Constituent Assembly and, later, the National Assembly. Before Madagascar achieved its political independence, there were even Malagasy who became ministers in the French government, while many less elevated elected offices became open to them, for example as mayors. In 1939 only a few thousand people had the right to vote, most of them town-dwellers; twenty years later universal suffrage was extended to the entire adult population.

The growth of a modern form of political participation was also the result of the anticolonial movement that emerged from a handful of civic associations in the 1920s. At first, these struggles were focused on the demand for Malagasy to enjoy full rights of French citizenship. The most pregnant symbol of the negation of republican values, the *Code de l'indigénat*—the administrative code that governed the lives of colonial subjects throughout the French empire—became the target of campaigns in favour of civil rights. By 1935, fewer than 1,500 Malagasy had actually managed to fulfil the exhaustive administrative procedures necessary to achieve the status of French citizen, and the difficulties in acquiring this status no doubt pushed elites in the direction of nationalism. However, there could also be a psychological cost to claiming French citizenship. Some people felt deeply torn between loyalty to the ancestral culture that was denigrated by colonial propaganda, and a French culture that was presented as superior. The tragic destiny of the French-language poet Jean-Joseph Rabearivelo,[34] who committed suicide in 1937, is an extreme case of this type of cultural schizophrenia[35] that played a role in the creation of Malagasy nationalism.

The rural world and the colonial economy

At the outset, this modern civil society was hardly representative of the population as a whole. Discussions of such matters as citizenship and civil rights were confined largely to the urban milieu, although there were some lobbies that tried to use colonial law, occasionally with success, to defend the rights of peasants, all too often cheated of their land by unscrupulous settlers and then forced to pay rent for occupying their own houses and dues for grazing their own cattle.

The vast majority of the population continued to live from agriculture and animal husbandry in innumerable hamlets that often consisted of no more than three or four houses. The pattern of dispersed settlement made administrative control difficult and also reduced the possibilities of social advancement for most Malagasy. Especially in the southern parts of the island, cattle-herders relied on raiding their neighbours rather than on breeding to increase the size of their herds. Farming techniques, on the other hand, especially for growing rice, had reached a high degree of sophistication in the highlands over centuries, as a result of population pressure. The colonial administration introduced new crops, including coffee, vanilla and cloves on the east coast and tobacco in the west, and gave attention to improving some traditional crops such as rice and beans.

In some areas farmers used a rotating slash-and-burn system known as *tavy*. This involved cutting down trees, setting fire to the undergrowth on the cleared ground, and sowing rice seeds in the ashes. This technique produces excellent harvests in the first year after planting, but the yield steadily declines in subsequent years. Farmers using this system moved their place of residence periodically as they searched for new land, returning to their old plots only when enough time had elapsed for the soil to restore itself. As the population grew, the agricultural cycle became correspondingly shorter, wearing out the soil and destroying the forest. Every year tens of thousands of hectares of rain forest were disappearing, and in many places the quality of the soil was changed permanently. The first official measures to protect the environment and the forest were decreed in 1927 and *tavy* was thereafter subject to increasing regulation. As a result, at times of political tension, *tavy* became a form of protest against the state.

Measures such as these had a marked effect on peasant life, but it was only a minority of successful farmers that drew any benefit. In the 1930s it was precisely this rural elite of successful farmers that produced most of Madagascar's exports, outperforming those French settlers who had opted for agriculture. In general, high-quality French agricultural enterprises were conspicuous by their absence. Throughout the colonial period there were never more than about 35,000 French citizens in Madagascar at any one time, most of them in the highlands and the main towns, and very few of them engaged in agriculture. Many of those who did have agricultural interests left their estates in the hands of a Malagasy overseer. The deterioration of soil quality made it imperative to introduce expensive, high-technology farming methods, but the few French nationals who settled on the land were poor, with the result that in 1949, for example, out of every 100 French planters, only 39 were making any use of chemical fertilizers for their coffee bushes. [36] But the main reason for the failure of French agricultural colonization was the scarcity of labour. With the government taking so many people for forced labour, there was a lack of manpower even in areas of high population density like the highlands, where a relatively high standard of living meant that people had less incentive than elsewhere to seek work on French-owned farms and plantations.

In these circumstances, trade became the main economic activity of colonial settlers. Réunionnais, Chinese, Indian[37] and Merina traders competed to do business with peasant farmers by fair means or foul. One technique was to lend money to farmers at a very high rate of interest at the start of the growing-season, which left the recipient still in arrears after making his repayment following the harvest. Methods like these gave farmers no opportunity to save money or invest in new technology, trapping them in a near-subsistence economy. The traders who had face-to-face contact with farmers were part of a pyramid structure, at the summit of which were three major companies that imported goods from France and exported Malagasy export products. This trio was formed by the Compagnie Lyonnaise, the Compagnie Marseillaise de Madagascar, and the Société Industrielle et Commerciale de l'Emyrne. Imported goods were distributed for sale by a chain of intermediaries that included the big firms' own local branches, so that a provincial branch of the Compagnie Marseillaise de Madagascar both bought local agricultural produce and sold the imported goods that local people needed. Before 1940, big companies invested only half as much as small settlers in plantations. Their investments were mostly in tertiary activities such as shipping and transport, banking and trade. Overall, out of 11.5 million francs invested in 1940, big business was responsible for 6.4 million, out of which 5.08 million went to its own enterprises.[38] Most banks, meanwhile, were profit-seeking operations with a low horizon, lending money for short terms at high rates of interest. A commercial structure like this did little to stimulate production.

It was a mix of international and local factors—the Second World War and the post-war international situation, later combined with the alarm-call of Madagascar's 1947 insurrection—that eventually persuaded the French metropolitan government to pay more attention to Madagascar's rural sector. In general terms, the war had a similar effect on other colonial powers, too, with the United Kingdom setting up its Colonial Development Corporation in 1948. Post-war attention to the rural sector was the context in which the government unveiled an ambitious investment policy aimed at stimulating economic development, the precursor of the development plans of the 1960s. The development fund FIDES (Fonds d'Investissement pour le Développement Economique et Social) was to be the source of finance for the ten-year plan promulgated on 30 April 1946. The new strategy of rural development involved a reorganization of local government, and the traditional village assemblies in the highlands, the *fokonolona,* were officially transformed into rural communes in 1950. By 1952, Madagascar's 105 communes[39] had an elected leadership but remained subject to higher authorities.

All things considered, an observer assessing rural conditions in Madagascar in the late 1950s could paint a positive picture, with 37,000 hectares of virgin land having been brought into cultivation, new irrigation work resulting in improved rice yields, and 6,000 tonnes of fertilizer being imported annually. There had also been improvements in animal husbandry methods. When it came to getting produce to market, the roads were vastly better than ever before: where there had been only 2,400 kilometres of roads and 1,300 cars in 1925, by 1960 there were

3,000 kilometres of all-weather roads and 28,000 kilometres of dirt roads, for 30,000 motor vehicles. The formal economy remained based on trade, mainly imports of manufactured goods from France and the export of agricultural products from Madagascar. The island had procured for itself no less than 80 percent of the world market in vanilla, and did good business in exporting cloves, to Indonesia especially.[40] The main boom in coffee production was in the period between 1930 and 1938, during which production increased from 6,000 to 41,000 tonnes, allowing the emergence of a class of small Malagasy planters that was to play an important role in politics after the promulgation of the famous *loi-cadre*, the law of 23 June 1956 that granted self-government at provincial level in French colonies.[41]

This was an import-heavy economy, with exports covering only 58 percent of the cost of imports in 1951. Thanks to the effort put into development, by the eve of independence exports had improved to equal 76 percent of imports. However, it is risky to read too much into these figures as they cover some rapid commodity price changes. In the late 1920s, for example, after coffee production had begun to take off, a sudden fall in world prices meant that producers were exchanging a bag of coffee for a bag of rice, one-to-one. To maintain their income Malagasy coffee-farmers had to increase production constantly, whereas French settlers were subsidized by the state—that is, by Malagasy tax-payers. In the same vein, it is not clear that the obligation to obtain imports primarily from France was as beneficial to Madagascar as it was to the metropole. Many basic imports could have been obtained at lower cost nearer to home, such as from South Africa or India. Moreover, the system of colonial preference gave French industry no incentive to modernize, since it faced no competition. The most important tendency in the economy was the growth in external trade as a whole, which increased twenty-fold over the colonial period. No inhabitant of Madagascar was unaffected by macro-economic changes on this scale. Villages and hamlets ceased to be the enclaves that many of them may once have been, if only because of the pressure put on villagers to work as sharecroppers, or due to the attentions of government officials on tour.

The rural areas remained under-governed, as measured by the number of government officials in proportion to the population. Yet, paradoxically, never in the whole history of Madagascar has the central government been more present in the life of the peasant than during the colonial period. Villagers had to pay taxes on even the most basic objects, such as domestic animals.[42] No village, no matter how remote, was safe from a visit by a district officer. When General Gabriel Ramanantsoa later came to power, in 1972 after the collapse of the First Republic, one of his first acts was to abolish the poll tax previously paid by every adult, as well as the cattle tax. These measures, although popular, were to lead to a notable decline in the authority of the state, an indication of the limits of the success achieved by Gallieni's 'moralizing taxes'—*l'impôt moralisateur*.

Madagascar's peasant societies had reached a complex stage of development. Of various new avenues for social advance, the main one was education. By 1934, some 48 per cent of Malagasy children of school age were enrolled in 2,132 educational institutions, of which 1,009 were officially classified as schools, 558 of them in the coastal regions.[43] In the province of Antananarivo, 73 per cent of children attended school, compared to only 20 per cent in Madagascar's southernmost province.[44] While metropolitan France at the same period had one school for every 515 inhabitants, there was one school per thousand in Antananarivo and one for 5,420 people in Tulear province.[45] These statistics confirm the impression that colonization had its greatest impact in the areas considered by the colonial administration to be the most useful economically. They also show that the early implantation of schools in the central highlands during the nineteenth century had given that area an enduring advantage in many aspects of social and economic development.

Christianity too opened windows onto a wider world, in contrast with local cults that often had little meaning outside a limited area. (Many protective charms and amulets, for example, were considered ineffective if they passed over water, in other words beyond a boundary.) Catholicism alone grew from 170 churches and 48 missionaries in 1880, catering for some 20,000 Malagasy Catholics, to boasting 400,000 parishioners in 1930, worshipping in 2,718 churches under the guidance of 190 missionaries. Catholic and Protestant missions as well as the government vied with each other to open schools and attract new adherents. Christianity's status as a universal religion did not preclude local appropriations, as witnessed by the number of healers. Some of these had great success among Christian communities, to the consternation of European missionaries, such as one Rakristina from the small provincial town of Miandrivazo, who in 1928 caused a sensation in Antananarivo by her healing activities. At the end of the 1920s, the impact of some such Christian healers led colonial administrators to consider them a threat of the same order as political agitators.[46] Churches also served as centres of social and even political exchange in other ways, as it was often after Sunday service that churchgoers gathered to hear someone reading aloud articles from the newspapers that had arrived from Antananarivo, leading to discussions of national news. Many preachers and priests were more or less involved in political activity, and provincial schoolteachers and men of the cloth were among the most important correspondents of the leaders of the anti-colonial movement. For some of the latter, like Aléxis Bezaka and Jacques Rabemananjara, two leaders from the east coast of the nationalist movement that was to burgeon at the end of the Second World War, a period in a mission school or a seminary became the classic path for a political career. Although few rural schoolchildren went beyond primary level, the very presence of primary-school graduates in the rural areas contributed to the formation of a more fine-grained social hierarchy. It was in this milieu that both the colonial government and the anti-colonial movement recruited their supporters. Ironically, both derived their values from France's republican and revolutionary tradition, for whereas the government promised assimilation, the anticolonial movement was based on the demand for universal citizenship.[47]

Further galvanizing influences on rural society stemmed from recruitment, both for the army and for forced labour. Recruitment for service in the First World War took place in every region of Madagascar, with obvious consequences when war veterans came home. Some of the 35,000 Malagasy linked by the solidarity of the trenches supported their former comrades-in-arms Jean Ralaimongo and Paul Dussac in their efforts on behalf of the civil rights movement, which, benefiting from the arrival of Léon Blum's Popular Front government in France in 1936, partially reconstituted itself as a Communist party. Similarly, after the Second World War, some Malagasy veterans of the French army were to emerge as leaders of the 1947 rising.[48]

On the whole, the rural standard of living remained very low throughout the colonial period in comparison with that of the towns. The great majority of rural households could only just survive financially and the average peasant was vulnerable to the slightest change of fortune. Circumstances like these reinforced ancient beliefs about the ineluctability of destiny and chance (*anjara* and *vintana* in Malagasy), for a Malagasy peasant had precious little control over his or her own life.

National independence and state sovereignty

When France was occupied by German troops in 1940, Madagascar's colonial authorities chose to support the pro-German government whose headquarters were at Vichy. In retaliation, the British government imposed an economic blockade on Madagascar, and then, in May 1942, fearing the possible use of Madagascar's seaports by Axis powers,[49] it despatched an expeditionary force to take control of the island. A contingent composed largely of East African and South African troops landed in the north and soon took temporary control of the entire island.

The invasion of Madagascar was a major blow to the prestige of French colonial government. 'For a long time', wrote a British official in the interim military administration, 'the most urgent task of our information services was the sterilisation of Vichy propaganda'.[50] The British military authorities allowed Malagasy anti-colonialist political leaders to enjoy a relatively wide freedom of speech in the months before they turned control of the island over to a Gaullist administration. Subsequently, the euphoria surrounding the liberation of metropolitan France from German occupation in 1944 provided further indirect encouragement to political expression in Madagascar. The Free French forces under General de Gaulle promised a new direction to policy in regard to the entire French empire at the famous Brazzaville conference of 1944, and, as the war drew to its close, reports of the Atlantic Charter and the creation of the United Nations were received in Madagascar, contributing to a belief that the old style of colonial government had gone forever.

Thus, when French colonial government was formally restored in Madagascar, the utmost confusion reigned. In some parts of the island, the disruption of the war years and the rapid arrival and departure of a British administration had created a perception that the colonial state had ceased to exist altogether. This was combined with a difficult economic situation, while the fact that the colonial government had had to rely exclusively on local resources during the war years had resulted in a doubling of the local tax burden, probably the most intense fiscal pressure experienced by Malagasy peasants during the whole colonial period.[51] Leading Malagasy political activists in Paris created the Mouvement Démocratique de la Rénovation Malgache in February 1946.[52] So rapidly did this news spread, at a time when the colonial government was not fully restored, that the MDRM was reckoned to have at least 200,000[53] members by the end of the year, with its headquarters in Antananarivo and branches island-wide. The advance of nationalism brought with it a myth that formal independence would bring with it freedom and prosperity and restore an authentically Malagasy society with a better life for all. The new French constitution of 27 October 1946 re-established the French empire in the form of the Union Française, under the terms of which former subjects, in Madagascar as in other colonies, became French citizens en masse.[54] Ironically, this was the fulfilment of the exact demand made just a few years earlier by Ralaimongo and his fellow-militants.

While the MDRM was itself a legal party, it was infiltrated from the beginning by clandestine radical groups, notably PANAMA (Parti Nationaliste Malagasy) and Jiny. These in turn were infiltrated by police informers. The MDRM's rank and file members held a great variety of different views and espoused a range of goals, varying from various forms of cohabitation with France to demands for immediate independence. Throughout the end of 1946 and the early months of 1947, feverish political activity surrounded the election of national deputies to the French parliament, and yet most of the population was excluded from voting in the series of elections that marked the return of French rule.

The strong sense of an interregnum in 1945–47 offered definite parallels with the *menalamba* rising fifty years earlier. In the political vacuum between the British departure and the reestablishment of French government, all manner of forces had free play, including the settling of local vendettas, agitation by nationalist militants and, conversely, counter-moves by sections of society that feared a nationalist movement that was often associated with leading families from the pre-1895 royal government. This tendency was represented in the PADESM party (Parti des Déshérités de Madagascar), created by an alliance of Merina who were of *mainty* status or who were descendants of slaves and some coastal elites well-disposed to the colonial government. Nevertheless, some major leaders of the MDRM arose from these very same groups, such as Aléxis Bezaka, Tata Max and Justin Bezara, all from coastal areas. PADESM's leaders, arguing that high-status Merina families would be the main beneficiaries of immediate independence, preferred the status quo to any rapid move to end Madagascar's colonial status.[55]

Throughout 1946 and the early part of 1947 there was increased violence, quite often targeting the many French settlers on the east coast who were of Réunionnais origin.[56] On the night of 29 March 1947, there were attacks on settlers or government offices in several different locations simultaneously, giving the impression of a planned rising. Targeting PADESM militants and government agents, the movement spread rapidly, and at one point the insurgents were active among over a quarter of the island's population, mostly in eastern regions of the island. The French government responded by arresting senior members of the MDRM, accusing them of fomenting the rising. The three deputies elected to the French parliament under the colours of the MDRM, along with several other leaders of the party, were convicted of high treason and received death sentences, subsequently commuted. Many of the MDRM's less well-known leaders died in battle or were executed, such as Lieutenant Randriamaromanana and Samuel Rakotondrabe.[57] Large numbers of party militants were arrested and banished to isolated areas.

The wave of arrests of senior MDRM officials deprived the rising of its most obvious potential leaders, making space for a second generation of leaders to emerge during 1947 from among World War Two veterans returning home.[58] Deprived of its leaders, the insurgency took the form of an armed social movement that was often inarticulate and incoherent. Badly organized and poorly armed, the insurgents were eventually overcome by a combination of armed civilians, militias, and the armed forces. The rising was essentially confined to the provinces of Tamatave and Fianarantsoa, especially the areas along the east coast. French troops, themselves poorly equipped, conducted a brutal counter-insurgency campaign, making extensive use of an ostentatious violence designed to intimidate.[59] The ferocity of repression as well as internal divisions within the population aggravated ethnic tensions and created a social trauma that was to last for decades.[60] Figures for the number of victims of the rising vary, but they are of the order of several tens of thousands, a substantial number in a population of some four million.[61] These deaths were caused by skirmishes and by the repression that was to last until the early 1950s, as well as by the hunger, sickness and forced migration that were a consequence of war and counter-insurgency. The main political consequence of the rising was to leave the political field open to PADESM, which was able to score heavily in elections after 1947 by default, since its MDRM rival lay in ruins. France's timid post-war attempts at political liberalization came to an abrupt halt. Nevertheless, there is no doubt that the 1947 rising marked a turning-point in the relationship with France.

The high degree of participation in the 1947 rising was a symptom of just how unpopular colonial rule had become, and one of the few positive consequences of the rising was the greater attention that the colonial government now paid to rural matters. More generally, the tragic 1947 rising fostered the feeling that freedom and citizenship could come about only through independence. But the move towards national sovereignty was also being driven by international events, including the French defeat in Indochina in 1954 and the beginning of the independence movement in Algeria. After legislative elections on 2 January 1956, the need for reform of the colonial system was so obvious that the French parliament adopted a fast-track procedure that was to lead within six months to the *loi-cadre* of 23 June 1956, opening the way to universal suffrage in the colonies combined with administrative decentralization under the control of elected assemblies responsible for their own affairs. Each colonial territory was endowed with its own assembly, the embryo of a future government.[62] Promulgation of the *loi-cadre* in Madagascar and the release of the 1947 detainees coincided with the emergence of a new political elite from the provinces, many of them associated with the PADESM party. A majority of the newcomers, now splintering into a multitude of small regional and ethnic factions, favoured a form of independence that would leave room for a large measure of collaboration with France. They had little fear of the more extreme nationalists, who had been weakened by repression.

The passage from colonialism to independence, although propelled by rapid legislative changes, can also be seen as part of a more gradual process by which the French government and French interests sought the form of association that they found most congenial. In the space of six and a half decades, the colonial state had taken the form initially of a protectorate, then of a colony administered directly by a governor-general, and later of an overseas territory whose people had the status of French citizens, before finally transmuting into a self-governing state within a French Community that turned out to be short-lived. Even after the declaration of independence, a handful of Frenchmen continued to sit in the government of the new sovereign state as cabinet ministers. France retained military bases at Antsiranana (the former Diego Suarez) and Antananarivo, while French technical assistants were present in every government ministry, even after the declaration of independence. The Malagasy franc, the symbol of national sovereignty, was part of the franc zone, and the French treasury controlled Malagasy monetary policy. Continuing dependence on France was henceforth mediated by a Malagasy state endowed with the conventional attributes of sovereignty. In truth, independence may be considered not as the description of a political reality, but as an ideology—one of the many produced during the twentieth century.

The independence myth

By the end of the 1950s, international opinion was running strongly in favour of, at the very least, a relaxation of the tight bonds between European metropoles and their colonial possessions. Powerful voices argued for complete decolonization. General de Gaulle's return to power in May 1958 and his inauguration of France's Fifth Republic set in motion an orderly process of decolonization that had enough momentum to carry the support of almost all political factions in both France and Madagascar. This, however, was achieved by ignoring or over-riding many of the norms associated with a democracy.

A powerful impetus to change came from a visit to Madagascar by De Gaulle early in his presidency, canvassing support for a new constitutional dispensation to be confirmed by referendum. Speaking at a public meeting in Antananarivo on 22 August 1958 he declared that 'in just a few weeks, by agreeing to the proposals that will be put to you, you will embark with France and the other [colonial] territories towards a brighter future. I know what your response will be'. What stuck in the memory of many Malagasy who heard De Gaulle's speech was the last part of his oration, when the General announced that 'tomorrow, you will be a state once more, as you were in the days when the royal palace was occupied by your own kings'.[63] As he made this remark, he gestured towards the queen's palace, the nineteenth-century royal edifice high on the ridge above the stadium where he was speaking.

Standing alongside the French president during his speech was Philibert Tsiranana. Born in 1910, and described in official legend as a cattle-herder, Tsiranana was a former schoolteacher from a Tsimihety family influential in the north of Madagascar. He was a founder-member of the PADESM party, regarded by its enemies as a lackey of the colonial government. But Tsiranana had also been a member both of a Communist study-group and, later, of the SFIO, the French section of the Socialist International, the ticket on which he was elected to the French Union as a deputy for Madagascar in 1956. He became the vice-president of Madagascar's executive body, elected by the provincial assemblies established in France's colonies by the *loi-cadre* of 1956, serving alongside a French high commissioner. Thus, the Tsiranana who shared the platform with De Gaulle, as the general explained the constitutional referendum that was to establish France's Fifth Republic and open the way towards Madagascar's First Republic, was an old political hand.

The *loi-cadre* had endowed French colonies with their own autonomous government, and in Madagascar's case the members of this body had been chosen by means of the first-ever elections in which the entire adult population of the island could participate. But those elections also took place in a political vacuum that was a consequence of French repression of the 1947 rising, leaving PADESM without serious challenge. The government installed under the terms of the *loi-cadre* inherited from PADESM a practice of collaboration with the colonial authorities that did not reflect the full range of public opinion but that was the point of view of the most active part of the political elite. Dominated by people from the coastal areas, PADESM was notably anti-Merina, but anti-Merina rhetoric was not enough to keep all members of the government united. In the year of the *loi-cadre*, 1956, Philibert Tsiranana created a new formation, the Parti Social-Démocrate (PSD), that proclaimed itself to be in favour of something called 'moderate independence'. He managed to win support from elements of both the old PADESM camp and from some of its former opponents, thus putting together a group strong enough to receive formal nomination from Madagascar's parliament. Less openly, he also enjoyed the blessing of the French Socialists who dominated the ministry of colonies in Paris.

Opposed to Madagascar's governing coalition was another formation that was hardly more coherent than the PSD. Its common denominator was the aspiration to 'real independence', the precise content of which was never specified—a pro-independence congress organized by the opposition, held in Tamatave in early May 1958, pronounced itself in favour of 'Independence first and discussion later'.[64] Subsequently, the opposition formed itself into a new party, the Party for Madagascar's Independence, known by its Malagasy initials as AKFM,[65] in preparation for elections. The AKFM's ranks contained a range of opinion that included communists[66] and nationalists of various stripes.

The question put to Madagascar's voters in the constitutional referendum of September 1958 was written by the French government. It offered to France's colonies a choice between three types of relationship. The options, as France's high commissioner outlined them in a radio broadcast a few days before the vote, were as follows: 'to be part of the Republic with the status of overseas territory ..., to become a department of France ..., or to form a state that will have the power to confer on itself a republican status ... and that will deal with the French republic on a basis of equality ... within the larger community'.[67] France's high commissioner also advised Malagasy on the choice they should make: 'we wish to live with you as brothers ... in this community of free peoples where you will be our equals ... In the whole of History it is unusual that men obtain ... the full quality of a free citizen of a free country while a whole range of economic and social advantages are guaranteed by another state.' Accusing groups opposed to a 'yes' vote of being 'inspired by foreigners', France's most senior representative in the island warned the public: 'do not allow yourselves to be carried away by a handful of troublemakers trained in methods that are, and always will be, foreign to this country.'[68]

The 'yes' camp won a convincing victory. The AKFM-led opposition was able to persuade no more than 30 per cent of the electorate to cast its vote against the referendum. Thereafter, the provincial assemblies elected under the terms of the *loi-cadre*, meeting in Antananarivo just a couple of weeks later, on 14 October 1958, pronounced themselves in favour of independence, and Tsiranana was henceforth to consider this as the real date of independence. He gave a major speech in the main square of the Andohalo district of Antananarivo's upper town, the spot where in earlier times sovereigns used to address their subjects, and the square was promptly renamed the Place de la République. On the following day, the French authorities repealed the law of annexation dating from 6 August 1896 whereby Madagascar had formally become a French colony. The provincial assemblies renamed themselves the Constituent National Assembly and the cabinet declared itself to be the provisional government of a new state headed by Philibert Tsiranana.

A new constitution was drafted, and officially adopted on 28 April 1959 by the Constituent National Assembly. Notwithstanding the existence of ethnic tensions at least among political elites, and consequent demands for a federal structure that would give political expression to ethnic difference, the new state was unitary in character. The system nevertheless maintained some of the decentralized structures that had been established in 1956 by the *loi-cadre*. The two chambers of parliament re-elected Tsiranana as president of the republic on 1 May 1959.

The adoption of a new constitution at the same time that Madagascar retained its allegiance to the French community gave independence an ambiguous flavour. Tsiranana, for example, still held the title of Minister-Counsellor of the French Community, and he served as a member of France's delegation to the United Nations in 1959. Opposition supporters considered that the adoption by a provisional body of such an important document as a constitution, and the unseemly unanimity of the various organs that had chosen Tsiranana as president, were signs of manipulations engineered by Tsiranana and his French friends to ensure their tenure of power.

In effect, municipal elections held on 11 October 1959 threw a different light on politics during the weeks when Madagascar was regaining its formal sovereignty. In spite of a relatively low voter turnout, the 1959 municipal elections revealed that the opposition had majority support in the major towns, with Antananarivo and Diego Suarez being won by the AKFM and Tamatave, Madagascar's second city, by a local Christian Democrat party led by Aléxis Bezaka, a former member of the MDRM who had allied himself to the AKFM. Tuléar pronounced itself in favour of another nationalist party, MONIMA. Created in 1958, MONIMA[69] ('Madagascar for the Malagasy') was led by an Antandroy customary chief, Monja Jaona. Of all Madagascar's main towns, only Majunga did not fall into the hands of parties opposed to Tsiranana and his governing PSD. The rural areas, on the other hand, voted solidly for the PSD. In fullness of time, Tsiranana and his government manoeuvred to neutralize little by little the town halls that had fallen into the hands of the opposition, starting with the smaller towns. In the end, the PSD appointed a delegate-general in Antananarivo over the head of the city's elected mayor. Throughout the remainder of the First Republic, Antananarivo was to remain directly under central state control in spite of the fact that the opposition AKFM party regularly won elections there.

Firmly rooted in the capital city but otherwise increasingly marginalized, the AKFM came to be seen as essentially a Merina ethnic party. This was in spite of the fact that it had a significant base in Diego Suarez, for example, a town governed by a communist mayor during the first years of Madagascar's independence. Notwithstanding its particular ethnic flavour, there can be no doubt that, on balance, the AKFM became the main opposition party. Inspired by an eastern European style of socialism, it made no secret of its links with the French Communist Party and with international communism generally, and it indeed contained a significant number of crypto-communists. But for all its communist sympathies, at the end of the 1950s the AKFM was in essence a nationalist party.

Aiming to cut the ground from under the feet of the AKFM opposition, Tsiranana emphasized his own nationalist credentials and worked in favour of a greater degree of sovereignty for the new Malagasy state. French and Malagasy authorities embarked on a series of negotiations in early 1960 that were to result in the signature on 26 June of a cooperation agreement[70] defining the terms of future collaboration between the two states. The 26th of June 1960 has been celebrated as Madagascar's independence day ever since then. In the month following, Tsiranana triumphantly accompanied back to Madagascar the three MDRM parliamentarians convicted in connection with the 1947 rising, who had been living in exile in France since their release from prison. Tsiranana claimed for himself the title 'the father of independence', although in Madagascar itself, there were still many people obliged to live in internal exile, away from their place of origin. The seal of international approval was set on Madagascar's status when it was admitted to membership of the United Nations on 21 September 1961.

Throughout the First Republic, French consuls sat as members of the provincial assemblies that had the power to decide provincial budgets. As one writer noted, 'officer-cadets from the Malagasy army are trained at the military academy in Antsirabe by instructors who are mostly French officers or teachers ... Military equipment is supplied

The head of Malagasy military intelligence is a French ...ieur Moine...'.[71] The French army had its own bases in ... The island of Sainte Marie even continued to enjoy a ...as as both French and Malagasy. French was enshrined in Madagascar's constitution as the official language. Government foreign policy was based on the maintenance of relations with France and followed France's line in most respects, with the addition of an almost obsessive anti-communism.

The PSD government[72]

Opposition criticism tended to concentrate on Tsiranana's questionable legitimacy since, according to opposition leaders, his position was based on his appointment by organs of a provisional character. It was in this atmosphere that the first legislative elections to be held in the new sovereign state took place on 4 September 1960. The seven electoral districts offered 107 seats to be occupied by deputies mandated for a period of five years. Twenty-seven parties, with 444 candidates between them, competed for the votes of some 2.5 million people, of whom only 1.9 million actually voted. The participation of so many parties provided a veneer of democratic pluralism, but government candidates benefited from the text of a manipulative electoral law. Thus, the PSD received 62.91 per cent of votes cast, against 13.10 per cent for the AKFM. This gave the PSD 82 parliamentary seats and attracted to its side deputies from some smaller parties, bringing the number of parliamentarians in support of the government to 104 out of 107. The electoral law, by helping the PSD to a position of supremacy, not only marginalized the opposition, but also decimated the PSD's own allies.

With a strong executive arm and a tame legislature, Tsiranana was later to confide to the French daily *Le Monde*:[73] 'We allow the opposition to exist, but not to act'. Political life in the First Republic was in effect a bipolar system in which the PSD faced the AKFM. But another political force existed, at least potentially, in the form of Christianity, and throughout the 1960s some leading lights of the PSD were deeply concerned by the possibility of a political party supported by the Catholic church. The AKFM was led from its creation by the Reverend Richard Andriamanjato, the pastor of the prestigious church of the queen's palace, the successor of such famous nationalist churchmen as Reverend Ravelojaona. His congregation belonged to the FJKM (Fiangonan'i

Jesoa Kristy eto Madagasikara), a grouping of Protestant churches that included branches of the old London Missionary Society .

Odd as it may sound, then, the first legislative elections in a sovereign Madagascar, in 1960, confirmed the PSD's anti-democratic tendencies. By 1961, the PSD appeared all-powerful. It could dictate policy to the government, as it was to do, for example, in 1967, when the party suggested the development of diplomatic links with South Africa, at the height of the apartheid period. At the zenith of the PSD's power, party members were even authorized to arrest suspected wrongdoers and hand them over to the police. Another sensitive point concerned the PSD's regionalist character. The Merina/coastal dichotomy was a mainstay of PSD ideology, and regionalist factions coexisted inside the party. First elected as head of state in May 1959 by unanimous vote of a parliamentary college, Tsiranana was subsequently re-elected in 1965 and January 1972 by massive popular majorities, but always with the support of the government machine. Strong administrative control guaranteed a certain degree of institutional and political stability and encouraged the public perception of a peaceful country, but ensured also that the forces undermining it remained hidden from view. In spite of all the fine words about national unity, politics was governed by a subterranean logic of ethnic and regional calculation. Inside the PSD itself, northerners, especially the Tsimihety, the president's own ethnic group, tended to be opposed to a southern faction led by the home affairs minister, André Resampa. Electoral fraud confirmed the PSD's formal hegemony while hiding from view the conflicts that existed deep within the bowels of the regime.

As for the administrative structure of the First Republic, this was little different from what it had been in 1946, when France, reasserting its position after the Second World War, had created a range of new institutions. Madagascar remained divided into six provinces (Tananarive, Tamatave, Diego-Suarez, Majunga, Fianarantsoa and Tulear), each governed by an elected general council and a provincial commissioner appointed by the central government. The provinces were divided into 18 prefectures, themselves further sub-divided into sub-prefectures, districts and cantons. Seven hundred and fifty communes were empowered to choose their own mayors in the same way as parliamentary deputies, giving the illusion of a system that was democratic. As in colonial times, a large percentage of Madagascar's economic resources was earmarked for financing this heavy administrative machine. The economy remained oriented towards overseas and could finance only a limited percentage of the cost of government policies, with French development aid accounting for the rest. Under the terms of its cooperation agreements, Madagascar was obliged to deposit its foreign exchange reserves in the French treasury, while the Malagasy franc remained linked to the French currency, leaving little room for Madagascar's rulers to conduct a genuinely independent financial policy. On the positive side, this was a system that provided a high degree of financial stability. The one source of income that Madagascar's rulers could control at their own discretion was taxes. These were raised in the same manner as during the colonial period, strengthening the conviction among some nationalist parties, such as MONIMA, that nothing had really changed.

Pragmatism was generally the dominant feature of decision-making in a vast country that remained thinly-populated, essentially rural, and potentially rich in agricultural resources. Take-off into economic development in such circumstances faced numerous obstacles including the small size of peasant holdings, poor communication infrastructure, soils that required inputs of fertilizer, and inadequate water and energy provision. The huge concessions held by French import-export companies and private European coffee and tobacco estates were too few in number and too backward technologically to play a decisive role in the economy. The creation of a small number of new factories gave the illusion of a great step forward, but for the most part, the state's financial investments, plus aid from the French government and from the European Development Fund, were used to oil the economic machine inherited from colonial times. A business-as-usual policy did little to raise average incomes, which remained very unequal between different social categories and geographical regions. On the other hand, there were no hold-ups in the supply of strategic goods and no shortages of consumer products.

The terminal crisis of the Tsiranana regime began in 1971, when the president became seriously ill. The prospect of his departure brought into view the subterranean forces that had actually been present since the founding of his regime. Conflicts between different factions within the government and the ruling party were evident in the appointment of no less than four competing vice-presidents. In April 1971, the government's heavy-handed methods of tax collection set off a peasant rebellion in the south, which MONIMA claimed to have organized.[74] The government's brutal reaction resulted in as many as 2–3,000 deaths.[75] Shortly after these events, Interior Minister André Resampa, generally regarded as the strong man of the ruling party and the government, was arrested on 1 June 1971 on a charge of plotting a coup with American and Chinese support, and exiled to the island of Sainte Marie. Yet in January 1972, Tsiranana stood as the sole candidate for presidential elections and received a third seven-year mandate with the support of no less than 99 per cent of voters. The scale of his victory is an index of the dubious methods used to secure re-election.

Madagascar, sometimes hailed in the French-language press as the *île heureuse* ('The fortunate island'), had lived through the first decade of its formal independence without apparent difficulty, unlike quite a few of its sister-states in mainland Africa. But in 1971–2, it was to undergo a crisis, unforeseen by any of the key players, that was not only political in nature, but social above all. In its first decade of existence as a sovereign state, Madagascar's population had increased at an astonishing speed, from 5,183,000 in 1960 to 7,321,000 in 1970.[76] There was an unprecedented mass of young people, without any concomitant economic expansion that could provide them with a livelihood. A whole society was in search of a new mode of existence, amounting to perhaps the most profound crisis in Madagascar's history. This crisis was to last for a long time.

7

AN ISLAND IN THE WORLD 1973–2002

Majunga, 21 July 2005. The French president, Jacques Chirac, in a speech delivered during an official visit to Madagascar, formally announces his regret for what he calls the 'crimes of French colonization in 1947'. His Malagasy counterpart, Marc Ravalomanana, makes a rather suprising reply. He states that, since he himself was born in 1949, the insurrection that occurred two years earlier is of minimal concern. For him, the future of the island's relationship with France is more important than the past.[1]

It is quite possible that the majority of the island's population is inclined to a similar view, since most of them were born after the end of formal colonial rule. If so, then their attitude has been shaped by the experiences of the final decades of the twentieth century.

Broadly speaking, the period from the 1970s to the early twenty-first century was one of severe trial and recurring political instability in Madagascar. Among the traumatic events of these years have been the 1971 peasant rising in which thousands lost their lives, the urban riots and demonstrations of 1972 in which youth played a vanguard role, political intrigues that resulted in the assassination of a head of state three years later, disguised coups and attempted coups, and rapid swings of political fortune, often extra-constitutional.

Economic decline has been the consequence of a profound malaise rather than its cause. At the heart of Madagascar's difficulties has been population growth of staggering proportions—as in continental Africa, probably 'of a scale and speed unique in human history'.[2] The astonishing increase in the number of people has resulted in a very youthful population and the burgeoning of towns and cities.

Madagascar's society or societies have been struggling to find new ways of functioning and of coexisting ever since they were unified under a single political authority at the end of the nineteenth century. Patronage by France, a source of reassurance for part of the island's population, has been seen by another part of the same population as one of the main obstacles to a quest for new ways of living together. But identifying the Other as an explanation for the excesses that have marked this search for novelty in social relations does not resolve any fundamental problems; it does little more than postpone the necessity for self-examination that was also characteristic of Madagascar's late twentieth century. Malagasy have been drawn down this path by a confrontation with the world beyond the ocean that has become ever-more intense, and from which they were shielded for several generations by French patronage. The events of the last third of the twentieth century illustrate the fact that the real obstacle to confronting the world is not so much specific individuals or particular groups, indigenous or foreign, as society itself.

Malagasy society (by this time, it is perhaps permissible to speak in the singular) has attained a degree of sophistication quite distinct from that of earlier centuries. We may take as an example the 'mystical force of primacy'[3] known in Malagasy as *hasina,* which for centuries regulated relations between rulers and their subjects, as well as social life more generally. Nowadays, the vertical dimension in which *hasina* is thought to function is called into question by new horizontal solidarities. Power has mutated; these days, it is legitimated by elections, even manipulated ones. Between those individuals or social groups that are held to incarnate collective authority, on the one hand, and the citizenry at large, on the other hand, there exists a category of ever more numerous intermediaries, including associations more or less closely connected to the Christian churches, political parties, newspapers and private radio stations. There has been a parallel evolution concerning the stigma of slavery, which never disappeared during either the colonial period or the First Republic, notwithstanding the rhetoric of equality. Perhaps more effective than republican law and political discourse in working against the memory of slavery are certain indigenous mechanisms of ritual and religion, some of them very old.[4] Historical change has accelerated. Developments worldwide have obliged Malagasy to make choices with unprecedented speed, sometimes implying the abandonment of paths previously followed over centuries. At the same time, they are subject to frustrating delays.

Perhaps Madagascar's experience of the acceleration of history since the 1960s would be best described as a trauma, except that the word 'trauma' suggests that the Malagasy are victims, denying their role as agents of their own history. In any event, the true prologue was the street-protests of 1972.

1972

The harbinger of the downfall of the First Republic was a strike in favour of better conditions by medical students at the university in Antananarivo. This soon spread to students from other faculties and then to high schools all over the island. Originally organized by the youth wing of the main opposition party, the AKFM, the strike soon spun out of control, gaining in strength and scale but remaining non-violent. The rapid spread of the strike movement was an indication of the enormous political potential of the millions of young people who composed the majority of the population. Drawing on a deep reservoir of popular support, the strike gained the backing of trades unions and adopted a new set of demands. The depth of frustration with the PSD government was clear.[5]

It was not only in the political field that youth began to assert its influence, but in society more generally, including in artistic and cultural fields. The musical group Mahaleo was the founder of an artistic movement known as *vokatry ny tany* ('locally made'). The members of Mahaleo were only school students when the group was formed in 1970. Singing about sex and drugs like their age-mates in Europe and North America, their backing music, played on acoustic instruments, was generally regarded as authentically Malagasy. They and other new artists were heroes of the student movement.

The trigger for the spread of the protests that had begun in the capital was the death on 8 May 1972 of seventeen-year old school-student Modeste Randrianarisoa, while he was being held in police custody in Ambalavao, a town in Fianarantsoa province. Beyond its political implications, Randrianarisoa's death was interpreted by youth in every part of the island as a sign of the restrictions they felt in a society that had always been dominated by respect for age. Just two years earlier, the police were arresting young women wearing mini-skirts and forcibly shaving the heads of any young men who dared to grow their hair, both fashions being regarded as affronts to decency. In this restive atmosphere, news of Modeste Randrianarisoa's death spread almost instantly through schools and colleges all over the island, inspiring a vast movement of solidarity. Just one day after his death school students in Diego Suarez and Fort Dauphin, at the two opposite ends of Madagascar, over a thousand kilometres apart, went on strike. Thereafter, hardly a day went by without news of support from other areas.[6] Opting for a hard-line response, the government arrested 400 of the student movement's leaders and deported them to the prison-island of Nosy Lava. The demonstrators promptly focussed their demands on the release of the detainees, gaining further support from various other sectors of society.[7] The students were joined by the new movement known as the ZWAM[8] (Zatovo Western Andevo Malagasy—'Malagasy Western Slave Youth' or 'Zatovo Warriors' Association of Madagascar' or various other interpretations), a youth movement strongly influenced by fledgling groups on the far left of the political spectrum. The ZWAM was the first organization in Madagascar to be formed by the descendants of slaves, all of them young. Devoted followers of the spaghetti westerns then popular in Antananarivo's cinemas, they roamed the streets of the capital in cowboy hats. It was a mobilization of the city's lumpenproletariat.[9]

On 13 May 1972, security forces opened fire with live ammunition on a demonstration in Antananarivo's main avenue, causing several deaths. This event brought the ecumenical church movement into the fray, as it made a public show of support for the strikers by organizing a religious service in commemoration of the victims. Clerics of various denominations formed a delegation to President Tsiranana to press for the liberation of the student-leaders held at Nosy Lava.[10] Others in the protest movement now began to direct their ire at the government itself, denouncing French cultural imperialism and calling for the revision of the cooperation agreements with France that were central to the PSD's legitimacy, the date of their signature in 1960 being the official anniversary of Madagascar's independence. On 18 May an ailing Tsiranana resigned and handed power to the chief of staff of the armed forces, General Gabriel Ramanantsoa, thereby inaugurating a transition period.

Ramanantsoa was from an aristocratic Merina family, descended from leading courtiers of the old monarchy. Married to a Frenchwoman, he had served in the French army in several colonial campaigns.

While the military took control of the state, the protest movement began to take on the classic form of left-wing revolutionary movements, organizing itself around committees modelled on the Russian soviets of 1917. These were known as the KIM (Komity Iombonan'ny Mpitolona, 'United Militants' Committees'), grouping university and school students, teachers and workers. These committees were active particularly in Antananarivo and other towns. Some rural areas saw the creation of KIT (Komity Iombonan'ny Tantsaha, 'Peasants' Committees') that called for land redistribution. KIM and KIT committees convened a self-styled people's congress that was intended to chart the country's future following the collapse of the First Republic. This people's congress became a forum for rhetorical excess, providing the caretaker military government with an opportunity to bolster its own legitimacy by organizing a constitutional referendum in which voters were asked to state their support for the interim administration. Ninety-six per cent of those voting in the referendum, held on 8 October 1972, supported the government. As during the First Republic, this very high figure was obtained by the government's administrative machine generating support for the incumbent authority, a reflex of obedience deeply ingrained in the island's peasantry. The youth, in sole control of the protest movement for some weeks, now lost the initiative as military men of a slightly more senior generation asserted their power. Unlike the young instigators of *'mai 72'*, as the movement was known, the military men who now wielded power could actually remember the colonial period.

Armed with the legitimacy provided by a provisional constitution, General Ramanantsoa had a five-year mandate to restore stability. Parliament was abolished, and replaced by a purely consultative body known as the People's National Development Council.[11] The transitional government was composed largely of technocrats, although it also included two men who were destined subsequently to serve as heads of state, Albert Zafy and Didier Ratsiraka. But the transitional government had only limited success in calming political agitation, which had taken on an ethnic complexion. On 25 January 1975, under threat from a faction within the armed forces, Ramanantsoa dissolved his government after just 28 months in office. On 5 February he handed power to his former interior minister, Colonel Richard Ratsimandrava, a gendarmerie officer who had commanded the repression of the rising that had shaken the south of the island in April 1971.[12]

Himself the descendant of a former slave family from Imerina, the new president had a radical programme, aiming to revive the KIM committees, this time in rural areas. The new committees were to be called *fokonolona*,[13] the name of a village council in Imerina. His aim was nothing less than for the *fokonolona* gradually to replace the state itself in order to create a radically decentralized form of government. This vision of the mass mobilization of the peasantry was an idea much in vogue on the Malagasy left, first articulated by Jean Ralaimongo in the 1930s.[14] In Ratsimandrava's hands it was combined with an ideology of development, comparable to the philosophies of authenticity being propounded at the same period by some leaders in Africa, notably Tanzania's prestigious head of state, Julius Nyerere.

Just one week after his accession to the presidency, on 11 February 1975, Ratsimandrava was assassinated while he was being driven through the narrow, winding streets of Antananarivo's upper city. His killers were former members of the palace guard of the old PSD government, but the precise nature of Madagascar's first high-level political murder of modern times remained unclear even after the trial of some 300 people, including Tsiranana, had resulted in a handful of minor convictions. There was no lack of potential suspects, as Ratsimandrava had created an impressive number of enemies, notably rivals among the ambitious young officers who surrounded him and other political opponents, including extremists from the defunct PSD. One future president, Didier Ratsiraka, is reported to have had foreknowledge of Ratsimandrava's death.[15] Other enemies included French neocolonial networks, sometimes collectively known as *la Françafrique,* whose position was under threat. Some time before his death, Ratsimandrava had publicly castigated French companies established in previous decades, that still had a major share in Madagascar's economy, and they were afraid that they would be nationalized.

There were also deadly ethnic tensions among Madagascar's political elites.[16] A section of the army led by officers claiming to be champions of the *côtier* population entered into open revolt. An influential current within the elites was opposed to any suggestion of power passing into the hands of the descendant of a slave. Those who thought this way were, at the very least, not inconvenienced by the murder of Ratsimandrava, who joined King Radama II as one of the very few leaders in Madagascar to be assassinated while they were in office.

Following Ratsimandrava's death, between 11 February and 15 June 1975, power passed into the hands of a military directorate of eighteen senior officers from all branches of the armed forces. This interim administration banned all political parties and succeeded in restoring some sense of calm. One member of the junta was the young naval officer Didier Ratsiraka, who emerged as its leading figure. Presenting himself in public as being the choice of his peers, Ratsiraka became preeminent. In order to provide a legal basis for his personal prominence, he organized a referendum on 21 December 1975 that required voters to state their opinion on three questions rolled into one. These were as follows:

> For a new society and as a guarantee of justice and social equality, do you accept the Charter of the Socialist Revolution and the Constitution that will implement it, and Captain Didier Ratsiraka as President of the Republic?

After the military directorate had left power there was a settling of scores. Some former members were sentenced to long terms of imprisonment, and others died in mysterious accidents. The least unfortunate were given minor jobs and left undisturbed.

These high-level manoeuvres seemed far removed from the day-to-day concerns of the majority of Malagasy, and indeed from the preoccupations of the youth who had spearheaded the *mai* 72 movement that brought down the First Republic. Nevertheless, the plots of elites, and the murder of a head of state, were the signs of more profound problems.

The Democratic Republic of Madagascar

Once again thanks to the weight of the government admininistrative machine, 96 per cent of voters approved the new constitution, Ratsiraka, and the Charter of the Socialist Revolution known as the Maoist-sounding *Boky mena* ('Red Book'). The ministers and officials of Captain Ratsiraka's new government now proceeded to reorganize the state into forms familiar from some other socialist dispensations in Africa, featuring notably an inflated executive branch and a legislative entirely at its command—the People's National Assembly, consisting of 137 deputies elected for five years. At the top of the governmental pyramid, elected by popular vote for a renewable mandate of seven years, the head of state was simultaneously head of the armed forces and also leader of the Vanguard of the Malagasy Revolution (AREMA), the political party he established after his election.

According to the website of the French embassy in Antananarivo, the changes now taking place could be summarized as follows :

> After Independence, under the presidency of Philibert TSIRANANA, relations between France and Madagascar were very stable. The accession of Didier RATSIRAKA and his Marxist orientation had, in the period between 1975 and 1980, immediate and significant negative repercussions on these relations, notably the nationalization of French businesses, confiscation of the land and collectivization of the plantations of former settlers, separation from the franc monetary zone and the francophone community, and 'Malgachization' and the abandonment of French as a subject of study at both primary and secondary levels of education.[17]

To be more precise, the divorce with France actually began somewhat earlier, in 1972, when Ratsiraka was still serving as foreign minister in Ramanantsoa's military government. It was in this capacity that this debonaire young officer was responsible for renegotiating Madagascar's cooperation agreement with France and, the following year, for its withdrawal from the franc zone. Nor was Ratsiraka alone in calling for a radical review of relations with France, as Ratsimandrava himself had singled out the major colonial trading companies for criticism, and the AKFM party had been calling for their nationalization even in the 1960s. The action of the Malagasy government in closing French military bases and disputing French sovereignty over a scattering of small islands (Glorieuses, Europa, Juan de Nova, Bassas da India, and Tromelin) was in pursuit of a policy that had even been advocated by one wing of the old PSD.

Nevertheless, the Second Republic was genuinely innovative in its adoption of a foreign policy known as *'tous azimuts'* ('all directions'). This involved aligning Madagascar's foreign policy more closely with the Soviet bloc and North Korea, both of which had been demonized by the Tsiranana regime. This pro-third world and anti-imperialist strategy soon ran up against some hard realities. Madagascar's condemnation of Indonesia for its 1975 invasion of East Timor, for example, was not repeated after Indonesia had threatened to cease purchases of

Madagascar's cloves, of which it was the main buyer. Abandonment of Tsiranana's good relations with apartheid South Africa benefited some neighbouring countries but brought no tangible benefit to Madagascar. Closer ties to the USSR and North Korea did little to promote development. In the last resort, France remained the island's leading trade partner and most important aid donor.

As far as economic policy was concerned, successive governments after the fall of the First Republic were aiming to build a socialist economy, in effect formulating policies on the basis of ideas from the late 1950s. The first wave of nationalizations was in 1973, targeting the main French trading companies with colonial-era roots. This was soon followed by public ownership of leading sectors of the economy including banks, insurance companies and strategic industries. Other firms were reconstituted as mixed public-private partnerships, and by 1977, the state controlled more than 60 per cent of the economy. The long-term purpose of these measures, according to the Red Book, was to turn all public concerns into socialist companies. The harsh reality was that they contributed to the spread of corruption at the highest levels of the state, up to and including some members of the president's family, on a grand scale. In one incident, an entire goods-train, complete with cargo, disappeared between Tamatave and Antananarivo. The French consul in Tamatave wrote: 'The scandal provoked by this matter, if the public were in full possession of the facts, and if due process of law were followed, would be so great, that the government prefers not to publish the report into the affair'.[18]

The drive towards a socialist economy was taking place at the time of the most severe global economic turbulence since the Second World War, most notably the oil price rise of 1973, the delinking of the dollar from gold and the dismantling of the fixed exchange system, and worldwide inflation.[19] Yet, the economy was supposed to be not merely satisfying people's basic living requirements, but also financing an ambitious programme of state development. Building on the ideas of the martyred Ratsimandrava, the government was aiming to make the village assembly or *fokonolona* into the most basic organ of a socialist and democratic state with a view to putting development into the hands of the people. The 11,380 *fokontany* (the territory of each *fokonolona*), a thousand of which were situated in urban areas, functioned as direct democracies. Here, according to Ratsiraka, 'the citizen's views are solicited every single day ... A decentralized society ... gives broad responsibilities to all'.[20] These measures were presented in ideological terms as an authentic, Malagasy-style democracy, comparable to Tanzania's famous *ujamaa*. But this system soon lost the confidence of its supposed beneficiaries among the peasantry and the urban proletariat, becoming a fief of the governing party.[21] In local elections held on 20 March and 29 May 1977, AREMA took 88.2 percent of the seats in *fokontany* nationwide, and successive elections confirmed AREMA's leading position at every level of government.

On 29 December 1976, existing political parties were required to join the National Front for the Defence of the Revolution, intended as a first step towards a one-party state. The central pillar of this National Front was Ratsiraka's own AREMA, the country's largest party, with some 30,000 branches. Most members of the government and the Supreme Revolutionary Council were AREMA members. Other parties included in the National Front for the Defence of the Revolution were Vonjy, a breakaway from the old PSD; the AKFM; and the Christian Democrat party UDECMA. In the event, Ratsiraka never succeeded in dismantling the multi-party system entirely. MONIMA, the inspiration of the peasant rising in the south in 1971, was the first party publicly to denounce the gap between the socialism professed by Ratsiraka and the recourse to the administrative and political manipulations that were in evidence during successive elections. When it came to relations with the peasantry, the new state was hardly any different from the PSD. For the rural populations, expressing ostensible obedience to the wishes of the government—*fanjakana* in Malagasy, a word carrying overtones of the precolonial monarchies—was considered to be a guarantee against bullying and intimidation or worse. One left-wing party, the MFM (Mpitolona ho an'ny Fanjakan'ny Madinika), created during the events of 1972, consistently stayed outside the big revolutionary tent erected by AREMA.

While the government worked to provide a legal and legitimate base for its new structures, there was growing poverty, and, in the countryside, increasing insecurity. The wave of nationalizations caused a lack of consumer products and gross inefficiencies in the collection of crops from farmers in the rural areas. Shortages became the norm, meaning that people had to queue to buy rice, cooking oil, flour, sugar, and even salt. Black-market trade, smuggling and fraud, petty or not so petty, became part of most people's daily reality. Socialism Malagasy-style had no answer to the arrival of growing numbers of young people on the labour market. Ratsiraka's response was to call for patience.[22]

In 1978 the government tried to nationalize schools controlled by the mainstream Christian missionary churches, and in doing so it made formidable enemies. Both the Catholics and the FJKM Protestant church mobilized against these measures on the grounds of freedom of both religion and thought, and they joined two other mission-originated churches, the Lutherans and the Anglicans, to form the FFKM (Fiombonan'ny Fiangonana Kristianina Malagasy – the Council of Christian Churches in Madagascar). On 14 June 1979, in a declaration signed by the leaders of the four main churches, the FFKM announced that 'the church has the duty to seek the national interest, and to speak its mind even when its words may be disagreeable'.[23] From this time onwards, the FFKM was consistently opposed to the socialist government and used its resources to support human rights groups and an election-monitoring organization.

The reforms enacted in the name of socialism cost money. By the late 1970s the state budget was three times what it had been in 1972, and the government resorted to printing money as a short-term solution. Seeing the difficulties ahead, it went in search of scapegoats. In the course of a speech in November 1977, Ratsiraka announced the discovery of a plot said to have been organized by apartheid South Africa with accomplices inside Madagascar. The community of Shi'ite Muslims of Indian origin, known locally as Karana, was repeatedly the victim of scapegoating by the government, as were Comoran communities in the north of the island, who were subject to large-scale massacres.[24] In a similar vein of political manipulation, the government attempted to mobilize Merina of slave descent as a political constituency.

By the early 1980s, Madagascar's decline had reached bottom. Per capita income had declined by some 20 per cent since the First Republic. Factories for assembling French cars under licence, set up in the 1960s when the population was a mere six million, were now being closed despite the fact that the population (and therefore the potential market for cars) was now considerably larger. The middle class was acquiring some of the traits of a proletariat, as was evidenced by changing tastes in music. In the 1960s, musical groups such as Ny Railovy or Ny Voanio or the musician Henri Ratsimbazafy played electric instruments and sang in French about love, family and work, imitating French stars who themselves modelled their acts on American originals. The ultimate in this vein was the group Surf, which was actually based in France and offered to a francophone public cover-versions of American hits like *If I Had a Hammer*. In the 1970s, acoustic music made a comeback, in the hands of younger artistes offering biting lyrics in Malagasy about poverty and migration. The group Mahaleo, for example, included in its repertoire *Lendrema*, a song about the descendant of a slave, socially and economically marginalized.

Indeed, there were many people living a life not unlike that of the fictional Lendrema. Three out of every four people were living beneath the poverty line, compared to less than two out of four under the First Republic. The policy of rapid investment inaugurated in 1978 with a view to developing a modern industrial sector led to nothing so much as a massive increase in public debt. Useless white-elephant development projects were created purely to service grand corruption. In Tamatave, a massive flour mill was built in a region that did not produce a single grain of wheat; if it had ever worked, it could have provided in one week enough flour to last the whole island for a year. There was a general decay in the quality of infrastructure, as was pointed out by the administration of a later mayor of Antananarivo, Marc Ravalomanana, in 1999: 'The construction of the most important infrastructure ... was carried out in the period between 1910 and 1930. Since then, the city has seen very little new infrastructure', the city council lamented.[25] The number of mouths to feed was growing faster than the amount of food. Whereas in 1975 Madagascar imported 70,000 tonnes of rice, seven years later it was importing five times as much. Yet, perhaps figures like these need to be interpreted with a certain prudence, as they reflect the formal aspect of the economy rather than its informal face. In the villages, the collapse of agricultural collectives combined with the failure of state-run crop-marketing services to force farmers into self-sufficiency. The reality in the towns was that the informal economy permitted the survival of a population whose numbers continued to grow not just from births, but also from continued immigration from the rural areas.

It is clear that fast-track socialism was a failure of impressive proportions in its economic aspects especially. Nevertheless, there was a more positive side to it. The socialist government's aim of breaking loose from the suffocating embrace of France and opening the island to other political cultures, notably by way of the thousands of young people sent for training in Soviet bloc countries, and the new valorization of indigenous culture, did have the effect of creating a sentiment of pride and self-worth. This was no negligible achievement.

Liberalism

Notwithstanding its anti-imperialist rhetoric, on 27 June 1980 a government unable to service its debts announced that it had reached agreement with the International Monetary Fund and the World Bank[26] and accepted a structural adjustment plan. It was tantamount to an admission that the Democratic Republic of Madagascar had failed.

Looking at these events in a longer perspective, the radical change in strategy signalled by agreement with the IMF can be considered a major event in Madagascar's history. To be sure, the immediate consequence was to accentuate economic and political inequalities,[27] making the 1980s years of recession interspersed by riots. The most serious disturbances were those connected with the kung fu martial arts clubs that had become very popular among middle- and upper-class youth from *hova* and *andriana* families in Antananarivo. Kung fu enthusiasts attacked members of the youth militias, generally composed of the descendants of slaves, that the government used as its enforcers on the streets of the capital city. In response, in 1985 the government sent the army to crush the kung fu enthusiasts in the gymnasiums that were their strongholds, killing dozens. Ratsiraka remained in power throughout, winning the 1982 presidential elections with 80 percent of votes cast. This was in spite of the fact that the policies recommended by the World Bank and the IMF were far removed from the principles of the Red Book. Each devaluation of the Malagasy franc stood in flagrant contradiction to the anti-imperialist sentiments that continued to punctuate the speeches of a president whose spindoctors presented him as 'the respected leader', *filoha hajaina*. After agreeing in 1982 to increase prices paid to rice-farmers,[28] the government gradually cut itself adrift from the poorer urban strata that were its political base and that were represented in official rhetoric as the proletariat.

In Antananarivo, the soup kitchens organized by the state and the ruling party in recompense for their change in political line had the effect of keeping the descendants of slaves in a state of dependency.

As for the rural areas, the most basic unit of Malagasy socialism, the *fokonolona*, had no success in eliminating insecurity and poverty. In 1986, the United Nations reckoned that in the world league-table of wealth, Madagascar was 186th out of 204 states and territories.[29] It was the poorest state in the southwest of the Indian Ocean, poorer even than the Comoro Islands, with a gross domestic product of just $210 dollars per head, compared to $470 in the Comoros. The musical group Mahaleo composed a bitterly ironic song concerning the government's efforts at oil prospection, endlessly on the verge of bearing fruit, but never quite doing so. 'Waiting for Bemolanga', they sang, with reference to the name of the oil-field, 'is hoping for a stone to give birth'.

One by one, the institutions of the Second Republic expired, and the political landscape was remodelled. In 1985, for the first time since Madagascar had regained its sovereignty twenty-five years earlier, the AKFM party lost control of Antananarivo's city hall. With the fall of the AKFM went the last illusions of the independence era. The ultra-left MFM party became ultra-liberal, implicitly accepting that for the general welfare of the population, both feet needed to be planted in the global economy. Madagascar had little choice other than to find the best possible position it could within that dispensation. In the newspapers, references to 'the international community' and 'aid donors' largely replaced mention of France. Yet France remained the main source of foreign assistance. Like other donors, the French government imposed conditionalities that Madagascar was obliged to respect, at least in principle, on pain of being considered a failed state. Figures from the Organization for Economic Cooperation and Development indeed suggest that there was a correlation between what the Malagasy government did and how much aid money it was receiving.[30]

In the run-up to presidential elections in 1989, opposition politicians staked out their pitch in favour of multi-party democracy, claiming that this was the system that best fitted a liberal economy such as that which Madagascar now had, and called for changes to the constitution. But they failed to achieve a cross-party democratic alliance, leaving Ratsiraka to be re-elected with 60 percent of votes cast, although a high percentage of these votes were fraudulent. [31] This meant that Ratsiraka could now start on his third seven-year mandate. No amount of vote-rigging could hide the fact that Ratsiraka's authority was slipping away, as indicated by the low turnout in legislative elections.

By this time, liberal economic reforms were at last producing some positive results, and between 1988 and 1990, economic growth finally overtook population growth. But any government led by Didier Ratsiraka was poorly placed to benefit from this improvement, as his name alone was indelibly associated with a socialism that had failed. His 1989 election victory did nothing to silence the opposition, which was now demanding a transitional administration on the model of democratization processes in several African countries. The Council of Christian Churches, the FFKM, offered its services as a mediator, proposing to hold a national conference that would assemble what it called the '*forces vives de la nation*' ('the living forces of the nation'). Eighty political parties and various other associations agreed to take part, but the government parties twice refused. Albert Zafy, a professor of medicine, born in 1927, was appointed as president of the Forces Vives, which now took on an organizational form. Zafy had served from 1972 to 1975 as minister of health in General Ramanantsoa's administration, sitting in the same cabinet as Ratsiraka, at that time foreign minister. Ratsiraka's refusal to take part in the national conference proposed by the FFKM turned the Forces Vives into a rally of opposition parties having the backing of the churches.

On 1 May 1991, the Forces Vives called for an unlimited general strike aimed at forcing Ratsiraka to accept a transitional government and general elections. Two months later, Ratsiraka made a partial concession, dissolving the government and appointing the mayor of Antananarivo to head a transitional government. Despite pleas from both sides to intervene, the army stayed neutral. Ratsiraka was able to persuade some of the more moderate opposition parties to join the new government, still under his own presidency. The hardcore opposition, known as the Forces Vives Rasalama, responded by appointing its own shadow government, forcibly taking over government ministries to install its own appointees. In the provinces, Ratsiraka's supporters adopted similar tactics to nominate their people as provincial governors in pursuit of a radical form of federalism, calculated to reawaken ethnic sentiments. The veteran nationalist leader Monja Jaona, still faithful to the ideology of difference that had been prevalent earlier in his career, sided with Ratsiraka and accused the Merina and the people of Antananarivo in general of being opposed to the *côtier* population.

Madagascar thus had two parallel governments, only one of which had international recognition. The tensions generated by such a dangerous situation culminated on 10 August 1991 in a massacre in front of the walls of the presidential palace at Iavoloha, ten kilometres outside Antananarivo. The presidential guard opened fire on a crowd of demonstrators, causing several deaths, although the exact number was never established. Captured on video, footage of these events circulated overseas and was played and replayed in bars and video salons all over the island, often accompanying Jackie Chan films or horror films—in keeping with this company, video clips of the events at the presidential palace were often given lurid titles such as *Massacre at Iavoloha*. Viewers could hear a soundtrack featuring a president holed up in his bunker and ordering his guards to fire, while a helicopter circled overhead, dropping grenades on the crowd and forcing people to scatter through fields sown with mines.

In the end, after discreet negotiations, a transitional administration was established that had opposition support, and representatives of the FFKM took up key positions. A series of conferences in the provinces followed by a national forum in Antananarivo drafted a new constitution[32] that was eventually adopted by referendum in August 1992.

This was the birth of Madagascar's Third Republic. It received a Christian baptism at the hands of the ecumenical organization, the FFKM. The leading role played by the churches in this political drama was the immediate consequence of the general failure of the population to find any other form of organization that had remained intact throughout the Ratsiraka years.

The Third Republic

The third and most recent constitution of the Malagasy Republic is novel in many ways, perhaps most importantly in that it reduces the powers of the president. The head of state is now elected for five years only, and may serve no more than two terms. Fifteen years after its promulgation, the Third Republic may now be seen to have inaugurated an extended period of transition, first under the presidency of Albert Zafy (1993–1997), later after a return to power by Ratsiraka (1997–2002), and most recently under Marc Ravalomanana.

Henceforth, the FFKM, the federation of the four historic churches, is an essential component of any political dispensation in the island.

This organization includes Madagascar's leading Christian intellectuals,[33] many of whom cut their teeth writing in favour of ecumenism in the 1960s. The experience of the Second Vatican Council and the general euphoria of the first years of independence later led this generation of clerics in the direction of church unification, via translations and retranslations of the Bible. In 1975, one group of Christian intellectuals described themselves as 'acting as a spiritual guide and defender of values both human and Christian, which the Malagasy socialist revolution has sometimes appeared to ignore, or even to abuse'.[34] At a time when Marxism and nationalism appeared to be losing their former dynamism, and with the advent of the Third Republic, the section of the intelligentsia aligned with the FFKM gradually supplanted other groups and individuals who had been more prominent in the post-independence years, not least as the universities declined as places of knowledge, becoming instead waiting-rooms whose primary aim was to occupy young adults who in any event were most unlikely to find salaried jobs.[35] Madagascar's six universities were increasingly unable to reproduce a secular intellectual elite capable of competing with the products of mission education. In the late 1980s, quotations from the Bible and religious services began to replace public debate in secular form.

One short-term, and highly negative, effect of the turn towards religious language was that it left politicians free to continue manipulating the law and the institutions of government and politics. In February and March 1993,[36] eight candidates stood in presidential elections that eventually saw Albert Zafy, leader of the Forces Vives, pitted against Ratsiraka. Zafy won easily in the second round of voting. Parliamentary elections produced a majority for the Forces Vives, although this coalition was now revealed to be a brittle one, riven by ethnic and political rivalries, grouping factions with little in common other than their opposition to Ratsiraka. In the space of just three years, the government was reshuffled some ten times and saw three prime ministers come and go, one of whom was formally censured by the National Assembly. The old royal palace in Antananarivo burned down in a mysterious case of arson. In economic matters, one faction of the government took a populist line, combined with more personal interests, in a search for unconventional finance. International adventurers and fraudsters beat a path to the presidential palace, the most sensational such case involving a prince from a minor European royal family in a sordid partnership with the son of a veteran national politician. Several senior figures were tainted by similar financial scandals.

The atmosphere of no-holds-barred economic liberalism was felt at every level of society. Across the island, people recognized the new omnipresence of the free market. A popular *salegy* dance tune, by the singer Jaojoby, was called *Samy mandeha, samy mitady* ('Everyone for Himself'). In some rural areas, there was a series of bizarre incidents of young men stealing bones from ancestral tombs and offering them for sale.[37] In a society in which ancestral remains are still the object of religious reverence, this was a sign not only of the penetration of market-forces into every sector of life, but of a most disturbing moral and even spiritual confusion that was threatening the very texture of social life.

Exasperated by government profligacy, corruption and indiscipline, in 1994 the World Bank suspended its programme in Madagascar, promptly followed by the IMF and other donors. On 17 September 1995 President Zafy arranged another constitutional referendum intended to reestablish a strong executive presidency and to reaffirm his position in the face of the National Assembly. But a year later, a majority of deputies voted to impeach the president, and a new prime minister took his place as chief negotiator in restoring relations with the donors and in order to prepare fresh elections. The former president Didier Ratsiraka observed these developments from his place of exile in Paris, and in 1996 returned home to campaign once more, claiming a mission to save the nation as a candidate in presidential elections held in 1997. During the poll, a substantial part of the electorate abstained altogether, finding neither Zafy nor Ratsiraka to their taste. This was to the advantage of Ratsiraka, who won the election by a narrow 50,000 votes. A victorious Ratsiraka again changed the constitution, eliminating the articles concerning impeachment. Parliamentary elections, however, did not produce a majority for his party, now renamed ARES. Ratsiraka's partisans were divided, not least by their interests in corruption and clientelism.[38] One minister, claiming slave descent as a ground for his personal political legitimacy, succeeded in placing several members of his family in key positions,[39] and there were many similar cases. The president himself was not above suspicion. During his election campaign, Ratsiraka claimed that he had lived in exile in Paris from 1996 in a modest council flat. Yet in

November 1997, just a few months after his return to power, he was able to buy an apartment in the fashionable Paris suburb of Neuilly for an estimated $1.4 million.[40]

For aid donors and businesspeople, the new Ratsiraka, a fervent convert to liberalism, remained marginally more reassuring than the chaotic political opposition. As new elections approached in 2001, Ratsiraka seemed to have every chance of re-election. With 88 percent of respondents to an opinion poll believing that politicians were motivated primarily by personal gain,[41] the existing political class was clearly unable to represent the aspirations of Malagasy citizens towards a better society, and this role was instead filled by Christian churches and new religious movements. In this respect, the resurgence of churches as institutional channels of politics reflects not just the result of the vacuum caused by Ratsiraka during his socialist period, but a profound reorientation of popular ideas about society and people's relationship to the invisible world of spiritual belief that has parallels in many parts of the former colonized world.[42] Alongside the growth of 'born-again' Christian communities, reverence for older cults of nature and the ancestors continue to flourish, particularly among the poorer strata of society.[43] In the last decades of the twentieth century, some Malagasy began to attend mosques, including in the highlands. Today, there is a Muslim FM radio station. Especially in the west and south of the island, where Islamized immigrants landed many centuries ago, there has been something of a self-conscious return to the past. Islamic organizations have sprung up with no connection to the Comoran communities, leading to the development of a distinctly heterodox indigenous version of Islam. Few Malagasy Muslims go on pilgrimage and there are few Qur'anic schools. There may be as many as two and a half million Muslims in Madagascar.

The return of religion to a position of political prominence was certainly hastened by the unrestrained economic liberalism that put extreme financial pressure on much of the population. A worker in the government's much-vaunted industrial processing zone was considered fortunate with a wage of just $40 per month. No political party formulated a programme that came close to addressing the needs of this section of society.

2002

The rise of Marc Ravalomanana from obscurity is a perfect illustration of the decay of Madagascar's political class and the established parties. After the failure of socialism, none had any particular programme. All were more or less devalued by corruption and nepotism. Ravalomanana, by contrast, initially made a career in business, and for much of his life had no allegiance to any political party. When he emerged as a presidential candidate in 2001, his political experience was limited to less than three years as mayor of Antananarivo.

Marc Ravalomanana was born on 19 December 1949 in a village close to the capital city. He claims to be a self-made man who transformed a small family business into an agro-industrial firm regarded as one of the most successful in Madagascar. Certainly he has made a fortune in the manufacture of dairy products—including, according to some opponents and commercial rivals, by some astute and even dubious purchases on international markets. By 2001, his company, Tiko, employed some 5,000 people directly and had a further 10,000 farmers under contract to provide milk and fruit for its factories. At least before his first presidential campaign, he appeared to many as the very model of a local success story.[44]

On the face of it, Ravalomanana's political career began when he was elected mayor of Antananarivo in 1999 after providing discreet support to opposition parties, including one led by Norbert Ratsirahonana, a prime minister under Zafy. As mayor, Ravalomanana was popular for making improvements to the capital and widely admired for his willingess to stand up to government bullying.[45] In a city whose sensibilities are still marked by the memory of the nineteenth-century Christian martyrs, he was able to turn to his advantage whatever measures the government took to stop him.[46] He in fact enjoyed considerable support from the churches, being himself the national vice-president of the powerful FJKM church, the main Protestant denomination.

There were altogether six candidates for the presidential elections held on 16 December 2001. What counted most in the eyes of voters was not their manifestos, but the personalities involved. The incumbent president, Didier Ratsiraka, long since self-promoted to the rank of admiral, described himself as 'an officer by profession, a politician by accident'.[47] His strengths included the support of provincial governors and councillors. For many people, he symbolized the corruption of an aging and illegitimate political class running a 'brigand state'.[48] A second candidate was ex-President Albert Zafy, who remained stuck in a political alliance whose sole common denominator was hostility to Ratsiraka. Ravalomanana, precisely because he was a political neophyte, represented the prospect of change. Among his major assets were the support of the churches and of an administrative machine based in the Antananarivo city hall, both of which were to play key roles in building him a custom-made political party and a popular following. Ravalomanana soon emerged as the main opposition contender and gathered the anti-Ratsiraka camp behind him. He conducted an American-style campaign, handing out tee-shirts, baseball caps and other trinkets with the Tiko logo. Not least, he succeeded in winning the support of many people in coastal areas, attracted by the hopes generated by his personal success story. For the first time one of the unspoken rules of Malagasy politics was broken, with a Merina of *fotsy* status being poised to win presidential elections.

On election day, voter turnout was higher than for many years, with voters concentrated on the two rivals Ratsiraka and Ravalomanana. A major innovation was the use by the Ravalomanana campaign team of a fleet of helicopters that enabled party workers to visit polling-stations within hours of the polls and to collect the first estimates of voter returns. The results were published on the Internet and picked up by newspapers and by Ravalomanana's private television and radio station long before the official count had been made. According to figures gathered by his own party machine, Ravalomanana was in the lead after the first round of voting and had perhaps won outright. Similar estimates were made by an independent election-monitoring body, which estimated that Ravalomanana had garnered 50.5 percent of votes on the first round, and Ratsiraka 37.7 percent.[49] These results, however, were not only unofficial but were based on an incomplete count of votes cast.

On 25 January 2002, the Constitutional Court finally published the official figures, claiming that Ravalomanana had received 46.2 percent of votes cast, and Ratsiraka 40.9 percent.[50] This meant a second round of voting, giving Ratsiraka a second opportunity. Ravalomanana's supporters promptly called for a recount. When Ratsiraka duly refused, both camps began flexing their muscles, with Ravalomanana's supporters launching a general strike in the capital, and Ratsiraka's people responding by setting up roadblocks in the provinces. The situation turned into nothing less than a low-intensity civil war, although there were no more than a hundred victims according to official figures. Still, the tension and the dangerous atmosphere created by steady low-level violence were very real, continuing through the first half of 2002. By July, Ratsiraka's supporters had blown up key bridges on roads connecting Antananarivo to the provinces, and Ratsiraka had hired a team of mercenaries. Intercepted by the French authorities, the foreign fighters never made it as far as Madagascar. Finally, in July 2002, after the army had mobilized 2,000 men in a clear threat to intervene, Ravalomanana emerged as the winner and was recognized by the diplomatic community as the new president of Madagascar. The extended crisis had caused the loss of billions of dollars in damage and cancelled investment.

The significant role played by foreign powers in the competition for the presidency was a further significant innovation associated with the titanic political struggle that marked the beginning of the twenty-first century in Madagascar. Algeria provided Ratsiraka with a planeful of military equipment even before the affair of the foreign mercenaries and the French role in grounding them. The Organization of African Unity, even as it was mutating into the African Union, attempted to mediate but made no progress. The Senegalese president Abdoulaye Wade was accepted by both sides as a mediator and managed to convene a meeting in Dakar that resulted in signature of a peace agreement, which, however, was subsequently ignored.

The election of 2002, and the unprecedented role played by the international community in its solution, is perhaps a good point to end the story of Madagascar. For, since its turn to liberalism in the 1980s, one of the most notable developments has been Madagascar's diversification of its orientation in the world. France continues to remain Madagascar's most important bilateral donor, [51] not least with the aim of stimulating cultural activities with a view to keeping Madagascar in the French-speaking world, and France also supplies direct aid to the state, which remains unable to finance itself from its own resources. It is perhaps no surprise that Madagascar, now under a businessman-president who is also a prominent Christian, became a firm favourite of the US administration led by President George W. Bush. The US government, like numerous American non-governmental organizations, sees the protection of biodiversity as a high priority: television has made Madagascar's flora and fauna famous throughout the world. On American television, a well-known children's programme is introduced by a cartoon lemur, who proclaims in Malagasy *'mangatsiaka!'* ('cool!'). Ironically, the great interest in the island's natural environment is paralleled by that of multinational companies interested in its mineral resources, whose activities permanently alter the sites where they dig for the earth's riches.

Outside the world of government aid and major investment, small traders from Madagascar now travel regularly to China to buy goods for resale at home. They compete with Chinese migrants who have created a veritable Chinatown in the middle of Antananarivo. From southern Asia come legions of gem-traders in search of Madagascar's semi-precious stones. In just a few months they founded an entire new town at Ilakaka, the site of a major seam of sapphires,[52] which has now grown almost to the size of Tamatave. It is the only place in the world that can boast a Thai hospital staffed by Malagasy doctors. Nor is Ilakaka Madagascar's only gemstone boomtown.[53] There are now traders from Africa who own shops in Antananarivo, while traditional links to the Comoros and Mauritius continue to blossom. The arrival of the Internet in large and middle-sized towns is linking young people to the wider world[54] and providing them with new skills, spreading beyond schools and universities. Institutions as august as France's National Library are outsourcing computer-based work to firms in Madagascar headed by a new generation of young entrepreneurs.

The hybridization of old norms with the values and forms of a mass democracy[55] remains the means for people to access modernity and prosperity, twenty-first century style. It permits both rulers and citizens to contemplate a more extensive opening of Madagascar to the world. For good, or for ill.[56]

CONCLUSION

The history of Madagascar concerns the common experiences of people whose origins, ever more distant as time has gone by, lay on various shores of the Indian Ocean or even further afield. Throughout their history Madagascar's people have contrived to organize themselves into distinct communities while remaining in contact, direct or indirect, with the world across the sea, even though the Big Red Island has always been on the margins of the main trade-routes, not least because it has never produced much that has been of importance to others. At the end of this chain of historical experience is today's Republic of Madagascar, about a half-century old. This state is now the main vehicle for the collective journey through time of the island's people.

It is possible to read this story in a positivist sense, as a long journey towards a single, inevitable destination—namely, the gradual unification of people of disparate origin, and the building of a nation. But such a point of view poses problems, as there have always been centrifugal forces at work alongside the very human propensity to seek ways of living together. Tensions between centrifugal and centripetal elements, and an intensity of communication that is perhaps surprising in such a large island, have created networks of mutual dependency between Madagascar's inhabitants that have culminated in the situation today. Elements of dialogue and of conflict were not solely the result of isolation, but have also been the product of the regional networks of exchange that criss-cross the western Indian Ocean. It was not Madagascar's inexorable destiny to become one country under the rule of a single government.[1] This outcome is best understood as the result of a long series of particular struggles and patterns of interaction.

As we noted at the outset, the story of Madagascar has speeded up. In the early centuries, a sail-journey from Asia to the Big Island might occupy several weeks.[2] In the 1930s, a steamer to France took about three weeks.[3] Nowadays, Madagascar is served by numerous airlines and is joined to the rest of the world by instantaneous electronic communication. While Madagascar's people have been the main actors in their own story, the possibilities for action have always been shaped by factors like these.

In the introduction to this book, we suggested certain themes that have been visible throughout the island's history. In the present conclusion, it is perhaps useful to consider how some of these same themes have been translated in practical terms and how they are perceptible today.

Demography

Madagascar is even now rather thinly populated, and within living memory contained extensive areas that were almost devoid of permanent settlement. Population density is not a question of numbers alone, but of the relationship of people to a country's usable surface-area, in other words the area that can be inhabited without an alteration of the land's surface that goes beyond the residents' technical capacities.

Early migrants seem to have settled the land at a time when the natural environment was becoming notably more fragile.[4] For the early settlers, the natural environment was both an enemy and the source of nurture. Details of this relationship between people and ecology remain a matter for further research.[5] There is scattered evidence of the importance of the relationship at various points in time, for example in the name of one of the earliest, semi-mythical, Sakalava kings, from the early seventeenth century. His posthumous name is Andriamandazoala, literally the 'Prince Who Cuts Down the Forest', most probably a reference to the clearing of land to create pasture for the cattle that were so central to the fortunes of his dynasty.

Madagascar has never been subject to really massive waves of migration or invasion. The first known permanent transfer of population to the island, in the seventh or eighth century, was followed by further small-scale arrivals spread over a long period. Austronesian ships of this early period were of impressive size and performance, and direct migration from Austronesia to Madagascar may have continued up to the time of the Portuguese navigators. Although the island was known to Arab sailors and geographers from the seventh century or earlier, demographic information concerning the Afro-Asian zone of navigation,[6] between the Comoros, Madagascar and Africa to the south of Kilwa, is in short supply. The intensity of commercial exchange in this zone seems to have increased as a result of a rise in mineral exports from southern Africa, but no author writing at that time with reference to al-Qomr, Buki and Waqwaq—some of the variety of often vague names that may have designated Madagascar, and often the Comoros as well—suggested that the islands were of much commercial importance. According to two modern authors, it was 'the islands' lack of "viability"' that is 'probably the reason for the paucity of information concerning them stemming from Arab-language geographers, encyclopaedias and chroniclers before the fifteenth century'.[7]

The relative lack of documentation concerning Madagascar in the early centuries of its settlement suggests that not only its commercial production but also its population was rather insignificant. Yet the social and political arrangements of the early settlers were to have long-lasting implications for the island's demography. From the earliest periods, Madagascar's population was characterized by the existence of specific areas of settlement of greater or lesser density. For centuries, fevers or other natural phenomena, together with threats of a social nature such as the slave trade and the vagaries of politics, were the causes of what appears to have been a relatively high death-rate, balanced by the high birth-rate of populations that were overwhelmingly agrarian. This precarious equilibrium, maintained over many centuries, resulted in a rate of population growth so low as to amount to virtual stagnation, even into the colonial period. Early in the twentieth century, General Gallieni wrote: [8]

> we are confronting very considerable difficulties ... with the widely dispersed nature of the population, of our military posts, of our settlers, and with the apathy and indifference of our Malagasy, of our compatriots, of our soldiers themselves, and, I might almost say, of our doctors, all of whom have become more or less fatalistic, like most of our colonial officers, especially in regard to malarial fever. It is accepted that in the colonies, especially Madagascar, everyone has fever, and that no one escapes.

Population estimates made before colonial times are highly unreliable, not least because they were based on highly variable methods of calculation, producing some spectacular contradictions. In 1776, the Polish-Hungarian adventurer Benyowski, self-proclaimed emperor of Madagascar although working for the French government, estimated in a report to Paris that the population of the Big Island was between 250,000 and 300,000. This is about fifteen times lower than the figure suggested some fifty years later by the missionary William Ellis, who, in his 1838 *History of Madagascar*, estimated a population of four and a half million,[9] basing himself on a census by King Radama I's royal administration. Contemporary estimates were generally around the mark of between two and a half million and three million people[10] and acquired a degree of scientific precision only when the French colonial administration investigated the matter in the twentieth century.

It seems that in the earliest period, the general tendency of population movement was a gradual diffusion from north to south. Early centres of population were in the northwest, northeast and southeast, and the last two at least have been among the main clusters of population ever since. The highlands became a zone of refuge for new arrivals unable to establish themselves in the main estuaries, already quite densely populated, and consequently the highlands also acquired a relatively high density of population from quite an early date. These central areas later became zones of refuge for people escaping from the attentions of slave-raiding kingdoms based on the coast, during the period when seaborne trade was controlled by Muslim-dominated thalassocracies before ceding influence to the chartered East India companies of rival European powers. Paradoxically, however, the highlands were also for at least two centuries the main area where slaves were recruited. The south of Madagascar, chronically short of water, appears always to have been rather thinly populated other than at nodes of overseas trade. The latter have also been points of emigration from the island.

Just as the data from before the twentieth century are not good enough to permit accurate estimates of total population figures,[11] nor do they make it easy to discuss with precision the consequences of social and political upheavals on overall demographic patterns. It is unclear, for example, what was the effect of the Antalaotra slave trade or of the later European slave trade on the overall population profile. Although men seem to have formed the majority of slaves destined for export, there were also women who suffered the same fate. Slave exports, apparently running at a level of between 1-3,000 per annum from the early seventeenth to the early nineteenth centuries,[12] do not appear to have brought about a change in the ratio of men to women so great as to cause major new patterns of sexual behaviour, such as a more intensive practice of polygamy. One modern historian, however, has detected a change in the sexual division of labour in Imerina that he attributes to the effects of the slave trade and military service.[13] Nor does the transfer of population brought about by slave-raiding seem to have led to any durable population increase in the Sakalava kingdoms, as occurred in parts of West Africa for example, and Madagascar's west coast remains an area of low population to this day despite the fact that the Sakalava kingdoms were major slave-traders for two centuries or more. The rather sparse population of the west today may even be the result of people escaping en masse from the attentions of slave-traders; Sakalava kings may have preferred to raid the more densely populated highlands rather than take the trouble of enslaving the more scattered populations closer to hand. The relative scarcity of the population has contributed to the formation of a landscape in the west wilder and less obviously man-made than that of the highlands, even though Majunga had established itself as one of the leading ports of the southwestern Indian Ocean by the late eighteenth century, taking over the role previously enjoyed by Mazalagem Nova.

Interestingly, the only slave-trading kingdom that seems to have acquired a substantial number of new, permanent, inhabitants as a result of this activity was the Kingdom of Madagascar, with its capital in Antananarivo. The heartland of the Kingdom of Madagascar may have received a small net influx of population in the decades before the internal slave trade was suppressed following the imposition of French rule. Yet in other respects the Kingdom of Madagascar showed a profligate disregard for human life. A Malagasy doctor in the early twentieth century, trying to estimate the effects of deaths from the *tangena* poison ordeal, reckoned that it had caused the disappearance of no less than two per cent of the highland population,[14] or some 3,000 people per year throughout the reign of Queen Ranavalona I. During the same period, tens of thousands more lives were lost through the government's domestic policies, most notably large-scale forced labour.[15] A disproportionate number of the victims of state violence were freemen.[16] That the central highlands remained relatively densely populated in spite of loss of life on this scale—and perhaps even greater during the military campaigns of Radama I—was due to the import of slaves into this region. In other words, the import into central Imerina of large numbers of slaves may not have significantly changed the overall numbers of people living there, but did have a major effect on its social composition and, consequently, on political relations between governors and governed.

On the whole, it seems that Madagascar's demographic history may bear some resemblance to that of the nearby continent of Africa. In mainland Africa, there was a very gradual increase over centuries,[17] with setbacks caused by natural calamities and social and political factors including the initial shock of colonization. High birth-rates remained common throughout all these phases. The introduction of mass hygiene by the colonial authorities caused a detectable fall in mortality rates. Thereafter, numbers increased rapidly. An acceleration in the speed of historical time coincided with that of population growth, the one influencing the other. So it was in Madagascar, too. At the beginning of the twentieth century, when the first fairly systematic census was conducted, the number of people was somewhere around two and a half million. At the end of the colonial period, there were about 6 million Malagasy. The best estimates are that today there are some 19 million, and that in another generation there will be twice as many. Life expectancy has increased steadily but slowly.

This rapid increase has also coincided with the growth of towns. The first colonial census suggested an urban population of less than ten per cent; in 2007, between 35 and 40 per cent of the population lived in towns. Coupled with this is the low average age of the population. The 1993 census[18] estimated that 45 per cent of the 12.2 million population was under the age of 15. By 2007, well over half the population was under the age of 18. The rise in the number of young people no doubt has an effect on society that goes beyond simple figures, as the structures of society, economy and politics adapt to new ways of behaviour and to new needs, which appear with startling speed. In the field of politics, for example, one of the first signs of the emergence of a specific youth movement was the creation in 1913 of the nationalist association Vy, Vato, Sakelika. It was later suppressed by the colonial authorities with more than 400 arrests, including many minors. One of the roots of the crises of the 1970s was also the importance of youth, demonstrated by new forms of musical and artistic expression that continued to reverberate to the end of the last century. These were signs of a new cultural dynamism.

Civilization and culture

How an originally tiny population, slowly multiplying into millions before the population explosion of the mid-twentieth century, contrives to develop common idioms of understanding over time, has a great deal to do with language. Language is more than a means of communication. It is above all a vehicle for the articulation of those repertoires of values that are often considered to constitute a recognizable culture. The spoken word is only one component of culture, with other elements including art, politics, music and so on. 'Culture is experience-induced in people', Fredrik Barth has remarked, 'so to identify it, we must be able to point to those experiences. We must also accept ... that culture must constantly be generated by those experiences from which people learn.'[19]

In the case of Madagascar, there is evidence from many fields of long-standing and intensive interactions between inhabitants of different regions of the island. The older meanings of the word 'commerce' give some idea of the historical content of these exchanges. In old Malagasy, *fihaonana* designated a place for long-distance commerce.[20] The earliest known sites of regular internal trade within the island, these early market-places were loaded with ambiguous meaning. According to nineteenth-century memory, 'in all these markets, people did business with one another, following which, people returned to their homes and began shooting at each other again, only to meet again at the next market-day if there was something to sell'.[21] Among the commodities traded were human beings, sold into the slave trade or put up for ransom after capture in war. There are still many Malagasy place-names, generally at the confines of the island's areas of densest settlement, whose meanings recall that commerce took place there. A common civilization as well as a common language are testimony to the frequency of communication between people from an early date.

As we have seen, the modern Malagasy language has its distant origins in the speech of the ships' crews that landed in the island in the seventh or eighth centuries. Their language was sufficiently robust to impose itself on waves of migrants, whose linguistic additions and imports did not change it fundamentally. A language, however, is a living thing, neither rigid nor uniform. It may vary from one location to another in the form of dialects, and according to social environment or even individual style, in the form of accents. Language also changes over time. Accordingly, to speak of the unity of a language is quite compatible with recognizing the existence of variety within it, as with ancient Greek, a single recognizable tongue despite the existence of Ionian and Doric versions. The pan-Hellenism that was articulated by the great philosophers of antiquity did not preclude the Greeks from fighting wars with one another or enslaving one another throughout the classical period. And yet this was also the period that eventually witnessed the rise of Athenian democracy. Something comparable seems to have been true of Madagascar in earlier centuries. Linguists have found evidence that there were at least two modes of speech present among the earliest immigrants to Madagascar, possibly corresponding to different languages, and almost certainly to different social classes. However, it has been conclusively established that a single recognizable dialect has never corresponded to a single ethnic identity in any period for which sufficient evidence exists to permit a judgment.[22]

In language as in other aspects of culture, centrifugal and centripetal elements have always coexisted, producing tensions that stimulate change. A Malagasy-speaker can make himself difficult to understand by speaking a 'deep' dialect, but he can also draw on common elements that make communication easier. Throughout Madagascar's known history, the use of another tongue or dialect has never been an obstacle to islanders communicating with one another. Two hundred years ago, Andriamahazonoro (died 1828),[23] the counsellor of King Radama I, drafted the 1817 treaty with Britain in *sorabe* script written in the southeastern dialect. Only later was the document translated into English and French. This treaty was to be the legal instrument of Madagascar's formal entry into the international diplomatic system then under construction.

The earliest immigrants, given their small numbers, could hardly reproduce the complex monarchies they may have known in their places of origin, such as the Sumatran kingdom of Srivijaya, that depended on dense populations for their prosperity. But the idea of hierarchy was present from the inception. Everywhere in Madagascar, power was to become connected to religious ideology, further combining over time with material interests, such as control of cattle and of the slave trade. Documents from the period when Madagascar became integrated into the Islamic commercial networks of the Indian Ocean suggest the existence in the island of several 'sultanates',[24] presumably political units organized around a chief or other ruler, that were links in the chain of seaborne trade. Even at that early date, slaves were among the merchandise exchanged. The existence of such political entities is attested by oral traditions conserved by the descendants of both rulers and ruled. It was the pioneering archaeologist Pierre Vérin[25] who systematically investigated the existence in northern Madagascar of stone-built towns ruled by Muslim princes coexisting with communities settled by non-Muslims, a pattern frequent at that time in East Africa and further afield. Careful study of early waves of immigration throws light on the mechanisms by which Madagascar's people assimilated new migrants and new ideas, suggesting how it transpired that the inhabitants of the Comoros adopted Islam slowly but completely, while the people of Madagascar generally did not,[26] at least not until very recently. Madagascar's distance from the centres of Islamic orthodoxy, its marginal position in long-distance trade networks and its relative lack of strategic commodities, not to speak of the island's sheer size, all conspired to enable Madagascar to develop in its own way.

Meanwhile, some at least of the island's people habitually travelled from one region to another for trade or for other reasons, taking regular routes that are still used by cattle-drovers to this day. Distinct political communities influenced one another or even fused.[27] Traders crisscrossed the island, including its mountainous interior. One of the island's biggest markets emerged far inland, in Antananarivo. This was the famous *zoma* market that was held every Friday—the Muslim holy day—until it was stopped by the city's mayor in the 1990s as a result of the congestion that made the city centre virtually impassable for a part of the week. New commercial centres have sprung up in other areas of the capital. Yet some of the old sales-pitches remain, now the haunt of sex-workers; the site of one of the old slave-markets is today a park favoured by male prostitutes.

Ethnicity and slavery

Both slavery and political entities under the rule of a chief or monarch seem to have existed in Madagascar from a very early date indeed. Given the longevity of the institutions of domestic bondage, we may even say that the principle of servility was constitutive of Madagascar's civilization from its origins, as was the idea of sacred monarchy. The latter, however, has received far more attention from historians.

In thinking about the history of the relationship between hierarchy and subordination, and that of the relations between geographically disparate groups, it is essential to avoid the temptation of projecting today's categories into the past, such as the nineteenth-century idea of a state that is 'owned' by a nation of citizens equal in law. Nor should we suppose that today's ethnic groups existed in the more distant past. To investigate this matter further, it is necessary to consider some of the nuances of ethnicity.

'Ethnicity is a world-wide social fact', the historian John Lonsdale informs us. 'All human beings make their cultures within communities that define themselves against "others" '.[28] Madagascar's people have lived in communities from the earliest times, and it was within these that communal values developed. Centripetal and centrifugal elements coexisted even in small-scale societies. Lonsdale has made a famous distinction between what he calls 'moral ethnicity'—the civic virtues that develop in small communities—and 'political tribalism', a distinctive component of modern state politics. 'Moral ethnicity' he defines as 'that contested internal standard of civic virtue against which we measure our personal esteem.' It is, he notes, 'very different from the unprincipled "political tribalism" with which groups compete for public resources'.[29] If we consider ethnicity in Madagascar in this light, it becomes clear both that it is of considerable antiquity, and that it has changed greatly in nature over time. Regarding the longevity of groups in Madagascar, we may note that Flacourt mentioned several distinct population groups and that he, like still earlier writers, was struck by the extreme variety of the island's inhabitants. In the kingdom of Madécasse he found the complex dual hierarchies of 'blacks' *(mainty)* and 'whites' *(fotsy)*. Some of the groups whose names he recorded were clearly forebears of those still existing today, such as the ones he called 'Machicorois' (today's Masikoro) or 'Séclaves' (Sakalava).

In short, some group-names that are current today have existed for more than three hundred years and Madagascar's inhabitants have recognized the existence of differences among themselves for as long as we can determine. Perhaps the first question that needs to be asked is the extent to which such perceptions of difference were the basis of social organization and political action in the past. We may then investigate the extent of the changes in political and social arrangements that have taken place behind the designation of an unchanging group-name.

Modern studies of ethnicity have been strongly marked by the experience of twentieth-century colonial government, much concerned with the identification of what Gallieni called 'races', supposedly immutable identities that were rationalized by colonial ethnographers in the 1920s and 1930s as eighteen distinct Malagasy 'tribes' or 'peoples'. The unchanging existence of such groups has been taken as a fact by far too many subsequent writers on Madagascar. The reality of ethnicity is historical above all: it is never static, being permanently inscribed neither in the human genome nor even on the landscape. Not all Sakalava have lived from cattle-herding. Not all Vezo are nomadic fishermen. Not all Merina are specialists in irrigated riziculture.

If we inquire into the historicity of ethnicity and its relationship to notions of inequality, we may note that in the eighteenth century, the best protection against capture by slave-raiders was often to place oneself under the protection of a king who promised protection, himself in search of the voluntary allegiance that might legitimize his own rule. Similar procedures may have existed earlier, too. Subjection to a monarch became the content of a contract negotiated in regard to a constituency founded on civic virtues. It was largely through alliances of convenience such as these, or political conjunctures of a similar type, that the distinctive communities later to be identified as ethnic groups were created and reproduced themselves. The *Tantaran' ny Andriana*, the famous collection of oral traditions first transcribed in the mid-nineteenth century, recall King Andrianampoinimerina in much this way, notwithstanding the fact that he was perhaps the leading slave-trading monarch of his time. A Merina identity—a political identity—was actually a rather late creation.[30] The case of a smaller and less well known group, the Marofotsy, is instructive precisely because the Marofotsy were never considered by colonial ethnographers to be one of Madagascar's eighteen 'races', 'tribes' or 'ethnic groups'. Originally constituted largely by fugitives from a variety of existing groups, and including escaped slaves, the collectivity later to be dubbed Marofotsy was formed in the 1820s in the course of negotiations with King Radama I, then embarking on his bid to subdue the entire island. The group succeeded in receiving from the king recognition of a collective status as free persons. Subsequently the Marofotsy obtained other privileges from Radama's successors, via a complex strategy of alliances.[31] It is interesting to note that the Marofotsy were prominent in the *menalamba* movement of resistance to French conquest. Despite the iniquities of the Kingdom of Madagascar that was overthrown by the French, for the Marofotsy, the old royal government had offered a political compact that had been generally satisfactory and that promised to be better than anything offered by the incoming colonial administration as far as leaders like the *menalamba* chief Rabezavana could judge.[32]

Histories of this sort are not unusual. The foundation of a distinct group with a political identity was often based on a core population whose long historical existence became identified as an ethnicity in a modern sense only later. The ethnographer Jacques Faublée noted in 1954 concerning the Bara, one of the eighteen colonially-designated ethnic groups, that 'formerly, the Bara kingdoms, except at a few points, were separated from one another by depopulated zones ... These days, new migrants have settled in these deserted areas and the various tribes mix with one another there ... Bara society exists only in regard to traditional boundaries'.[33] Although Faublée did not develop the idea contained in this observation, he, just as Flacourt's informants had done three centuries previously, was in fact presenting an ideological discourse when he invoked the idea of 'traditional boundaries' and of kingdoms that had been separated 'formerly'. In this respect there is no good reason to suppose that the practices of the people of the Bara area of south-central Madagascar as recorded fifty years ago by Faublée were significantly different from what they had been in earlier centuries.

The spaces between human societies are not impermeable: in between population cores live intermediate groups, through whom interactions take place. Significant historical ruptures, such as the death of powerful sovereigns or changes of dynasty, may make such intermediate groups temporarily more visible to outsiders than usual inasmuch as they may use the circumstances to try and negotiate a superior status for themselves in an emerging new dispensation. Groups of this sort function as buffers between more numerous and powerful groups, and their members maintain concurrent allegiances, playing off greater powers one against the other in pursuit of a classic strategy of the weak in face of the powerful. A Marofotsy could quite easily move between the larger groups known as Sihanaka, Sakalava and Merina—three of the eighteen colonially-recognized ethnicities—creating and maintaining relationships that were often described in terms of kinship. A good example of this process is Rainianjanoro, a general of the old royal army who assisted the French military in their conquest of Madagascar, serving as a senior intelligence officer. Throughout his career of royal service Rainianjanoro was considered a Merina from a *mainty* group, but in securing the surrender of various insurgent groups in north-central Madagascar he also had resort to a Sakalava identity, and described himself as a Marofotsy when negotiating the surrender of the *menalamba* chief Rabezavana, as Rainianjanoro himself described in his memoirs.[34]

A status of a sort similar to that of the Marofotsy, on the margins of major groups, may be recognized in the histories of such groups as the Vorimo, the Voromahery, the Hirijy and the Afomarolahy, all of which have historically played off the ambitions of more powerful groups in their own interest. 'To imagine the existence of a new "tribe" may be the best way to look outward, to embrace social progress', Lonsdale has observed.[35] It is notable that marginal or flexible groups like these have rarely attracted the attentions of historians other than at moments of upheaval, when they make sudden appearances in narratives organized around the fortunes of larger groups. Yet, in their habits and in the interactions that constitute the ordinary texture of history, they, too, represent an important element in the story of Madagascar. The major groups whose ethnonyms are the most widely known—Merina, Sakalava, Bara and others—are the expression of a generalized political relationship rather than of the more tangible realities of daily life. These major groups have all been formed by political processes out of clusters of much smaller groups, sometimes even out of hundreds of them. Thus, a history of Madagascar needs to take into account the existence not only of the major political constructions considered to be ethnic groups, but also of the smaller groups of which these have been composed, or which have existed at their margins, excluded either voluntarily or otherwise. Histories of the major ethnic groups often reflect no more than the result of collecting the oral histories of those families and dynasties who have aspired to rule.

Interactions between groups have from time to time generated conflict, sometimes violent. But violence has never been the only form of intercourse between Madagascar's groups. History has been made in the first instance by more mundane and peaceful exchanges, implying the existence of a variety of mechanisms for regulating differences, or, it might be said, for politics.[36] Language, religious practices and political models have circulated between one part of the island and another, just as people and goods have done. Officials of indigenous religious cults or shrines have often had to travel to one of the island's spiritual centres for their initiation,[37] transcending group borders. In some indigenous cults, the Sakalava king Andriamisara is remembered as an ally of the Merina King Andrianampoinimerina, although they in fact lived some two centuries apart.[38] Their cohabitation in popular memory is an indication of the extent to which one group has borrowed cults from another. Quite often, the winners of political and military exchanges have assimilated some of the values of the weaker groups that they have vanquished. Throughout most of Madagascar's history, violent conflicts were not a sign that normal mechanisms of social interaction had been disrupted. However violent they may have been, they were limited to specific areas of the island and were normally concerned with access to resources. This has changed only with the use of ethnicity as a mobilizing tool of modern politics, the 'political tribalism' that is characteristic of the contemporary period and that has accompanied the formation of a central state. Even now, in spite of attempts by rival politicians competing to mobilize people, inter-group violence often retains some of its older character.[39]

Changing and malleable, group identities and group interactions are both more numerous and more complex than is implied by the existence of maps that show ethnic groups living in bounded territories, produced in increasing numbers from the nineteenth century, but most particularly during the colonial period. We may take as an example the Joshua Project, the ambitious programme of worldwide evangelization organized by a US Christian missionary group.[40] Using similar criteria to colonial ethnographies, the Joshua Project identifies the existence of some fifty ethnic groups in Madagascar instead of the favoured colonial number of eighteen. In reality, the 'traditions' by reference to which an ethnicist ideology justifies the existence of an ethnic group both appear and disappear according to their social usefulness. Traditions and groups are validated in popular speech by reference to ancestors, themselves more virtual than real. Few Malagasy can actually identify their ancestors further back than the eighteenth century at most, the only exceptions being a small number of families that are descended from leading royal dynasties.

The notion of kinship is nevertheless a powerful ideological tool. The Christian churches and some politicians have taken to referring to all Malagasy as being linked by *fihavanana*, the principle of common descent, inviting their countrymen to view their interconnectedness through the prism of kinship. Similar notions representing the nation as a relation between each citizen and a motherland or fatherland, for whose sake children are ready to shed their blood, have of course gained massive political currency in other parts of the world. But in the present case there is a further aspect of the rhetoric of kinship that needs particular investigation. That is the extent to which it masks the question of slavery. Considered an existentially impure being, a slave cannot be part of a family of free persons.

Slavery or servitude has changed in form and in substance between the time, more than a thousand years ago, when ships' crews setting out on a long ocean voyage were organized in an apparently strict hierarchy,[41] and the twenty-first century, when the condition of slavery is defined by international laws and conventions.[42] But, if wealthy Malagasy families still own slaves today, even when they are living in the centre of Paris,[43] it is because it is a durable feature of Malagasy civilization. It is interesting to note the existence of a modern myth that not just some of the early settlers of Madagascar, but all of them, were slaves who had been expelled from a country of origin in southeast Asia. One of Madagascar's leading novelists has recently written:[44]

> I have always wondered why my ancestors were cast out to sea. I am still angry with the Malays and those who identify with them ... Did you know that in Malay, the word *olona*, which for us means 'person', means 'slave'? So our ancestors were slaves who, being surplus to requirements, were sent to die abroad.

Historically speaking,[45] it is far more likely that the leaders of these early maritime expeditions were relatively powerful and wealthy people who were accompanied by others of lower status.

While the evidence concerning those early centuries is slender, for later periods there is progressively more evidence that slavery was an important element in the constitution of society. Social relations were subject to the existence of hierarchies in which notions of purity and impurity featured strongly. Kings and their families claimed to be of external origin, of an objectively different sort from ordinary people. Slavery was a form of subjection and dependency that became more extreme with the increased importance of long-distance trade, as rulers became liable to export recalcitrant subjects. The rise of powerful kingdoms four centuries or more ago was based on extended relations with Muslim traders and, later, with Europeans, whether the freebooting pirates who were so prominent in Madagascar in the late seventeenth century, or with chartered companies. There have always been those who have protested with their feet against pressure or oppression of this sort, by migrating. Flight has been a constant feature of Malagasy society, favoured by the island's vast size. Clusters of fugitives and escaped slaves have formed sizeable groups that were hierarchical in their turn, reproducing some of the features of their societies of origin. To this day, individuals can avoid the implacable logic of inequality only with the greatest difficulty.

Slavery is not only a pillar of Malagasy civilization but also a widespread human propensity. Slave status is not the same in all societies and all historical periods. Although it would be unwise to romanticize the condition of domestic slaves in Madagascar's past, it should be emphasized that servility in Madagascar was often considered by Europeans to be mild in comparison with the brand of slavery they enforced in their own colonies. The relationship of inequality, political authority and geographical location remains a largely unexplored aspect of Madagascar's history, and it is noteworthy that, in the entire academic history of the country, there have been only two conferences on the subject of domestic slavery, and that the few published works on the question have for the most part been written by foreigners.[46]

During the centuries when commercial slavery was developing in size and intensity, it was the interior of Madagascar that served as the main reservoir for the slave-trading kings of the coast. Some of the places where slaves changed hands to begin their journey to the coast and towards the oblivion of exile[47] were locally known as *famohizankova* ('Where Freedom is Lost'). These spots, situated on the edge of the central highlands, were where the unfortunates who had been earmarked for export had their last glimpse of their homeland. The relative intensity of the slave trade during the seventeenth and eighteenth centuries presented the societies of the central highlands from which so many slaves were recruited with a profound moral problem concerning the nature of social and political bonds.[48] It was out of this crisis that a compact emerged binding the king of Imerina and his subjects, whereby subjects were given guarantees that they would not be enslaved, and they pledged unfailing allegiance in return. But since the external trade of the central highlands, and thus the supply of money, depended largely on slavery, it was necessary to seek a supply of slaves elsewhere. It was partly from this logic that a politics of expansion arose, designed to capture slaves rather than to occupy or administer territory, as well as from the strategic pressures caused by European attempts to wrest control of the slave trade.[49] Thereafter, during the short century that the Kingdom of Madagascar existed, slaves were kept for domestic use rather than exported. Paradoxically, slaves soon came to be subject to easier conditions than freemen, being exempt from the *fanompoana* that was a duty of 'free' subjects to a monarch. The *corvées* performed by freemen rather than the work done by slaves became the most ostentatious form of forced labour and almost certainly the most oppressive. Some slaves, doing business on behalf of their masters in distant parts of the island, even prospered to the point of owning slaves of their own. People of servile status sometimes occupied senior positions at royal courts in various parts of the island. Nevertheless, even if forced labour by subjects was more important than the work of slaves, as others have pointed out,[50] the fact remains that the Kingdom of Madagascar was built on a system of slavery. When the district of Imamo rose in revolt in the 1860s, the rising was repressed mercilessly, with many deaths and the enslavement of part of a population that had a long historical association with Imerina. The Kingdom of Madagascar signed treaties and passed laws concerning slavery and the slave trade, and maintained procedures for recognition of manumission or the recognition of free status, such as that negotiated by the Marofotsy in the 1820s.

In 1896, when the French Resident-General Hippolyte Laroche decreed the abolition of slavery, colonial officials estimated the number of people of servile status at some 400,000, of whom half lived in the central highlands, close to Antananarivo. This was a substantial proportion of the entire population of the island. Moreover, not even the formal abolition of slavery brought an end to the reality of servile status, as the colonial system was built on a system of forced labour that recalled many aspects of the obligation of *fanompoana* owed to officials of the old royal government. In 1930, the Geneva Slavery Convention condemned forced labour[51] as a form of slavery. An inquiry by the colonial government in the same year concluded that the reality of slavery was disappearing, but this was clearly a pious hope.[52] The opportunities offered by modern political systems to at least some sections of the population to express their views brought the social question of servile status into the formal political arena. When a political party was created in 1946 that aimed to represent the descendants of slaves and *côtiers* (groups from the coastal regions) in the face of a nationalist movement that was perceived as being dominated by descendants of the former slave-owning classes, the new party received the blessing of the colonial administration, which thereby implicitly recognized the continuation of the social fact of servile status. The politicization of this issue was further entrenched with the adoption of universal suffrage in 1956. At the end of the twentieth century, the stigma of slave ancestry still weighed quite heavily on a section of the population, such as in a Betsileo village located on the southern fringes of the highlands.[53] The stigmatization of a substantial number of Malagasy remains a challenge to democracy for the foreseeable future. Conversely, even in the present century, some individuals have been able to claim ministerial positions in part by asserting that they are of slave descent, claiming a status reminiscent of that of the powerful *mainty*[54] generals in the old Kingdom of Madagascar. The great variety of status within the catch-all category designated by the English word 'slave' is evidence of the urgent need for further research into this question.

Like monarchy, language and music, slavery has been both a medium and a result of interaction between groups. Another paradox of servitude concerns space. Flight has often served as one of the means of escaping from servile status, at least temporarily, and this has been made possible by the existence of empty spaces. Yet it has generally proved impossible for any group to live in close proximity to, or in the margins of, more highly organized societies while evading the control of their main authorities. Sooner or later, the latter finish by exerting control over margins and groups, or at least by attempting to integrate them into their bosom. Thus, space seems to have played a role in both the maintenance of servitude and in its reproduction.

Space and time

The archives of Dutch traders of the seventeenth and eighteenth century provide eloquent evidence that Madagascar's open spaces and the formidable distances between settlements have never been an obstacle to the interaction between individuals and groups that has been a motor of the island's history. News of the arrival of a ship in search of a cargo of slaves in a northwestern port was quite soon known further south and in the highlands, hundreds of kilometres away.[55] There was a sailing season, dictated by the monsoon winds, which meant that local slave-traders could prepare themselves for the start of a new business year. More generally, we read of European slave-traders arriving and making their wishes known, waiting several weeks for their local trade partners to assemble the slaves for export.[56] The slave export trade thus encouraged the development of regular axes of exchange, which were also routes for the transmission of other goods and of political models and channels of social contact. The terminus of many of the networks established along these routes was the main seaports, which contained a high proportion of people who had travelled and who spoke many languages—even in the seventeenth century, this included Malagasy-speakers who were also fluent in Swahili, Arabic, Portuguese, English, Dutch or French. It was thanks to such institutionalized commercial practices as these that the time-scales of intercontinental trade came to overlay the conceptions of time associated with the agricultural year. The days of the week in the Malagasy language are the same as in the Arabic language.

In most other respects, time was regulated by the rhythms of the agricultural year, even in military matters. When the demand for slaves was most intense, kings would assemble an army of peasants to take part in raids, often at strategic moments of the agricultural season. Betsimisaraka traditions, for example, recall campaigns made at harvest-time, when enemies were busy with their crops and when maximum booty might be assured. In other contexts, a temporary truce might be called to fight off the threat posed by the arrival of a swarm of locusts.[57] The slave trade encouraged the emergence of 'robber barons',[58] petty rulers in the densely-populated highland regions in the seventeenth and eighteenth centuries who abandoned the life of farmers to specialize to a greater or lesser extent in the profession of violence. Radama I was one of their successors.

The problems faced by Radama's armies in the early nineteenth century were due to the fact that they still relied to a large extent on the techniques and logistics of the peasant armies of former times, which lived from the land. But Radama I imposed on his subjects a new form of political time, that of the state. This had a profound effect, to the extent that even today, the areas once dominated by the Kingdom of Madagascar are those where citizens not only demand rights from the state, but also where they are most likely to fulfil their obligations to it. The province of Antananarivo is the one where citizens register deaths with state officials and where censuses are easiest to organize and implement.[59]

If time is first and foremost a social idea, so, too, is space. Denser populations encourage the shrinking of distances, not least because information may thereby spread faster, even in the absence of electronic media. In the early stages of the national strikes of May 1972, the school-student Modeste Randrianarisoa died at a police station in Fianarantsoa province on 8 May. News of his death spread so fast that protests took place in some other towns in the province on the very same day. When the interior ministry ruled that Randrianarisoa's body could not be buried in his home town of Ambatolampy, as would be customary, and that he should be buried the following day in the town where he had died, the news swept through schools and towns right across Madagascar. On 9 May, schools in Diego Suarez and Fort Dauphin, well over a thousand kilometres apart, went on strike. The next day it was the turn of schools in Tuléar and Morondava.[60] It was largely the speed and size of the student movement that eventually brought down President Tsiranana's government.

Not all sections of society share the same sense of distance and time. Christian time is oriented towards the future, and even towards eternity, but it is the formal profession of only some 40–50 per cent of the population. Large numbers of Christians also remain faithful to local cults. Conversion to Christianity has been by means of a local brand of monotheism and by considering immortality as a condition to be reached by becoming an ancestor. The royal ancestors of the old kingdoms still retain their influence[61] in part due to the national state, which uses the support-base of the historic monarchies to boost its own power, and in so doing provides cohesion to an ensemble of social forces.

If some of the dissimilarities in perceptions of time and space have faded over the years, differences in levels of development seem to have become a structural feature of Madagascar's history. Some present-day politicians have turned this theme into the main plank of their ideology and the basis of their political appeal, representing themselves as spokespersons for particular regions or population groups said to be disadvantaged. We need to ask whether such regional differences today are greater or smaller than they were in the past, such as may be gauged, for example, by comparing the modest dwelling of King Andrianampoinimerina, a replica of which stands at his first capital in Ambohimanga, close to Antananarivo, and the more splendid palace of his near-contemporary King Andrianahevenarivo of the Sakalava kingdom of Boina, described by a contemporary Dutch visitor.[62] It would be interesting to compare these differences of material wealth with those existing, say, between town-dwellers and rural populations in the mid-nineteenth century.[63]

New factors affecting the standards of living of different sections of the population include the use of mobile phones, internet, the development of satellite television, and so on. In 2005, there were only 90,000 regular internet users, or a mere 0.5% of the population.[64] Madagascar's connection to fibre-optic cables will certainly improve communication with the rest of the world but will also create new opportunities for those who know how to seize them. New fractures between the privileged and the non-privileged are not related purely to material standards of living but are cognitive, above all. Even in major universities, most lecturers and professors do not have email addresses, while many students regularly surf the Internet and download lecture-notes from websites.

Differences in perceptions of time and social distance are notably the consequence of a problem that successive governments, going right back to colonial times, have been unable to solve—how to achieve an economic growth rate that is consistently higher than the rate of population growth. As long as this problem remains unresolved, differences will be aggravated as the average age of the population goes down and large numbers of young Malagasy especially share planetary time, following the emergence of China and India as Indian Ocean great powers. Since 89% of India's trade is via the Indian Ocean, the Indian government has very discreetly installed in the north of Madagascar a monitoring station enabling it to maintain surveillance over its sea-lanes.[65] Chinese investment and immigration are increasing, with Chinese quarters springing up in various parts of Madagascar. Many Malagasy traders these days buy their wholesale stocks directly from sources in China or

Asia more generally. France remains Madagascar's number one commercial partner, but is increasingly signalling its wish to link its policy in the region to that of the European Union as a whole.

In the economic field, the international financial institutions are becoming major partners of the Malagasy state even while they have little understanding of the country at ground-level—far less than the missionaries of the nineteenth century, or colonial administrators, or the French *coopérants* of the post-independence years. As in continental Africa, structural adjustment programmes, first unveiled in the 1980s, have placed a premium on privatization and market liberalization, resulting in greater poverty and in de-industrialization. They have been followed by poverty-reduction programmes that have helped to boost economic growth but have done little to create new jobs. The tensions that exist between foreign intervention and the resources of an island culture remain drivers of change, as they have so many times before.

At the end of this journey into the past of Madagascar and its people, it is perhaps useful—though risky—to close with a few words about the future. The country remains one of the poorest in the world, with a per capita income of just $857 per head, or slightly more than two dollars per day.[66] If statistics like this, produced in airconditioned offices, were completely accurate, then most Malagasy would be dead : common sense suggests that some sources of wealth and income are not being measured. Talk of Madagascar's enormous potential is equally clichéd. To be sure, China's industrial takeoff has made it viable for a Canadian mining company to open one of the world's largest open-cast nickel mines, increasing Madagascar's Gross National Product by some ten per cent in one bound. Other, similarly massive mining ventures are in prospect, including in the oil sector. Tourism is growing fast, particularly in ecotourism, but with its 300,000 visitors per year Madagascar still lags behind neighbouring Mauritius, for example, which has exploited its far more limited resources skilfully.

A country's only true wealth remains its people, and especially its youth. Their force lies in their capacity to derive positive value from their acquired experience—in other words, their history. Tourist brochures and guidebooks often refer to the strong link between Madagascar's present and its past. But, like everywhere else in the world, the future also depends on the past.

NOTES

INTRODUCTION

1 E.g. Hubert Deschamps, *Histoire de Madagascar* (1960; 4th edn, Berger-Levrault, Paris, 1972). This was for years the standard general history of Madagascar, and is still worth consulting. It has since been superseded by Pierre Vérin, *Madagascar* (1990; new edn, Karthala, Paris, 2000).

2 For scholarly research on this issue, see e.g. Didier Nativel and Faranirina V. Rajaonah (eds), *Madagascar et l'Afrique: entre identité insulaire et appartenances historiques* (Karthala, Paris, 2007), and, on language, a succession of articles by Sander Adelaar that are listed in the bibliography.

3 Best known by its Malagasy title, *Tantaran' ny Andriana*. First published in Malagasy in the nineteenth century, the standard French edn (translated by G.S. Chapus and E. Ratsimba) is *Histoire des rois* (revised edn, vols I–III, V, Edns de la Librairie de Madagascar, Antananarivo, 1974–8). This will henceforth be abbreviated to *TA*.

4 *Firaketana ny fiteny sy ny zavatra Malagasy* (publication in instalments, Imprimerie industrielle, Antananarivo, 1937–63).

5 Sir Mervyn Brown, *A History of Madagascar* (Damien Tunnacliffe, London, 1995), updating the same author's earlier *Madagascar Rediscovered: A history from early times to independence* (Damien Tunnacliffe, London, 1978).

6 Steven M. Goodman and Jonathan P. Benstead (eds), *The Natural History of Madagascar* (University of Chicago Press, Chicago and London, 2004).

7 http://droit.francophonie.org/doc/html/mg/con/fr/1994/1994dfmgcofr1.html

8 See e.g. Karen Middleton (ed.), *Ancestors, Power and History in Madagascar* (Brill, Leiden, 1999), many of the contributors to which have also published important monographs.

9 *L'Etrangère intime: essai d'anthropologie de la civilisation de l'ancien Madagascar* (2 vols, Edns des archives contemporaines, Paris, 1986).

10 cf. 'Introduction', in Françoise Raison-Jourde (ed.), *Les Souverains de Madagascar* (Karthala, Paris, 1983), pp.7–68.

11 See chapter one.

12 Ignace Rakoto (ed.), *L'Esclavage à Madagascar: aspects historiques et résurgences contemporaines* (Musée d'art et d'archéologie, Antananarivo, 1997). This is the published record of an international conference held in Antananarivo from 24–28 Sept. 1996. Jean-Roland Randriamaro, *PADESM et luttes politiques à Madagascar* (Karthala, Paris, 1997) provides an oblique commentary on the question of social inequality in the late colonial period. Sandra Evers, *Constructing History, Culture and Inequality: The Betsileo in the extreme southern highlands of Madagascar* (Brill, Leiden, 2002) includes material on persons of slave descent.

13 Notably Gwyn Campbell, *An Economic History of Imperial Madagascar, 1750–1895: The rise and fall of an island empire* (Cambridge University Press, 2005). On an earlier period, Thomas Vernet, 'Slave trade and slavery on the Swahili coast, 1500–1750', in Paul Lovejoy, Behnaz A. Mirzai and Ismael M. Montana (eds), *Slavery, Islam and Diaspora* (Africa World Press, Trenton NJ, in press).

14 Pier M. Larson, *Ocean of Letters: Language, literacy and longing in the western Indian Ocean* (forthcoming).

15 A metaphor suggested by Jean-François Baré, cited in Raison-Jourde, 'Introduction', *Les Souverains*, pp. 64–5.

16 Raison-Jourde, 'Introduction', *Les Souverains*. An important re-reading of state formation is Gilbert Ratsivalaka,'Madagascar dans le sud-ouest de l'océan Indien (c.1500–1824)' (doctorat d'Etat, University of Nice, 1995).

17 John Iliffe, *Africans: The history of a continent* (2nd edn, Cambridge, 2007), p. 2.

18 Cf. Philippe Beaujard, 'The Indian Ocean in Eurasian and African world-systems before the sixteenth century', *Journal of World History*, 16, 4 (2005), esp. pp.459–60.

19 Laurent Berger, 'Les raisons de la colère des ancêtres Zafinifotsy (Ankaraña, Madagascar): l'anthropologie au défi de la mondialisation' (doctoral thesis, Ecole des Hautes Etudes en Sciences Sociales, Paris, 2006), pp. 247–66.

20 Jan Vansina, *De la tradition orale: essai de méthode historique* (Musée royal de l'Afrique centrale, Brussels, 1961).

21 At the time of writing, six provinces have been replaced by 22 smaller regions.

1. SETTLEMENT 400–1099

1 Michael N. Pearson, *Port Cities and Intruders: The Swahili coast, India, and Portugal in the early modern era* (The Johns Hopkins University Press, Baltimore and London, 1998), pp. 51–3.

2 William H. McNeill, 'The changing shape of world history', in Philip Pomper, Richard H. Elphick and Richard T. Vann (eds), *World History: Ideologies, structures and identities* (Blackwell, Oxford and Malden MA, 1998), p. 32.

3 In this study, we follow current convention in referring to the southeast Asian archipelago and its cultures in antiquity as Austronesia. We use the name Indonesia only when referring to geographical aspects corresponding to the modern entity of that name.

4 The name Borneo is still official usage in English and in Malaysian Malay. The name Kalimantan is used by Indonesians to designate primarily that part of the island that belongs to the Republic of Indonesia.

5 Otto Chr. Dahl, *Migration from Kalimantan to Madagascar* (Institute for Comparative Research in Human Culture, Serie B: Skrifter, LXXXII, Norwegian University Press, Oslo, 1991), pp. 85–7. For evidence that Madagascar was known to the ancient Greeks, see Yves Janvier, 'La géographie gréco-romaine a-t-elle connu Madagascar? Le point de la question', *Omaly sy anio,* 1–2 (1975), pp. 11–41; a collection of old sources has been published online by the University of Washington: see http://depts.washington.edu/uwch/silkroad/index.shtml, file 'Historical texts'.

6 Philippe Beaujard, 'Les arrivées austronésiennes à Madagascar : vagues ou continuum?', part 1, *Etudes océan Indien*, 35–6 (2003), p. 59, note 2.

7 Philippe Pariat, 'Les échanges en océan Indien à la période antique', May 2004:

http://aphgreunion.free.fr/articlepariat.htm

8 Jean-Pierre Domenichini, 'Le monde enchanté des Anciens', in *Madagascar et le christianisme* (Agence de cooperation culturelle et technique, Karthala and Ambozontany, Paris and Antananarivo, 1993), p. 16.

9 Robert E. Dewar, 'Were people responsible for the extinction of Madagascar's subfossils, and how will we ever know?', in Steven M. Goodman & Bruce D. Patterson (eds), *Natural Change and Human Impact in Madagascar* (Smithsonian Institution Press, Washington and London, 1997), p. 367.

10 R.D.E. MacPhee and D. Burney, 'Dating of modified femora of extinct dwarf hippopotamus from southern Madagascar: implications for constraining human colonization and vertebrate extinction events', *Journal of Archaeological Science*, 18, 6 (1991), pp. 695–706.

11 David A. Burney, 'Theories and facts regarding Holocene environmental change before and after human colonization', in Goodman and Patterson, *Natural Change,* p. 82.

12 Robert Dewar and Solo Rakotovololona, 'La chasse aux subfossiles: les preuves du onzième siècle au treizième siècle', *Taloha,* 11 (1992), p. 10.

13 Dewar, 'Were people responsible?', pp. 368–9.

14 Burney, 'Theories and facts', p. 85.

15 Henry Wright and Jean-Aimé Rakotoarisoa, 'Cultural transformations and their impacts on the environments of Madagascar', in Goodman and Patterson, *Natural Change,* p. 312.

16 Dewar and Rakotovololona, 'La chasse aux subfossiles', p. 6.

17 Dewar, 'Were people responsible?', pp. 369–70.

18 R. Battistini and P. Vérin, 'Man and the environment in Madagascar: past problems and problems of today', in R. Battistini and G. Richard-Vindard (eds), *Biogeography and Ecology in Madagascar* (W. Junk, The Hague, 1972), p. 319.

19 Pierre Vérin, *The History of Civilization in North Madagascar* (A.A. Balkema, Rotterdam, 1986), p. 39.

20 On the early use of cowries, Claude Allibert, 'Des cauris et des hommes. Réflexion sur l'utilisation d'une monnaie-objet et ses itinéraires', in Claude Allibert and Narivelo Rajaonarimanana (eds), *L'Extraordinaire au quotidien: variations anthropologiques* (Karthala, Paris, 2000), pp. 57–79.

21 See note 6, above.

22 Alexander Adelaar, 'The Austronesian languages of Asia and Madagascar: a historical perspective', in Alexander Adelaar and Nikolaus P. Himmelman (eds), *The Austronesian Languages of Asia and Madagascar* (Routledge Language Family Series, Routledge, London and New York, 2005), p. 1, gives a figure of 270 million. In a personal communication, Sander Adelaar updates this to 300 million speakers of Austronesian languages today.

23 'Introduction', in Peter Bellwood, James J. Fox and Darrell Tryon (eds), *The Austronesians: Historical and comparative perspectives* (Dept of Anthropology, Research School of Pacific and Asian Studies, Australian National University, Canberra, 1995), p. 5.

24 Otto Chr. Dahl, *Malgache et Maanjan* (Egede-Instituttet, Oslo, 1951), pp. 9–10.

25 Stephen Ellis, 'Un texte du XVIIème siècle sur Madagadascar', *Omaly sy anio*, 9 (1979), pp. 151–66.

26 Cf. Emil Birkeli, *Les Vazimbas de la côte ouest de Madagascar: notes d'ethnologie* (Mémoires de l'Académie malgache, fascicule XXII, Tananarive, 1936),

pp. 13–14.

27 This is discussed by Raymond K. Kent, *Early Kingdoms in Madagascar 1500–1700* (Holt, Rhinehart and Winston, New York, 1970), chapter one, who calls it 'the myth of the white king'.

28 'Malagasy' is a nationalist construction whose use by the indigenous population does not predate the nineteenth century. In this text we have tried hard to avoid applying the word anachronistically to earlier periods. However, there are some junctures where this becomes unavoidable for the sake of narrative clarity.

29 The phrase was used by Hubert Deschamps. See Jean-Pierre Domenichini, ' "La plus belle enigme du monde" ou l'historiographie coloniale en question', *Omaly sy anio*, 13–14 (1981), pp. 57–76.

30 Dahl, *Malgache et Maanjan,* p. 23.

31 Sander Adelaar, personal communication.

32 S. Supomo, 'Indic transformation: the Sanskritization of *Jawa* and the Javanization of the Bhārata', in Bellwood *et al.* (eds), *The Austronesians*, p. 292.

33 M.E. Hurles, B.C. Sykes, M.A. Jobling and P. Forster, 'The dual origin of the Malagasy in island southeast Asia and East Africa: evidence from maternal and paternal lineages', *American Journal of Human Genetics*, 76, 5 (2005), pp. 894–901.

34 O.W. Wolters, *The Fall of Srivijaya in Malay History* (Lund Humphries, London, 1970), pp. 8–18.

35 UNESCO, *Relations historiques à travers l'océan Indien: compte rendu et documents de travail de la réunion d'experts sur 'Les contacts historiques entre l'Afrique de l'Est d'une part et l'Asie du Sud-Est d'autre part, par les voies de l'océan Indien,' Maurice, 15–19 juillet 1974* (*Histoire générale de l'Afrique*, Etudes et documents no.3, Paris, 1980), p. 147, note 1.

36 O.W. Wolters, *Early Indonesian Commerce: A study of the origins of Srivijaya* (Cornell Univ Press, Ithaca, NY, 1967), p. 240.

37 James Scott, International Institute for Asian Studies (Leiden) annual lecture, published in *IIAS Newsletter,* 19 (June 1999), p. 3.

38 Wolters, *The Fall of Srivijaya in Malay History*, p. 18.

39 Pierre Vérin, 'Histoire ancienne du nord-ouest', special number of *Taloha* (1972), pp. 54–7.

40 Dahl, *Migration from Kalimantan,* pp. 49–55.

41 K. Alexander Adelaar, personal communication.

42 Dahl, *Migration from Kalimantan,* pp. 114–21.

43 K. Alexander Adelaar, 'Malay influence on Malagasy: linguistic and culture-historical implications', *Oceanic Linguistics*, 28, 1 (1989), pp. 9–11.

44 K.A. Adelaar, 'Borneo as a cross-roads for comparative Austronesian linguistics', in Bellwood *et al.* (eds), *The Austronesians,* pp. 78–82.

45 Vérin, 'Histoire ancienne du nord-ouest', p. 58.

46 Ibid.

47 Pierre-Yves Manguin, cited in K. Alexander Adelaar, 'Towards an integrated theory about the Indonesian migrations to Madagascar', in P. N. Peregrine, I. Peiros and M. Feldman (eds), *Ancient Human Migrations: A multidisciplinary approach* (University of Utah Press, Salt Lake City UH, forthcoming).

48 Including e.g. Adelaar and Manguin.

49 Pierre-Yves Manguin, 'The southeast Asian ship: an historical approach', *Journal of Southeast Asian Studies,* XI, 2 (1980), pp. 266–76.

50 Otto Chr. Dahl, 'Bantu substratum in Malagasy', *Etudes océan Indien,* 9 (1988),

p. 94.

51 Dahl, *Malgache et Maanjan*, pp. 105–7.

52 Randall L. Pouwels, 'East African coastal history', *Journal of African History*, 40, 2 (1999), pp. 285–6.

53 Dahl, 'Bantu substratum in Malagasy', p. 126.

54 Adelaar, 'Towards an integrated theory'.

55 Battistini and Vérin, 'Man and the environment in Madagascar', pp. 318–9.

56 Pierre Boiteau, *Contribution à l'histoire de la nation malgache* (Editions sociales, Paris, 1958), pp. 30–4.

57 K.A. Adelaar, 'New ideas on the early history of Malagasy', in H. Steinhauer (ed.), *Papers in Austronesian Linguistics no. 1* (Pacific Linguistics series, A-81, Department of Linguistics, Research School of Pacific Studies, Australian National University, Canberra, 1991), p. 4. This thesis is argued by K. Alexander Adelaar in a succession of papers.

58 Roger Blench, 'The ethnographic evidence for long-distance contacts between Oceania and East Africa', in Julian Reade (ed.), *The Indian Ocean in Antiquity* (Kegan Paul International, London, 1996), pp. 417–38.

59 Dahl, *Migration from Kalimantan*, p. 88.

60 Paul Ottino, 'Le moyen age de l'océan Indien et les composantes du peuplement de Madagascar', *Asie du sud-est et le monde insulindien*, VII (1976), p. 3; a translation of the *Periplus* can be found online at http://depts.washington.edu/uwch/silkroad/index.shtml, file 'historical texts'. Claude Allibert, in a note on p. 471 of his magisterial edition of Flacourt, suggests that the *Periplus* may mention Madagascar as Menuthias Island: Etienne de Flacourt (Claude Allibert, ed.), *Histoire de la Grande Isle Madagascar* (1658; Karthala, Paris, 1995).

61 James Hornell, 'The outrigger canoes of Madagascar, East Africa and the Comoro Islands', *Mariner's Mirror*, 30 (1944), pp. 3–18, 170–85. With regard to Madagascar, see Jean-Pierre Domenichini, 'Pirogues et bateaux cousus à Madagascar', *Tsingy* (forthcoming). On the musical controversy, A.M. Jones, *Africa and Indonesia: The evidence of the xylophone and other cultural and musical factors* (Brill, Leiden, 1964) and 'The influence of Indonesia: the musicological evidence reconsidered', *Azania*, IV (1969), pp. 131–45. For an evaluation, Roger Blench, 'Evidence for the Indonesian origins of certain elements of African culture: a review, with special reference to the arguments of A.M. Jones', *Journal of the International Library of African Music*, undated extract, in library of the Koninklijk Instituut voor Taal-, Land- en Volkenkunde, Leiden, catalogue number a 1592 N. On artistic influences, see Marc Leo Felix, 'Good ideas go a long way: similarities in the artistic typology of East Africa, Indonesia and Madagascar', *The World of Tribal Arts*, 2, 2 (1995), pp. 46–53.

62 Pierre Vérin, 'Origines malgaches: histoire culturelle et archéologie de Madagascar, mise au point et commentaire', in Conrad P. Kottak *et al.* (eds), *Madagascar: Society and history* (Carolina Academic Press, Durham, NC, 1986), p. 50.

63 Christopher Ehret, *An African Classical Age: Eastern and southern Africa in world history, 1000 BC to AD 400* (University Press of Virginia and James Currey, Charlottesville, VA and Oxford, 1998), p. 21; Louis Molet and Paul Ottino, 'Madagascar entre l'Afrique et l'Indonésie', *L'Homme*, XII, ii (1972), pp. 128, 131. Molet and Ottino do not reject A.M. Jones's suggestion that Austronesian seafarers may even have traded with the Atlantic coast of Africa.

64 Claude Allibert, *Les Apports austronésiens à Madagascar, dans le canal de Mozambique et en Afrique zambézienne: éléments de réflexion à partir de deux*

auteurs négligés (INALCO, Paris, 1990), pp. 39–51.

65 Shihan de S. Jayasuriya and Richard Pankhurst, 'On the African diaspora in the Indian Ocean region', in Shihan de S. Jayasuriya and Richard Pankhurst (eds), *The African Diaspora in the Indian Ocean* (Africa World Press, Trenton, NJ, 2003), p. 9.

66 Alexandre Popovic, *The Revolt of African Slaves in Iraq in the 3rd/9th Century* (French edn 1976; Markus Wiener, Princeton, NJ, 1999).

67 Gabriel Ferrand, 'Les voyages des Javanais à Madagascar', *Journal Asiatique*, 10th series, XV, 2 (1910), pp. 300–1.

68 Bakoly Domenichini-Ramiaramanana and Jean-Pierre Domenichini, 'Madagascar dans l'océan Indien avant le XIIIè siècle : présentation de données suggérant des orientations de recherche', *Nouvelles du Centre d'art et d'archéologie, Université de Madagascar,* 1 (1983), pp. 15–17.

69 Philippe Beaujard, 'L'Afrique de l'Est, les Comores et Madagascar dans le système-monde avant le XVIe siècle', in Nativel and Rajaonah (eds), *Madagascar et l'Afrique*, pp. 29–102.

70 Dahl, *Migration from Kalimantan,* pp. 87–8.

71 Denys Lombard, *Le Carrefour javanais: essai d'histoire globale* (3 vols, Editions de l'Ecole des hautes études en sciences sociales, Paris, 1990), 2, p. 30.

72 'Wakwak', entry by F. Viré, in *The Encyclopaedia of Islam* (new edn, Brill, Leiden, 2002).

73 Quoted in Domenichini-Ramiaramanana and Domenichini, 'Madagascar dans l'océan Indien avant le XIIIè siècle', p. 7.

74 Ibid., p. 11. Dahl, *Malgache et Maanjan*, pp. 358–66, discusses various other possible Austronesian connections of the word Waqwaq.

75 Pierre Vérin, Conrad Kottak, and P. Gorlin, 'The glottochronology of Malagasy speech communities,' *Oceanic Linguistics,* 8 (1970), pp. 26–83.

76 Derek Nurse and Thomas Spear, *The Swahili: Reconstructing the history and language of an African society, 800–1500* (Univ. of Pennsylvania Press, Philadelphia, 1985), pp. 65–7.

77 Cf. Wright and Rakotoarisoa, 'Cultural transformations', p. 310.

78 Vérin, 'Origines malgaches: histoire culturelle et archéologie de Madagascar', pp. 45–52.

79 Chapter two.

80 Rafolo Andrianaivoarivony, 'Mixed cultures of Madagascar and the other islands', in M.A. al-Bakhit, L. Bazin and S.M. Cissoko (eds), *History of Humanity, vol. IV: From the seventh to the sixteenth century* (UNESCO, Paris, 2000), pp. 531–5.

81 Pierre Boiteau, 'Les proto-Malgaches et la domestication des plantes', *Bulletin de l'Académie malgache,* new series, LV, I–II (1977), pp. 22–5.

82 Cf. Barthélémy Manjakahery, 'Le site d'Erimoho dans l'histoire des hautes vallées de la Menakompy, centre-sud de Madagascar' (doctoral thesis, University of Paris I, 1997).

83 Paul Ottino, 'The mythology of the highlands of Madagascar and the political cycle of the Andriambahoaka', in Yves Bonnefoy (ed.), *Mythologies: A restructured translation of* Dictionnaire des mythologies et des religions des sociétés traditionnelles et du monde antique (Chicago University Press, Chicago, 1991), p. 961, argues in favour of a direct Indian connection, but without solid linguistic evidence.

84 Adelaar, 'New ideas on the early history of Malagasy', pp. 1–4, 18–20.

85 Adelaar, 'Borneo as a cross-roads for comparative Austronesian linguistics', pp. 78–82.
86 K.A. Adelaar, 'Malagasy culture-history: some linguistic evidence', in Julian Reade (ed.), *The Indian Ocean in Antiquity* (Kegan Paul International, London, 1996), pp. 490–1.
87 Adelaar, 'Borneo as a cross-roads', p. 80.
88 Cf. Henry T. Wright, 'Early communities on the island of Maore and the coasts of Madagascar', in Conrad P. Kottak *et al.* (eds), *Madagascar: Society and history* (Carolina Academic Press, Durham, NC, 1986), pp. 84–5.
89 Ottino, *L'Etrangère intime.*
90 David Hurvitz, 'The "Anjoaty" and embouchures in Madagascar', in Conrad P. Kottak *et al.* (eds), *Madagascar: Society and history* (Carolina Academic Press, Durham, NC, 1986), p. 107, note 2, and p. 110.
91 Ibid., p. 116.
92 Philippe Beaujard, 'Madagascar, au confluent des mondes austronésien, bantou et islamique' (unpublished, Présentation de travaux en vue de l'habitation à diriger des theses, Ecole des hautes études en sciences sociales, Paris, 1998), pp. 216, 223.
93 K. Alexander Adelaar, 'An exploration of directional systems in West Indonesia and Madagascar', in Gunter Senft (ed.), *Referring to Space: Studies in Austronesian and Papuan languages* (Clarendon Press, Oxford, 1997), pp. 53–78.
94 Domenichini, 'Le monde enchanté des Anciens'.
95 Conrad P. Kottak, *The Past in the Present: History, ecology and cultural variation in highland Madagascar* (University of Michigan Press, Ann Arbor, MI, 1980), p. 72.
96 Boiteau, 'Les proto-Malgaches', pp. 22–5.

2. TRANSFORMING THE ISLAND 1100–1599

1 Robert E. Dewar, 'The archaeology of the early settlement of Madagascar', in Reade, *The Indian Ocean in Antiquity*, pp. 472–3.
2 Chantal Radimilahy, *Mahilaka: An archaeological investigation of an early town in northwestern Madagascar* (Dept. of Archaeology and Ancient History, University of Uppsala, 1998).
3 Neville Chittick, 'L'Afrique de l'Est et l'Orient: les ports et le commerce avant l'arrivée des Portugais,' in UNESCO, *Relations historiques à travers l'océan Indien*, pp. 19–20; Vérin, *The History of Civilisation in North Madagascar,* p. 4.
4 Henry T. Wright and Fulgence Fanony, 'L'évolution des systèmes d'occupation des sols dans la vallée de la rivière Mananara au nord-est de Madagascar', *Taloha,* 11 (1992), p. 37.
5 Ibid.
6 Chantal Radimilahy, 'Archéologie de l'Androy', *Recherche, pédagogie et culture,* XI, 55 (1981), p. 63.
7 David Rasamuel, 'Alimentation et techniques anciennes dans le sud malgache à travers une fosse à ordures du XIè siècle', *Etudes océan Indien,* 4 (1984), pp. 81–91.
8 Claude Allibert and Pierre Vérin, 'Linguistique, archéologie et l'exploration du passé malgache', in Øyvind Dahl (ed.), *Language, a Doorway between Human Cultures: Tributes to Dr Otto Chr. Dahl on his ninetieth birthday* (Novus forlag, Oslo, 1993), p. 35; Andrianaivoarivony, 'Mixed cultures of Madagascar'.

9 Beaujard, 'Les arrivées austronésiennes', p. 87.
10 Wright and Rakotoarisoa, 'Cultural transformations', p. 325.
11 Ibid., pp. 327–8.
12 Chapter one.
13 Humberto Leitão (ed.), *Os dois descobrimentos da ilha da São Lourenço mandado fazer pelo vice-rei D. Jerônimo de Azevedo* (Centro de estudos históricos ultramarinos, Lisbon, 1970), p. 201.
14 Anon (Rabozaka?), 'Notes d'histoire malgache', c.1914, unpaginated ms. in the library of the Académie malgache, Antananarivo.
15 Claude Allibert, introduction to *Etudes océan Indien,* 27–8 (1999), special number on 'Navires, ports, itinéraires', p. 8.
16 Jean-Claude Hébert, 'Madagascar et Malagasy : un double nom de baptême', *Bulletin de Madagascar*, 302–3 (1967), pp. 599–600. Adelaar, 'Towards an integrated theory about the Indonesian migrations to Madagascar', doubts the likelihood of the Bugi/Buki connection.
17 Hébert, 'Madagascar et Malagasy', p. 583.
18 Louis Molet, *Le Bain royal à Madagascar: explication de la fête malgache du fandroana par la coutume disparue de la manducation des morts* (no publisher given, Antananarivo, 1956).
19 Cited by Rasamuel, *Fanongoavana*, p. 189.
20 Quoted by Pierre Vérin, 'Madagascar', in *The Encyclopaedia of Islam*, new edition, vol. 5 (Brill, Leiden, 1986), p. 940.
21 Jean-Pierre Raison, 'Le noir et le blanc dans l'agriculture ancienne de la côte orientale malgache', *Etudes océan Indien*, 15 (1992), pp. 199–216
22 Rasamuel, *Fanongoavana.* See esp. pp. I–II of the foreword by Beaujard and Blanc-Pamard.
23 Flacourt, *Grande Isle,* p. 125, claims that Matitanana in the southeast was the most populated area of the island in the mid-17th century, although he also mentions (pp. 115, 123) the dense population of the highlands.
24 Ibid., p. 123.
25 Jean-Pierre Raison, *Les Hautes terres de Madagascar* (2 vols., Karthala, Paris, 1984), esp. chs three and four.
26 Andrianaivoarivony, 'Mixed cultures of Madagascar'..
27 Cf. Terence Ranger, 'African Traditional Religion', in Stewart Sutherland and Peter Clarke (eds), *The Study of Religion, Traditional and New Religion* (Routledge, London, 1991), pp. 106–14.
28 Thomas Spear, 'Early Swahili history reconsidered', *International Journal of African Historical Studies,* 33, 2 (2000), pp. 265–6.
29 Pearson, *Port Cities*, pp. 55–6.
30 Robert S. Burrett, 'Pre-colonial gold mining', *Heritage of Zimbabwe*, 15 (1996), p. 60.
31 Chittick, 'L'Afrique de l'Est et l'Orient, p. 18.
32 See chapter seven.
33 Pearson, *Port Cities*, pp. 46–9, 161.
34 Lombard, *Le Carrefour javanais*, 2, p. 30.
35 Ottino, 'Le moyen age de l'océan Indien', pp. 6–8.
36 Christiane Rafidinarivo Rakotolahy, 'Le référent de l'esclavage dans les représentations transactionnelles marchandes à Madagascar', *Journal des Africanistes* 70, 1–2 (2000), p. 134.
37 Claude Allibert, 'Un voyageur turc dans l'océan Indien au XVIe siècle, *Etudes*

océan Indien, 10 (1988), pp. 33–4.

38 The Indian Ocean slave trade lasted longer than the far better known Atlantic slave trade, and was at times hardly less intensive. Only in recent years has this been the subject of the research it deserves. On Madagascar's role as a depot for African slaves in the 19th century, see Campbell, *An Economic History,* chapter nine.

39 Quoted by Auguste Toussaint, *Histoire de l'océan Indien* (Presses universitaires de France, Paris, 1961), p. 55.

40 Dahl, *Migration from Kalimantan to Madagascar*, pp. 89–90.

41 K.Alexander Adelaar, 'Asian roots of the Malagasy: a linguistic perspective', *Bijdragen tot de Taal- Land- en Volkenkunde*, 151, 3 (1995), p. 339.

42 Ferrand, 'Les voyages des Javanais à Madagascar', p. 281. Malaysian schoolchildren are today taught that Madagascar is part of the Malay world, as Solofo Randrianja observed during a visit to Malaysia in 2002.

43 D.G. Keswani, 'Influences culturelles et commerciales indiennes dans l'océan Indien, de l'Afrique et Madagascar à l'Asie du sud-est', in UNESCO, *Relations Historiques à travers l'océan Indien*, p. 40.

44 Toussaint, *Histoire de l'océan Indien,* p. 59.

45 Ottino, 'Le moyen age de l'océan Indien', pp. 5–6.

46 Cf. Gabriel Rantoandro, 'Une communauté mercantile du nord ouest : les Antalaotra', *Omaly sy Anio*, XX (1983–1984), pp. 195–210.

47 Pierre Vérin, 'Les apports culturels et la contribution africaine au peuplement de Madagascar', in UNESCO, *Relations historiques à travers l'océan Indien*, p. 108.

48 Vérin, *Madagascar*, p. 65.

49 Hébert, 'Madagascar et Malagasy', p. 592.

50 Reproduced *hors-texte* in vol. 1 of Edouard Ralaimihoatra, *Histoire de Madagascar* (2 vols., Société malgache d'édition, Antananarivo, 1965).

51 N.-J. Gueunier, J-C. Hébert, F. Viré, 'Les routes maritimes du Canal de Mozambique d'après les routiers arabo-swahilis', *Taloha,* 11 (1992), p. 79.

52 Ludvig Munthe, *La Tradition arabico-malgache: vue à travers le manuscrit A-6 d'Oslo et d'autres manuscrits disponibles* (Lutheran Printing House, TPFLM, Antananarivo, 1982), p. 79.

53 Philippe Beaujard, *Le Parler secret arabico-malgache du sud-est de Madagascar: recherches étymologiques* (L'Harmattan, Paris, 1998).

54 Munthe, *La Tradition arabico-malgache*, p. 17.

55 Adelaar, 'Borneo as a cross-roads', p. 80.

56 Munthe, *La Tradition arabico-malgache*, p. 7.

57 Beaujard, *Le Parler secret*, p. 9.

58 Hendrik Frappé, 'Korte beschrijving van 't Eiland Madagascar of St. Laurens aan de Westsijde', fol. 19, 1715, South African Library, Cape Town, MSD 3, recorded that children born in western Madagascar on Sunday or Tuesday were killed, even the king's. This manuscript has been translated and edited by Piet Westra and James C. Armstrong (eds), *Slave Trade with Madagascar: The journals of the Cape Slaver* Leijdsman, *1715* (Africana Publishers, Cape Town, 2006).

59 Leitão, *Os dois descobrimentos.*

60 Flacourt, *Grande Isle.*

61 Ottino, *L'Etrangère intime*, 1, p. 6.

62 Leitão, *Os dois descobrimentos*, p. 240.

63 Ottino, *L'étrangère intime*, 1, pp. 48–9.

64 Cf. Gabriel Ferrand, 'Les îles Râmny, Lâmery, Wâkwâk, Komor des géographes arabes, et Madagascar', *Journal asiatique*, 10th series, X (1907), pp. 442–5; see also Boiteau, *Contribution*, pp. 43–4.

65 Ferrand, 'Les îles Râmny, Lâmery', pp. 437, 443–4.

66 Munthe, *La Tradition arabico-malgache*, p. 17. The large corpus of primary sources on the Zafiraminia includes Mariano's description in Leitão, *Os dois descobrimentos*; Flacourt, *Grande Isle*, p. 146; Gabriel Ferrand, 'La légende de Raminia d'après un manuscrit arabico-malgache de la Bibliothèque nationale', *Journal asiatique*, 9th series, XIX (1902), pp. 185–230; Ravalarivo, 'Histoire des Rafindraminia' (manuscript no. 2773 III, Grandidier papers, Muséum national d'histoire naturelle, Paris).

67 Beaujard, 'Les arrivées', p. 108.

68 Alain Delivré, *L'Histoire des rois d'Imerina: interprétation d'une tradition orale* (Klincksieck, Paris, 1974), p. 233; cf. E. Ramilison, *Ny Loharanon' ny Andriana nanjaka teto Imerina, etc.* (2 vols, Imprimerie Ankehitriny, Antananarivo, 1951–2).

69 Ottino, 'The mythology of the highlands', p. 973.

70 Rasamuel, *Fanongoavana*, pp. I–II.

71 Peter Bellwood, *Prehistory of the Indo-Malaysian Archipelago* (1985; revised edn., University of Hawai'i Press, Honolulu, 1997), pp. 122–3.

72 Lombard, *Le Carrefour javanais*, 3, pp. 9–14.

73 Ibid., p. 89.

74 Ibid., pp. 19–21, 56–61.

75 Ibid., pp. 93–5.

76 Gabriel Rantoandro, 'Des royaumes concentriques de Java au «Royaume de Madagascar» : les fondements d'un héritage présumé', in Françoise Raison-Jourde and Solofo Randrianja (eds), *La Nation malgache au défi de l'ethnicité* (Karthala, Paris, 2002), pp. 107–23.

77 Beaujard, 'Les arrivées', p. 108.

78 Paul Ottino, 'Quelques brèves remarques sur les études de parenté et d'organisation sociale à Madagascar', *Asie du sud-est et monde insulindien,* III, 2 (1972), p. 119–20.

79 Battistini and Vérin, 'Man and the environment in Madagascar', pp. 326–8.

80 Beaujard, 'Madagascar, au confluent des mondes austronésien, bantou et islamique', p. 14.

81 Ottino, *L'étrangère intime*, 1, pp. 49–50.

82 Cf. Raison-Jourde, 'Introduction', *Les Souverains de Madagascar,* p. 18. Groups of Islamized immigrants are listed by Gabriel Ferrand, *Les Musulmans à Madagascar et aux îles Comores* (3 vols, E. Leroux, Paris, 1891–1902), 2, p. 1.

83 Quoted in Ferrand, 'Les îles Râmny, Lâmery', p. 514.

84 Flacourt, *Grande Isle*, p. 128.

85 *Filohabe* in classical Malagasy.

86 Beaujard, 'L'Afrique de l'Est, les Comores et Madagascar', p. 66.

87 Christian Pelras, *The Bugis* (Blackwell, Oxford, 1996), pp. 81–2.

88 As discussed in Kent, *Early Kingdoms*, chapter one.

89 Paul Ottino, 'La hiérarchie sociale et l'alliance dans le Royaume de Matacassi', *Asie du sud-est et le monde insulindien*, IV, 4 (1973), p. 54.

90 Raison, 'Le noir et le blanc dans l'agriculture ancienne de la côte orientale malgache'.

91 Beaujard, 'Les arrivées', p. 84.

92 Ibid., p. 107.
93 Boiteau, *Contribution*, p. 50.
94 Until the early 19th century, Europeans generally referred to the population of the central highlands as Hova, including both noble *(andriana)* and commoner *(hova)* groups. After that date, they increasingly tended to use the word Merina to designate the main highland ethnic group. See Pier Larsen, 'Desperately seeking the "Merina" (central Madagascar): reading ethnonyms and their semantic fields in African identity histories', *Journal of Southern African Studies*, 22, 4 (1996), pp. 541–60. Here, we distinguish between *hova* as a category of the population and Hova as an ethnic group in something resembling today's sense.
95 Wright and Rakotoarisoa, 'Cultural transformations', p. 325.
96 Pierre Vérin, 'L'Imerina et le peuplement de Madagascar: les hypothèses confrontées aux nouvelles découvertes', *Taloha*, 12 (1994), p. 26.
97 Leitaõ, *Os dois descobrimentos*, pp. 71, 207.
98 Rasamuel, *Fanangoavana*.
99 Philippe Beaujard, *Princes et paysans: les Tanala de l'Ikongo* (Harmattan, Paris, 1983), pp. 35–9.
100 Vérin, 'Les apports culturels', pp. 109–110.
101 Gabriel Ferrand, 'L'origine africaine des malgaches', *Journal Asiatique,* 10th series, XII (1908), p. 466.
102 Vérin, *History of Civilisation*, p. 49.
103 Pierre Vérin, 'L'origine indonésienne des malgaches : indices culturels et archéologie', *Bulletin de Madagascar,* 259 (1967), pp. 958–61.
104 Vérin, 'Les apports culturels', pp. 109–10.
105 Robert Drury (Capt. Pasfield Oliver, ed.), *Madagascar; or Robert Drury's Journal, During Fifteen Years' Captivity on that Island* (1729; T. Fisher Unwin, London, 1890), pp. 265–6. As with *hova*/Hova (see note 94), we distinguish between *vazimba* as a generic concept and Vazimba as an existing social or ethnic group.
106 Birkeli, *Les Vazimbas de la côte ouest de Madagascar*.
107 Pearson, *Port Cities,* pp. 70–1, 72.
108 Boiteau, *Contribution*, p. 52.
109 Battistini and Vérin, 'Man and the environment', pp. 318–9.
110 The most systematic attempt to examine the African origins of kingship in Madagascar is Kent, *Early Kingdoms*.
111 Deschamps, *Histoire de Madagascar*, pp. 22–3; see also the comments in Kent, *Early Kingdoms*, pp. 30–87.
112 Scott lecture, in *IIAS Newsletter*, p. 45.
113 Ibid.
114 Ottino, 'Quelques brèves remarques', p. 123.

3. ROYALTY AND THE RISE OF KINGDOMS 1600–1699

1 Flacourt, *Grande Isle* p. 145.
2 Ibid., p. 124.
3 Ibid., pp. 145–6.
4 See above, Introduction.
5 See e.g. Maurice Bloch, *From Blessing to Violence: History and ideology in the circumcision ritual of the Merina of Madgascar* (Cambridge University Press,

Cambridge, 1986).

6 James Sibree, *The Great African Island* (Trubner, London, 1880), p. 326.

7 E.g. 'Relâche du navire «Le Barneveld»', 1719, in Alfred Grandidier *et al.* (eds), *Collection des ouvrages anciens concernant Madagascar* (henceforth, *COACM*) (Comité de Madagascar, Paris, 1905), vol. 5, p. 24.

8 Flacourt, *Grande Isle,* p. 95.

9 Cf. ibid., p. 171.

10 Respectively Nacquart and Du Bois, both quoted by Allibert in ibid., pp. 55–6.

11 Westra and Armstrong, *Slave Trade*, p. 127.

12 Flacourt, *Grande Isle*, p. 190.

13 Suggested by Beaujard, 'Madagascar, au confluent des mondes austronésien, bantou et islamique', pp. 189–90.

14 Abbé Aléxis Rochon (trans. Jos. Trapp), *An Account of the Island of Madagascar*(1792), published with Pasfield Oliver, *Madagascar; or Robert Drury's Journal*, pp. 362–3.

15 Remains of which are on display in the Centre d'art et archéologie in Antananarivo. See David Rasamuel, 'Observations sur la fabrication et l'usage des poteries malgaches : l'évolution de la poterie malgache durant le second millénaire de notre ère', *Nouvelles du Centre d'art et archéologie*, 3–4 (1985–6), pp. 13–19 ; also, Rasamuel, *Fanongoavana*, pp. 193–5, with a photo of one of these dishes on p. 74.

16 Flacourt, *Grande Isle*, p. 190.

17 Drury, *Madagascar*, p. 181.

18 Ibid., p. 277.

19 Flacourt, *Grande Isle*, p. 169.

20 Boiteau, *Contribution,* p. 50.

21 Drury, *Madagascar*, p. 181.

22 Note by Allibert in Flacourt, *Grande Isle*, p. 503, note 8 (comment on ch.XXVI).

23 Ibid., p. 129.

24 Note the use of the term 'castes' by Georges Condominas, *Fokon'olona et collectivités rurales en Imerina* (Berger-Levrault, Paris, 1960), pp. 119–30.

25 Father Nacquart, quoted by Allibert in his introduction to Flacourt, *Grande Isle*, p. 63.

26 Ibid., p. 172.

27 Ibid.

28 Ibid.

29 Journal of the *Schuylenburg*, published in Stephen Ellis and Solofo Randrianja, 'Les archives de la Compagnie néerlandaise des indes orientales et l'histoire de Madagascar: l'expédition du navire de la VOC, le *Schuylenburg*, septembre 1752', in Ignace Rakoto (ed.), *La Route des esclaves, système servile et traite dans l'est malgache* (L'Harmattan, Paris, 2000), pp. 47–74.

30 Flacourt, *Grande Isle,* p. 172.

31 Ibid.

32 See the remarks by Claude Allibert in ibid., p. 505, note 13.

33 Rafolo Andrianaivoarivony, 'Habitats fortifiés et organisation de l'espace dans le Vonizongo (centre ouest de Madagascar. Le cas de Lohavohitra' (doctoral thesis, University of Paris I, 1989), p. 441.

34 Flacourt, *Grande Isle,* p. 165.

35 Ibid., p. 96.

36 Leitaõ, *Os dois descobrimentos*, pp. 71, 207.
37 Ellis, 'Un texte du XVIIe siècle sur Madagascar', p. 157.
38 Drury, *Madagascar*, pp. 277–8.
39 Rainitovo, *Tantaran' ny Malagasy manontolo* (3 vols., J. Paoli et fils, Tananarive, 1932), 2, pp. 211–12.
40 Suggested by Jean-Claude Hébert: see Radimilahy, *Mahilaka*, p. 20.
41 Leitaõ, *Os dois descobrimentos*, p. 204.
42 Flacourt, *Grande Isle,* p. 115.
43 Pier M. Larson, 'Colonies lost: God, hunger, and conflict in Anosy (Madagascar) to 1674,' *Comparative Studies of South Asia, Africa and the Middle East*, 27, 2 (2007), pp. 345–66.
44 Drury, *Madagascar*, p. 111.
45 Flacourt, *Grande Isle*, p. 301.
46 Ibid., p. 171; Drury, *Madagascar*, p. 200.
47 Cf. Flacourt, *Grande Isle*, pp. 150–5. The well-known scholar and medical doctor Albert Rakoto-Ratsimamanga (1907–2001) came from a family with a traditional knowledge of herbal medicine. He developed medicines based on local knowledge that have received worldwide recognition. Members of his family continue in practice.
48 Beaujard, 'Les arrivées', pp. 86–90.
49 Pierre Vérin and Narivelo Rajaonarimanana, quoted in Umar Danfulani, 'Sixteen figure divination in Africa', *Africana Marburgensia*, XXX, i (1997), pp. 32, 35.
50 Drury, *Madagascar*, p. 176.
51 Flacourt, *Grande Isle*, p. 176.
52 Westra and Armstrong, *Slave Trade*, p. 129.
53 Anon., 'An Acco[t] of the present comodityes that are imported & exported at Madagascarr and the manner of dealing with the natives', undated [1692?], Rawlinson ms. A.334, Bodleian Library, Oxford.
54 René Barendse, *The Arabian Seas: The Indian Ocean world of the seventeenth century* (M.E. Sharpe, Armonk, NY, 2002), p. 69.
55 Dennis O. Flynn and Arturo Giraldez, 'Born with a "silver spoon": the origin of world trade in 1571', *Journal of World History*, 6, 2 (1995), p. 13.
56 Toussaint, *Histoire de l'océan Indien,* p. 120.
57 Jan de Vries and Ad van der Woude, *The First Modern Economy: Success, failure and perseverance of the Dutch economy 1500–1815* (Cambridge University Press, 1997).
58 Radimilahy, *Mahilaka*, p. 33.
59 Ellis, 'Un texte du XVIIe siècle', p. 157.
60 Berger, 'Les raisons de la colère des ancêtres Zafinifotsy', pp. 247–66.
61 Leitaõ, *Os dois descobrimentos*, p. 62.
62 Ellis, 'Un texte du XVIIe siècle', p. 159.
63 Note by Jean-Aimé Rakotoarisoa, in *Recherche, pédagogie et culture,* IX, 55 (1981), pp. 105–6.
64 W. Ph. Coolhaas, *Generale Missiven van Gouverneurs-Generaal en Raden aan Heren XVII der Verenigde Oostindische Compagnie* (vol.1, Nijhoff, The Hague, 1960), p. 50.
65 Leitao, *Os dois descobrimentos,* p. 67.
66 Ibid., pp. 208, 215.
67 Ibid., p. 258.
68 Manuel Faria y Sousa, *Asia Portuguesa*, vol. 3 (Antonio Craesbeeck, Lisbon,

1675), part 3, ch.XII, p. 308.

69 South African State Archives, Cape Town, Council of Policy, C.2244: journal of the *Voorhout*, pp. 100–1.

70 Nationaal Archief, The Hague, VOC 4012, fols.704r–705v: 'Appendix of cort relas van situatie van 't eilant magelage, etc.', appendixed to the journal of the *Voorhout*, 1676–7.

71 Ibid, fol.696v, entry for 15 Sept. 1676.

72 Cf. Pierre Vérin, *Madagascar*, pp. 68–73.

73 Report by Mariano, *COACM*, 2, p. 14.

74 Raison-Jourde, 'Introduction', *Les Souverains*, pp. 18–26.

75 See above, pp. 77–8.

76 Flacourt, *Grande Isle*, p. 173.

77 Raison-Jourde, 'Introduction', *Les Souverains*.

78 Kent, *Early Kingdoms*, ch. five, argues that the Maroseraña were recent immigrants from Africa, bringing ideas of royal authority from Zimbabwe.

79 Pierre Vérin, 'Les anciens habitats de Rezoky et d'Asambalahy', *Taloha*, 4 (1971), pp. 29–45.

80 Cf. Malanjaona Rakotomalala, Sophie Blanchy and Françoise Raison-Jourde, *Madagascar: les ancêtres au quotidien* (L'Harmattan, Paris, 2001).

81 Leitaõ, *Os dois descobrimentos*, p. 66.

82 Beaujard, 'Madagascar, au confluent des mondes', p. 216.

83 Westra and Armstrong, *Slave Trade*, p. 125.

84 Cf. R.M. Andriamanjato, *Le Tsiny et le tody dans la pensée malgache* (Présence africaine, Paris, 1957).

85 Flacourt, *Grande Isle*, p. 173.

86 Ibid.

87 Bakoly Domenichini-Ramiaramanana, *Du ohabolana au hainteny: langue, littérature et politique à Madagascar* (Karthala, Paris, 1983).

88 Ottino, *L'Etrangère intime*, esp. the short summary in vol.2, pp. 519–21.

89 Lee Haring (ed.), *Ibonia: Epic of Madagascar* (Bucknell University Press, Lewisburg, PA, 1994).

90 François Noiret, *Le Mythe d'Ibonia, le grand Prince (Madagascar)* (Karthala, Paris, 2008) p. 28.

4. THE SLAVE-TRADER KINGS 1700–1816

1 See Kent, *Early Kingdoms*, ch. five, for the argument that the ruling dynasty of the Sakalava had its roots in central southern Africa.

2 Historians sometimes refer to 'the Sakalava kingdom' in the singular, although there were several rival kingdoms of this name coexisting with each other.

3 Westra and Armstrong, *Slave Trade*, p. 129.

4 Cf. Pier M. Larson, *History and Memory in the Age of Enslavement: Becoming Merina in highland Madagascar, 1770–1822* (James Currey, Oxford, 2000), *passim*.

5 Westra and Armstrong, *Slave Trade*, p. 129.

6 Flacourt, *Grande Isle*, p. 302.

7 Gerald Berg, 'The sacred musket: tactics, technology and power in eighteenth-century Madagascar', *Comparative Studies in Society and History*, 27, 2 (1985), pp. 261–79.

8 According to Jacques Lombard, *La Royauté sakalava: formation, développe-*

ment, et effondrement, du XVIIe au XXe siècle. Essai d'analyse d'un système politique (ORSTOM, Antananarivo, 1973), pp. 25–27, Lahifotsy was the fourth in the dynastic line, but there are other versions.

9 Kings in Madagascar may have several names, including one from before their reign, a second during their reign, and a third that is given posthumously. This makes precise identification an often arduous task.

10 James C. Armstrong, 'Madagascar and the slave trade in the seventeenth century', *Omaly sy Anio*, 17–20 (1983–4), p. 220.

11 Lombard, *La Royauté sakalava*, pp. 25–27.

12 Cf. Charles Guillain, *Documents sur l'histoire, la géographie et le commerce de la partie occidentale de Madagascar* (Imprimerie royale, Paris, 1845), pp. 24, 26; also, South African State Archives C.2250, log of the *Neptune*, supercargo John Godfried Krause, 1760, p. 102: entry for 19 Oct. 1760.

13 Jeremias Brons to Gov.-gen. W. van Outhoorn, 14 Jan. 1695, published in H.C.V. Leibbrandt, *Précis of the Archives of the Cape of Good Hope. Letters Received, 1695–1708* (W.A. Richards & Sons, Cape Town, 1896), pp. 28–31.

14 Description by the sieur de la Merveille, 1708, in *COACM*, 3, p. 619, note 1.

15 Guillain, *Documents*, pp. 22–3.

16 Rigsarkivet, Copenhagen: archives of the Vestindisk-Guineisk Kompagni, box 219: journal of Charles Barrington, pt 4, p. 60, 18/29 Jan. 1738.

17 Guillain, *Documents*, p. 38.

18 Ibid., pp. 20–2.

19 'Description de Madagascar et de l'île d'Anjouan par Jean Ovington' (1690), *COACM,* 3, p. 198.

20 As noted by a visitor: 'Deux voyages à Madagascar de J. van der Meersch' (1645–6), *COACM,* 3, p. 457.

21 Voyage of the *Barneveld*, 1719, *COACM*, 5, p. 24.

22 See below, notes 39–41.

23 Edwin Fagereng, *Une famille de dynasties malgache* (Instituttet for Sammenlignende Kulturforskning, Oslo, 1971), pp. 40–1.

24 Memoir of the pirate Cornelius, 1703–5, in *COACM*, 3, pp. 615–22.

25 Voyage of *De Brack*, 1741, in *COACM*, 6, p. 189. So great was this susceptibility to strong drink on the part of the Sakalava kings that, according to one modern historian, alcohol and in-marrying were among the main causes of the eventual decline of the Sakalava monarchy: Manassé Esoavelomandroso, 'Antagonisme des *Fanjakana*', in *Madagascar et le christianisme* (Ambozontany and Karthala, Antananarivo and Paris, 1993), p. 49.

26 Westra and Armstrong, *Slave Trade*, p. 129.

27 Ibid.

28 Wendy Wilson-Fall, *Malagasy Free Black Settlement in Hanover County, Virginia, During Slavery : The intriguing story of Lucy Andriana Renibe Winston* (Hanover County Black Heritage Society and Hanover County Historical Society, Ashland, VA, 2007), p. 19.

29 Rigsarkivet, Copenhagen: Barrington's journal, pt.IV, p. 69, entry for 20/31 Jan. 1738.

30 I.e. the Arab/Antalaotra slaving fleet from Anjouan in the Comoros.

31 Journal of the *Barneveld*, 1719, in *COACM*, 5, p. 33.

32 Rigsarkivet, Copenhagen: Barrington's journal, pt.IV, p. 71, 20/31 Jan. 1738.

33 Westra and Armstrong, *Slave Trade*, p. 129.

34 Memoir of the pirate Cornelius, *COACM*, 3, pp. 615–22.

35 Various unsuccessful attempts have been made to identify this person among the fair number of pirates named Tom who are known to have visited Madagascar.

36 Stephen Ellis, 'Tom and Toakafo: The Betsimisaraka kingdom and state formation in Madagascar, 1715–1750', *Journal of African History* 48, 3 (2007), pp. 439–55.

37 The only biography has never been published: Nicolas Mayeur, 'Histoire de Ratsimila-hoe, Roi de Foule-pointe et des Bé-tsi-miçaracs', 1806, British Library, add. mss. 18129, fols.82–143.

38 Ibid., fols. 84v–85r.

39 Armstrong, 'Madagascar and the slave trade', p. 216.

40 Thomas Vernet, 'Slave trade and slavery', p. 4 of chapter offprint.

41 Ibid., p. 34. Barendse, *Arabian Seas*, p. 259, quotes a similar figure of 3–4,000 slaves per year exported from Madagascar to the Swahili coast, with a further 1–3,500 being exported annually to Mogadishu or points further north. Estimates of a similar magnitude are made by Arne Bialuschewski, 'Pirates, slavers, and the indigenous population in Madagascar, c.1690–1715', *International Journal of African Historical Studies*, 38, 3 (2005), p. 415, and Markus Vink, ' "The world's oldest trade": Dutch slavery and slave trade in the Indian Ocean in the seventeenth century', *Journal of World History*, 14, 2 (2003), pp. 144–5.

42 Noted by Mariano in 1613. See also Ellis 'Un document du XVIIe siècle', p. 157. On the purchase of slaves in Imerina a hundred years later, see Nationaal Archief, The Hague, VOC 10813: journal of *De Brak* [or *Brack*], 1742, entry for 29 Sept. 1742, recording that from Ambolambo [central highlands] 'slaves are annually transported to Massaleeg…'

43 Raombana (ed S. Ayache), *Histoires* (2 vols, Ambozontany, Fianarantsoa, 1980, 1994), 1, p. 111.

44 British Library, add. mss. 18129, fol.25r: Mayeur to Froberville, 4 April 1806.

45 Julien-Pierre Du Maine de la Josserie, 'Idée de la Côte occidentale de Madagascar, depuis Ancouala au nord, jusqu'à Mouroundava désigné par les Noirs sous le nom Menabe', *Annales des voyages, de la géographie, et de l'histoire*, XI (1810), pp. 27–8.

46 Ibid.

47 Cf. Flacourt, *Grande Isle*, p. 475, note 1 by Allibert, concerning ch. six.

48 Kent, *Early Kingdoms*, ch. five.

49 Mentioned e.g. by Flacourt, *Grande Isle*, p. 184 in the form of the adjective *masina*. On *hasina*, Delivré, *L'Histoire des rois*, pp. 140–71.

50 Cf. Ottino, *L'Etrangère intime*, 1, pp. 9–10.

51 Cf. above, p. 43.

52 Raison-Jourde, 'Introduction', *Les Souverains*, especially pp. 18–35.

53 Voyage of *De Brak/De Brack*, in *COACM*, 6, pp. 52–196.

54 Westra and Armstrong, *Slave Trade*, p. 129.

55 Flacourt, *Grande Isle*, p. 148.

56 Ibid., p. 302.

57 Westra and Armstrong, *Slave Trade*, p. 109.

58 Rigsarkivet, Copenhagen: Barrington's journal, pt.IV, p. 14, entry for 9/20 Jan.1738, with a similar formulation at p. 19, entry for 10/21 Jan. 1738.

59 Letter by Mariano, written at Mozambique, 20 August 1617, *COACM*, 2, p. 253.

60 See e.g. the engraving of Rafaralahy, governor of Foulpointe, in the frontispiece to volume 1 of William Ellis, *History of Madagascar* (2 vols, Fisher & Son,

London and Paris, 1838).

61 Most obviously the *Tantaran' ny Andriana*.

62 Cf. Raison-Jourde, *Les Souverains*.

63 Argued by Larson, *History and Memory*, p. 27.

64 Cf. Ferrand, *Les Musulmans*, 1, p. 32.

65 Lombard, *Le Carrefour javanais*, 3, pp. 89–127, 130–42.

66 James Sibree, *Madagascar and its people* (The Religious Tract Society, London, 1870), p. 301 (quotation); H.F. Standing, 'The tribal divisions of the Hova Malagasy', *Antananarivo Annual*, III (1887), p. 360.

67 Adrien Mille, *Contribution à l'étude des villages fortifiés de l'Imerina ancien (Madagascar)* (Musée d'art et d'archéologie de l'Université de Madagascar, Antananarivo, 1970).

68 Raombana, *Histoires,* 1, p. 135.

69 Ibid.

70 Ibid., p. 129.

71 Nicholas Mayeur, 'Voyage dans le sud et dans l'intérieur des terres et particulièrement au pays d'Hancove (janvier à décembre 1777)', *Bulletin de l'Académie malgache*, old series, XI (1913), pp. 139–76; 'Voyage au pays d'Ancove (1785)', *Bulletin de l'Académie malgache*, old series, XII (1913), pp. 13–42.

72 Anrianaivoarivony, 'Habitats fortifiés et organisation de l'espace dans le Vonizongo', p. 441.

73 Mayeur, 'Voyage dans le sud', p. 167.

74 Cf. Françoise Raison-Jourde, *Bible et pouvoir à Madagascar au XIXe siècle : invention d'une identité chrétienne et construction de l'Etat (1780–1880)* (Karthala, Paris, 1991), pp. 189–91.

75 Ibid., p. 106.

76 As reported by a French agent in Fort-Dauphin to the governor of Bourbon: Archives départementales, Ile de la Réunion, France, series 1 M 48c: de Roland to de Freycinet, 20 June 1822.

77 Ranaivo G. Ratsivalaka, *Les Malgaches et l'abolition de la traite européenne des esclaves (1810–1817). Histoire de la formation du Royaume de Madagascar* (Editions Hery Arivo, Antananarivo, 1999), pp. 76, 82.

78 See the biographical sketch by Louis Molet in F. Ranaivo, *Hommes et destins (Dictionnaire biographique d'Outre-mer)*, vol. 3 (Publication de l'Académie des sciences d'outre-mer, Travaux et mémoires, new series 9, Paris and Nice, 1979), pp. 24–6.

79 Larson, *History and Memory*, pp. 183–91.

80 Charles Renel, *Les Amulettes malgaches, ody et sampy*, special number of *Bulletin de l'Académie malgache*, new ser., II (1915), pp. 241–2.

81 Raombana, *Histoires*, 1, p. 149.

82 Edward A. Alpers, 'Madagascar and Mozambique in the nineteenth century: the era of the Sakalava raids (1800–1820)', *Omaly sy Anio*, 5–6 (1977), pp. 37–53.

83 J-M. Filliot, *La Traite des esclaves vers les Mascareignes au XVIIIe siècle* (ORSTOM, Paris, 1974), p. 51. Campbell, *Economic History*, p. 55, suggests that the Mascarenes imported about 160,000 slaves between 1610 and 1810, of which 45 per cent were from Madagascar. Both figures imply a rather lower level of exports from Madagascar than is implied by eye-witness descriptions. Cf. note 98.

84 Larson, *History and Memory*, chapter two; Campbell *Economic History*, esp. p. 56.

85 Jean-Pierre Raison, 'Perception et réalisation de l'espace dans la société merina',

Annales : économies, sociétés, civilisations, 32, 3 (1977), pp. 426–9.

86 Delivré, *L'histoire des rois*, p. 160, p. 382 n.79.

87 The phrase is borrowed from Maurice Bloch, 'La séparation du pouvoir et du rang comme processus d'évolution. Une esquisse du développement des royautés dans le centre de Madagascar', in Raison-Jourde, *Les Souverains*, pp. 265–98.

88 Until recently, mistakenly given by most authors as 1810. See Delivré, *L'Histoire des rois*, p. 227, and Larson, *History and Memory*, p. 296, n.105.

89 'Relation d' un voyage en Imerina effectué du 6 avril au 24 mai 1808, par Barthélémy Hugon', British Library, add. mss.18137, fol.17.

90 André Coppalle, 'Voyage dans l'intérieur de Madagascar et à la capitale du roi Radama pendant les années 1825 et 1826', *Bulletin de l'Académie malgache*, VIII (1910), pp. 42–3: diary entry for 3 February 1826.

91 James Sibree, 'The Sakalava: their origin, conquests and subjugation', *Antananarivo Annual,* 1 (1878), pp. 461–3.

92 Raombana, *Histoires*, 1, p. 247.

93 Another version is given by Raombana (*Histoires*, 2, p. 15), who claims that Radama was 28 years old or more.

94 Larson, *History and Memory*, p. 220.

95 Chardenoux to Farquhar, 13 Sept. 1816, in Jean Valette, 'La mission de Chardenoux auprès de Radama Ier (1816)', *Bulletin de Madagascar*, 207 (1963), p. 668.

96 L. Carayon, 'Voyage dans l'intérieur de Madagascar', *L'Annuaire des voyages et de la géographie* (1847), p. 83; Guillaume Grandidier, *Histoire politique et coloniale* (3 vols, Imprimerie officielle, Antananarivo, 1942–58), 1, p. 120, note 2 (a).

97 Raombana, *Histoires*, 1, pp. 19, 29.

98 William Ellis, *The Martyr Church*: *A narrative of the introduction, progress and triumph of Christianity in Madagascar* (John Snow, London, 1870), p. 7.

99 Journal of James Hastie for 17, 26 August, 11 September 1817, in James Sibree and Antoine Jully, 'Le voyage de Tananarive en 1817. Manuscrits de James Hastie', *Bulletin de l'Académie malgache*, II (1903), pp. 181, 186–7, 252.

100 Jean Valette, 'Un mémoire de Rondeaux sur Madagascar', *Bulletin de l'Académie malgache*, new series, XLIV–II (1966), p. 123.

101 Ratsivalaka, *Les Malgaches et l'abolition de la traite européenne des esclaves.*

102 Mary K. Jones, 'The slave trade at Mauritius, 1810–29' (B.Litt. thesis, Univ of Oxford, 1936), p. 52.

103 The papers are deposited in the British Library, add. mss. 18117–18141.

104 Jones, 'The slave trade at Mauritius, pp. 60–1; see also the detailed account in Ratsivalaka, *Les Malgaches et l'abolition de la traite européenne des esclaves.*

5. THE KINGDOM OF MADAGASCAR 1817–1895

1 Jean Valette, 'Le traité passé entre Radama Ier et Jean René. Le 9 juillet 1817', *Bulletin de Madagascar*, 222 (1964), pp. 957–9; the background is examined in meticulous detail by Ratsivalaka, *Les Malgaches et l'abolition de la traite européenne des esclaves.*

2 Stephen Ellis, 'The history of sovereigns in Madagascar: new light from old sources', in Didier Nativel (ed), forthcoming.

3 Raison-Jourde, *Bible et pouvoir*, p. 287.

4 Estimate by Chardenoux, quoted in Valette, 'La mission de Chardenoux', pp. 697–700.

5 Ellis, *The Martyr Church,* p. 16.
6 Estimate by James Hastie, quoted in Larson, *History and Memory*, p. 218.
7 Archives of the World Council of Christian Missions, School of Oriental and African Studies, London: LMS Incoming letters, 2/2/D: Griffiths to Arundel, 20 December 1825.
8 Larson, *History and Memory*, pp. 237–9.
9 Ludvig Munthe, *La Bible à Madagascar: les deux premières traductions du Nouveau Testament malgache* (Avhandlinger Utgitt av Egede Instituttet, Oslo, 1969).
10 Sir Henry Singer Keating, 'Travels in Madagascar, Greece and the United States' [travels in 1825]: Bodleian Library, Oxford, Eng. Mss. C.29, p. 82.
11 Ibid., pp. 78–9.
12 National Library of Wales, Aberystwyth: NLW 19157E: Jones and Griffiths to Phillips, 30 April 1823.
13 Archives de la République Malgache, Antananarivo: SS5, manuscript by Rainandriamampandry, fol.114.
14 Ludvig Munthe, Charles Ravoajanahary and Simon Ayache, 'Radama I et les Anglais: les négociations de 1817 d'après les sources malgaches («sorabe» inédits)', *Omaly sy anio*, 3–4 (1976), pp. 50–1.
15 Claudine Caillon-Filet, 'Jean Laborde et l'océan Indien' (thèse de doctorat, University of Aix-en-Provence, 1978), p. 63 et seq.
16 Antoine Jully, 'La politique des races à Madagascar', *Revue de Madagascar*, 1st series, 9, 1 (1907), p. 11.
17 Campbell, *An Economic History*, pp. 112–33.
18 Archives of the World Council of Christian Missions, LMS Incoming 4/4/A: Freeman to Philip, 14 May 1833.
19 Jean-Baptiste Piolet, *Madagascar et les Hova* (Delagrave, Paris, 1895), pp. 131–2.
20 Centre des Archives d'Outre-Mer (CAOM), Aix-en-Provence, France : MAD 11 (25), liasse 2: 'Notice sur le Royaume d'Emirne...', Sept. 1825, by Lt. de vaisseau Duhautcilly.
21 P. Fruitet, 'Activités économiques du Napoléon de Lastelle, Jean Laborde et François Lambert à Madagascar', mémoire no. 55 (1945–6), Ecole nationale de la France outre-mer, Paris.
22 William Ellis, *Madagascar Revisited* (John Murray, London, 1867), p. 91.
23 Alfred Grandidier (trans. J. Sibree), 'Property and wealth among the Malagasy', *Antananarivo Annual*, VI (1898), pp. 224–33.
24 Françoise Raison-Jourde, 'Les Ramanenjana: une mise en cause populaire du christianisme en Imerina, 1863,' *Asie du sud-est et le monde insulindien*, 7, 2–3 (1976), pp. 271–93.
25 G. Grandidier, *Histoire politique et coloniale*, 2, p. 51, text and note 1.
26 Ibid., p. 187, text and note 3.
27 Deschamps, *Histoire de Madagascar*, p. 207.
28 CAOM MAD 371 (1008): Resident-general Laroche to Colonial Minister Lebon, 12 July 1896.
29 Letter from Radilifera to Alfred Grandidier, 10 Jan. 1877, quoted in Raymond Decary, *Coutumes guerrières et organisation militaire chez les anciens Malgaches* (2 vols, Editions maritimes d'outre-mer, Paris, 1966), 2, p. 60.
30 Rainianjanoro, *Fampandrian-tany sy tantara maro samy hafa* (Friends' Foreign Mission Association, Antananarivo, 1920), pp. 35–6.
31 Robert Kestell-Cornish, *Journal of a Tour of Exploration in the North of Mada-*

gascar (Society for the Propagation of the Gospel, London, 1877), pp. 19–20, entry for 23 July 1876.

32 Joseph Sewell, *Remarks on Slavery in Madagascar, with an address on that subject, delivered at Antananarivo* (E. Stock, London, 1876), p. 8.

33 Joseph Mullens, *Twelve Months in Madagascar* (Nisbet, London, 1875), pp. 326–7.

34 Campbell, *An Economic History*, pp. 218–42.

35 James Sibree, *South-East Madagascar: Being notes of a journey through the Tanala, Taimoro and Taisaka countries in June and July 1876* (A. Kingdon, Antananarivo, no date), pp. 36–7.

36 Ibid., pp. 55–6.

37 Ibid., p. 37.

38 Ibid., p. 56.

39 Archives of the Catholic archbishopric, Andohalo, D.20: Diary of Fr M. Finaz, p. 208 of original diary (Dec. 1855).

40 Ibid.

41 Piolet, *Madagascar et les Hova*, pp. 100–1.

42 See Simon Ayache, *Raombana l'historien : introduction à l'édition critique de son œuvre* (Ambozontany, Fianarantsoa, 1976).

43 Raombana (ed. S.Ayache), 'Annales', A2, 691–3 of original ms. (unpublished typescript, Académie malgache, Antananarivo).

44 Stephen Ellis, 'Witch-hunting in central Madagascar, 1828–61', *Past and Present*, 175 (2002), pp. 90–123.

45 Anon., 'Historique des affaires de Madagascar', Institut de recherche scientifique de Madagascar, Antananarivo, ms. 0767.

46 Françoise Raison-Jourde, 'Du service sacré à la corvée de travail. Réflexions sur le fanompoana à Madagascar, XVIIe–XIXe siècles', unpublished paper read at a symposium held at the School of Oriental and African Studies, London, 28 November 1986.

47 One of the few available discussions is in Campbell, *An Economic History*, chapter six. This is, however, rather unconvincing — e.g. on p. 137, Campbell presents a graph suggesting that the population of Madagascar increased from some 2.5 million to 6 million people in just eight years, between 1861 and 1869. According to the same graph, the population diminished by an equally massive proportion in the five years following, thereafter once more increasing at a similarly unbelievable rate.

48 Raymond Decary, 'La population de Madagascar', *Bulletin de l'Académie malgache*, new series, XXVIII (1947–8), p. 29. This figure is regarded by Decary as an underestimate. However, more recent studies use slightly lower figures.

49 Sibree, *Madagascar and its People*, p. 284.

50 Archives of the Catholic archbishopric, Andohalo, D 63: Mgr. Jean-Baptiste Cazet, 'Esclavage à Madagascar', 1 March 1890, among notes presented to Cardinal Siméoni in Sept. 1891.

51 Estimate by C. Savaron, quoted in Françoise Raison-Jourde, 'Familiarisation de l'esclavage, asservissement des libres. Le paradoxe merina d'une mutuelle privation du désir de liberté', in Ignace Rakoto (ed.), *L'Esclavage à Madagascar : aspects historiques et résurgences contemporaines* (actes du Colloque international sur l'esclavage, Antananarivo 24–28 sept 1996) (Musée d'art et d'archéologie, Antananarivo, 1997)', p. 117.

52 Richard Baron, 'Political and social review of the last decade', p. 19, document

annexed to *Antananarivo Annual and Madagascar Magazine,* 6 (1900), Rhodes House Library, Oxford.

53 Raombana (ed. Ayache), 'Annales', A2, 444–5 of original text.

54 Gwyn Campbell, 'The history of nineteenth-century Madagascar: "le royaume" or "l'empire" ?', *Omaly sy anio*, 33–6 (1994), pp. 331–80. Cf. the remarks on the Sakalava kingdoms above, pp. 108–9. The first reference to the Kingdom of Madagascar as an 'empire' appears to be by Louis Carayon, a French officer who had experienced the empire of Napoleon Bonaparte: *Précis historique sur le people ova, suivi de l'appréciation des derniers événemens de Tamatave* (Gide, Paris, 1845), p. 10.

55 Cf. John Darwin, *After Tamerlane: The global history of empire since 1405* (Allen Lane, London, 2007), p. 23.

56 As recommended by Pier M. Larson, 'Popular historians in the Vakinankaratra: the art of historical memory in highland Madagascar', p. 15, unpublished ms.

57 Cf. Jacques Faublée, *L'Ethnographie de Madagascar* (Editions de France et d'outre-mer, Paris, 1946), p. 124.

58 S. Ellis, 'The history of sovereigns in Madagascar'.

59 US National Archives and Records Administration, Washington, D.C., consular records, US Cons. III (viewed on microfilm at the French National Archives, Paris, 253 Mi 35): V.F. Stanwood, 'Commerce of the West Coast of Madagascar in the hands of white men', 1 Dec. 1880.

60 Walter Bagehot, 'The danger of lending to semi-civilized countries', in Norman St John Stevas (ed.), *The Collected Works of Walter Bagehot*, vol. 10 (*The Economist*, London, 1978), p. 419.

61 Ministère des Affaires étrangères, Paris, Madagascar (old series), correspondance politique, vol. 30 : C. Le Myre de Vilers, 'Situation économique et financière', 14 Dec. 1888, f. 43.

62 Ellis, 'Witch-hunting in central Madagascar'.

63 Quotation from M. Finaz in Raison-Jourde, *Bible et pouvoir*, p. 150.

64 William Ellis, *Three Visits to Madagascar* (John Murray, London, 1857), pp. 398, 402 (quotation).

65 Raison-Jourde, *Bible et pouvoir*, p. 152.

66 Ellis, *Three Visits*, pp. 118–9.

67 Raison-Jourde, *Bible et pouvoir*, pp. 197–290.

68 Figures proposed by William Ellis but regarded by Françoise Raison-Jourde as rather exaggerated : see her 'Un tournant dans l'histoire religieuse merina du XIXe siècle: la fondation des temples protestants à Tananarive entre 1861 et 1869', *Annales de l'Université de Madagascar*, xi (1970), p. 15.

69 On Radama II, see Françoise Raison-Jourde, 'Radama II, ou le conflit du réel et de l'imaginaire dans la royauté merina', in C.-A. Julien *et al.* (eds), *Les Africains* (9 vols, Jeune Afrique, Paris, 1977), 8, pp. 275–311.

70 Coppalle, 'Voyage dans l'intérieur de Madagascar', *Bulletin de l'Académie malgache*, VIII (1910), p. 37, noting a conversation on 18 Jan. 1826. Italics in original.

71 Archives of the World Council of Christian Missions, LMS Incoming 6/4/B: Ellis to Tidman, 6 November 1863.

72 Cf. Gerald M. Berg, 'Radama's smile: domestic challenges to royal ideology in early nineteenth-century Imerina', *History in Africa*, 25 (1998), pp. 69–92.

73 Jacques Dez, 'La monarchie merina et le développement agricole', *Terre Malgache/Tany Malagasy*, X (1971), pp. 232, 235.

74 Stephen Ellis, *The Rising of the Red Shawls: A revolt in Madagascar, 1895–1899* (Cambridge University Press, Cambridge, 1985), pp. 94–100.
75 W. Ellis, *Madagascar Revisited*, pp. 108–9.
76 Sibree, *Madagascar and Its People*, p. 230.
77 S. Ellis, *Red Shawls*, pp. 21, 48.
78 *TA*, 2, 389.
79 E.g. Solofo Randrianja, 'Les Marofotsy à la conquête de la liberté vers 1820', in S. Randrianja (ed.), *Madagascar: Ethnies et ethnicité* (CODESRIA, Dakar, 2004), pp. 79–136.
80 C. Le Myre de Vilers, 'Le traité hova', *Revue de Paris* (15 Nov. 1895), p. 229; W.E. Cousins, 'The abolition of slavery in Madagascar, with some remarks on Malagasy slavery generally', *Antananarivo Annual and Madagascar Magazine*, V (1896), p. 448.
81 Larson, *Ocean of Letters*.
82 Mohamed Ahmed Saleh, 'Les Comoriennes de Zanzibar et le culte des esprits *kibuki* malgaches', in Nativel and Rajaonah, *Madagascar et l'Afrique,* pp. 425–37.
83 On US interests, see Christine Mullen Kreamer, 'Objects as envoys, an introduction', p. 18, in Christine Mullen Kreamer and Sarah Fee (eds), *Objects as Envoys: Cloth, imagery and diplomacy in Madagascar* (Smithsonian Institution, Washington, DC, 2002), and Edgar Krebs and Wendy Walker, 'Madagascar in the minds of foreigners', in ibid., pp. 121–48.
84 Gustave Julien, *Institutions politiques et sociales de Madagascar* (2 vols, Guilmoto, Paris, 1909), 2, pp. 504–34.
85 'Brief summary of important events in Madagascar from 1878 to 1881', *Antananarivo Annual and Madagascar Magazine,* V (1881), pp. 115–7.
86 James Richardson, 'The coronation of Ranavalona III', *Antananarivo Annual and Madagascar Magazine*, VII (1883), p. 103.
87 Archives of the World Council of Christian Missions, LMS Incoming, 24b/2/A : Baron to Thompson, 31 Jan. 1894.
88 W. Ellis, *History of Madagascar*, 2, 342.
89 S. Ellis, *Red Shawls*.
90 Listed in A. Martineau, *Madagascar en 1894* (Flammarion, Paris, no date), pp. 151–75.
91 Ibid., p. 136 et seq.
92 Cf. Guy Jacob, 'La France et Madagascar de 1880 à 1894 : aux origines d'une conquête coloniale' (Atelier national de reproduction des thèses, Lille, 1997).
93 Archives départementales de l'Orne, Alençon, France: Le Myre de Vilers papers, dossier 19: Note by Le Myre de Vilers, 12 pp. , c.1893.
94 See e.g. various works by Manassé Esoavelomandroso, including 'La province maritime orientale du "Royaume de Madagascar" à la fin du XIXe siècle (1882–1895)', 2 vols., (thèse de doctorat, Universities of Paris and Antananarivo, 1976) ; and 'Le mythe d'Andriba', *Omaly sy Anio*, 1–2 (1975), pp. 43–73.

6. THE FRENCH PERIOD 1896–1972

1 Manassé Esoavelomandroso, 'La «révolte de l'est» (novembre 1895-février 1896): essai d'explication', *Omaly sy anio* 21–2 (1985), pp. 33–46.
2 Ralaimihoatra, *Histoire*, 2, p. 211.
3 Guy Jacob, '*Fahavalisme* et troubles sociaux dans le Boina à la fin du XIXème

siècle', *Annales de Madagascar*, série Lettres et Sciences humaines, 6 (1967), pp. 21–32.

4 Stephen Ellis, *Un complot colonial à Madagascar: L'affaire Rainandriamampandry* (Karthala, Paris, 1990).

5 S. Ellis, *Red Shawls.*

6 Faranirina V. Esoavelomandroso, 'Les Sadiavahe: essai d'interprétation d'une révolte dans le Sud (1915–1917)', *Omaly sy anio,* 1–2 (1974), p. 164.

7 Solofo Randrianja, *Société et luttes coloniales à Madagascar (1896–1946)* (Karthala, Paris, 2001), p. 100.

8 Deschamps, *Histoire de Madagascar*, p. 281.

9 In the entire colonial period, only 10% of French overseas investment went to French colonies, mostly from small savers. See Henri Brunschwig, 'Politique et économie dans l'empire français d'Afrique noire, 1870–1914', *Journal of African History*, 11, 3 (1970), pp. 401–17.

10 Jean Fremigacci, 'L'administration coloniale : les aspects oppressifs', *Omaly sy anio*, 7–8 (1978), pp. 209–37.

11 Guy Jacob, 'Gallieni et "l'impôt moralisateur" à Madagascar: théorie, pratiques et conséquences (1901–1905)', *Revue française d'histoire d'outre-mer*, 74, 277 (1987), pp. 431–73.

12 Albert Ralaikoa, 'Aspects monétaires de la mainmise coloniale à Madagascar', *Omaly sy anio,* 37–38, (1993–1995), pp. 199–206.

13 Stock-market crashes and financial scandals were other aspects of Gallieni's governorship: see Charles Richard, 'Le gouvernement de Victor Augagneur à Madagascar' (Thèse de doctorat, University of Paris, 1969), p. 4.

14 Paul Seguy, membre de la Chambre de commerce d'Antananarivo, 'L'œuvre de la France à Madagascar', in 'Entreprises et produits de Madagascar', *Tana-Journal*, 1 (1949).

15 Daniel Rainibe, 'Une condition indigene?', *Omaly sy anio,* 15 (1982), p. 121.

16 CAOM, Mad C 330 : rapport d'inspection, Dec. 1936.

17 The SMOTIG system was later to be revived by the Malagasy state under Didier Ratsiraka (1975–1991) in the form of national service, with the difference that recruits were employed as teachers, and for one year only.

18 Deschamps, *Histoire de Madagascar*, p. 287.

19 Faranirina V. Esoavelomandroso, 'Résistance à la médecine en situation coloniale : la peste à Madagascar', *Annales : économies, sociétés, civilisations*, 36–2, 1 (1981), pp. 168–90. Up to the present day, periods of economic distress have also corresponded to sporadic and limited outbreaks of bubonic plague.

20 D. Nemours, *Madagascar et ses richesses* (Editions Pierre Roger, Paris, 1930), pp. 283, 294.

21 V. Rafrezy Andrianarivelo and I. Randretsa, *Population de Madagascar : situation actuelle et perspectives d'avenir* (Ministère de la recherche scientifique et technique pour le développement, Antananarivo, 1985), p. 20.

22 This comparatively low figure, half the size of estimates made in pre-colonial times, may simply reflect the differences in calculations based on the population of Antananarivo proper compared to those incorporating the suburban areas.

23 Faranirina V. Esoavelomandroso-Rajaonah, 'Des rizières à la ville. Les plaines de l'ouest d'Antananarivo dans la première moitié du XXème siècle', *Omaly sy anio*, 29–32 (1989–90), p. 332.

24 Archives de la République Malgache, Antananarivo, 11 D 14: M. Olivier's speech to Délégations économiques et financières, 17 October 1927.

25 Louis Chevalier, *Madagascar: populations et ressources* (Presses universitaires de France, Paris, 1952), p. 108.

26 Faranirina V. Esoavelomandroso, 'Différentes lectures de l'histoire : quelques réflexions sur la V.V.S.', *Recherches, pédagogie et culture*, IX, 50 (1981), pp. 100–111.

27 CAOM, Mad C 354 d 957 : dossier Dussac.

28 Cf. S. Randrianja, F. Vergès, Hai Quang Ho, C. Rakotolahy, Z. Hussein, T. Malbert, 'Cartographie d'une zone de contacts', in G. Kobou (ed.), *Les Economies réelles en Afrique/Real Economies in Africa* (Codesria, Dakar, 2003), pp. 129–202.

29 *Ny Tari-dalana*, June 1937, p. 7.

30 S. Randrianja, 'Jean Ralaimongo', in Jean Maitron (ed.), *Dictionnaire biographique du mouvement ouvrier français, Tome XIX : de la Première à la Seconde guerre mondiale* (Éditions ouvrières, Paris, 1983).

31 Esoavelomandroso-Rajaonah, 'Des rizières à la ville', pp. 322–3.

32 H. Ly Tio Fane Pineo, *La Diaspora chinoise dans l'océan Indien occidental* (ACOI, Aix-en-Provence, 1981), p. 185.

33 Esoavelomandroso-Rajaonah, 'Des rizières à la ville', p. 332.

34 Moradewun Adejunmobi, *J. J. Rabearivelo: Literature and lingua franca in colonial Madagascar* (Peter Lang, New York, 1996).

35 Cf. Randi Deguilhem, 'Turning Syrians into Frenchmen: the cultural politics of a French non-governmental organization in Mandate Syria (1920–67)—the French Secular Mission schools,' in *Islam and Christian-Muslim Relations,* 13, 4 (2002), pp. 449–60.

36 Jean Fremigacci, 'La colonisation à Vatomandry-Mahanoro. Espérances et désillusions (1895–1910)', *Omaly sy anio*, 3–4 (1976), pp. 167–249.

37 In fact mostly Muslims originating from the Indian subcontinent, including Indians as well as Pakistanis after the independence of both countries in 1947.

38 Boiteau, *Contribution*, p. 234.

39 Rojo Razoaliarinirina, 'Les nationalistes citadins de Tamatave de la Deuxième guerre mondiale à l'indépendance (1939–1960)' (mémoire de maîtrise en histoire, Université de Tamatave, 1999), pp. 7–36.

40 Chevalier, *Madagascar*; René Gendarme, *L'Economie de Madagascar: diagnostic et perspectives de développement* (Editions Cujas, Paris, 1963).

41 M. Massiot, *L'Administration publique à Madagascar : évolution de l'organisation administrative et territoriale de Madagascar de 1896 à la proclamation de la République Malgache* (L.G.D.J., Paris, 1971), pp. 406–34.

42 Fremigacci, 'L'administration coloniale : les aspects oppressifs'.

43 CAOM, FM 52 B 16 : rapport Guernut (inspection des colonies).

44 The schooling rates in other provinces are between these two figures. The exact figures should be treated with care, but they do give some idea of comparative levels.

45 CAOM, FM 52 B 16 : rapport Guernut (inspection des colonies).

46 CAOM, Province de Tananarive, 0023 : affaires religieuses.

47 Solofo Randrianja, 'Les valeurs de 1789 et leur utilisation par les forces politiques à Madagascar entre les deux guerres', in Guy Jacob (ed.), *Regards sur Madagascar et la Révolution française* (CNAPMAD, Antananarivo, 1990), pp. 159–66.

48 Raymond K. Kent, *The Many Faces of an Anti-Colonial Revolt: Madagascar's long journey into 1947* (Foundation for Malagasy Studies, Albany, CA, 2007),

pp. 230, 239.

49 Although the immediate motive was probably fear that Japan might use Madagascar's harbours, there was also a German plan to send European Jews to Madagascar: see Eric Jennings, 'Writing Madagascar back into the Madagascar Plan', *Holocaust and Genocide Studies*, 21, 2 (2007), pp. 187–217.

50 National Archives of the United Kingdom, FO 371/42213: report by the British consulate in Antananarivo, 22 December 1943.

51 Solofo Randrianja, 'Les Britanniques et Madagascar pendant la Deuxième guerre mondiale', in E. Combeau-Mari and E. Maestri (eds), *Le Régime de Vichy dans l'océan Indien* (SEDES, CRESOI, La Réunion, 2002), pp. 163–76.

52 R.W. Rabemananjara, *Madagascar : histoire de la nation malgache* (Imprimerie Lanchaud, Paris, 1952), p. 170.

53 Alain Spacensky, *Madagascar : cinquante ans de vie politique, de Ralaimongo à Tsiranana* (Nouvelles Editions Latines, Paris, 1970), p. 50, was researched using confidential data from colonial police archives.

54 Massiot, *L'Administration publique à Madagascar*, p. 337.

55 See the interview with Georges-Louis Berante, a colonial government employee and chief of staff of Philibert Tsiranana in 1958, cited in Randriamaro, *PADESM et luttes*, pp. 357–8.

56 Kent, *Many Faces*, pp. 175–8, 186, 208.

57 See e.g. Pastor Jean Vernier's testimony in Randriamaro, *PADESM et luttes*, pp. 266–7.

58 Kent, *Many Faces*, p. 239.

59 See e.g. the memoir of Jacques Rabemananajara, the poet and MDRM politician, on his detention between 12 and 15 April 1947, cited in Jacques Tronchon, *L'Insurrection malgache de 1947: essai d'interprétation historique* (Maspero, Paris, 1974), p. 285.

60 Jennifer Cole, *Forget Colonialism? Sacrifice and the art of memory in Madagascar* (Univ. of California Press, Berkeley, CA, 2001).

61 Exact figures for the numbers of victims are the matter of considerable controversy. During his visit to Madagascar on 21–22 July 2005, President Jacques Chirac cited a range of between 15,000 and 150,000 victims. For debates on these figures, see *L'Express de Madagascar*, July 2005. For a succinct account, see Jean Fremigacci, 'La vérité sur la grande révolte de Madagascar', *L'Histoire*, 318 (March 2007), pp. 36–43.

62 Massiot, *L'Administration publique à Madagascar*, pp. 405–34. Frederick Cooper, *Africa Since 1940: The past of the present* (Cambridge University Press, 2002), pp. 77–81, provides a concise account of French colonial policy.

63 CAOM, 6 (13) D 6: text of De Gaulle's speech in Antananarivo, 22 August 1958.

64 *Lakroan'i Madagasikara*, 1271, 5 August 1958.

65 Cf. Philippe Leymarie, 'L'AKFM malgache (1958–1968)', *Revue française d'études politiques africaines*, 98 (1974), pp. 71–90.

66 Gisèle Rabesahala, *Que vienne la liberté, Ho tonga anie ny fahafahana* (Océan éditions, La Réunion, 2006), chapters 2–4.

67 CAOM, 6 (3) D 6: transcript of radio broadcast by the Haut commissaire de la république, 22 Sept. 1958.

68 A confidential 9-page document sent to all senior administrative personnel in early September 1958 contains a list of arguments to be used against those recommending a 'no' vote in the referendum: 'the offer made by France to its over-

seas peoples, which she requests them to accept in September, aims to establish relations between the French republic and an independent Malagasy state on a new basis'. CAOM, 6 (3) D 6, memorandum entitled 'Eléments de contre propagande', 15 Sept. 1958, p. 6, distributed by the commissioner of Tuléar province to his staff.

69 Gérard Althabe, 'Le Monima', *Revue française d'études politiques africaines*, 86 (1973), pp. 71–6.

70 Philippe Leymarie, 'Les accords de coopération franco-malgaches', *Revue française d'études politiques africaines*, 78 (June 1972), pp. 55–60.

71 Ibid., pp. 56, note 3 and 58, note 7; see also XXX, 'Le poids de l'assistance technique', *Revue française d'études politiques africaines*, 78 (June 1972), pp. 64–70.

72 See Roger Pascal, *La République malgache* (Berger-Levrault, Paris, 1965).

73 22 May 1964.

74 Gérard Althabe, 'Les manifestations paysannes d'avril 1971', *Revue française d'études politiques africaines*, 78 (1972), pp 71–7.

75 Gérard Althabe, *Anthropologie politique d'une decolonisation* (L'Harmattan, Paris, 2000), pp. 32–3.

76 Andrianarivelo Rafrezy and Randretsa, *Population de Madagascar*, p. 31 ; Michel Le Bris, 'La nouvelle classe en chiffres', *Les Cahiers de l'Ecole Nationale de la Promotion Sociale*, Antananarivo, 2–3 (1971), pp. 7–57.

7. AN ISLAND IN THE WORLD 1973–2002

1 Philippe Randrianarimanana , 'Iles et cocotiers : le président malgache ne s'encombre pas la mémoire', *Le Courrier international*, 25 juillet 2007.

2 Iliffe, *Africans*, p.2.

3 Bloch, *From Blessing to Violence,* p 41.

4 Rakotomalala et al, *Les ancêtres au quotidien*, esp. pp.317–28.

5 Gérard Althabe, 'Les luttes sociales à Tananarive en 1972', *Cahiers d'études africaines*, XX, 4, no.80 (1980), pp.440–7.

6 Rémi Rahajarizafy, *Mey 1972* (1973; Librairie mixte, Antananarivo, 1975), p.37.

7 Willy Razafinjatovo, interview by Tiana Rajaona, *La Gazette de la Grande île,* 13 May 2005.

8 Solofo Randrianja, 'Présentation des travaux en vue de l'habilitation à diriger des thèses' (unpublished, Université de Paris VII-Denis Diderot, 2003), p. 315.

9 The question of slave descent remains a taboo subject in the whole of Madagascar. See Sandra Evers, 'Solidarity and antagonism in migrant societies on the Southern highlands', in Rakoto (ed), *L'Esclavage à Madagascar*, pp.339–45; and Sandra Evers, 'Stigmatization as a self-perpetuating process', in Sandra Evers and Marc Spindler (eds), *Cultures of Madagascar: Ebb and flow of influences* (International Institute for Asian Studies, Leiden, 1996), pp.157–85.

10 Rémi Ralibera, *Souvenirs et témoignages malgaches, de la colonisation à la IIIème République* (Foi et Justice, Antananarivo, 2008), p.129.

11 See www.assemblee-nationale.mg/fr/historique.php

12 See above, p.185.

13 Cf. Condominas, *Fokonolona et collectivités rurales en Imerina.* See also U.S. Library of Congress, 'The fokonolona and traditional governance', http://countrystudies.us/madagascar/28.htm

14 Solofo Randrianja, 'La notion de royauté dans le mouvement d'émancipation malgache entre les deux guerres', in Raison-Jourde, *Les Souverains,* pp. 409–26.
15 According to Ralibera, *Souvenirs et témoignages malgaches,* pp. 147–64.
16 Ibid., pp. 133–46.
17 http://www.ambafrance-mada.org/article.php3?id_article=255
18 Report to the ambassador, 12 February 1976: Archives diplomatiques, Nantes, Tananarive 235; see also 'Un exploit de la police tamatavienne', *Madagascar Matin,* 26 January 1976.
19 J.K. Galbraith, *Money: Whence it came, where it went* (Pelican edn., Harmondsworth, 1976), pp.296–314.
20 Interview in *Le Monde,* 28 December 1977, p. 7.
21 Charles Cadoux and Jean du Bois de Gaudusson, 'Madagascar, 1979–1981, un passage difficile', in *Annuaire des pays de l'océan Indien*, VII (Centre national de la recherche scientifique et Presses universitaires d'Aix-Marseille, Paris and Aix-en-Provence, 1980), pp. 357–87.
22 Charles Cadoux, 'Les élections générales de 1982–1983 à Madagascar : des élections pour quoi faire?', *L'Année africaine 1983* (A. Pedone, Paris, 1985), pp. 67–85.
23 Cf. ' "Les maux qui nuisent la Nation". Déclaration des responsables des quatre églises chrétiennes de Madagascar', *Eglise et société à Madagascar* (5 vols., Foi et Justice, Antananarivo, 1990–2000), 3, pp. 58–64.
24 'Les évènements de Majunga : une manœuvre de provocation impérialiste', *Madagascar Renouveau*, 1er trimestre (1977), pp. 17–19; Andriamirado, 'Un banal fait divers (incident comoro-malgache de décembre 1976)', *Madagascar Matin*, n°1450 (12 March 1977) ; see also the account of the Majunga massacre by J.-M. Devillard in *Le Monde*, 16–17 Jan. 1977. For an academic assessment, J.-L. Calvet, 'Madagascar', *Annuaire des pays de l'océan Indien*, no. III (Presses universitaires d'Aix-Marseille, 1978), p. 374.
25 http://www.iarivo-town.mg
26 World Bank, *Madagascar: Recent economic developments and prospects*, report PUB2357, 30 November 1980: www-wds.worldbank.org
27 Philippe Hugon, 'La crise économique de Madagascar et l'intervention du Fonds monétaire international', *Canadian Journal of African Studies*, 20, 2 (1986), p. 191.
28 Philippe Hugon, 'La crise économique et les politiques d'ajustement' , *Annuaire des Pays de l'océan indien*, IX (1982–1983), (Aix-en-Provence 1982), pp. 471–92.
29 According to *Midi Madagascar* of 2 July 2001, quoting the World Health Organization, the socialist government presided over a fall in life expectancy from 54 to 45 years for men and from 56 to 48 for women.
30 'Evolution de l'APD à Madagascar 1984–2004': http://www.diplomatie.gouv.fr/fr/pays-zones-geo_833/madagascar_399/presentation-madagascar_992/economie_1863.html
31 Françoise Raison-Jourde, 'Une transition achevée ou amorcée?', *Politique africaine*, 52 (1993), p. 6.
32 Charles Cadoux, 'La constitution de la Troisième République malgache', *Politique africaine*, 52 (1993), pp. 58–66.
33 Ralibera, *Souvenirs et témoignages malgaches,* pp. 186–94.
34 Ibid., p. 193.
35 Tim May, 'L'avenir des universités, espaces de reflexion et/ou lieux d'attente?',

Codesria Bulletin, 1–2, (2004), pp. 63–5.

36 François Roubaud, *Les Elections présidentielles à Madagascar 1992–1996 : un essai de géographie électorale* (Madio, Antananarivo, 1997).

37 This phenomenon became steadily more serious and was to prove long-lasting: in mid-2001, the police discovered a gang in Mandritsara in possession of tens of kilograms of human bones. See *Madagascar Tribune*, 5 July 2001.

38 E.g. *Madagascar Tribune*, 13 November 2001.

39 *Madagascar Tribune*, 10 July 2001.

40 *Lettre de l'océan Indien*, 2 November 2001.

41 *L'Express de Madagascar*, 19 July 2001.

42 Cf. Stephen Ellis and Gerrie ter Haar, *Worlds of Power: Religious ideas and political practice in Africa* (C. Hurst & Co., London, 2004), esp. chapters one and seven.

43 Rakotomalala et al, *Les Ancêtres au quotidien*.

44 For an exploration of Ravalomanana's appeal, see Luke Freeman, 'Why are some people powerful?', in Rita Astuti, Jonathan Parry and Charles Stafford (eds), *Questions of Anthropology* (Berg, London, 2007), pp.281–306.

45 *L'Express de Madagascar*, 29 June 2001.

46 *L'Express de Madagascar*, 30 June, 5 July 2001.

47 Jean-Jacques Bozonnet, 'Didier Ratsiraka, l'ami caméléon', *Le Monde*, 10 May 2002.

48 Françoise Raison-Jourde and Jean-Pierre Raison, 'Ravalomanana et la troisième indépendance?', *Politique africaine*, 86 (2002), special issue on 'Madagascar, les urnes et la rue', p. 12.

49 Richard Marcus, *Political Change in Madagascar: Populist democracy or neo-patrimonialism by another name?* (Paper no.89, Institute of Security Studies, Pretoria), p.6.

50 Mireille Razafindrakoto and François Roubaud, 'Le scrutin présidentiel du 16 décembre 2001: les enjeux d'une élection contestée', *Politique africaine*, 86 (2002), pp.20–1.

51 According to the French ministre déléguée à la Coopération, au développement et à la francophonie, Brigitte Girardin, in 2007: http://www.diplomatie.gouv.fr/fr/pays-zones-geo_833/madagascar_399/presentation-madagascar_992/economie_1863.html

52 Rosaleen Duffy, 'Gemstone mining in Madagascar: transnational networks, criminalisation and global integration', *Journal of Modern African Studies*, 45, 2 (2007), pp.185–206.

53 Andrew Walsh, ' "Hot money" and daring consumption in a northern Malagasy sapphire-mining town', *American Ethnologist,* 30, 2 (2003), pp.290–305.

54 Jennifer Cole, 'Fresh contact in Tamatave, Madagascar: sex, money, and intergenerational transformation', *American Ethnologist,* 31, 4 (2004), pp.571–86.

55 The most complete study of this process is probably Didier Galibert, 'Les gens de pouvoir : territoire et légitimités à Madagascar' (2 vols, thèse de doctorat, Université de la Réunion, 2006).

56 Apparently for the first time, an epidemic of chikugunya fever reached Madagascar from Réunion in 2005.

CONCLUSION

1 Cf. Ratsivalaka, 'Madagascar dans le sud-ouest', p. 906.

2 Above, p. 17.
3 Above, pp. 163, 165.
4 Personal communication from the geographer M. Petit, July 2006.
5 Cf. Goodman and Patterson, *Natural Change and Human Impact in Madagascar*.
6 This phrase is taken from Jean Devisse, 'Les Africains, la mer et les historiens', *Cahiers d'études africaines*, XXIX, 3–4, 115–116 (1989), p. 410.
7 François Viré and Jean-Claude Hébert, ' Madagascar, Comores et Mascareignes à travers la Hawiya d'Ibn Mâgid (866H/1462)', *Omaly sy anio*, 25–26 (1987), p. 58.
8 Gallieni to Grandidier 1 June 1904, in Joseph-Simon Gallieni, *Lettres de Madagascar, 1896–1905* (Société d'éditions géographiques, maritimes et coloniales, Paris, 1928), p. 149.
9 Quoted by Chevalier, *Madagascar, populations et ressources*, p. 32.
10 Campbell, *An Economic History*, p. 137, fig. 1, shows a wide range of estimates for the 19th-century population.
11 The main study of demography is Campbell, *An Economic History*, chapter six.
12 Larson estimates that between 1729 and 1820, some 113,400 slaves were exported from Madagascar, of which 60,732 were from the central highlands. See 'A census of slaves exported from Central Madagascar to the Mascarenes between 1775 and 1820', in Rakoto, *L'Esclavage à Madagascar*, p. 142. On the earlier Antalaotra slave trade, see Vernet, 'Slave trade and slavery on the Swahili coast'.
13 Larson, *History and Memory*, p. 124.
14 Dr Ravelonahina , 'Les causes de la dépopulation à Madagascar', unpublished thesis cited by Chevalier, *Madagascar: Populations et ressources,* p. 66. Ravelonahina probably took these figures directly from Ellis, *History of Madagascar*,1, p. 487.
15 On poison ordeals, see Ellis, 'Witch-hunting in central Madagascar'; on forced labour, Campbell, *An Economic History*, pp. l12–33.
16 Ellis, 'Witch-hunting in central Madagascar', p. 116.
17 Catherine Coquery-Vidrovitch, *Afrique noire: permanences et ruptures* (2nd rev. edn., L'Harmattan, Paris, 1992), pp 17–65 ; Iliffe, *Africans*, esp. pp. 1–5.
18 Dominique Waltisperger, Pierre Cantrelle and Osée Ralijaona, *La Mortalité à Antananarivo de 1984 à 1995* (Centre français sur la population et le développement, Paris, 1998), p. 1.
19 Fredrik Barth, 'Ethnicity and the concept of culture', paper presented to the conference on 'Rethinking Culture', Harvard University, 1995: http://www.tau.ac.il/tarbut
20 *TA*, 3, p. 246.
21 Ibid., p. 247.
22 Solo Raharinjanahary, 'Langues, dialectes et ethnies à Madagascar', in Randrianja, *Madagascar, ethnies et ethnicité*, pp. 137–202.
23 Louis Molet, 'Andriamahazonoro', in Ranaivo, *Hommes et destins,* 3, pp. 24–26.
24 Francis Zafindrandremitambahoaka Marson, ' Les sultanats musulmans à Madagascar : la filiation de la civilisation des échelles commerciales arabes et la survivance islamique dans certaines royautés malgaches' (doctoral thesis, Université de Perpignan, 2007).

25 Pierre Vérin, *Les Echelles anciennes du commerce sur les côtes nord de Madagascar* (Service de reproduction des thèses de l'université, Lille, 1975).

26 Raymond Delval, 'Migrations, minorités et échanges en Océan Indien, XIX siècle. Table ronde', *Etudes et documents*, 11 (1978), Université de Provence, p. 94.

27 Raison, 'Introduction', *Les Souverains.*

28 John Lonsdale, 'Moral ethnicity and political tribalism', in Preben Kaarsholm and Jan Hultin (eds), *Inventions and Boundaries : Historical and anthropological approaches to the study of ethnicity and nationalism* (Occasional paper 11, International Development Studies, Roskilde University, 1994), p. 131.

29 Ibid.

30 Larson, *History and Memory.*

31 Randrianja, 'Les Marofotsy'.

32 S. Ellis, *Red Shawls*, esp. pp. 149–50.

33 Jacques Faublée, *La Cohésion des sociétés bara* (Presses universitaires de France, Paris, 1954), p. 4.

34 Rainianjanoro, *Fampandrian-tany*, pp. 9–11.

35 Lonsdale, 'Moral ethnicity and political tribalism', p. 131.

36 Concerning e.g. the kingdom of Boina, see Marie-Pierre Ballarin, *Les Reliques royales sakalava, source de légitimation et enjeu de pouvoir : Madagascar XVIII–XXème siècles* (Karthala, Paris, 2000), pp. 171–8.

37 Rakotomalala et al, *Les ancêtres au quotidien.*

38 Ibid., p. 42.

39 See e.g. Roger Rafidison, 'Les affrontements ethniques dans le sud-est pendant la période coloniale : une interrogation sur le passé de la région', *Omaly sy anio*, 37–38 (1993–4), pp. 261–70. The same was true of the anti-Comoran pogroms in 1977, which involved the looting of businesses owned by traders of foreign origin in several parts of the island.

40 http://www.joshuaproject.net/countries.php?rog3=MA .

41 Cf ch. one.

42 The Slavery Convention signed at Geneva on 25 September 1926 defines slavery as 'the status or condition of a person over whom any or all of the powers attaching to the right of ownership are exercised' (article 1.1). The slave trade includes 'all acts involved in the capture, acquisition or disposal of a person with intent to reduce him to slavery; all acts involved in the acquisition of a slave with a view to selling or exchanging him; all acts of disposal by sale or exchange of a slave acquired with a view to being sold or exchanged, and, in general, every act of trade or transport in slaves' (article 1.2): http://www.ohchr.org/english/law/slavery.htm#wp1034147

43 'Traite de personnes : un garçon vierge est « loué » à Ar. 40.000', *La Tribune de Madagascar*, 26 juillet 2007.

44 Michèle Rakotoson, *Lalana* (Éd. de l'Aube, La Tour d'Aigues, 2002), pp. 162, 164.

45 Ch. one.

46 In addition to works by Rakoto, Evers and others cited in the bibliography, see also e.g. David Graeber, 'Painful memories,' *Journal of Religion in Africa*, 27, 4 (1997), pp. 374–400.

47 Larson, *Ocean of Letters*, shows how a substantial Malagasy diaspora remained in existence in places where slaves were exported for several generations.

48 Larson, *History and Memory.*

49 Ratsivalaka, 'Madagascar dans le sud-ouest'.

50 Campbell, *An Economic History*, p. 114.

51 Defined as '...all work or service which is exacted from any person under the menace of any penalty and for which the said person has not offered himself voluntarily' : article 2 (1) of the Forced Labour Convention, 1930, which entered into force on 15 June 1932. http://www.itcilo.it/actrav/english/common/C029.html

52 Cf. the report by the administrator Poirier, 18 Nov. 1929, ARM D 840.

53 Cf. Evers, 'Stigmatization as a self-perpetuating process'.

54 During most of Madagascar's history, the status of *mainty* has not resembled that of servility. Only since the nineteenth century has there been an increasing tendency to include those of *mainty* origin in a vague category of 'former slaves': Benjamina Ramantasoa Ramarcel, '*Mainty=andevo*, un amalgame statutaire de l'Imerina', in Rakoto, *L'Esclavage à Madagascar*, pp. 147–60.

55 See e.g. Resolutions of the Council of Policy, Cape Town, C121, pp. 48–74, 8 January 1743, concerning the *Brak*: available online at http://databases.tanap. net/cgh/

56 See e.g. Westra and Armstrong, *Slave Trade.*

57 Mayeur, 'Voyage au pays d'Ancove (1785)', p. 32.

58 Maurice Bloch, 'The disconnection between power and rank as a process: an outline of the development of kingdoms in central Madagascar', *Archives européennes de sociologie*, XVIII, I (1977), pp. 107–48, who describes these rulers as 'really gangs of brigands'; a French version appears in Raison-Jourde, *Les Souverains*, pp. 265–98.

59 Cf. Waltisperger *et al., La Mortalité à Antananarivo de 1984 à 1995.*

60 Rahajarizafy, *Mey 1972*, p. 37.

61 The pioneering study of royal possession cults in the Republic of Madagascar is Gérard Althabe, *Oppression et libération dans l'imaginaire : les communautés villageoises de la côte orientale de Madagascar* (Maspero, Paris, 1969). Subsequent work includes Jean-François Baré, *Pouvoir des vivants, langage des morts: idéo-logiques sakalave* (Maspero, Paris, 1977); Gillian Feeley-Harnik, *A Green Estate: Restoring independence in Madagascar* (Smithsonian Institution Press, Washington DC, 1991); Lesley A. Sharp, *The Possessed and the Dispossessed: Spirits, identity, and power in a Madagascar migrant town* (University of California Press, Berkeley, CA,1993); and Michael Lambek, *The Weight of the Past: Living with history in Mahajanga, Madagascar* (Palgrave Macmillan, London, 2002).

62 Ellis and Randrianja, 'Les archives de la Compagnie néerlandaise des indes orientales et l'histoire de Madagascar', pp. 48–9.

63 See e.g. the account by the Austrian traveller Ida Pfeiffer, *Voyage à Madagascar* (1862; Karthala, Paris, 1981), with an introduction by Faranirina Esoavelomandroso.

64 Solofo Randrianja, 'Madagascar', in David Levinson and Karen Christensen (eds), *Global Perspectives on the United States*, vol. 2 (Berkshire Publishing, Great Barrington, MA, 2007), p. 386.

65 *Asia Times,* 2 August 2007.

66 United Nations Development Programme, *Human Development Report*, http://hdr.undp. org/hdr2006/statistics/countries/country_fact_sheets/cty_fs_MDG.html

APPENDIX I

ACRONYMS

AKFM	Antokon' ny Kongresin' ny Fahaleovantenan' iMadagasikara
AMI	Assistance Médicale Indigène
AREMA	Avant-garde de la Révolution Malgache
ARES	Alliance pour le Redressement Economique et Social
ARM	Archives de la République Malgache
AVI	Asa Vita no Ifampitsarana
BCE	Before the Common Era
CAOM	Centre des Archives d'Outre-mer
CE	Common Era
COACM	*Collection d'ouvrages anciens concernant Madagascar*
FFKM	Fiombonan'ny Fiangonana Kristianina eto Madagasikara
FIDES	Fonds d'Investissment pour le Développement Economique et Social
FJKM	Fiangonan'i Jesoa Kristy eto Madagasikara
ILO	International Labour Organization
IMF	International Monetary Fund
KIM	Komity Iombonan'ny Mpitolona
KIT	Komity Iombonan'ny Tantsaha
LMS	London Missionary Society
MDRM	Mouvement Démocratique de la Rénovation Malgache
MFM	Mpitolona ho an'ny Fanjakan'ny Madinika; later, Mpitolona ho an'ny Fandrosoan' i Madagasikara
MONIMA	Madagascar Otronin' ny Malagasy
PADESM	Parti des Déshérités de Madagascar
PANAMA	Parti Nationaliste Malagasy

PSD	Parti Social-Démocrate
SADC	Southern African Development Community
SFIO	Section Française de l'Internationale Ouvrière
SMOTIG	Service de la Main d'Oeuvre pour les Travaux d'Intérêt Général
TA	*Tantaran' ny Andriana*
UDECMA	Union des Démocrates Chrétiens de Madagascar
USSR	Union of Soviet Socialist Republics
VOC	Verenigde Oostindische Compagnie
VVS	Vy, Vato, Sakelika
ZWAM	Zatovo Western Andevo Malagasy

APPENDIX II

GLOSSARY

al-Qomr	One of the names for Madagascar used by Arab navigators and geographers, it is also the origin of the name Comoro Islands.
Ambaniandro	('Under the Sun'), a name initially designating all free subjects of King Andrianampoinimerina. Later subject to a process of ethnicization, the term came to mean the inhabitants of, or people originating from, the region of Imerina.
Andafiavaratra	The leading military and commercial faction of the ruling elite in the Kingdom of Madagascar. Leading members of this group resided on the north side (*avaratra)* of the queen's palace.
andevo	'Slave', literally 'of the home'.
Andriamanitra hita maso	'The visible god', i.e. the sovereign.
andriambahoaka	A ruler claiming universal sovereignty.
andriana	Normally translated as 'noble'. In Imerina, the oldest groups in this category have tended to be degraded to make way for new groups related to more recent rulers. In France such groups might be referred to as *noblesse d'Empire*. A whole village or an entire region might be considered as *andriana*, in contradiction to the more restricted European notion of nobility or aristocracy.
anjara	Destiny
Antalaotra	'People of the sea', a general term designating Islamized traders from the Comoros, East Africa and the Persian Gulf, often referred to in older European texts as 'Arabs' or 'Moors'.
Antandroy	Name of an ethnic group.
Antemoro	Name of an ethnic group.
Avaradrano	Originally, a kingdom with a capital at Ambohimanga. Later, a province of Imerina. The name is

	also used to designate groups originating on the north bank of the Ikopa river.
Bara	Name of an ethnic group.
Betsileo	Name of an ethnic group.
Betsimisaraka	Name of an ethnic group.
Bezanozano	Name of an ethnic group.
Boky mena	('Red Book'), the charter of the socialist revolution, annexed to the constitution of the Second Republic.
Buki, Buqi	An old Swahili word designating Madagascar and its people.
Buqqiyin	People from Madagascar. See *Buki*
Code de l'indigénat	The administrative regulations applied to colonial subjects.
deka	(Derived from *aides-de-camp*), junior officers attached to generals of the royal army.
fahavalo	'Enemies' in Malagasy. A name used by French colonial soldiers to designate Malagasy insurgents.
fandroana	In Imerina, the feast of the royal bath, traditionally held on the first day of the lunar month of Alahamady but fixed in 1883 on 22 November.
fanjakana	The government, the state.
fanompoana	Royal service, originally owed to the sovereign as an act of allegiance, but turned in the nineteenth century into a system of forced labour.
fihaonana	A meeting place; in earlier times, a market.
fihavanana	Kinship
firenena	Descent-groups often labelled by Europeans as 'clans' or 'tribes'.
foko	Many anthropologists translate with 'deme', following Maurice Bloch. In all of Madagascar, a *foko* is a social group with a specific cultural identity. In Imerina, *foko* also have specific territories, but in some other parts of the island they do not.
fokonolona	Traditional village assemblies in the highlands, extended by colonial authorities and then by the socialist regime to the whole of Madagascar.
fokontany	The administrative territory of each *fokonolona* under the socialist government of the 1970s and 1980s.
fotsy	'Whites', non-servile groups.
hainteny	Oral literature and poetry

hasina — A spiritual quality traditionally considered the essence of social and political organization, opposed to the forces of disorder and wildness; blessing or spiritual power.

Hova/hova — An old word originally used to describe free peasant communities without masters. Until the early nineteenth century, Europeans generally referred to the population of the central highlands as Hova, including both noble *(andriana)* and commoner *(hova)* groups. Thereafter, they increasingly tended to use the word Merina to designate the ethnic group living in this region. The present book distinguishes between *hova* (a category of the population of central Madagascar) and Hova (an old word designating the population of a specific region).

Imerina — The central region of Madagascar.

Jiny — A secret society that played a role in the 1947 rebellion.

karana, karany — An ethnic label used to designate a person of Indian or Pakistani origin, whether Muslim or not.

karazana — See *foko*.

lahatra — Hidden destiny, an integral part of the cosmos.

lamba — A large cloth worn as a garment, wrapped around the upper body like a Roman toga; by extension, textiles.

lava-sofina — 'Long ears', an old name applied to inhabitants of the highlands because of their practice of lengthening their ear-lobes with heavy ear-rings.

Madecasse, Matacasse, etc. — Originally, the subjects of a kingdom that existed in the southeast of Madagascar in the seventeenth century; probably the origin of the word 'Malagasy', later used to designate all the inhabitants of the island.

mainty — 'Blacks', a category of the population distinguished from *fotsy* ('whites'); formerly, *mainty* were considered privileged servants of the sovereign. In recent decades the word has been wrongly used to designate slaves or the descendants of slaves.

Maroseraña — A Sakalava royal dynasty.

Masikoro — Name of an ethnic group.

menabe, Menabe — Royal domain-lands; also, the name of a leading Sakalava kingdom.

menalamba	'Those who wear red togas', the name given to an anti-French rebellion that lasted from 1896-1898.
menakely	An area belonging to a fief-holder.
Merina	Name of an ethnic group.
Mozambiques, Mojambikas, Masombika	Generic term for African slaves in Madagascar.
mpanjaka	Sovereign.
ombiasy	A particular class of ritual expert, often itinerant.
philoubei (in classical Malagasy, *filohabe)*	A name used on the east coast to designate a headman.
ramanenjana	Name of a possession cult, best known for preceding the murder of King Radama II in 1863.
ray amandreny	'Father and mother', used in a gerontocratic society as a respectful title for persons in authority.
Sadiavahe	'Those who wear bark-cloth', the name given to an anti-French rebellion in 1915-1917.
Sakalava	Name of an ethnic group.
sampy	A group talisman.
sorabe	('Big writing'). Malagasy texts written in Arabic script, introduced by Islamized immigrants at a relatively early date and regarded as a potent religious technology. The oldest surviving manuscript written in this esoteric script dates from the seventeenth century.
sikidy	A technique of divination.
sombily	The act of slaughtering cattle, derived from the Malay *semblih*, itself a corruption of the Arabic *bismillah*, 'in the name of God'.
Tanala	('Forest People'): name of an ethnic group.
tangena	Ordeal by poison.
tavy	Rotating slash-and-burn agriculture.
tompon-tany	'Masters of the land', the name taken by a social group claiming to be descended from the first inhabitant of a particular location.
tompon-drano	'Masters of the waters', the name taken by a social group claiming to be descended from the first inhabitant of certain coastal locations.
vazaha	'Foreigner', especially a European or other Westerner.
vazimba, Vazimba	Formerly used to designate the supposed aboriginal inhabitants of Madagascar; also the name of a specific ethnic group.

vintana	Fortune.
vita Malagasy	'Made by Malagasy', i.e. made in Madagascar.
volamena	'Red silver', i.e. gold. The name of a branch of the Maroseraña dynasty.
Vorimo	Name of an ethnic group, associated with a rising on the east coast in 1895-96.
Vy, Vato, Sakelika	(VVS: 'Iron, Stone, Network'), the name of a secret society formed by young intellectuals that existed from 1913-1916, often considered the first modern nationalist organization.
Waqwaq	An Arabic name designating Madagascar and its inhabitants in early period, but also used to designate some other territories.
zoma	Friday.

APPENDIX III

BIOGRAPHIES

Many Malagasy proper names begin with the honorific titles Ra- or Andriana-. Names have a meaning, such as Andriamandazoala ('The Prince who Destroys the Forest'), the mythical first king of the Sakalava Maroseraña dynasty. For readers intimidated by the length of many proper names in the text, a good rule is to concentrate on the main substance of the name rather than the honorific titles.

ANDRIAMAHAZONORO (died 1828): One of ten Antemoro clerics summoned to Antananarivo as counsellors to King Andrianampoinimerina. He later served King Radama I also, teaching the king to write in Arabic script and acting as a diplomatic adviser. He participated in the negotiations leading to the British treaties of 1817 and 1820, was also part of a delegation that travelled to Britain and met King George IV on 21 April 1821, and was murdered during the coup of 1828.

ANDRIAMANDISOARIVO (posthumous name): see Tsimenata.

ANDRIAMASINAVALONA (ruled c.1675–c.1710): The first ruler to impose political unity on the region of Imerina, creating a kingdom around his capital, Antananarivo. The king's name was also applied to his descendants; the Andriamasinavalona became a category of nobility later used by successive monarchs to incorporate various minor rulers whom they wished to honour. Foreigners, such as the French trader Napoléon de Lastelle, could also be incorporated into this group.

ANDRIANAMPOINIMERINA ('The King at the Heart of Imerina') (c.1750–1809): Came to power as the ruler of Ambohimanga, a small town north of Antananarivo, in 1778. From there he conquered the whole of the highland province of Imerina to become its undisputed ruler. He also conquered several neighbouring kingdoms to create a powerful inland state.

ANDRIANDAHIFOTSY, also known as Lahifotsy, Lightfoot, etc. (c.1614–1683). One of the first kings in the Maroseraña dynasty, he created the first powerful Sakalava kingdom, becoming a major slave trader.

BRUTO CHAMBANGA: A ruler of the Madécasse region, who met the Jesuit Luis Mariano in 1613. According to Mariano, *bruto* was an honorific term indicating royal status. It is probably of Austronesian origin.

DRURY, ROBERT (1687–c.1733): English sailor who was shipwrecked in Madagascar, enslaved, and spent some sixteen years there. He later wrote (probably with professional assistance) a memoir that remains a key source on the history of southern Madagascar.

DUSSAC, PAUL LÉON ALFRED (1877–1938): The son of a veteran of the Paris Commune who emigrated to Réunion Island, Dussac settled first in Mayotte and then, after the First World War, in Madagascar. His left-wing republican views earned him the suspicion of the colonial administration. Working with Jean Ralaimongo, he became one of the leaders of the anticolonial movement in Madagascar. He was appointed secretary-general of the Communist Party in Madagascar after the formation of the Popular Front government in Paris in 1936.

ELLIS, WILLIAM (1794–1872): British missionary and author of a two-volume history of Madagascar published in 1838 on the basis of material supplied by missionaries from the London Missionary Society. Ellis also published other books on Madagascar based on his own subsequent travels to the island.

FARQUHAR, ROBERT TOWNSEND (1776–1830): A Scottish colonial official, appointed the first British governor-general of the Mascarene Islands after their capture from the French in 1810. As governor of the new British colony of Mauritius, Farquhar sought to implement Britain's 1807 ban on the slave trade. Seeking diplomatic contacts in Madagascar, one of the main regional sources of slaves, Farquhar sent a series of ambassadors to the neighbouring island, leading to the treaty with King Radama I signed on 23 October 1817.

FLACOURT, ETIENNE DE (1607–1660): Born into a noble family at Orléans, Flacourt was appointed as administrator of the French East India Company post at Fort Dauphin (Taolagnaro). He published the first full-length book on

Madagascar, which remains an indispensable source on the island's history. Claude Allibert is the editor of a modern re-edition.

GALLIENI, JOSEPH-SIMON (1849–1916): French army officer appointed Madagascar's first governor-general in 1896. He held this position until 1905, achieving the conquest of the whole island. Gallieni was awarded the rank of marshal posthumously in 1921.

JEAN-RENÉ (1773–1826): Born in Mauritius of a French father employed by the Compagnie des Indes and a Malagasy mother from Fort-Dauphin. In 1798 Jean-René was appointed as an interpreter for the French agent at Tamatave. After the town's occupation by British forces, the British government in Mauritius assisted Jean-René to become king of Tamatave. In 1817 Jean-René formally recognized Radama I as king of Madagascar and continued to retain great influence.

LAHIFOTSY: see Andriandahifotsy.

RABEMANANJARA, JACQUES (1913–2005): One of the founders of the nationalist Mouvement Démocratique de la Rénovation Malgache (MDRM), elected to the French National Assembly as a deputy for Madagascar in 1946. He was condemned to forced labour in connection with the insurrection of 1947 and amnestied in 1956. A minister and vice-president during the First Republic (1960–1972), he went into exile in 1975. Rabemananjara stood unsuccessfully as a candidate for the presidency in 1991 before returning to France. He is also widely known as a French-language writer.

RADAMA I (1793–1828): A son of King Andrianampoinimerina, Radama's talents were recognized by his father at an early age, and he already led military expeditions as a teenager. Radama succeeded to the throne of Imerina in 1809 and gained recognition from the British government as king of Madagascar in 1817. Radama resolved to abolish slave exports from his kingdom, and invited British missionaries to work in Imerina. He established a standing army, launching military expeditions throughout Madagascar, and a permanent civil service.

RADAMA II (1829–1863): Also known as Prince Rakoto before his accession, Radama was the son of Queen Ranavalona I and was officially regarded as the son of King Radama I, although in fact born a year after the latter's death. Strongly influenced by the French consul Jean Laborde, when Radama came to power he abolished forced labour and made sweeping changes to the government, attracting the opposition of powerful interests. Radama was murdered on 11 May 1863. In nationalist historiography, Radama II is generally regarded as an incompetent king who fatefully compromised with imperialist interests.

RAINILAIARIVONY (1828–1896): A grandson of one of King Andrianampoinimerina's generals, Rainilaiarivony dominated the government of Antananarivo from the 1860s until his overthrow by French troops in 1895. In 1864 he replaced his brother as prime minister, and he subsequently married the last three queens of Madagascar. He installed Protestantism as the official state religion by converting, together with Queen Ranavalona II, in 1869.

RALAIMONGO, JEAN (1884–1943): Jean Ralaimongo was the preeminent figure in the struggle for citizens' rights during the colonial period. Born in today's province of Fianarantsoa, at the age of seven he was captured by bandits, witnessing the murder of several family members, and became a slave. He received his freedom in 1898 as a result of anti-slavery legislation enacted by the colonial government. He then began his school education, becoming interested in republicanism and freemasonry. He volunteered for service in the First World War, partly in the hope of obtaining French citizenship, a goal he never achieved in spite of support from other Malagasy war veterans and from left-wing organizations in France. In the course of his political activities, Ralaimongo befriended other anti-colonial luminaries including Ho Chi Minh. In 1921 he returned to Madagascar and threw himself into the campaign for citizenship. Moving to Diego Suarez, he founded the anti-colonial newspaper *L'Opinion*. In 1929 Ralaimongo was arrested and relegated to the remote town of Port Bergé where he stayed until receiving an amnesty from the Popular Front government in 1936. He returned to Antananarivo in triumph and participated in the establishment of the Communist Party, continuing to press for citizens' rights for all. The Communist Party was banned in 1939. Ralaimongo died on 10 August 1943.

RAMANANTSOA, GABRIEL (1906–1979): A former officer of the French army, and chief of staff of the Malagasy army during the First Republic, he served as president of Madagascar's military government from 1972 to 1975.

RANAVALONA I (1788?–1861): Ranavalona was crowned queen of Madagascar after the death of her husband Radama I in 1828. She continued his military expeditions aimed at conquering outlying regions of the island. Government policy under Ranavalona frequently clashed with British and French interests. After she had issued a series of decrees aimed at restricting missionary activity, most British missionaries left Madagascar in 1836.

RAOMBANA (1809–1855): Born in Imerina into a royal family that had been eclipsed by the dynasty of King Andrianampoinimerina, Raombana was educated in England. Twin brother of a later minister of foreign affairs, he became private secretary to Queen Ranavalona I. Raombana is known above all for his history of Madagascar written in English, amounting to over 6,000 manuscript pages. The published edition has been edited by Simon Ayache.

RASETA, JOSEPH DELPHIN (1886–1979): Born into a Merina Protestant family, Raseta was trained as a doctor. He was a member of the nationalist secret society Vy Vato Sakelika (VVS), suppressed by the colonial government in 1916. He later joined Jean Ralaimongo in his anti-colonial campaigns, and in 1937 he collaborated with Ralaimongo, Paul Dussac and others in the establishment of a Malagasy Communist Party. Interned by the colonial administration from 1941 to 1943, Raseta was elected to the Constituent Assembly in Paris in 1945. He was a founder-member of the nationalist MDRM party in February 1946 and, later that year, was elected to the French National Assembly as a deputy for Madagascar. He was probably the single most important leader of the 1947 rising. Convicted and imprisoned in France, he returned to Madagascar only in 1960.

RATSIMANDRAVA, RICHARD (1931–1975): Born into a *mainty* family of servile origin in Imerina, Ratsimandrava joined the French army, serving in Morocco and Algeria. He became head of Madagascar's gendarmerie in 1969 and commanded the repression of an insurrection in the south of the island in 1971. Ratsimandrava became interior minister in the military government of 1972, developing a policy of radical decentralization. Sworn in as head of state on 5 February 1975, he was murdered in Antananarivo six days later.

RATSIRAKA, DIDIER IGNACE (1936–): His father was a leader of the Parti des Déshérités de Madagascar (PADESM) party in the Moramanga region and his mother, Céline Velonjara, was the daughter of one of PADESM's national leaders. A naval captain, Ratsiraka was appointed foreign minister in the military government of 1972–75. Taking power in 1975 after Ratsimandrava's assassination, he went on to establish a socialist government. Ratsiraka's first presidency lasted until 1993, when he lost elections to Albert Zafy. In 1997 he was reelected, but he was again defeated at the ballot box in December 2001, this time by Marc Ravalomanana. Ratsiraka's refusal to accept this result led to seven months of violent conflict. Ratsiraka departed for voluntary exile in France in July 2002.

RATSIMILAHO (c.1695–1750): son of an English pirate and a mother from Madagascar, he was the founder of the Betsimisaraka kingdom.

RAVALOMANANA, MARC (1949–): Born in a suburb of Antananarivo into an impoverished family of high traditional status, Ravalomanana amassed a fortune as the owner of a dairy business. With help from the World Bank, he turned this into an international company, Tiko S.A. In 1999 he was elected mayor of Antananarivo as head of a movement known as Tiako Iarivo, subsequently relabelled Tiako'i Madagasikara ('I Love Madagascar'). In 2001 he became vice-president of the Church of Jesus Christ in Madagascar (FJKM), the Protestant church that claims the allegiance of almost half of Madagascar's Christians. In December 2001 Ravalomanana stood as an opponent to Didier Ratsiraka in presidential elections. A dispute over the election results led to a low-intensity civil war throughout the first half of 2002, from which Ravalomanana emerged victorious. Ravalomanana was re-elected on 3 December 2006.

RAVELOJAONA, REVEREND (1879–1956): Educated at Protestant schools during the pre-colonial period, Ravelojaona became a schoolteacher in 1897. In 1904–5 he travelled to Europe on behalf of a Christian organization. In 1908 he was appointed pastor of the prestigious church of Ambohitantely in Antananarivo, formerly the church favoured by the royal family, and was to retain this post for the rest of his life. He published in Malagasy-language journals, writing one widely-noticed piece comparing Madagascar to Japan after the latter's 1905 military victory over Russia. His writings influenced the young founders of the Vy Vato Sakelika (VVS) nationalist society. Tried and acquitted of membership of the VVS, Ravelojaona joined the French army and served in the First World War. Returning to Madagascar in 1920, he became an active cultural nationalist. In 1939 he was elected as a member of the Conseil Supérieur des Colonies.

RAVOAHANGY-ANDRIANAVALONA, JOSEPH (1893–1970): Born at Fianarantsoa into a high-status Merina family, Ravoahangy's medical studies were interrupted in 1915 when he was sentenced to life imprisonment for his membership of the Vy Vato Sakelika (VVS) nationalist organization. He was amnestied in 1922 and completed his medical studies. Moving to Diego-Suarez, he joined Jean Ralaimongo and others in political campaigning. Following a demonstration in Antananarivo on 19 May 1929, Ravoahangy-Andrianavalona was banished by the colonial government for five years to the town of

Maintirano. He returned to Antananarivo in 1936 and became a founder of the Communist Party. In 1945 he was elected to the Constituent Assembly and the following year he became a founder-member of the MDRM nationalist party before being elected as a deputy for Madagascar in the French National Assembly. Following the outbreak of the 1947 insurrection, he was convicted and sentenced to death. Although this was later commuted, he did not return to Madagascar in 1960. He occupied several minor posts under the First Republic.

TOAKAFO, also known as Andrianamboniarivo (posthumous name) (c.1688–1732): the second Sakalava king of Boina. Developing a close relationship with European pirates and other foreign traders, he built a powerful army and became the most powerful king in Madagascar.

TSIMENATA, also known as Chimenate etc. and by his posthumous name of Andriamandisoarivo (c.1668–c.1709): the first Sakalava king of Boina. Younger son of Andriandahifotsy.

TSIRANANA, PHILIBERT (1912–1978) : A schoolteacher by profession, Tsiranana was a founder-member of the Parti des Déshérités de Madagascar (PADESM) in 1946. Initially with the support of the colonial government, PADESM aimed to rally the *mainty* groups in Imerina, plus other populations from the coastal areas, in opposition to the nationalist MDRM party. In 1956 Tsiranana was elected as a deputy for Madagascar and in the same year he founded the Parti Social-Démocrate (PSD) with other moderates from PADESM. In July 1958, the Representative Assembly elected him president of the government. Prior to the referendum held in September 1958, he campaigned to keep Madagascar within the French Community. At a congress of provincial counsellors on 14 October 1958, he presided over the establishment of the Malagasy Republic and the creation of a National Assembly. On 29 April 1959, the National Assembly voted for a constitution and, on 1 May, it elected Philibert Tsiranana as the first president of the Malagasy Republic. Independence was officially declared on 26 June 1960. Under Tsiranana's presidency, Madagascar retained strong links with France. On 17 May 1972, an ailing Tsiranana, under pressure from a youth revolt, handed power to the army chief of staff, General Gabriel Ramanantsoa. Tsiranana played no further significant political role.

ZAFY, ALBERT (1927–): Born in the north of the island, trained as a cardiologist, Zafy became a minister in the military government led by General Ramanantsoa in 1972. He campaigned for a 'no' vote in the 1976 constitutional referendum that was designed to legitimize the coup d'état by Captain Didier Ratsiraka, previously a member of the same military administration. In 1989, Zafy became the president of the opposition movement known as the Forces Vives and founded the Union Nationale pour la Démocratie et le Développement (UNDD). Propelled by a wider movement in favour of democracy, the opposition chose Zafy to stand against Ratsiraka as its candidate for presidential elections in 1993. Zafy won the elections with 53 % of the votes. Aiming to create a strong executive presidency, Zafy clashed with members of his party who were in favour of a parliamentary system. Amid personal and political conflicts and widespread corruption, Zafy was impeached by the National Assembly in 1997 on the grounds that he had violated the constitution. He was defeated by a resurgent Ratsiraka in presidential elections in 1997. In presidential elections in 2001, he finished in third place, subsequently becoming a leader of the opposition to President Marc Ravalomanana.

BIBLIOGRAPHY

ARCHIVES

Denmark
Rigsarkivet, Copenhagen: archives of the Vestindisk-Guineisk Kompagni: boxes 219-21, papers concerning Charles Barrington and the ship *Grewinde ef Laurwigen.*

France
Archives départementales de la Réunion, St-Denis.
Archives départementales de l'Orne, Alençon: Le Myre de Vilers papers.
Archives diplomatiques, Nantes.
Archives du Ministère des Affaires étrangères, Paris.
Centre des archives d'Outre-Mer (CAOM), Aix-en-Provence.

Madagascar
Archives de la République Malgache, Antananarivo.
Archives of the Catholic archbishopric, Andohalo.

The Netherlands
Nationaal Archief, The Hague: archives of the United East India Company (VOC). See also the website http://www.tanap. net/

South Africa
South African State Archives, Cape Town: archives of the Council of Policy. See also the website http://www.tanap. net/

United Kingdom
British Museum, London: Farquhar papers, Add. Mss. 18117–18141.
Archives of the World Council of Christian Missions, School of Oriental and African Studies, London: papers of the London Missionary Society.
National Archives of the United Kingdom (formerly the Public Record Office), Kew : Foreign Office papers.
National Library of Wales, Aberystwyth: Neuaddlwyd and Aberaeron papers, NLW 19157E.

USA
US National Archives and Records Administration, Washington D.C., con-

sular records, US Cons. III (viewed on microfilm at the French National Archives, Paris, 253 Mi 35).

UNPUBLISHED MANUSCRIPTS AND THESES

Anrianaivoarivony, Rafolo, 'Habitats fortifiés et organisation de l'espace dans le Vonizongo (centre ouest de Madagascar). Le cas de Lohavohitra' (doctoral thesis, University of Paris I, 1989).

Anon., 'An Acco[t] of the present comodityes that are imported & exported at Madagascarr and the manner of dealing with the natives', undated [1692?], Rawlinson ms. A.334, Bodleian Library, Oxford.

Anon., 'Historique des affaires de Madagascar', Institut de recherche scientifique de Madagascar, Antananarivo, ms. 0767.

Anon (Rabozaka?), 'Notes d'histoire malgache', c.1914, unpublished ms. in the library of the Académie malgache, Antananarivo, unclassified.

Baron, Richard, 'Political and social review of the last decade', document annexed to *Antananarivo Annual and Madagascar Magazine,* 6 (1900), Rhodes House Library, Oxford.

Beaujard, Philippe, 'Madagascar, au confluent des mondes austronésien, bantou et islamique' (Présentation de travaux en vue de l'habitation à diriger des thèses, Ecole des hautes études en sciences sociales, Paris, 1998).

Berger, Laurent, 'Les raisons de la colère des ancêtres Zafinifotsy (Ankaraña, Madagascar) : l'anthropologie au défi de la mondialisation' (doctoral thesis, Ecole des hautes études en sciences sociales, Paris, 2006).

Caillon-Filet, Claudine, 'Jean Laborde et l'Océan Indien' (doctoral thesis, University of Aix-en-Provence, 1978).

Esoavelomandroso, Manassé, 'La province maritime orientale du "Royaume de Madagascar" à la fin du XIXe siècle (1882–1895)', (2 vols, doctoral thesis, Universities of Paris and Antananarivo, 1976).

Frappé, Hendrik, 'Korte beschrijving van 't Eiland Madagascar of St. Laurens aan de Westsijde', 1715, South African Library, Cape Town, MSD 3. This manuscript has been translated and published by Piet Westra and James C. Armstrong (eds), *Slave Trade with Madagascar: The journals of the Cape Slaver* Leijdsman, *1715* (Africana Publishers, Cape Town, 2006).

Fruitet, P. , 'Activités économiques du Napoléon de Lastelle, Jean Laborde et François Lambert à Madagascar', mémoire no.55 (1945–6), Ecole Nationale de la France Outre-Mer, Paris.

Galibert, Didier, 'Les gens de pouvoir : territoire et légitimités à Madagascar' (2 vols, doctoral thesis, University of Réunion, 2006).

Jones, Mary K., 'The slave trade at Mauritius, 1810–29' (B.Litt. thesis, University of Oxford, 1936).

Keating, Sir Henry Singer, 'Travels in Madagascar, Greece and the United States' [travels in 1825]: Bodleian Library, Oxford, Eng. Mss. C.29.

Larson, Pier M., 'Popular historians in the Vakinankaratra: the art of historical memory in highland Madagascar', unpublished ms.

Manjakahery, Barthélémy, 'Le site d'Erimoho dans l'histoire des hautes vallées de la Menakompy, centre-sud de Madagascar' (doctoral thesis, University of Paris I, 1997).

Marson, Francis Zafindrandremitambahoaka, 'Les sultanats musulmans à Madagascar : la filiation de la civilisation des échelles commerciales arabes et la survivance islamique dans certaines royautés malgaches' (doctoral thesis, University of Perpignan, 2007).

Mayeur, Nicolas, 'Histoire de Ratsimila-hoe, Roi de Foule-pointe et des Bé-tsimiçaracs', British Museum, add mss. 18129, fols.82–143.

Rainandriamampandry, 'Tantarany Madagascar', drafts in the Archives de la République Malgache, series SS.

Raison-Jourde, Françoise, 'Du service sacré à la corvée de travail. Réflexions sur le fanompoana à Madagascar, XVIIe-XIXe siècles', unpublished paper read at a symposium held at the School of Oriental and African Studies, London, 28 November 1986.

Randrianja, Solofo, 'Présentation des travaux en vue de l'habilitation à diriger des thèses' (University of Paris VII-Denis Diderot, 2003).

Raombana (ed.S.Ayache), 'Annales', unpublished typescript, Académie malgache, Antananarivo.

Ratsivalaka, Gilbert, 'Madagascar dans le sud-ouest de l'océan Indien (c.1500–1824)' (2 vols, Doctorat d'Etat, University of Nice, 1995).

Ravalarivo, 'Histoire des Rafindraminia' (manuscript no. 2773 III, Grandidier papers, Muséum national d'histoire naturelle, Paris).

Razoaliarinirina, Rojo, 'Les nationalistes citadins de Tamatave de la Deuxième guerre mondiale à l'indépendance (1939 – 1960)' (Master's thesis, history, University of Tamatave, 1999).

Richard, Charles, 'Le gouvernement de Victor Augagneur à Madagascar (1905–1910)', (doctoral thesis, University of Paris, 1969).

NEWSPAPERS AND MAGAZINES

Asia Times

Le Courrier international, Paris

L'Express de Madagascar, Antananarivo

La Gazette de la Grande île, Antananarivo

Lakroan'i Madagasikara, Antananarivo

Lettre de l'océan Indien, Paris

MADAGASCAR

Madagascar matin, Antananarivo
Madagascar renouveau, Antananarivo
Madagascar tribune, Antananarivo
Midi Madagascar, Antananarivo
Le Monde, Paris
Tana-Journal, Antananarivo
Ny Tari-dalana, Antananarivo
La Tribune de Madagascar, Antananarivo

INTERNET PUBLICATIONS

Antananarivo city hall: www.iarivo-town.mg

Barth, Fredrik, 'Ethnicity and the concept of culture', paper presented to the conference on 'Rethinking Culture', Harvard University, 1995: www.tau.ac.il/tarbut

Embassy of France, Madagascar: www.ambafrance-mada.org/article.php3?id_article=255

Forced Labour Convention, 1930: www.itcilo.it/actrav/english/common/C029.html

La Francophonie: www.droit.francophonie.org/doc/html/mg/con/fr/1994/1994dfmgcofr1.html

Grandidier archives: the archives of Alfred and Guillaume Grandidier are currently being put online. Some items may be consulted at www.fonds-grandidier.mg

Joshua Project: www.joshuaproject.net/countries.php?rog3=MA

Ministry of Foreign Affairs, France, 'Evolution de l'APD à Madagascar 1984–2004': www.diplomatie.gouv.fr/fr/pays-zones-geo_833/madagascar_399/presentation-madagascar_992/economie_1863.html

National Assembly, Madagascar: www.assemblee-nationale.mg/fr/historique.php

Pariat, Philippe, 'Les échanges en océan Indien à la période antique', May 2004: aphgreunion.free.fr/articlepariat.htm

The Periplus of the Erytrean Sea: www.depts.washington.edu/uwch/silkroad/index.shtml, 'Historical texts'.

The Slavery Convention: www.ohchr.org/english/law/slavery.htm#wp1034147

TANAP is a project to publish online the archives of the Dutch East India Company, the VOC:www.tanap. net

United Nations Development Programme, *Human Development Report*: www.hdr.undp.org/hdr2006/statistics/countries/country_fact_sheets/cty_fs_MDG.html

U.S. Library of Congress, 'The fokonolona and traditional governance', www.countrystudies.us/madagascar/28.htm

World Bank, *Madagascar: Recent economic developments and prospects*, report PUB2357, 30 November 1980: www-wds.worldbank.org

PUBLISHED BOOKS AND ARTICLES

Adejunmobi, Moradewun, *J. J. Rabearivelo, Literature and lingua franca in colonial Madagascar* (Peter Lang, New York, 1996).

Adelaar, K.Alexander, 'Malay influence on Malagasy: linguistic and culture-historical implications', *Oceanic Linguistics*, 28, 1 (1989), pp. 2–46.

Adelaar, K.Alexander, 'New ideas on the early history of Malagasy', in H. Steinhauer (ed.), *Papers in Austronesian Linguistics no. 1* (Pacific Linguistics series, A-81, Department of Linguistics, Research School of Pacific Studies, Australian National University, Canberra, 1991), pp. 1–22.

Adelaar, K.Alexander, 'Malagasy culture-history: some linguistic evidence', in Reade (ed.), *The Indian Ocean*, pp. 487–500.

Adelaar, K.Alexander , 'Asian roots of the Malagasy: a linguistic perspective', *Bijdragen tot de Taal- Land- en Volkenkunde*, 151, 3 (1995), pp. 325–56.

Adelaar, K. Alexander, 'Borneo as a cross-roads for comparative Austronesian linguistics', in Bellwood et al, *The Austronesians,* pp. 75–95.

Adelaar, K. Alexander, 'An exploration of directional systems in West Indonesia and Madagascar', in Gunter Senft (ed.), *Referring to Space: Studies in Austronesian and Papuan languages* (Clarendon Press, Oxford, 1997), pp. 53–78.

Adelaar, K. Alexander, 'The Austronesian languages of Asia and Madagascar: a historical perspective', in Alexander Adelaar and Nikolaus P. Himmelman (eds), *The Austronesian Languages of Asia and Madagascar* (Routledge Language Family Series, Routledge, London and New York, 2005), pp. 1–42.

Adelaar, K. Alexander, 'Towards an integrated theory about the Indonesian migrations to Madagascar', in P. N. Peregrine, I. Peiros and M. Feldman (eds), *Ancient Human Migations: A multidisciplinary approach* (University of Utah Press, Salt Lake City UH, forthcoming).

Allibert, Claude, 'Un voyageur turc dans l'océan Indien au XVIe siècle, *Etudes océan Indien,* 10 (1988), pp. 9–39.

Allibert, Claude, *Les Apports austronésiens à Madagascar, dans le canal de Mozambique et en Afrique zambézienne : éléments de réflexion à partir de deux auteurs négligés* (INALCO, Paris, 1990).

Allibert, Claude, 'Tradition et modernité à Madagascar', introduction to De Flacourt, *Grande Isle*, pp. 11–85.

Allibert, Claude, Introduction to *Etudes océan Indien,* 27–8 (1999), special number on 'Navires, ports, itinéraires', pp. 7–9.

———, 'Des cauris et des hommes. Réflexion sur l'utilisation d'une monnaie-objet et ses itinéraires', in Claude Allibert and Narivelo Rajaonarimanana (eds), *L'Extraordinaire au quotidien: variations anthropologiques* (Karthala, Paris, 2000), pp. 57–79.

———, and Pierre Vérin, 'Linguistique, archéologie et l'exploration du passé malgache', in Øyvind Dahl (ed.), *Language, a Doorway between Human Cultures: Tributes to Dr Otto Chr. Dahl on his ninetieth birthday* (Novus Forlag, Oslo, 1993), pp. 29–38.

Alpers, Edward A., 'Madagascar and Mozambique in the nineteenth century: the era of the Sakalava raids (1800–1820)', *Omaly sy anio*, 5–6 (1977), pp. 37–53.

Althabe, Gérard, *Oppression et libération dans l'imaginaire : les communautés villageoises de la côte orientale de Madagascar* (Maspero, Paris, 1969).

———, 'Les manifestations paysannes d'avril 1971', *Revue française d'études politiques africaines*, 78 (1972), pp 71–7.

———, 'Le Monima', *Revue française d'études politiques africaines*, 86 (1973), pp. 71–6.

———, 'Les luttes sociales à Tananarive en 1972', *Cahiers d'études africaines*, XX, 4, no.80 (1980), pp. 407–47.

———, *Anthropologie politique d'une décolonisation* (L'Harmattan, Paris, 2000).

Andriamanjato, R.M., *Le Tsiny et le tody dans la pensée malgache* (Présence africaine, Paris, 1957).

Andrianaivoarivony, Rafolo, 'Mixed cultures of Madagascar and the other islands', in M.A. al-Bakhit, L. Bazin and S.M. Cissoko (eds), *History of Humanity, vol. IV: From the seventh to the sixteenth century* (UNESCO, Paris, 2000), pp. 531–5.

Andrianarivelo, V.Rafrezy, and I. Randretsa, *Population de Madagascar : situation actuelle et perspectives d'avenir* (Ministère de la recherche scientifique et technique pour le développment, Antananarivo, 1985).

Armstrong, James C., 'Madagascar and the slave trade in the seventeenth century', *Omaly sy anio*, 17–20 (1983–4), pp. 211–33.

Ayache, Simon, *Raombana l'historien : introduction à l'édition critique de son œuvre* (Ambozontany, Fianarantsoa, 1976).

Bagehot, Walter, 'The danger of lending to semi-civilized countries', in Norman St John Stevas (ed.), *The Collected Works of Walter Bagehot*, vol.10 (The Economist, London, 1978), pp. 419–23.

Ballarin, Marie-Pierre, *Les Reliques royales sakalava, source de légitimation et enjeu de pouvoir : Madagascar XVIII-XXème siècles* (Karthala, Paris, 2000).

Baré, Jean-François, *Pouvoir des vivants, langage des morts: idéo-logiques sakalave* (Maspero, Paris, 1977).

Barendse, René, *The Arabian Seas: The Indian Ocean world of the seventeenth century* (Sharpe, Armonk NY, 2002).

Battistini, René, and Pierre Vérin, 'Man and the environment in Madagascar: past problems and problems of today', in R. Battistini and G. Richard-Vindard (eds), *Biogeography and Ecology in Madagascar* (W. Junk, The Hague, 1972), pp. 311–37.

Beaujard, Philippe, *Princes et paysans: les Tanala de l'Ikongo* (L'Harmattan, Paris, 1983).

———, *Le Parler secret arabico-malgache du sud-est de Madagascar : recherches étymologiques* (L'Harmattan, Paris, 1998).

———, 'Les arrivées austronésiennes à Madagascar : vagues ou continuum?', part 1, *Etudes océan Indien*, 35–6 (2003), pp. 59–147.

———, 'The Indian Ocean in Eurasian and African world-systems before the sixteenth century', *Journal of World History*, 16, 4 (2005), pp. 411–65.

———, 'L'Afrique de l'Est, les Comores et Madagascar dans le système-monde avant le XVIe siècle', in Nativel and Rajaonah, *Madagascar et l'Afrique*, pp. 29–102.

Bellwood, Peter, *Prehistory of the Indo-Malaysian Archipelago* (1985; rev. edn, University of Hawai'i Press, Honolulu HI, 1997).

———, James J. Fox and Darrell Tryon (eds), *The Austronesians: Historical and comparative perspectives* (Dept of Anthropology, Research School of Pacific and Asian Studies, Australian National University, Canberra, 1995).

Berg, Gerald M., 'The sacred musket: tactics, technology and power in eighteenth-century Madagascar', *Comparative Studies in Society and History*, 27, 2 (1985), pp. 261–79.

———, 'Radama's smile: domestic challenges to royal ideology in early nineteenth-century Imerina', *History in Africa*, 25 (1998), pp. 69–92.

Bialuschewski, Arne, 'Pirates, slavers, and the indigenous population in Madagascar, c.1690–1715', *International Journal of African Historical Studies*, 38, 3 (2005), pp. 401–25.

Birkeli, Emil, *Les Vazimbas de la côte ouest de Madagascar: notes d'ethnologie* (Mémoires de l'Académie malgache, fascicule XXII, Antananarivo, 1936).

Blench, Roger, 'Evidence for the Indonesian origins of certain elements of African culture: a review, with special reference to the arguments of A.M.

Jones', *Journal of the International Library of African Music*, undated extract, in library of the Koninklijk Instituut voor Taal-, Land- en Volkenkunde, Leiden, catalogue number a 1592 N.

———, 'The ethnographic evidence for long-distance contacts between Oceania and East Africa', in Julian Reade (ed.), *The Indian Ocean*, pp. 417–38.

Bloch, Maurice, 'La séparation du pouvoir et du rang comme processus d'évolution. Une esquisse du développement des royautés dans le centre de Madagascar', in Raison-Jourde, *Les Souverains de Madagascar*, pp. 265–98. An English version exists as 'The disconnection between power and rank as a process: an outline of the development of kingdoms in central Madagascar', *Archives européennes de sociologie*, XVIII, I (1977), pp. 107–48.

———, *From Blessing to Violence: History and ideology in the circumcision ritual of the Merina of Madgascar* (Cambridge University Press, Cambridge, 1986).

Boiteau, Pierre, *Contribution à l'histoire de la nation malgache* (Edns sociales, Paris, 1958).

———, 'Les proto-Malgaches et la domestication des plantes', *Bulletin de l'Académie malgache*, new series, LV, i–ii (1977), pp. 21–6.

'Brief summary of important events in Madagascar from 1878 to 1881', *Antananarivo Annual and Madagascar Magazine*, V (1881), pp. 115–26.

Brown, Mervyn, *Madagascar Rediscovered: A history from early times to independence* (Damien Tunnacliffe, London, 1978).

———, *A History of Madagascar* (Damien Tunnacliffe, London, 1995).

Brunschwig, Henri, 'Politique et économie dans l'empire français d'Afrique noire, 1870–1914', *Journal of African History*, 11, 3 (1970), pp. 401–17.

Burney, David A., 'Theories and facts regarding Holocene environmental change before and after human colonisation', in Goodman and Patterson, *Natural Change*, pp. 75–89.

Burrett, Robert S., 'Pre-colonial gold mining', *Heritage of Zimbabwe*, 15 (1996), pp. 57–69.

Cadoux, Charles, 'Les élections générales de 1982–1983 à Madagascar : des élections pour quoi faire?', *L'Année africaine 1983* (A. Pedone, Paris, 1985), pp. 67–85.

———, 'La Constitution de la Troisième République malgache', *Politique africaine*, 52 (1993), pp. 58–66.

———, and Jean du Bois de Gaudusson, 'Madagascar, 1979–1981, un passage difficile', in *Annuaire des pays de l'océan Indien*, VII (Centre national de la recherche scientifique et Presses universitaires d'Aix-Marseille,

Paris and Aix-en-Provence, 1980), pp. 357–87.

Callet, François (trans. G.S. Chapus and E. Ratsimba), *Histoire des rois* (rev. edn, vols I–III, V, Edns de la Librairie de Madagascar, Antananarivo, 1974–8). Better known by its Malagasy title, *Tantaran' ny Andriana.*

Calvet, J.-L., 'Madagascar', *Annuaire des pays de l'océan Indien, volume III 1976* (Presses Universitaires d'Aix-Marseille, Paris and Aix-en-Provence, 1978), pp. 347–94.

Campbell, Gwyn, 'The history of nineteenth-century Madagascar: "le royaume" or "l'empire" ?', *Omaly sy anio*, 33–6 (1994), pp. 331–80.

———, *An Economic History of Imperial Madagascar, 1750–1895: The rise and fall of an island empire* (Cambridge University Press, 2005).

Carayon, Louis, 'Voyage dans l'intérieur de Madagascar', *Annuaire des voyages et de la géographie,* 4 (1847), pp. 53–126.

———, *Précis historique sur le people ova, suivi de l'appréciation des derniers événemens de Tamatave* (Gide, Paris, 1845).

Chevalier, Louis, *Madagascar : populations et ressources* (Presses universitaires de France, Paris, 1952).

Chittick, Neville, 'L'Afrique de l'Est et l'Orient: les ports et le commerce avant l'arrivée des Portugais,' in UNESCO, *Relations historiques à travers l'océan Indien*, pp. 15–25.

Cole, Jennifer, *Forget Colonialism? Sacrifice and the art of memory in Madagascar* (University of California Press, Berkeley, 2001).

———, 'Fresh contact in Tamatave, Madagascar: sex, money, and intergenerational transformation', *American Ethnologist,* 31, 4 (2004), pp. 571–86.

Condominas, Georges, *Fokon'olona et collectivités rurales en Imerina* (Berger-Levrault, Paris, 1960).

Coolhaas, W. Ph.,*Generale Missiven van Gouverneurs-Generaal en Raden aan Heren XVII der Verenigde Oostindische Compagnie* (vol.1, Nijhoff, The Hague, 1960).

Cooper, Frederick, *Africa Since 1940 : The past of the present* (Cambridge University Press, 2002).

Coppalle, André, 'Voyage dans l'intérieur de Madagascar et à la capitale du roi Radama pendant les années 1825 et 1826', *Bulletin de l'Académie malgache,* VII (1909), pp. 3–49 (pt.1) ; VIII (1910), pp. 25–64 (pt.2). Republished by Edns de la Lanterne magique, Besançon, 2006.

Coquery-Vidrovitch, Catherine, *Afrique noire: permanences et ruptures* (2nd rev. edn., L'Harmattan, Paris, 1992).

Cousins, William E., 'The abolition of slavery in Madagascar, with some remarks on Malagasy slavery generally', *Antananarivo Annual and Madagascar Magazine,* V (1896), pp. 446–50.

Dahl, Otto Chr., *Malgache et Maanjan* (Egede-Instituttet, Oslo, 1951).

———, 'Bantu substratum in Malagasy', *Etudes océan Indien,* 9 (1988), pp. 91–132.

———, *Migration from Kalimantan to Madagascar* (Institute for Comparative Research in Human Culture, Serie B: Skrifter, LXXXII, Norwegian University Press, Oslo, 1991).

Danfulani, Umar, 'Sixteen figure divination in Africa', *Africana Marburgensia,* XXX, i (1997), pp. 24–45.

Darwin, John, *After Tamerlane : The global history of empire since 1405* (Allen Lane, London, 2007).

De Vries, Jan, and Ad van der Woude, *The First Modern Economy: Success, failure, and perseverance of the Dutch economy, 1500–1815* (Cambridge University Press, 1997).

Decary, Raymond, 'La population de Madagascar', *Bulletin de l'Académie malgache*, new series, XXVIII (1947–8), pp. 29–47.

———, *Coutumes guerrières et organisation militaire chez les anciens Malgaches* (2 vols, Editions maritimes d'outre-mer, Paris, 1966).

Deguilhem, Randi, 'Turning Syrians into Frenchmen: the cultural politics of a French non-governmental organization in Mandate Syria (1920–67)—the French Secular Mission schools,' in *Islam and Christian-Muslim Relations,* 13, 4 (2002), pp. 449–60.

Delivré, Alain, *L'Histoire des rois d'Imerina : interprétation d'une tradition orale* (Klincksieck, Paris, 1974).

Delval, Raymond, 'Migrations, minorités et échanges en océan Indien, XIX siècle. Table ronde', *Etudes et documents*, 11 (1978), Université de Provence.

Deschamps, Hubert, *Histoire de Madagascar* (1960 ; 4th edn, Berger-Levrault, Paris, 1972).

Devisse, Jean, 'Les Africains, la mer et les historiens', *Cahiers d'études africaines*, XXIX, 3–4, 115–116 (1989), pp. 397–418.

Dewar, Robert E., 'The archaeology of the early settlement of Madagascar', in Reade, *The Indian Ocean in Antiquity*, pp. 471–86.

———, 'Were people responsible for the extinction of Madagascar's subfossils, and how will we ever know?', in Goodman and Patterson, *Natural Change and Human Impact in Madagascar*, pp. 364–77.

———, and Solo Rakotovololona, 'La chasse aux subfossiles: les preuves du onzième siècle au treizième siècle', *Taloha,* 11 (1992), pp. 5–13.

Dez, Jacques, 'La monarchie merina et le développement agricole', *Terre Malgache/Tany Malagasy*, X (1971), pp. 231–6.

Domenichini, Jean-Pierre, ' " La plus belle énigme du monde" ou l'historiographie coloniale en question', *Omaly sy anio*, 13–14 (1981), pp. 57–76.

Domenichini, Jean-Pierre, 'Le monde enchanté des Anciens', in *Madagascar et le christianisme* (Agence de cooperation culturelle et technique, Karthala and Ambozontany, Paris and Antananarivo, 1993), pp. 13–38.

———, 'Pirogues et bateaux cousus à Madagascar', *Tsingy* (forthcoming)

Domenichini-Ramiaramanana, Bakoly, *Du ohabolana au hainteny: langue, littérature et politique à Madagascar* (Karthala, Paris, 1983).

———, and Jean-Pierre Domenichini, 'Madagascar dans l'océan Indien avant le XIIIè siècle : présentation de données suggérant des orientations de recherche', *Nouvelles du Centre d'art et d'archéologie, Université de Madagascar,* 1 (1983), pp. 5–19.

Drury, Robert (Capt. Pasfield Oliver, ed.), *Madagascar; or Robert Drury's Journal, During Fifteen Years' Captivity on that Island* (1729; T. Fisher Unwin, London, 1890).

Du Maine de la Josserie, Julien-Pierre, 'Idée de la Côte occidentale de Madagascar, depuis Ancouala au nord, jusqu'à Mouroundava désigné par les Noirs sous le nom Menabe', *Annales des voyages, de la géographie, et de l'histoire*, XI (1810), pp. 20–52.

Duffy, Rosaleen, 'Gemstone mining in Madagascar: transnational networks, criminalisation and global integration', *Journal of Modern African Studies*, 45, 2 (2007), pp. 185–206.

Eglise et société à Madagascar (5 vols, Foi et justice, Antananarivo, 1990–2000).

Ehret, Christopher, *An African Classical Age: Eastern and southern Africa in world history, 1000 B.C. to A.D. 400* (University Press of Virginia and James Currey, Charlottesville, VA and Oxford, 1998).

Ellis, Stephen, 'Un texte du XVIIème siècle sur Madagadascar', *Omaly sy anio*, 9 (1979), pp. 151–66.

———, *The Rising of the Red Shawls: A revolt in Madagascar, 1895–1899* (Cambridge University Press, 1985).

———, *Un complot colonial à Madagascar : l'affaire Rainandriamampandry* (Karthala, Paris, 1990).

———, 'Witch-hunting in central Madagascar, 1828–61', *Past and Present*, 175 (2002), pp. 90–123.

———, 'Tom and Toakafo: The Betsimisaraka kingdom and state formation in Madagascar, 1715–1750', *Journal of African History*, 48, 3 (2007), pp. 439–55.

———, 'The history of sovereigns in Madagascar: new light from old sources', in Didier Nativel (ed.), forthcoming.

———, and Gerrie ter Haar, *Worlds of Power: Religious ideas and political practice in Africa* (C. Hurst & Co. and Oxford University Press, London and New York, 2004).

———, and Solofo Randrianja, 'Les archives de la Compagnie néerlandaise des indes orientales et l'histoire de Madagascar: l'expédition du navire de la VOC, le Schuylenburg, septembre 1752', in Ignace Rakoto (ed.), *La Route des esclaves, système servile et traite dans l'est malgache* (L'Harmattan, Paris, 2001), pp. 47–74.

Ellis, William, *History of Madagascar* (2 vols, Fisher & Son, London and Paris, 1838).

———, *Three Visits to Madagascar* (John Murray, London, 1857).

———, *Madagascar Revisited* (John Murray, London, 1867).

———, *The Martyr Church: A narrative of the introduction, progress and triumph of Christianity in Madagascar* (John Snow, London, 1870).

Esoavelomandroso, Faranirina V., 'Les Sadiavahe : essai d'interprétation d'une révolte dans le Sud (1915–1917)', *Omaly sy Anio* 1–2 (1974), pp. 139–71.

———, 'Différentes lectures de l'histoire : quelques réflexions sur la V.V.S.', *Recherches, pédagogie et culture*, IX (1981), 50, pp. 100–111.

———, 'Résistance à la médecine en situation coloniale : la peste à Madagascar', *Annales : économies, sociétés, civilisations*, 36, 2 (1981), pp. 168–90.

———, 'Des rizières à la ville. Les plaines de l'ouest d'Antananarivo dans la première moitié du XXème siècle', *Omaly sy anio*, 29–32 (1989–90), pp. 321–37.

Esoavelomandroso, Manassé, 'Le mythe d'Andriba', *Omaly sy anio*, 1–2 (1975), pp. 43–73.

———, 'Antagonisme des *Fanjakana*', in *Madagascar et le christianisme*, pp. 39–56.

———, 'La «révolte de l'est» (novembre 1895–février 1896): essai d'explication', *Omaly sy anio*, 21–2 (1985), pp. 33–46.

Evers, Sandra, 'Solidarity and antagonism in migrant societies on the Southern highlands', in Rakoto, *L'Esclavage à Madagascar*, pp. 339– 45.

———, 'Stigmatization as a self-perpetuating process', in Sandra Evers and Marc Spindler (eds), *Cultures of Madagascar: Ebb and flow of influences* (International Institute for Asian Studies, Leiden, 1996), pp. 157–85.

———, *Constructing History, Culture and Inequality: The Betsileo in the extreme southern highlands of Madagascar* (Brill, Leiden, 2002).

Fagereng, Edwin, *Une famille de dynasties malgaches* (Instituttet for Sammenlignende Kulturforskning, Oslo, 1971).

Faria y Sousa, Manuel, *Asia Portuguesa*, vol. III (Antonio Craesbeeck, Lisbon, 1675).

Faublée, Jacques, *L'Ethnographie de Madagascar* (Editions de France et d'outre-mer, Paris, 1946).

———, *La Cohésion des sociétés bara* (Presses universitaires de France, Paris, 1954).

Feeley-Harnik, Gillian, *A Green Estate: Restoring independence in Madagascar* (Smithsonian Institution Press, Washington DC, 1991).

Felix, Marc Leo, 'Good ideas go a long way: similarities in the artistic typology of East Africa, Indonesia and Madagascar', *The World of Tribal Arts,* 2, 2 (1995), pp. 46–53.

Ferrand, Gabriel, *Les Musulmans à Madagascar et aux îles Comores* (3 vols, E. Leroux, Paris, 1891–1902).

———, 'La légende de Raminia d'après un manuscrit arabico-malgache de la Bibliothèque nationale', *Journal asiatique*, 9th series, XIX (1902), pp. 185–230.

———, 'Les îles Râmny, Lâmery, Wâkwâk, Komor des géographes arabes, et Madagascar', *Journal asiatique*, 10th series, X (1907), pp. 434–566.

———, 'L'origine africaine des malgaches', Gabriel, *Journal Asiatique,* 10th series, XII (1908), pp. 353–500.

———, 'Les voyages des Javanais à Madagascar', *Journal Asiatique*, 10th series, XV, 2 (1910), pp. 281–330.

Filliot, J.-M., *La Traite des esclaves vers les Mascareignes au XVIIIe siècle* (ORSTOM, Paris, 1974).

Firaketana ny fiteny sy ny zavatra Malagasy (publication in instalments, Imprimerie industrielle, Antananarivo, 1937–63).

Flacourt, Etienne de (ed. Claude Allibert), *Histoire de la Grande Isle Madagascar* (1658 ; Karthala, Paris, 1995).

Flynn, Dennis O., and Arturo Giraldez, 'Born with a "silver spoon": the origin of world trade in 1571', *Journal of World History*, 6, 2 (1995), pp. 201–21.

Freeman, Luke, 'Why are some people powerful?', in Rita Astuti, Jonathan Parry and Charles Stafford (eds), *Questions of Anthropology* (Berg, Oxford, 2007), pp. 281–306.

Fremigacci, Jean, 'La colonisation à Vatomandry-Mahanoro. Espérances et désillusions (1895–1910)', *Omaly sy anio*, 3–4 (1976), pp. 167–249.

———, 'L'administration coloniale : les aspects oppressifs', *Omaly sy anio*, 7–8 (1978), pp. 209–37.

———, 'La vérité sur la grande révolte de Madagascar', *L'Histoire*, 318 (March 2007), pp. 36–43.

Galbraith, J.K., *Money: Whence it came, where it went* (Pelican edn., Harmondsworth, 1976).

Gallieni, Joseph-Simon, *Lettres de Madagascar, 1896–1905* (Société d'éditions géographiques, maritimes et coloniales, Paris, 1928).

Gendarme, René, *L'Economie de Madagascar: diagnostic et perspectives de développement* (Editions Cujas, Paris, 1963).

Goodman, Steven M., and Bruce D. Patterson (eds), *Natural Change and Human Impact in Madagascar* (Smithsonian Institution Press, Washington and London, 1997).

———, and Jonathan P. Benstead (eds), *The Natural History of Madagascar* (University of Chicago Press, Chicago and London, 2004).

Graeber, David, 'Painful memories,' *Journal of Religion in Africa*, 27, 4 (1997), pp. 374–400.

Grandidier, Alfred (trans. J. Sibree), 'Property and wealth among the Malagasy', *Antananarivo Annual and Madagascar Magazine*, VI (1898), pp. 224–33.

———, *et al.*, eds, *Collection des ouvrages anciens concernant Madagascar* (9 vols, Comité de Madagascar, Paris, 1903–20).

Grandidier, Guillaume, *Histoire politique et coloniale* (3 vols, Imprimerie officielle, Antananarivo, 1942–58).

Gueunier, N.J., J-C. Hébert, F. Viré, 'Les routes maritimes du Canal de Mozambique d'après les routiers arabo-swahilis', *Taloha,* 11 (1992), pp. 77–120.

Guillain, Charles, *Documents sur l'histoire, la géographie et le commerce de la partie occidentale de Madagascar* (Imprimerie royale, Paris, 1845).

Haring, Lee (ed.), *Ibonia: Epic of Madagascar* (Bucknell University Press, Lewisburg, PA, 1994).

Hébert, Jean-Claude, 'Madagascar et Malagasy: un double nom de baptême', *Bulletin de Madagascar*, 302–3 (1967), pp. 583–613.

Hornell, James, 'The outrigger canoes of Madagascar, East Africa and the Comoro Islands', *Mariner's Mirror,* 30 (1944), pp. 3–18 (pt. 1), 170–85 (pt. 2).

Hugon, Philippe, 'La crise économique et les politiques d'ajustement', *Annuaire des Pays de l'océan Indien*, IX (1982–1983), (Presses universitaires d'Aix-Marseille, Aix-en-Provence 1982), pp. 471–92.

———, 'La crise économique à Madagascar et l'intervention du Fonds monétaire international', *Canadian Journal of African Studies*, 20, 2 (1986), pp. 186–218.

Hurles, M.E., B.C. Sykes, M.A. Jobling and P. Forster, 'The dual origin of the Malagasy in island southeast Asia and East Africa: evidence from maternal and paternal lineages', *American Journal of Human Genetics*, 76, 5 (2005), pp. 894–901.

Hurvitz, David, 'The "Anjoaty" and embouchures in Madagascar', in Kottak *et al., Madagascar: Society and history*, pp. 107–20.

Iliffe, John, *Africans: The history of a continent* (2nd edn, Cambridge, 2007).

Jacob, Guy, '*Fahavalisme* et troubles sociaux dans le Boina à la fin du XIXème siècle', *Annales de Madagascar*, série Lettres et Sciences humaines, 6 (1967), pp. 21–32.

———, 'Gallieni et « l'impôt moralisateur » à Madagascar : théorie, pratiques et conséquences (1901–1905)', *Revue française d'histoire d'outre-mer*, 74, 277 (1987), pp. 431–73.

———, *La France et Madagascar de 1880 à 1894 : aux origines d'une conquête coloniale* (Atelier National de Reproduction des thèses, Lille, 1997).

Janvier, Yves, 'La géographie gréco-romaine a-t-elle connu Madagascar? Le point de la question', *Omaly sy anio,* 1–2 (1975), pp. 11–41.

Jennings, Eric, 'Writing Madagascar back into the Madagascar Plan', *Holocaust and Genocide Studies*, 21, 2 (2007), pp. 187–217.

Jayasuriya, Shihan de S., and Richard Pankhurst, 'On the African diaspora in the Indian Ocean region', in Shihan de S. Jayasuriya and Richard Pankhurst (eds), *The African Diaspora in the Indian Ocean* (Africa World Press, Trenton, NJ, 2003), pp. 7–17.

Jones, A.M., *Africa and Indonesia: The evidence of the xylophone and other cultural and musical factors* (Brill, Leiden, 1964).

———, 'The influence of Indonesia: the musicological evidence reconsidered', *Azania*, IV (1969), pp. 131–45.

Julien, Gustave, *Institutions politiques et sociales de Madagascar* (2 vols, Guilmoto, Paris, 1909).

Jully, Antoine, 'La politique des races à Madagascar', *Revue de Madagascar*, 1st series, 9, 1 (1907), pp. 3–17.

Kent, Raymond K., *Early Kingdoms in Madagascar 1500–1700* (Holt, Rinehart and Winston, New York, 1970).

———, *The Many Faces of an Anti-Colonial Revolt: Madagascar's long journey into 1947* (Foundation for Malagasy Studies, Albany, CA, 2007).

Kestell-Cornish, Robert, *Journal of a Tour of Exploration in the North of Madagascar* (Society for the Propagation of the Gospel, London, 1877).

Keswani, D.G., 'Influences culturelles et commerciales indiennes dans l'océan Indien, de l'Afrique et Madagascar à l'Asie du sud-est', in UNESCO, *Relations historiques à travers l'océan Indien*, pp. 37–50.

Kottak, Conrad P. , *The Past in the Present: History, ecology and cultural variation in highland Madagascar* (University of Michigan Press, Ann Arbor, MI, 1980).

———, Jean-Aimé Rakotoarisoa, Aidan Southall and Pierre Vérin (eds), *Madagascar: Society and history* (Carolina Academic Press, Durham, NC, 1986).

Kreamer, Christine Mullen, and Sarah Fee (eds), *Objects as Envoys: Cloth ,imagery and diplomacy in Madagascar* (Smithsonian Institution, Washington DC, 2002).

Krebs Edgar, and Wendy Walker, 'Madagascar in the minds of foreigners', in Kreamer and Fee (eds), *Objects as Envoys*, pp. 121–48.

Lambek, Michael, *The Weight of the Past: Living with history in Mahajanga, Madagascar* (Palgrave Macmillan, London, 2002).

Larson, Pier M., 'Desperately seeking the "Merina" (central Madagascar): reading ethnonyms and their semantic fields in African identity histories', *Journal of Southern African Studies*, 22, 4 (1996), pp. 541–60.

———, 'A census of slaves exported from central Madagascar to the Mascarenes between 1775 and 1820', in Rakoto, *L'Esclavage à Madagascar*, pp. 131–45.

———, *History and Memory in the Age of Enslavement: Becoming Merina in highland Madagascar, 1770–1822* (James Currey, Oxford, 2000).

———, 'Colonies lost: God, hunger, and conflict in Anosy (Madagascar) to 1674,' *Comparative Studies of South Asia, Africa and the Middle East*, 27, 2 (2007), pp. 345–66.

——— *Ocean of Letters: Language, literacy and longing in the western Indian Ocean* (forthcoming).

Le Bris, Michel, 'La nouvelle classe en chiffres', *Les Cahiers de l'Ecole nationale de la promotion sociale*, Antananarivo, 2–3 (1971), pp. 7–57.

Le Myre de Vilers, Charles, 'Le traité hova', *La Revue de Paris*, 2, 6 (1895), pp. 225–41.

Leibbrandt, H.C.V., *Précis of the Archives of the Cape of Good Hope. Letters Received, 1695–1708* (W.A. Richards & Sons, Cape Town, 1896).

Leitão, Humberto (ed.), *Os dois descobrimentos da ilha da São Lourenço mandado fazer pelo vice-rei D. Jerônimo de Azevedo* (Centro de estudos históricos ultramarinos, Lisbon, 1970).

Leymarie, Philippe, 'Les accords de coopération franco-malgaches', *Revue française d'études politiques africaines*, 78 (1972), pp. 55–60.

———, 'L'AKFM malgache (1958–1968)', *Revue française d'études politiques africaines*, 98 (1974), pp. 71–90.

Lombard, Denys, *Le Carrefour javanais: essai d'histoire globale* (3 vols, Editions de l'Ecole des hautes études en sciences sociales, Paris, 1990).

Lombard, Jacques, *La Royauté sakalava : formation, développement, et effondrement, du XVIIe au XXe siècle. Essai d'analyse d'un système politique* (ORSTOM, Antananarivo, 1973).

Lonsdale, John, 'Moral ethnicity and political tribalism', in Preben Kaarsholm and Jan Hultin (eds), *Inventions and Boundaries : Historical and anthropological approaches to the study of ethnicity and nationalism*

(Occasional paper 11, International Development Studies, Roskilde University, 1994), pp. 131–50.

Ly Tio Fane Pineo, H., *La Diaspora chinoise dans l'océan Indien occidental* (ACOI, Aix-en-Provence, 1981).

McNeill, William H., 'The changing shape of world history', in Philip Pomper, Richard H. Elphick and Richard T. Vann (eds), *World History: Ideologies, structures and identities* (Blackwell, Oxford and Malden, MA, 1998), pp. 21–40.

MacPhee, R.D.E., and D. Burney, 'Dating of modified femora of extinct dwarf hippopotamus from southern Madagascar: implications for constraining human colonization and vertebrate extinction events', *Journal of Archaeological Science*, 18, 6 (1991), pp. 695–706.

Madagascar et le christianisme (Ambozontany and Karthala, Antananarivo and Paris, 1993).

Manguin, Pierre-Yves, 'The southeast Asian ship: an historical approach', *Journal of Southeast Asian Studies,* XI, 2 (1980), pp. 266–76.

Marcus, Richard, *Political Change in Madagascar: Populist democracy or neopatrimonialism by another name?* (Paper no. 89, Institute of Security Studies, Pretoria).

Martineau, A., *Madagascar en 1894* (Flammarion, Paris, no date).

Massiot, Michel, *L'Administration publique à Madagascar : évolution de l'organisation administrative et territoriale de Madagascar de 1896 à la proclamation de la République Malgache* (L.G.D.J., Paris, 1971).

May, Tim, 'L'avenir des universités, espaces de reflexion et/ou lieux d'attente ?', *Codesria Bulletin*, 1–2 (2004), pp. 63–5.

Mayeur, Nicolas, 'Voyage au pays d'Ancove (1785)', *Bulletin de l'Académie malgache*, old series, XII (1913), pp. 13–42.

———, 'Voyage dans le sud et dans l'intérieur des terres et particulièrement au pays d'Hancove (janvier à décembre 1777)', *Bulletin de l'Académie malgache*, old series, XI (1913), pp. 139–76.

Middleton, Karen (ed.), *Ancestors, Power and History in Madagascar* (Brill, Leiden, 1999).

Mille, Adrien, *Contribution à l'étude des villages fortifiés de l'Imerina ancien (Madagascar)*, Musée d'art et d'archéologie de l'Université de Madagascar, Antananarivo, 1970).

Molet, Louis, *Le Bain royal à Madagascar : explication de la fête malgache du Fandroana par la coutume disparue de la manducation des morts* (no publisher given, Antananarivo, 1956).

———, 'Andriamahazonoro', in Ranaivo, *Hommes et destins,* III, pp. 24–26

———, and Paul Ottino, 'Madagascar entre l'Afrique et l'Indonésie', *L'Homme*, XII, ii (1972), pp. 126–35.

Mullens, Joseph, *Twelve Months in Madagascar* (Nisbet, London, 1875).

Munthe, Ludvig, *La Bible à Madagascar: les deux premières traductions du Nouveau Testament malgache* (Avhandlinger Utgitt av Egede Institut-tet, Oslo, 1969).

———, *La Tradition arabico-malgache : vue à travers le manuscrit A-6 d'Oslo et d'autres manuscrits disponibles* (Lutheran Printing House, TPFLM, Antananarivo, 1982).

———, Charles Ravoajanahary and Simon Ayache, 'Radama I et les Anglais : les négociations de 1817 d'après les sources malgaches (« sorabe » inédits)', *Omaly sy anio*, 3–4 (1976), pp. 9–104.

Nativel, Didier, and Faranirina V. Rajaonah (eds), *Madagascar et l'Afrique : entre identité insulaire et appartenances historiques* (Karthala, Paris, 2007).

Nemours, D., *Madagascar et ses richesses* (Editions Pierre Roger, Paris, 1930).

Noiret, François, *Le Mythe d'Ibonia, le grand Prince (Madagascar),* (Karthala, Paris, 2008).

Nurse, Derek, and Thomas Spear, *The Swahili: Reconstructing the history and language of an African society, 800-1500* (University of Pennsylvania Press, Philadelphia, 1985).

Ottino, Paul, 'Quelques brèves remarques sur les études de parenté et d'organisation sociale à Madagascar', *Asie du sud-est et monde insulindien,* III, 2 (1972), pp. 109–33.

———, 'La hiérarchie sociale et l'alliance dans le Royaume de Matacassi', *Asie du sud-est et le monde insulindien*, IV, 4 (1973), pp. 53–89.

———, 'Le moyen age de l'océan Indien et les composantes du peuplement de Madagascar', *Asie du sud-est et le monde insulindien,* VII (1976), pp. 3–8.

———, 'The mythology of the highlands of Madagascar and the political cycle of the Andriambahoaka', in Yves Bonnefoy (ed.), *Mythologies : A restructured translation of* Dictionnaire des mythologies et des religions des sociétés traditionnelles et du monde antique (Chicago University Press, Chicago and London, 1991), pp. 961–76.

———, *L'Etrangère intime : essai d'anthropologie de la civilisation de l'ancien Madagascar*, (2 vols, Editions des archives contemporaines, Paris, 1986).

Pascal, Roger, *La République malgache* (Berger-Levrault, Paris, 1965).

Pearson, Michael N. , *Port Cities and Intruders: The Swahili coast, India, and Portugal in the early modern era* (The Johns Hopkins University Press, Baltimore and London, 1998).

Pelras, Christian, *The Bugis* (Blackwell, Oxford, 1996).

Pfeiffer, Ida, *Voyage à Madagascar* (1862; Karthala, Paris, 1981), with an introduction by Faranirina Esoavelomandroso.

Piolet, J.-B., *Madagascar et les Hova* (Delagrave, Paris, 1895).

Popovic, Alexandre, *The Revolt of African Slaves in Iraq in the 3rd/9th Century* (French edn 1976; Markus Wiener, Princeton, NJ, 1999).

Pouwels, Randall L., 'East African coastal history', *Journal of African History,* 40, 2 (1999), pp. 285–96.

Rabemananjara, R.W., *Madagascar: histoire de la nation malgache* (Imprimerie Lanchaud, Paris, 1952).

Rabesahala, Gisèle, *Que vienne la liberté, Ho tonga anie ny fahafahana* (Océan éditions, La Réunion, 2006).

Radimilahy, Chantal, 'Archéologie de l'Androy', *Recherche, pédagogie et culture,* XI, 55 (1981), pp. 62–5.

———, *Mahilaka: An archaeological investigation of an early town in northwestern Madagascar* (Dept. of Archaeology and Ancient History, University of Uppsala, 1998).

Rafidinarivo Rakotolahy, Christiane, 'Le référent de l'esclavage dans les représentations transactionnelles marchandes à Madagascar', *Journal des Africanistes* 70, 1–2 (2000), pp. 123–44.

Rafidison, Roger, 'Les affrontements ethniques dans le sud-est pendant la période coloniale: une interrogation sur le passé de la région', *Omaly sy anio*, 37–38 (1993–1994), pp. 261–70.

Rahajarizafy, Rémi, *Mey 1972* (1973; Libraire mixte, Antananarivo, 1975).

Raharinjanahary, Solo, 'Langues, dialectes et ethnies à Madagascar', in Randrianja, *Madagascar, ethnies et ethnicité*, pp. 137–202.

Rainianjanoro, *Fampandrian-tany sy tantara maro samy hafa* (Friends' Foreign Mission Association, Antananarivo, 1920).

Rainibe, Daniel, 'Une condition indigene?', *Omaly sy anio,* 15 (1982), pp. 117–24.

Rainitovo, *Tantaran' ny Malagasy manontolo* (3 vols, J. Paoli et fils, Antananarivo, 1932).

Raison, Jean-Pierre, 'Perception et réalisation de l'espace dans la société merina', *Annales : économies, sociétés, civilisations*, 32, 3 (1977), pp. 412–32.

———, *Les Hautes terres de Madagascar* (2 vols, Karthala, Paris, 1984).

———, 'Le noir et le blanc dans l'agriculture ancienne de la côte orientale malgache', *Etudes océan Indien*, 15 (1992), pp. 199–216.

Raison-Jourde, Françoise, 'Un tournant dans l'histoire religieuse merina du XIXe siècle : la fondation des temples protestants à Tananarive entre 1861 et 1869', *Annales de l'Université de Madagascar*, xi (1970), pp. 11–56.

———, 'Les Ramanenjana : une mise en cause populaire du christianisme en Imerina, 1863,' *Asie du sud-est et le monde insulindien*, 7, 2–3 (1976), pp. 271–93.

———, 'Radama II, ou le conflit du réel et de l'imaginaire dans la royauté merina', in C.-A. Julien et al (eds), *Les Africains* (9 vols, Jeune Afrique, Paris, 1977), vol.8, pp. 275–311.

——— (ed.), *Les Souverains de Madagascar* (Karthala, Paris, 1983).

———, *Bible et pouvoir à Madagascar au XIXe siècle: invention d'une identité chrétienne et construction de l'Etat (1780–1880)* (Karthala, Paris, 1991).

———, 'Familiarisation de l'esclavage, asservissement des libres. Le paradoxe merina d'une mutuelle privation du désir de liberté', in Rakoto, *L'Esclavage à Madagascar*, pp. 117–30.

———, 'Une transition achevée ou amorcée ?', *Politique africaine*, 52 (1993), pp. 6–18.

———, and Jean-Pierre Raison, 'Ravalomanana et la troisième indépendance?', *Politique africaine*, 86 (2002), special number on 'Madagascar, les urnes et la rue', pp. 5–17.

Rakoto, Ignace (ed.), *L'Esclavage à Madagascar: aspects historiques et résurgences contemporaines* (actes du Colloque international sur l'esclavage, Antananarivo, 24–28 Sept 1996), (Musée d'art et d'archéologie, Antananarivo, 1997).

Rakotoarisoa, Jean-Aimé, note in *Recherche, pédagogie et culture,* IX, 55 (1981), pp. 105–6.

Rakotomalala, Malanjaona, Sophie Blanchy and Françoise Raison-Jourde, *Madagascar: les ancêtres au quotidien* (L'Harmattan, Paris, 2001).

Rakotoson, Michèle, *Lalana* (Éd. de l'Aube, La Tour d'Aigues, 2002).

Ralaikoa, Albert, 'Aspects monétaires de la mainmise coloniale à Madagascar', *Omaly sy anio,* 37–38 (1993–1995), pp. 199–206.

Ralaimihoatra, Edouard, *Histoire de Madagascar* (2 vols, Société malgache d'édition, Antananarivo, 1965).

Ralibera, Rémi, *Souvenirs et témoignages malgaches, de la colonisation à la IIIème République* (Foi et justice, Antananarivo, 2008).

Ramantasoa Ramarcel, Benjamina, '*Mainty=andevo*, un amalgame statutaire de l'Imerina', in Rakoto, *L'Esclavage à Madagascar*, pp. 147–60.

Ramilison, E., *Ny Loharanon' ny Andriana nanjaka teto Imerina, etc.* (2 vols, Imprimerie Ankehitriny, Antananarivo, 1951–2).

Ranaivo, F. (ed.), *Hommes et destins (Dictionnaire biographique d'outre-mer),* vol. 3 (Travaux et Mémoires, new series 9, Académie des sciences d'outre-mer, Paris and Nice, 1979).

Randriamaro, Jean-Roland, *PADESM et luttes politiques à Madagas-*

car (Karthala, Paris, 1997).

Randrianja, Solofo, 'La notion de royauté dans le mouvement d'émancipation malgache entre les deux guerres', in Raison-Jourde, *Les Souverains de Madagascar*, pp. 409–26.

———, 'Jean Ralaimongo', in Jean Maitron (ed.), *Dictionnaire biographique du mouvement ouvrier français, Tome XIX : de la Première à la Seconde guerre mondiale* (Éditions ouvrières, Paris, 1983).

———, 'Les valeurs de 1789 et leur utilisation par les forces politiques à Madagascar entre les deux guerres', in Guy Jacob (ed.), *Regards sur Madagascar et la Révolution française* (CNAPMAD, Antananarivo, 1990), pp. 159–66.

———, 'Les Marofotsy à la conquête de la liberté vers 1820', in S. Randrianja (ed.), *Madagascar : Ethnies et ethnicité* (CODESRIA, Dakar, 2004), pp. 79–136.

———, *Société et luttes coloniales à Madagascar (1896–1946)* (Karthala, Paris, 2001).

———, 'Les Britanniques et Madagascar pendant la Deuxième guerre mondiale', in E. Combeau-Mari and E. Maestri (eds), *Le Régime de Vichy dans l'océan Indien* (SEDES, CRESOI, La Réunion, 2002), pp. 163–76.

———, 'Madagascar', in David Levinson and Karen Christensen (eds), *Global Perspectives on the United States*, vol. 2 (Berkshire Publishing, Great Barrington, MA, 2007), pp. 385–8.

———, F. Vergès, Hai Quang Ho, C. Rakotolahy, Z. Hussein, T. Malbert, 'Cartographie d'une zone de contacts', in G. Kobou (ed.), *Les Economies réelles en Afrique/Real Economies in Africa* (CODESRIA, Dakar, 2003), pp. 129–202.

Ranger, Terence, 'African traditional religion', in Stewart Sutherland and Peter Clarke (eds), *The Study of Religion, Traditional and New Religion* (Routledge, London, 1991), pp. 106–14.

Rantoandro, Gabriel, 'Une communauté mercantile du nord ouest: les Antalaotra', *Omaly sy anio*, 20 (1983–1984), pp. 195–210.

———, 'Des royaumes concentriques de Java au royaume de Madagascar : les fondements d'un héritage présumé', in Françoise Raison-Jourde and Solofo Randrianja (eds), *La Nation malgache au défi de l'ethnicité* (Karthala, Paris, 2002), pp. 107–23.

Raombana (ed S. Ayache), *Histoires* (2 vols, Ambozontany, Fianarantsoa, 1980, 1994).

Rasamuel, David, 'Alimentation et techniques anciennes dans le sud malgache à travers une fosse à ordures du XIè siècle', *Etudes océan Indien*, 4 (1984), pp. 81–91.

———, 'Observations sur la fabrication et l'usage des poteries malgaches : l'évolution de la poterie malgache durant le second millénaire de notre ère', *Nouvelles du Centre d'art et archéologie*, 3–4 (1985–6), pp. 13–19.

———, *Fanongoavana: une capitale princière malgache du XIVe siècle* (Editions Arguments, Editions Quae, Paris and Versailles, 2007), with a foreword by Philippe Beaujard and Chantal Blanc-Pamard and a preface by Rafolo Andrianaivoarivony.

Ratsivalaka, Ranaivo G., *Les Malgaches et l'abolition de la traite européenne des esclaves (1810–1817). Histoire de la formation du Royaume de Madagascar* (Editions Hery Arivo, Antananarivo, 1999).

Razafindrakoto, Mireille, and François Roubaud, 'Le scrutin présidentiel du 16 décembre 2001 : les enjeux d'une élection contestée', *Politique africaine*, 86 (2002), pp. 18–45.

Reade, Julian (ed.), *The Indian Ocean in Antiquity* (Kegan Paul International, London, 1996).

Renel, Charles, 'Les amulettes malgaches, ody et sampy', special number of *Bulletin de l'Académie malgache*, new ser., II (1915), pp. 31–279.

Richardson, James, 'The coronation of Ranavalona III', *Antananarivo Annual and Madagascar Magazine,* VII (1883), pp. 102–110.

Rochon, Aléxis (trans. Jos. Trapp), *An Account of the Island of Madagascar*(London, 1792), published with Capt. Pasfield Oliver (ed.), *Madagascar; or Robert Drury's Journal, During Fifteen Years' Captivity on that Island* (T. Fisher Unwin, London, 1890).

Roubaud, François, *Les Elections présidentielles à Madagascar 1992–1996 : un essai de géographie électorale* (Madio, Antananarivo, 1997).

Saleh, Mohamed Ahmed, 'Les Comoriennes de Zanzibar et le culte des esprits *kibuki* malgaches', in Nativel and Rajaonah, *Madagascar et l'Afrique,* pp. 425–37.

Scott, James, International Institute for Asian Studies (Leiden) annual lecture, published in *IIAS Newsletter,* 19 (June 1999).

Sewell, Joseph, *Remarks on Slavery in Madagascar, with an Address on that Subject, Delivered at Antananarivo* (E. Stock, London, 1876).

Sharp, Lesley A., *The Possessed and the Dispossessed: Spirits, identity, and power in a Madagascar migrant town* (University of California Press, Berkeley, CA, 1993).

Sibree, James, *South-East Madagascar. Being notes of a journey through the Tanala, Taimoro and Taisaka countries in June and July 1876* (A. Kingdon, Antananarivo, no date).

———, *The Great African Island* (Trubner, London, 1880).

———, 'The Sakalava: their origin, conquests and subjugation', *Antananarivo*

Annual and Madagascar Magazine, 1, 4 (1878), pp. 456–68.

———, *Madagascar and its People* (The Religious Tract Society, London, 1870).

———, and Antoine Jully, 'Le voyage de Tananarive en 1817. Manuscrits de James Hastie', *Bulletin de l'Académie malgache*, II (1903), pp. 91–114 (pt. 1) ; pp. 173–192 (pt. 2) ; III (1903), pp. 241–69 (pt. 3) and III (1904), pp. 17–36.

Spacensky, Alain, *Madagascar: cinquante ans de vie politique* (Nouvelles éditions latines, Paris, 1970).

Spear, Thomas, 'Early Swahili history reconsidered', *International Journal of African Historical Studies,* 33, 2 (2000), pp. 257–90.

Standing, H.F., 'The tribal divisions of the Hova Malagasy', *Antananarivo Annual and Madagascar Magazine*, III (1887), pp. 354–65.

Supomo, S., 'Indic transformation: the Sanskritization of *Jawa* and the Javanization of the Bhārata', in Bellwood *et al.*, *The Austronesians*, pp. 291–313.

Toussaint, Auguste, *Histoire de l'océan Indien* (Presses Universitaires de France, Paris, 1961).

Tronchon, Jacques, *L'Insurrection malgache de 1947: essai d'interprétation historique* (Maspero, Paris, 1974).

UNESCO, *Relations historiques à travers l'océan Indien : compte rendu et documents de travail de la réunion d'experts sur 'Les contacts historiques entre l'Afrique de l'Est d'une part et l'Asie du Sud-Est d'autre part, par les voies de l'océan Indien,' Maurice, 15–19 juillet 1974* (*Histoire générale de l'Afrique*, Etudes et documents no. 3, Paris, 1980).

Valette, Jean, 'La mission de Chardenoux auprès de Radama Ier (1816)', *Bulletin de Madagascar*, 207 (1963), pp. 657–702.

———, 'Un mémoire de Rondeaux sur Madagascar', *Bulletin de l'Académie malgache*, new series, XLIV-ii (1966), pp. 113–29.

———, 'Le traité passé entre Radama Ier et Jean René, le 9 juillet 1817', *Bulletin de Madagascar*, 222 (1964), pp. 957–9.

Vansina, Jan, *De la tradition orale: essai de méthode historique* (Musée royal de l'Afrique centrale, Brussels, 1961).

Vérin, Pierre, 'L'origine indonésienne des malgaches : indices culturels et archéologie', *Bulletin de Madagascar,* no. 259 (1967), pp. 947–77.

———, 'Les anciens habitats de Rezoky et d'Asambalahy', *Taloha*, 4 (1971), pp. 29–45.

———, 'Histoire ancienne du nord-ouest de Madagascar', special number of *Taloha* (1972).

———, *Les Echelles anciennes du commerce sur les côtes nord de Madagascar* (Service de reproduction des thèses de l'université, Lille, 1975).

———, 'Les apports culturels et la contribution africaine au peuplement de Madagascar', in UNESCO, *Relations historiques à travers l'océan Indien*, pp. 103–24.

———, 'Origines malgaches: histoire culturelle et archéologie de Madagascar, mise au point et commentaire', in Kottak, *Madagascar: Society and history*, pp. 45–52.

———, *The History of Civilization in North Madagascar* (A.A. Balkema, Rotterdam, 1986).

———, 'Madagascar', in *The Encyclopaedia of Islam*, new edn, vol.V (Brill, Leiden, 1986).

———, 'L'Imerina et le peuplement de Madagascar: les hypothèses confrontées aux nouvelles découvertes', *Taloha*, 12 (1994), pp. 25–8.

———, *Madagascar* (1990; new edn, Karthala, Paris, 2000).

———, Conrad Kottak, and P. Gorlin, 'The glottochronology of Malagasy speech communities,' *Oceanic Linguistics*, 8 (1970), pp. 26–83.

Vernet, Thomas, 'Slave trade and slavery on the Swahili coast, 1500–1750', in Paul Lovejoy, Behnaz A. Mirzai and Ismael M. Montana (eds), *Slavery, Islam and Diaspora* (Africa World Press, Trenton, NJ, in press).

Vink, Markus, ' "The world's oldest trade": Dutch slavery and slave trade in the Indian Ocean in the seventeenth century', *Journal of World History*, 14, 2 (2003), pp. 131–77.

Viré, François, 'Wakwak', entry in *The Encyclopaedia of Islam* (new edn, Brill, Leiden, 2002).

———, and Jean-Claude Hébert, 'Madagascar, Comores et Mascareignes à travers la Hawiya d'Ibn Mâgid (866H/1462)', *Omaly sy anio*, 25–26 (1987), pp. 55–80.

Walsh, Andrew, ' "Hot money" and daring consumption in a northern Malagasy sapphire-mining town', *American Ethnologist*, 30, 2 (2003), pp. 290–305.

Waltisperger, Dominique, Pierre Cantrelle and Osée Ralijaona, *La Mortalité à Antananarivo de 1984 à 1995* (Centre français sur la population et le développement, Paris, 1998).

Westra, Piet, and James C. Armstrong (eds), *Slave Trade with Madagascar: The journals of the Cape Slaver* Leijdsman, *1715* (Africana Publishers, Cape Town, 2006).

Wilson-Fall, Wendy, *Malagasy Free Black Settlement in Hanover County, Virginia, During Slavery : The intriguing story of Lucy Andriana Renibe Winston* (Hanover County Black Heritage Society and Hanover County Historical Society, Ashland, VA, 2007).

Wolters, O.W., *Early Indonesian Commerce: A study of the origins of Srivijaya* (Cornell University Press, Ithaca, NY, 1967).

———, *The Fall of Srivijaya in Malay History* (Lund Humphries, London, 1970).

Wright, Henry T., 'Early communities on the island of Maore and the coasts of Madagascar', in Kottak, *Madagascar: Society and history*, pp. 53–87.

———, and Fulgence Fanony, 'L'évolution des systèmes d'occupation des sols dans la vallée de la rivière Mananara au nord-est de Madagascar', *Taloha,* 11 (1992), p. 16–64.

———, and Jean-Aimé Rakotoarisoa, 'Cultural transformations and their impacts on the environments of Madagascar', in Goodman and Patterson, *Natural Change,* pp. 309–30.

XXX, 'Le poids de l'assistance technique', *Revue française d'études politiques africaines*, 78 (1972), pp. 64–70.

INDEX